JFK ASSASSINATION LOGIC

RELATED TITLES FROM POTOMAC BOOKS

The Forgotten Terrorist: Sirhan Sirhan and
the Assassination of Robert F. Kennedy
by Mel Ayton

A Farewell to Justice: Jim Garrison, JFK's Assassination,
and the Case That Should Have Changed History
by Joan Mellen

John F. Kennedy: World Leader
by Stephen G. Rabe

JFK ASSASSINATION LOGIC

HOW TO THINK ABOUT CLAIMS OF CONSPIRACY

John McAdams

POTOMAC BOOKS
WASHINGTON, D.C.

Library of Congress Cataloging-in-Publication Data
McAdams, John, 1945–
  JFK assassination logic : how to think about claims of conspiracy / John McAdams.—1st ed.
    p. cm.
  Includes bibliographical references and index.
  ISBN 978-1-59797-489-9 (hardcover: alk. paper)
  ISBN 978-1-59797-579-7 (electronic edition)
  1. Kennedy, John F. (John Fitzgerald), 1917–1963—Assassination. 2. Conspiracies—United States—History—20th century. I. Title.
  E842.9.M38 2011
  364.15—dc22

                                              2011013869

Printed in the United States of America on acid-free paper that meets the American National Standards Institute Z39-48 Standard.

Potomac Books
22841 Quicksilver Drive
Dulles, Virginia 20166

First Edition

10 9 8 7 6 5 4 3 2

Contents

Acknowledgments

These acknowledgments will be briefer than is often the case in books of this sort, simply because of the difficulty of listing (or even recalling) everybody who has helped in some substantial way with this project. But I want to especially mention a cadre of JFK assassination researchers who have thoroughly investigated one or a few issues and essentially settled—to the satisfaction of any reasonable person—the issues they have tackled. Typically these researchers have published their work only in obscure JFK assassination journals, or on the Internet (especially on the newsgroup alt.assassination.jfk). But each has contributed to clearing away the mass of factoids, misinformation, and dubious claims that have littered the historical landscape.

These people include Dave Reitzes, Stephen Roy (aka Blackburst), Russ Burr, Todd Wayne Vaughan, Dave Perry, Mike Russ, Clint Bradford, Tony Marsh, Mark Zaid, Gordon Winslow, Barb Junkkarinen, Dale Myers, and Bob Artwohl. Add to these folks authors like Jean Davison (who published the splendid book *Oswald's Game* and continues to make valuable contributions), Josiah Thompson (who published the best of all conspiracy books, *Six Seconds in Dallas*, and likewise continues to research), and Patricia Lambert (who published the definitive treatment of Jim Garrison's "investigation" in New Orleans). Lambert and author Max Holland provided me hugely valuable support and advice in the early stages of this project.

Some people play a vastly valuable role behind the scenes, and Paul Hoch (longtime Berkeley researcher) and Gary Mack (curator of the Sixth Floor Museum in Dallas) stand out.

A couple of people have done splendid work making resources available to researchers: Jim Lesar of the Assassination Archives and Research Center, and Rex Bradford of the Mary Ferrell Foundation. The foundation's website contains a mass of primary source documents that have been used in this book, and indeed other recent assassination books.

Steven Dhuey read this manuscript and made a variety of extremely valuable suggestions and improvements.

Several of my Marquette research assistants have contributed to the project, but the three who have worked on it most recently and most intensively are Ethan Bercot, Matt Surey, and Brett McCaw. Among earlier research assistants, Magen Knuth stands out as having done excellent work and having written some fine essays for my website.

Three editors at Potomac Books, Elizabeth Demers, Vicki Chamlee, and Julie Gutin, helped move this project along to completion.

Finally, there is my wife, Lynda, who read Priscilla McMillan's *Marina and Lee* and became convinced that her husband's obsession is not such an odd one after all.

Preface

This is not a book telling you *what* to think about conspiracy theories. Instead, it provides advice on *how* to think about conspiracy theories. It mostly discusses the assassination of John F. Kennedy, since JFK theories are the iconic American conspiracy theories. They are also the ones the author knows best. But if you know how to think about one conspiracy theory, you will know how to approach just about all of them.

If you know how fragile witness testimony is as evidence, you will probably bring the appropriate skepticism to witness accounts supporting a 9/11 U.S. government conspiracy or sightings of Bigfoot or UFOs. If you know how clueless government bureaucrats can be, you won't so readily accept that a supposed "smoking gun" document proves what a conspiracy theorist says it proves. If you know how common it is for photographs to be misinterpreted, you will tend to ask, do these apparent anomalies in photos supposedly shot on the surface of the moon really show fakery?

I am going to be up-front: I don't think a conspiracy was involved in Kennedy's death. People who believe in a conspiracy and read this book won't necessarily—and indeed probably won't—change their minds. But hopefully they will reject many bogus conspiracy arguments and evidence, even while holding out for a particular piece of evidence or some tantalizing "unanswered question" that might be the tip-off to covert shenanigans. The fact that illogic and the misuse of evidence are frequently behind conspiracy theories doesn't mean they *always* are. After all, there are real conspiracies in the world. Watergate was one, and so was the plot to kill Abraham Lincoln and members of his cabinet. Those theories that can survive critical scrutiny can be the basis of a reasonable discussion among reasonable people.

Most of what I say here might seem to be little more than common sense even when using a bit of jargon to express the idea (for example, ad hoc assumptions). But to repeat an old platitude, common sense can be amazingly uncommon. In this book, I will show the reader how to evaluate conspiracy theories. If the testimony of a witness doesn't seem quite "right," the reader will know all the ways that the testimony might be wrong, ranging from outright lies (and we'll discuss several witnesses who have almost certainly been lying) to alleged memories reconstructed from diverse elements to bizarre statements that are typical of honest perceptions of traumatic and highly stressful events.

Everybody knows that writers, newscasters, and producers of documentaries can mislead their audiences by leaving out certain information. The reader of this book may be dismayed to discover how often these omissions happen.

If I say that one's conclusions should be based on the most reliable evidence and not on the least reliable evidence, that instruction will seem like an obvious truism. But the reader is likely to be surprised at the amount of evidence that will have to be disregarded when using this approach. With most key issues, one or two "killer" pieces of evidence will determine what we conclude. Conspiracy books, however, typically throw a bunch of stuff against the wall, hoping some of it will stick and create suspicion. Books fingering Lee Oswald as the lone assassin typically provide a coherent narrative but often embrace evidence that's not too reliable. In contrast, I stress the need to focus on the hard data. That material should determine the conclusion.

This book most emphatically does not address every issue surrounding the Kennedy assassination, but the issues I do treat usually generalize those I have not covered. Once I demonstrate how fragile witness testimony is, the reader will know to treat any new witness skeptically. Once evidence is shown to be solid—for instance, that Lee Harvey Oswald really did to go Mexico City—then the reader won't be overly impressed by this or that anomaly in a government document that conspiracists use to cast doubt on a particular fact.

While I can't deal with every one of the vast array of minor issues surrounding the assassination, there is one big issue that I won't cover: Lee Harvey Oswald's character or personality. It's certainly possible to paint a compelling picture of Oswald the striver who wanted to be somebody important; of Oswald the violent fellow who beat his wife and shot at another person, Gen. Edwin Walker; of Oswald the actor who liked to play spy games; of Oswald the deceiver who lied quite readily when it served his purposes; and of Oswald the callow Marxist who became enamored of the Soviet Union and later, when he was disillusioned with Russia, of Fidel Castro's Cuba.

And, most important, I won't deal with Oswald the loner and malcontent.

In the hands of writers like Jean Davison and Gerald Posner, such a portrait has great psychological force in convincing the reader that Oswald was the lone assassin. There is just one logical problem: if Oswald was the perfect sort of person to be a lone assassin, he was also the perfect sort of person to be made into a patsy. Any conspiracy looking for a patsy would want somebody who looked and behaved just like Oswald. So showing that Oswald was a loner, was violent, or was disillusioned only debunks conspiracy theories that portray him as a great patriot (something Jim Garrison did). It doesn't debunk any sort of sensible conspiracy theory.

I hope to thoroughly immerse the reader in the messiness of the historical record. This book is not similar to the standard conspiracy book that piles one piece of evidence atop another (often contradictory) piece of evidence to create a towering but ramshackle edifice. But neither is it a lone assassin book that, taking only an occasional detour to debunk this or that conspiracy argument, tells a coherent story from beginning to an end where, as in a Greek tragedy, Oswald meets his destiny.

Rather than telling the whole story, this book concentrates on the pieces. Getting the pieces right—that is, making sense out of the messy and often contradictory mass of evidence—cannot be bypassed as one cruises down the road to a nice, pat conclusion. Once you get the pieces right, you can play "connect the dots" and put together a coherent narrative about what happened. Of course, sometimes the dots can be connected more than one way, which is why there are legitimate differences about what actually took place. But the more pieces are firmly established, the fewer the plausible alternative theories. That's why some realities about the past can be established as truth.

So get ready for some history.

Chapter One

The Frailty of Witness Testimony

Witness testimony is found front and center in virtually every book on the assassination of President John F. Kennedy.

This is for reasons both good and bad. First, the bad. Witnesses are often highly unreliable. Their testimony is "all over the place." There is, in other words, a lot of "noise" (confused and inaccurate perception, contaminated memory) along with the "signal" (accurate information). This noise opens up the possibility of making a case regardless of what the case happens to be. For instance, do you want to prove a shooter was on the famous grassy knoll? Just choose one set of witnesses. Want to convict Lee Harvey Oswald? Just pick different witnesses. Indeed, the same witnesses may be used by people arguing for a conspiracy theory and by those arguing for a lone assassin: it all depends on which parts of the testimony are quoted.

A "good" reason, and a seductive one, for focusing on witness testimony is that it has emotive power. Witnesses are real people who have been through a traumatic experience and have real human reactions. We can easily identify with them. Thus even authors offering sound conclusions based on solid evidence can seldom resist the temptation to flesh out their narratives with witness testimony. Consider the 1993 PBS *Frontline* documentary "Who Was Lee Harvey Oswald?" that quotes Robert Oswald, brother of killer (or patsy) Lee Oswald, talking about his meeting with Lee after the latter's arrest:

> I was allowed to visit with him approximately eight to ten minutes. And I asked him, I said, "Lee, what the Sam Hill's going on?" He said, "I don't know what they're talking about." I said, "Lee, they have got you charged

with the death of the President, shooting a police officer. They've got your rifle. They've got your pistol. And you don't know what the Sam Hill's going on?" And I became kind of intense, at that point, and looking into his eyes. And he never did answer, but he finally said, "Brother, you won't find anything there." And before we could get back to discussing anything of substance and everything, he gets tapped on his shoulder and told, "That's the end of it."[1]

A poignant narrative indeed, especially if one knows how shocked and humiliated Robert was by his brother's arrest.[2] Unfortunately, Robert's subjective interpretation of Lee's rather inscrutable demeanor and comments has little if any probative value.

Even the most levelheaded writers want a compelling narrative. The result is that witness testimony plays far too large a role in JFK assassination books and videos. The best evidence—the "killer" evidence—usually involves fingerprints, handwriting, ballistics, and photographs. But these factors are often relegated to a paragraph or a sentence or two, and in conspiracy books are impugned and attacked as false.

WACKY WITNESSES

When people talk about witness testimony, two closely related issues have to be discussed: perception and memory. *Perception* is how sense impressions get processed and stored in memory. *Memory* can be defined as "the cognitive processes whereby past experience is remembered."[3] Impressions stored in the memory are not static; people do not have "flashbulb" memory. This archaic term (dating back to when photographers actually used flashbulbs) implies that a scene, illuminated for a fraction of a second, is permanently recorded in the mind, as a photograph in a photo album. But that's not the way memory works.

When false testimony is given quite early, in the hours or days following the assassination, we classify that as a perception problem. When false testimony is made years or decades after the assassination and especially when the testimony of a witness changes over time, that's a memory problem. Of course, this kind of changed testimony can be the result of simple lying, but an honest witness, retrieving a memory decades after the fact, could also be wrong. The witness's memory has malfunctioned.

All sorts of JFK assassination witnesses are relevant, but one class is especially important: witnesses in Dealey Plaza. Solid witness testimony of more than the three shots that Lee Oswald is supposed to have fired would strongly support (indeed, virtually prove) a conspiracy. Solid witness testimony of a shooter on the grassy knoll would prove a conspiracy.

Wacky Witness Perceptions

Some testimony is just plain wacky. It doesn't fit a theory of Oswald as a lone gunman, and it doesn't fit any reasonable conspiracy theory. It's just "out there." Some examples from Dealey Plaza witnesses follow.

J. C. Price. Price was sitting on the roof of the Union Terminal Annex building, situated above Dealey Plaza across from the grassy knoll. Price's statement on the day of the assassination showed that he believed that Kennedy and Texas governor John Connally were in separate cars in the motorcade. He said he heard five shots (the vast majority of witnesses heard three or fewer) "and then much later, maybe as much as five minutes later another one."[4] No witness reported anybody shooting at the presidential limo at Parkland Hospital, which is where the limo was five minutes after the shooting.

Bill Newman. Newman had been standing with his wife, Gayle, and their two children in front of the pergola in Dealey Plaza near Elm Street. He reported that when the shooting started, the president "jumped up in his seat." Newman went on to say that Kennedy "was standing up" as he came directly in front of the Newmans and was hit in the head. Abraham Zapruder's famous film shows Kennedy's actions during the entire shooting sequence, and he was seated the whole time.[5]

Sam Holland. Holland was standing on the triple underpass and watching the motorcade turn from Houston Street onto Elm and proceed directly toward him when the shooting started. He gave a statement to the sheriff's office on the afternoon of the assassination and stated that "after the first shot the president slumped over and Mrs. Kennedy jumped up and tried to get in the back seat to him and then the second shot rang out."[6] Mrs. Jacqueline Kennedy (who was sitting next to her husband) did jump up and start to crawl out onto the trunk of the presidential limo, which is probably what Holland was talking about. But if so, that action happened after the "head shot," which was the third shot in the consensus "lone assassin" scenario and the fourth or fifth or sixth shot in the conspiracy scenarios.

Austin Miller. Positioned on the railroad overpass on the west side of the plaza, Miller thought the shots came from inside the presidential limo, saying they came "from right there in the car."[7]

Some of the Dealey Plaza witnesses recount a different sequence of events. Marvin Faye Chism, for example, reported that

> the President's wife immediately stood over him, and she pulled him up, and lay him down in the seat, and she stood up over him in the car. The President was standing and waving and smiling at the people when the shot happened. . . . The two men in the front of the car stood up, and then when the second shot was fired, they all fell down and the car took off just like that.[8]

The Zapruder film, however, shows nobody in the presidential limo standing during any part of the shooting sequence, much less acting like a jack-in-the-box.

A. J. Millican was another witness who produced a Wild West shooting sequence.

> Just after the President's car passed, I heard three shots come from up toward Houston and Elm right by the Book Depository Building, and then immediately I heard two more shots come from the Arcade between the Book Store and the Underpass, and then three more shots came from the same direction only sounded further back.[9]

If Millican was right, there was certainly a conspiracy. But at least 188 witnesses in Dealey Plaza reported the number of shots they heard, and he is the only one who reported as many as eight.[10]

Respondings to Traumatic Events

What is going on here? One might expect that stress concentrates the mind and makes for more accurate perception. But in fact the relationship between stress (or arousal) and the efficiency of memory is curvilinear, according to the Yerkes-Dodson Law. At very low states of arousal, memory functions poorly and improves with increased stress. At very high levels of stress, however, it becomes degraded, perhaps because shock disrupts the storage of memories or perhaps because stress distracts people, making them more worried about their personal safety.[11]

So far, we have odd, isolated perceptions from single witnesses. But it's also possible to find multiple witnesses for things that simply did not happen.

FALSE RECOLLECTIONS: THE MOTORCYCLE COP

Five witnesses independently reported that, in the wake of the shooting in Dealey

Plaza, a motorcycle cop jumped the curb and drove his motorbike at least partway up the slope on the grassy knoll.

James Simmons, watching the motorcade from the triple underpass, claimed to have seen a motorcycle cop who "drove up the grassy slope toward the Texas School Book Depository Building, jumped off his motorcycle and then ran up the hill toward the Memorial Arches."[12]

Nolan Potter, who was also on the triple underpass, said that he noticed "a policeman drive his motorcycle up the slope towards the Texas School Book Depository Building."[13]

Sam Holland, just as the previous witnesses on the triple underpass, reported a motorcycle cop "tried to ride up the embankment on his motorcycle and it turned over about halfway up the embankment." Holland reported he then saw the officer "run on over to the fence with the gun in his hand."[14]

Curtis Freeman Bishop, also on the underpass, was interviewed by the Federal Bureau of Investigation (FBI), which reported that he "recalls seeing a motorcycle policeman drive up the grassy slope near the Texas School Book Depository Building."[15]

Lee Bowers was in a railroad signal tower behind the stockade fence that was atop the grassy knoll. In a filmed interview with researcher Mark Lane, Bowers reported seeing a cop who "rode a motorcycle up the incline coming up from the lower portion of Elm Street, and he rode perhaps two-thirds of the way up or more before he deserted his motorcycle."[16]

This testimony, from witnesses apparently describing the same occurrence, raises numerous questions. First, there is the "up the slope towards the Texas School Book Depository Building" language. The depository is about a hundred yards removed from the slope leading up to the stockade fence atop the grassy knoll. There is no slope in front of the depository, unless "in front of" means between the depository and the triple underpass, which it probably does for these witnesses. Then there is the question of how Bowers could have seen any such thing, given that the stockade fence would have blocked his view.

Numerous photos of Dealey Plaza in the seconds and minutes after the shooting exist, and none of them show an abandoned motorbike on the grassy slope. What does the photographic evidence show? A motorcycle officer parked near the curb on the north side of Elm Street and ran up the grassy slope toward the place where the triple underpass meets the stockade fence that tops the knoll.[17] The officer was Clyde Haygood, who, according to his testimony,[18] attempted to jump the curb but failed.

So where did all the false recollections about riding up the slope come from?

In 1992 an El Al cargo plane hit an apartment complex in the Netherlands. Ten months after the accident, a team of Dutch psychologists asked a group of respondents if they had seen the television film of the moment the plane had hit the apartment building. Fifty-five percent said they had, and a later follow-up study showed two-thirds of respondents saying they had seen that film. In fact, respondents recalled various details of the accident, such as whether the plane had been on fire, the angle at which it hit the building, and so on. But in reality, there was no such television film.

Apparently, respondents had heard about the crash and formed a mental image. They also may have seen images of the crash scene, and their minds filled in the missing data.[19]

In another case, Boston University researchers showed a group of students slides of a hand picking up oranges scattered across the floor of a supermarket and a woman picking up groceries. Then, between fifteen minutes and forty-eight hours later, the students were shown a group of slides and asked which of them they had seen before. Some of the slides they had indeed seen before, but others showed "cause" images (a fellow taking an orange from the bottom of a pile, a grocery bag ripping) that the students had never seen. A total of 68 percent of the students reported seeing at least one of the "cause" images.[20]

As researchers Dennis Ford and Mark Zaid insist, memory is a reconstruction. Yes, things you have actually seen can be part of your memory, but then things you have only heard about can also form into memories.[21] As the previous cases show, things you simply *inferred* can also become part of your memory. Here's a simple test for the average reader: have you ever wondered whether you turned off your stove? Perhaps you have a memory of having turned it off, but you can't remember whether you actually did that or whether you just mentally rehearsed doing that.

INTERPRETING WITNESS TESTIMONY:
JUST WHAT DID THE WITNESS SAY?

So far, I have discussed witnesses who gave a fairly concrete and intelligible version of their testimony, even if it was wrong. But often it can be difficult to sort out what the testimony actually *is*. Consider, for example, the question of whether witnesses heard shots from the Texas School Book Depository—which would be consistent with Lee Oswald being the shooter—or from the grassy knoll, which would certainly indicate a conspiracy. This determination might seem straightforward, but in fact it frequently isn't.

To begin, note that on November 22, 1963, virtually nobody was using the term "grassy knoll." Merriman Smith of United Press International first used it in a dispatch sent twenty-five minutes after the shooting.[22] The term simply wasn't in common use, and no witnesses actually used the term in early testimony.[23] Instead, the grassy knoll witnesses used such terms as "the railroad overpass" or "railroad tracks" or "monument" (presumably the pergola). There were other terms that witnesses might have used to mean the grassy knoll, including "the fence," "the trees," "the parking lot," "the rail yards," or "that monument there." Almost any location on the west side of the plaza north of Elm Street will be classified as the grassy knoll. (See the map in the photo insert.)

Not all depository witnesses used the term "depository" either. Charles Brehm, standing on the south side of Elm Street during the shooting, said the shots came from "one of the two buildings back at the corner of Elm and Houston Streets."[24] That description fits the depository perfectly, but it also fits the Dal-Tex Building and the County Records Building.[25] If witnesses were in the depository or standing directly in front of the depository, then saying the shots came from "overhead" usually was classified as coming from the depository.

If determining the direction of the shots *still* sounds pretty easy, consider this information: various tabulations of the reported direction of the shots have been made, and "Eyewitness Reports on the Source of the Shots Fired in Dealey Plaza" table presents two of them. In 1967 Josiah Thompson's book *Six Seconds in Dallas* published the pioneering tabulation of the source of the shots fired in Dealey Plaza.[26] Then, in the late 1970s, the House Select Committee on Assassinations (HSCA) did a similar tabulation.[27] How did the two compare?

Ignoring, for the moment, the large differences in the responses "don't know" and "other," it's striking that Thompson's work shows a clear majority of witnesses who actually specified the shots came from the direction of the knoll, and the HSCA data shows a rather lopsided majority saying they came from the depository. Are both reporting the same event?

They are, but the two reports have interpreted the eyewitness testimony differently. For example, Thompson classifies Abraham Zapruder, the fellow who shot the famous movie of the assassination, as a grassy knoll witness. He does so on the

Eyewitness Reports on the Source of the Shots Fired in Dealey Plaza

Source reported	Josiah Thompson	House Select Committee on Assassinations
Texas School Book Depository	25	46
Grassy knoll	33	20
Other	2	29
Heard shots from two directions	4	
Don't know (or not reporting a direction)	126	76
Total	190	171

Sources: Josiah Thompson, *Six Seconds in Dallas: A Micro-study of the Kennedy Assassination* (New York: Bernard Geis Associates, 1967), 25; 2 HSCA 122.

basis of a brief Secret Service report of its interview with Zapruder that says, "According to Mr. Zapruder, the position of the assassin was behind Mr. Zapruder."[28] But why did Zapruder say that (assuming that he did)? He later explained to the President's Commission on the Assassination of President Kennedy, also known as the Warren Commission, that he couldn't really tell where the shots came from since "there was too much reverberation." He thought that because the right side of Kennedy's head exploded, the shots came from the right front, and since "the police started running back of me, it looked like it came from the back of me."[29]

There is a simple rule for interpreting testimony: witness inferences don't count. The reader's inferences are at least as good as Zapruder's, and they are better if the reader knows a bit about wound ballistics. Only Zapruder's actual observations count as evidence.

Zapruder's is not the only case where there is apparently conflicting testimony about the source of the shots. Consider, for example, Bobby Hargis, the motorcycle cop riding just to the left of the presidential limo, off the bumper, and slightly behind JFK and Jackie. There are different versions of his testimony. The first was published in the *Houston Post* the day after the assassination.

DALLAS—A Dallas motorcycle officer who was riding two feet from the presidential car described to the Houston Post Friday what he saw when a sniper fired the shots that killed President Kennedy and wounded Gov. John B. Connally.

"When the first rifle bullet spewed into the open limousine," said Patrolman J.H. [*sic*] Hargis, "The President bent forward in the car."

. . . Hargis said he jumped off his motorcycle and began a search of the building from which the shots were fired.

"I knew it was high and from the right. I looked for any sign of activity in the windows, but I didn't see anybody."[30]

That description sounds straightforward enough, and any lone gunman theorist should be delighted to embrace it. Unfortunately, when Hargis testified before the Warren Commission, his testimony was rather different.

> **Stern:** Just a minute. Do you recall your impression at the time regarding the source of the shots?
>
> **Hargis:** Well, at the time it sounded like the shots were right next to me. There wasn't any way in the world I could tell where they were coming from, but at the time there was something in my head that said that they probably could have been coming from the railroad overpass, because I thought since I had got splattered, with blood—I was just a little back and left of—just a little bit back and left of Mrs. Kennedy, but I didn't know. I had a feeling that it might have been from the Texas Book Depository, and these two places was the primary place that could have been shot from.[31]

Which version should one believe? Luckily, there is other evidence. A photograph shot by Wilma Bond shows Hargis on foot, just returning to his motorcycle on Elm Street, after having parked it there and run over to the north side of the street and partway up the incline. A photo by Richard Oscar Bothun likewise shows Hargis headed west on Elm Street after having dismounted and looked around.[32] Hargis testified that he "couldn't locate anyone who looked suspicious, so I waited a few seconds then ran back to my motorcycle and went to the triple underpass to see if I could see anyone, but I didn't observe anything."[33] He eventually made it back to the depository.[34] Obviously, Hargis's actions were not those of somebody who knew that the shots came from the depository. But then where did the *Houston Post* account come from? One simple possibility is that the reporter messed up and confused Hargis (whose initials he got wrong) with some other witness. Another is that Hargis, talking to the reporter after he returned to the depository and learned that the shots had come from there, gave an account reflecting what he had learned later. Perhaps then, under oath in front of the Warren Commission, he was simply especially scrupulous about what he said.

A similar problem occurs with a witness named Emmett Hudson. Hudson was standing on the steps that led from Elm Street to the top of the incline and then to a walkway that ran behind the retaining wall and in front of the stockade fence. In his statement to the sheriff's office on the day of the assassination, he said, "The shots I heard definitely came from behind and above me."[35] That, of course, fits the grassy knoll theory perfectly.

But on November 26 the FBI interviewed him. Its report stated that Hudson

> said the shots sounded as if they were fired over his head and from some position to the left of where he was standing. In other words, the shots sounded as if they were fired by someone at a position which was behind him, which was above him, and which was to his left.

The FBI report went on to say that Hudson had been shown the Mary Moorman photograph as it appeared in the *Dallas Times Herald*. He pointed to "the corner of the Texas School Book Depository building appearing in such photograph and said the shots sounded as if they were coming from that building."[36]

There is just a slight problem here. The depository is not shown in the Moorman photograph.[37]

Hudson was the groundskeeper in Dealey Plaza and certainly knew which building was the depository. His testimony before the Warren Commission repeats that the shot came from the depository but with a bizarre twist. He told the commission that the shots came from "above and kind of behind." Warren Commission counsel Wesley Liebeler then asked, "You heard it come from sort of behind the motorcade and then above?" Hudson replied yes.[38] That exchange seems an absurd example of Liebeler leading the witness (Hudson had not said "motorcade"), unless the counsel had read the FBI report, which he almost certainly had. Hudson's testimony to the Warren Commission had another strange element to it: he said he was lying on the ground when he heard the third and last shot. But the Moorman photo, a film by Marie Muchmore, and a film by Orville Nix all show him standing at the time of the head shot.[39]

The HSCA solicited the last piece of testimony from Hudson. Chief Counsel G. Robert Blakey phoned him and pointed out the apparent contradiction between his sheriff's department affidavit and his Warren Commission testimony. Hudson said, "Everything I told the Warren Commission is correct." Blakey's terse note summarizes Hudson's testimony: "Don't think any shots from behind fence."[40] Thus Hudson is classified as a depository witness, although the issue is certainly debatable. One could argue that Hudson, when talking to the FBI and the Warren Commission, "regularized" his testimony—that is, he conformed it to what the media were reporting about a depository shooter—and then stuck with his story when Blakey called a decade and a half later.

Not all witness classifications are as complicated as the ones discussed thus far, but many are, or else all the tabulations would be consistent. My own tabulation shows fifty-six witnesses reporting shots from the depository, thirty-four from the grassy knoll, eight from other locations, and five from two locations.[41] I, of course, believe this tabulation is better than the others', but given the division of witness testimony here, it would be foolish to claim that this tabulation provides strong evidence of shots coming from the depository. Indeed, taking Thompson's tabulation at face value, it would not be strong evidence of shots from the knoll.

Conspiracy author Stewart Galanor points out that witnesses who worked for the government—cops, sheriff's deputies, Secret Service agents, and so on—were a good deal more likely to say the shots came from the depository than those people who did not work for the government. Indeed, Galanor's tabulation shows the government witnesses listed the depository twenty-six times and the knoll eight, whereas the nongovernment witnesses named the depository twenty-two times and the knoll forty-four.[42] Galanor asserts that the government employees are the sort "who traditionally tend to identify with the government's case," completely ignoring the fact that most were in the motorcade right out in the middle of Dealey Plaza, were well positioned to hear shots from either the knoll or the depository, and were less likely to be confused by echoes. If anything, their testimony is probably better than that of the nongovernment witnesses.

BEWARE OF AD HOC ASSUMPTIONS

In dealing with witnesses—and in dealing with evidence generally—one often encounters ad hoc assumptions. An assumption is ad hoc if there is no reason for making it *except* to let the data fit the theory.

A recent book by James Douglass, *JFK and the Unspeakable*, provides a classic example. Douglass strongly suggests that Lee Oswald was an FBI informant who had penetrated and helped authorities break up an assassination plot against JFK that was supposed to happen in Chicago during a scheduled visit on November 2, 1963.[43] One will have to leave aside minor quibbles, such as the fact that a thorough investigation by the HSCA concluded there was no such plot.[44] But what about Dallas, where the supposed "plot" clearly succeeded? Douglass believes that Oswald was still working for the FBI on the day of the Kennedy assassination and that he had expected to break up a second plot in Dallas. But then, Douglass explains, "any such hopes were in vain. The FBI had become part of the plot."[45] Douglass, of course, has no evidence that Oswald was an FBI informant at all or that the bureau had turned from being a protector of the president (in Chicago) to a part of the conspiracy (in Dallas). He makes that assumption only because he needs to explain Oswald's success in breaking up the Chicago plot and his failure to break up the Dallas plot.

But one can't rule out all ad hoc assumptions. Scientists will sometimes throw away observations that are considered outliers. When the data points will fit a neat pattern and one observation sticks out far from the rest, scientists often discard it. Scientists throw such observations away on the grounds that they reflect a measurement error of some sort. Maybe there was a short in the equipment, maybe somebody bumped the measuring device, and so forth.[46] One should not be too cavalier about deleting this information, since an outlier can be valid information and may in fact be the tip-off to something interesting.

When scientists throw away an outlier because it doesn't fit the model and because they can't explain it, they are making an ad hoc assumption. It might seem as if researchers should never discard data, but the truth is in any nontrivial research there is always some "noise" in the data.

In conducting research, one should prefer the theory that requires the fewest ad hoc assumptions. Otherwise, any theory can be made to fit the data. Some assassination theorists go wild, assuming that this or that or (after a while) most of the evidence has been tampered with, that most of the witnesses whose testimony implicates Oswald are lying, and that many people are engaged in a cover-up.

Minimizing ad hoc assumptions is the first cousin or, better, the brother of the "principle of parsimony," which holds that the simplest explanation is the one more likely to be true.[47] This notion is itself not nearly as simple as it sounds. A conspiracy running everything is indeed a simple theory. But it requires many ad hoc assumptions about faked evidence, lying witnesses, and so on. Oswald as the lone shooter would also seem to be an eminently simple theory, but to believe it, one would have to make multiple ad hoc assumptions about mistaken witnesses, government documents riddled with serious errors, and so-called mysterious circumstances that would have to be dismissed as not really relevant.

Ad Hoc Theorizing and the Dealey Plaza Witnesses

Although one has to be careful because of the possibility of systematic (rather than random) witness errors, it is sometimes hard to ignore a lopsided consensus of witness testimony. Josiah Thompson tabulated 172 witnesses who mentioned the number of shots they heard, and only 9 remembered four or more shots (with 5 more remembering "three or four" shots).[48] Likewise, the HSCA's analysis found that out of 169 witnesses who reported the number of shots they heard, 156 reported three or fewer.[49] Thompson had 136 witnesses and the HSCA had 132 witnesses reporting exactly three shots. So unless one wants to posit (entirely ad hoc) silenced shots, it's hard to avoid the conclusion that three shots were fired.

Also relevant might be the fact that few witnesses in Dealey Plaza—four in Thompson's tabulation and five in the author's—heard shots from two different directions.[50] If shots actually came from two directions, would not more people have heard them as coming from two directions? Stewart Galanor tries to deal with this problem by stating that "if 55 witnesses claim the shots came from the Depository and 35 claim they came from the Knoll, a sensible conclusion would be that both events happened since the number of witnesses to both events is substantial."[51] Unfortunately, to believe this assertion, you have to believe (entirely ad hoc) that six shots were fired in Dealey Plaza, three from each location, with 55 witnesses hearing the shots from the depository and none of the shots from the knoll while 35 others heard the shots from the knoll but none from the depository. Much more sensible is the notion that the shots came from only one direction, with the witnesses being confused as to what direction that was.

I will return to the concept of ad hoc assumptions throughout this book. Believing the theory that requires the fewest ad hoc assumptions, and with ad hoc assumptions known to be plausible, is the key to sanity in evaluating any conspiracy theory or, in fact, any theory at all.

WITNESS TESTIMONY OF A GRASSY KNOLL SHOOTER?

An iconic but entirely faceless figure in all JFK conspiracy theories is the grassy knoll gunman. As noted, it's easy to produce witnesses who thought the shots came from the grassy knoll (or someplace nearby); however, more witnesses thought the shots came solely from the depository. But what about witnesses who might have actually seen a grassy knoll shooter? Such testimony would inherently be more valuable than earwitness testimony, given that many earwitnesses were confused.

Ed Hoffman

One grassy knoll witness is a fellow named Virgil "Ed" Hoffman. A deaf-mute, he was apparently parked above the Stemmons Freeway on-ramp southwest of Dealey Plaza and could not see the motorcade while it was on Elm Street, but he did see the motorcade as it sped onto the ramp and headed toward Parkland Hospital. He also claims to have seen two men behind the famous stockade fence overlooking Elm Street. He saw one man, whom he called Suit Man, fire a rifle at Kennedy. The shooter then moved down the fence and tossed the rifle to someone Hoffman called Railroad Man (who, of course, was dressed like a railroad employee), who kneeled behind a signal box, disassembled the weapon, and put it into a toolbox. Both men then walked away.[52]

But just as many witnesses with particularly interesting stories to tell, Hoffman didn't say any such thing in his first recorded statements. An FBI report dated June 28, 1967, records him saying that "he observed two white males, clutching something dark to their chests with both hands, running from the rear of the Texas School Book Depository building. The men were running north on the railroad, then turned east, and Hoffman lost sight of both of the men."[53] The FBI followed up by talking to his father and brother, and both stated that Hoffman "has in the past distorted facts of events observed by him. . . . The father of Virgil Hoffman stated that he did not believe that his son had seen anything of value and doubted he had observed any men running from the Texas School Book Depository and for this reason had not mentioned it to the FBI."[54]

This statement might seem damning, but unlike other interesting witnesses, Hoffman has somewhat plausible excuses. He claims that, since he is a deaf-mute, the FBI had difficulty understanding exactly what he was saying. Further, he says that his father and brother were both afraid for his safety and thus tried to tamp down any report that he had seen something explosive.[55]

However, Hoffman's story has one serious flaw. Shortly after the shots rang out in Dealey Plaza, some of the railroad workers on the triple underpass ran behind the stockade fence to see if they could find a shooter. If Hoffman's account is accurate, these men—including Sam Holland, James Simmons, and Richard Dodd—would have seen the retreating shooter and his accomplice in railroad attire.[56] But Hoffman's shooter could not have merely walked down the length of the fence to the corner and handed off a rifle to his accomplice since the entire area was jammed with cars. Sam Holland told Mark Lane: "They were just bumper to bumper . . . just a sea of cars. You couldn't hardly get through them. We were jumping over the bumpers, over the hoods of the cars to work our way to the spot that we saw the smoke and heard the shot."[57]

Holland likewise told Eddie Barker of Dallas TV station KRLD that "it took quite a little while to thread our way through the cars, there's so many parked there . . . they were parked at every angle."[58] So Holland's testimony (and that of his buddies who ran with him behind the stockade fence) is the "killer" evidence that discredits Hoffman's account.

J. C. Price

One has to stretch to make J. C. Price into a conspiracy witness, but by stretching really hard, you can. Price was watching the motorcade from the roof of the union terminal annex high above the plaza, and as already discussed, his testimony had some wacky elements. After hearing a "volley of shots, I think five and then much later, maybe as much as five minutes later, another one," he said,

> I saw one man running toward the passenger cars on the railroad siding after the volley of shots. This man had a white dress shirt, no tie and khaki colored trousers. His hair appeared to be long and dark, and his agility running could be about 25 years of age. He had something in his hand. I couldn't be sure but it may have been a head piece.[59]

Price's time perceptions were obviously distorted, and there were probably a lot of people running around behind the stockade fence and on the triple underpass. So the account needed a bit of enhancement. In a 1966 interview with Mark Lane, Price said the man was "carrying something in his right hand" and added that it "could have been a gun."[60] Of course, given the vagueness of Price's testimony, it could have been a birthday gift for his Aunt Bessie.

Joe Marshall Smith

Smith was a Dallas cop who ran behind the stockade fence after the assassination and confronted a man who (in Smith's words) "showed me" Secret Service credentials. Since there were no Secret Service agents in Dealey Plaza (all had rushed to Parkland Hospital with the presidential limo), somebody actually flashing Secret Service credentials would have been suspicious indeed.

The HSCA investigated this incident and suggested that perhaps other government agents had been in Dealey Plaza. In particular, the committee members heard testimony that plainclothes U.S. Army intelligence people were in Dallas.[61] Dallas Police chief Jesse Curry told the Warren Commission that "U.S. Alcohol Tax" (presumably, Bureau of Alcohol, Tobacco, and Firearms [BATF]) personnel helped search the parking lot around the depository.[62] In addition to uniformed officers, the Dallas Police had plainclothes detectives assigned along the motorcade route.[63] Author Gerald Posner reports that he examined the badges of these organizations, and "several look alike." Further, "any of these law enforcement officials could have been confused with Secret Service agents."[64]

Joe Smith was clearly rattled. As he explained in his Warren Commission testimony, he had drawn his pistol but then thought, "This is silly." But the "Secret Service agent" had seen him coming with his drawn pistol and "right away he showed me who he was." There is one final fact that conspiracy books always omit. The alleged Secret Service agent remained in the parking lot and helped Smith and Deputy Seymour Weitzman check out the cars.[65]

Lee Bowers

Lee Bowers is a classic case of turning a man who flatly contradicts the idea of a grassy knoll shooter into a supporter of that theory. It's all a matter of quoting him selectively. Bowers was in a railroad signal tower behind the stockade fence and had a clear view of the area behind the fence.[66]

Bowers told the Warren Commission that at the time of the shooting, he was looking toward the motorcade (although the presidential limo was out of sight for most of the shooting sequence) and that "there seemed to be some commotion" on the high ground above Elm Street. Pressed by Warren Commission counsel to describe it, he said, "I just am unable to describe [it] rather than it was something out of the ordinary, a sort of milling around, but something occurred in this particular spot which was out of the ordinary, which attracted my eye for some reason, which I could not identify."[67] Of course, if Bowers had seen somebody behind the stockade fence shooting at Kennedy, that would have been quite easy to describe.

To make it even mildly conspiratorial, Bowers's testimony needs some enhancement. Mark Lane got Bowers to say that he had seen "some unusual occurrence— a flash of light or smoke or something which caused me to feel like something out of the ordinary had occurred there." Bowers insisted, "Now, what this was, I could not state at that time and at this time I could not identify it."[68]

Bowers's earliest testimony doesn't even mention the "commotion," as he put it, and certainly not the flash of light or smoke. Rather, he seemed obsessed with three cars that drove down the Old Elm Extension and into the area behind the stockade fence.[69] Of course, they may have been looking for a place to park. But then they may have been scouting for conspirators who were planning on shooting from the grassy knoll. If so, the whole plot must have been put together as some kind of quick improvisation, since the first of the cars came at about 12:10 p.m., the second at about 12:20 p.m., and the third car "some seven or nine minutes before the shooting."[70] Why some conspiracy would need three scout cars is a mystery, but Bowers seemed to think the whole thing was suspicious.

The other conspiratorial element to Bowers's testimony is that he saw two men, apparently behind the stockade fence. One he described as "middle-aged, or slightly older, fairly heavy-set, in a white shirt, fairly dark trousers." The other was a "younger man, about mid-twenties, in either a plaid shirt or plaid coat or jacket." Were they the shooting team? Were these guys suspicious? The Warren Commission counsel asked Bowers, "Were they standing together or standing separately?" His reply: "They were standing within 10 or 15 feet of each other, and gave no appearance of being together, so far as I know."[71]

When asked if the two men fled the scene as the first cop came up toward the fence, Bowers said no. He stated that one of them was still there when the cops arrived, although he could not say whether the other one left, since his clothing blended in with the foliage.[72]

It should be obvious by now that Bowers was not a conspiracy witness. Indeed, his testimony is strong evidence that there was no grassy knoll shooter, since he was perfectly positioned to see one, was clearly paying attention, and reported neither a shooter nor anything genuinely suspicious.

Other Witnesses

As a witness, Marilyn Sitzman proved to be similar to Bowers. An employee of Abraham Zapruder's, she had accompanied her boss to Dealey Plaza. She had been standing with him on a concrete pedestal during the shooting, since Zapruder had vertigo and would likely have tumbled off without her support. She was perfectly positioned to see a shooter behind the southwest–northeast leg of the stockade fence; indeed, she said she had looked to her right (in the direction of the fence) after the shooting.[73] But she never reported seeing a shooter.

There are a couple of additional accounts that might involve a grassy knoll shooter. One of the most interesting involves a shadowy figure that one can see in Mary Moorman's Polaroid photo, which she shot almost at the instant that Kennedy was hit in the head. It appears to show a man dressed in a police uniform shooting at Kennedy, with the muzzle flash of his rifle visible and partly obscuring the shooter's face. Next to him can be seen (if you really want to see him) a man, presumably an accomplice in a construction worker's hard hat.[74]

What is interesting is that none of these accounts corroborate any other; indeed, there isn't even the false corroboration in which one account is apparently derived from another. "Badge man" in the police uniform is not in the location where Hoffman claimed to see a shooter but rather behind the north–south leg of the fence.[75] No witness confirmed a man in a Dallas Police uniform (although this filtered into much later accounts, such as that of Beverly Oliver). Joe Smith's "Secret Service agent" was not dressed in a police uniform but in the civilian clothing a federal agent might wear. Nobody saw anybody resembling "hard-hat man" behind the stockade fence at the time of the shooting. Likewise, the suit man and the railroad man are unique in Hoffman's account, and the fellow that Price saw running doesn't resemble anybody other witnesses described.

All this looks like "noise" and not "signal," at least as evidence of a grassy knoll shooter. There is no reason to doubt that J. C. Price saw a man running or that Lee Bowers saw two men doing nothing at all suspicious or that Hoffman saw two men running, as he apparently first told the FBI. The British television documentary *The Men Who Killed Kennedy* tried to conflate Bowers's account, the latter-day Hoffman account, and the badge man/hard-hat man evidence as all proving a grassy knoll shooter. But this attempt requires overlooking massive discrepancies among the three.

In the following chapters, other evidence bears on the existence of a grassy knoll shooter. But for now the witness testimony proves little. The best witness, Lee Bowers, seems to contradict the idea, and the other witnesses contradict each other.

Chapter Two

Problems of Memory

So far, this book has dealt with problems of perception, or cases where sensory impressions appear to have gotten badly confused before being stored in memory. But, of course, I can't rule out that these contradictions involve memory problems. There is plenty of opportunity for memories to become altered and distorted if a person is interviewed days or weeks, not to speak of months or years, after the event.

But what about testimony that changes? Sometimes—and this book looks at some colorful and cockamamy cases—the witness is telling tall tales. But more commonly, witnesses are merely misremembering.

ALYEA: CHICKEN BONES ON THE FIFTH FLOOR

News photographer Tom Alyea was shooting the president's visit to Dallas for WFAA-TV and was lucky enough to get into the depository soon after the 12:30 p.m. shooting and before it was sealed off by the police. His film is an important historical document. But in the 1990s Alyea gave a bit of testimony that raised some eyebrows. It had long been reported that the police found the remains of a chicken lunch on the depository's sixth floor while searching it in the minutes after the assassination.[1]

But Alyea insisted that story was wrong. At the Reporters Remember conference in Dallas in 1993, he said,

All right, on the fifth floor—I'm going to get questions on this—I was walking with this officer, plainclothesman, and we see a sack on the floor. And a

Dr Pepper bottle. I said fifth floor. He hit it with his toe. Some chicken bones came out of it.[2]

This comment wasn't a random misstatement. Alyea insisted to author Connie Kritzberg later in the 1990s that the chicken bones, Dr Pepper bottle, and so on, were found on the fifth floor.[3] But what about all the Dallas cops who said they saw the remains of the lunch on the sixth floor?[4] Depository employee William Shelley also reported the same thing.[5] So did the fellow who actually ate the lunch, Bonnie Ray Williams.[6]

Alyea gave an oral history to Columbia University on December 19, 1963. At the time, he said,

they were conducting a systematic search. It boiled down to the sixth floor. After a while it was obvious that the assassin was not in the building. . . . There was a stack [of boxes] with a stack of chicken bones on it. There was a Dr Pepper bottle which they dusted for fingerprints. The fingerprints were not Oswald's.[7]

One could perhaps fuss and fume and question the "cover-up" of the chicken bones on the fifth floor, but Alyea didn't believe there was a conspiracy and outspokenly condemned conspiracy theories. The necessary conclusion, quite simply, is that his memory failed him.

MALCOLM COUCH: A WILD AND WOOLLY DEALEY PLAZA SCENARIO

Malcolm Couch was a news photographer riding in the motorcade who jumped out of the car as it reached the depository and captured some dramatic footage of the aftermath of the shooting.[8] On November 22, 2000, his hometown newspaper recorded his memories of that scene.

Local Resident, Former TV Reporter Remembers Kennedy Assassination: Couch's Memories Remain Clear 37 Years Later

CLIFTON—Mal Couch, a citizen of the Womack community, and a former television reporter and cameraman for ABC-TV in Dallas, can remember Nov. 22, 1963, like it was yesterday.

. . . "At the scene, people were still lying on the ground, some protecting their children. Others were running. Policemen were scattering in every direction with shotguns and pistols drawn.

"I started toward the building where I had seen the rifle in the window. Then I saw something very weird. There was a trail of blood from the spot where the shooting occurred to the entrance of the Texas School Book Depository. I pointed it out to a man with me.

"Just then an FBI man stepped out of the building, and in his hand was an object dripping blood. It looked like a piece of hairy flesh. I know I didn't imagine this. The scene is very clear to me."[9]

A vivid image indeed. Unfortunately, there is no independent corroboration of any such piece of hairy flesh dripping blood, and the account seems to contradict the testimony Couch made to the Warren Commission. Then, he reported seeing a "pool" (not a trail) of blood near the depository. Asked whether there was "anything else you noticed by this pool of blood," Couch replied that there was nothing.[10] Neither Couch nor Alyea seem to be lying. But when a witness says, "I didn't imagine this. The scene is very clear to me," and a reporter says, "Memories remain clear 37 years later," beware.

MORE WITNESSES WHO CHANGED THEIR STORIES

One of the more interesting Dealey Plaza witnesses is a fellow named Phil Willis, a retired officer in the U.S. Army Air Corps who had been at Bellows Field, Hawaii, when the Japanese attacked Pearl Harbor. As a pilot, he had also fought in the Battle of Midway and the Guadalcanal campaign. He apparently had a knack for being where historic things happen, since he (along with his wife and two daughters) was also at the corner of Houston and Elm Streets when Kennedy was shot in Dealey Plaza.[11]

Willis can be found in various conspiracy videos supporting the idea of a grassy knoll shooter. In a 1993 video, he claimed,

The final shot had to come from the grassy knoll . . . somewhere in that area to hit him in the side . . . over the ear. There was at least one shot came [sic] from that direction, and it took the top of his head off and blew his brains out and backwards. And . . . um . . . I would swear that over my mother's grave to this day.[12]

But what did he say in 1964? Before the Warren Commission, when he was asked whether he actually observed the president when he was hit in the head, he responded, "No, sir; I did not. I couldn't see that well, and I was more concerned about the shots coming from that building." When asked what building was that, he replied, "The Texas School Book Depository Building." Warren Commission counsel Liebeler pressed further: "You were pretty sure?" Willis replied, "I felt certain. I even looked for smoke, and I knew it came from high up."

Acting as though the issue was not yet entirely resolved, Liebeler asked, "So you did not actually observe the President at the time he was hit in the head?" Willis said, "No, sir. . . ."[13]

At the trial of Clay Shaw, a New Orleans businessman, in 1969, Willis repeated that he had heard the shots from the Texas School Book Depository.[14] So what is going on here?

It's tempting to say that Willis was lying in his later statements, telling a good story to delight conspiracy believers. But given the discussion about false memories, he really might have formed a mental image of Kennedy's head being hit by a shot that had to have come from the grassy knoll. However, he might also have been influenced by his wife, Marilyn Willis, who believed that Kennedy's brains blew out backward and upward at the moment of the head shot.[15] Given that memory is a reconstruction, he might well have "remembered" seeing Kennedy being shot in the head. Actually, if you look at his later statement carefully, he doesn't literally say he saw Kennedy get hit in the head but just that it happened. Still, he ought to have been more circumspect about what he was willing to swear over his mother's grave.

OTHER WITNESSES WHO CHANGED THEIR STORIES

Witnesses who have changed their stories are a dime a dozen in this case, especially if one reads conspiracy books. Consider, for example, the question of whether Lee Harvey Oswald shot Officer J. D. Tippit less than an hour after Kennedy was shot in Dealey Plaza. Conspiracists challenge the Warren Commission on this point by claiming that Oswald entered the Texas Theatre (where he was eventually arrested) too early to have shot Tippit. For example, the 1988 television documentary *The Men Who Killed Kennedy* (Part 4, "The Patsy") quotes the employee who collected tickets and manned the concession stand, Warren "Butch" Burroughs, as saying, "We started the movie at one o'clock, and I was counting candy behind the candy case. And he . . . Oswald slipped in around . . . between 1:00 and 1:07."[16]

Likewise, Burroughs in 1987 told author Jim Marrs that Oswald had come into the Texas Theatre "only minutes after the feature started, which was exactly

1:00 p.m." Burroughs then ups the ante by claiming that about 1:15 p.m., Oswald came to the concession stand and bought some popcorn.[17]

If Oswald was in the Texas Theatre shortly after 1:00 p.m., he could not have been at Tenth Street and Patton Avenue around 1:15 p.m. and shot J. D. Tippit, as the Warren Commission concluded.

The problems with Burrough's later testimony are massive, however. In the first place, it contradicts that of Johnny Calvin Brewer, who saw Oswald in the vestibule of his shoe store after news of both killings—Kennedy's and Tippit's—had been broadcast. Oswald was slinking around, looking suspicious, while cop cars with their sirens blaring drove up and down West Jefferson Boulevard in front of the store. Brewer then followed Oswald to the nearby Texas Theatre. None of this action could have happened before the Tippit's shooting was reported on Dallas Police radio at about 1:16 p.m. Of course, the testimony of Julia Postal, the woman who worked in the theater's box office (but who was standing out on Jefferson and watching the police cars), meshes seamlessly with that of Brewer. Postal said she had stepped out of the box office and saw a man who ducked into the theater.[18] She later identified the man as Oswald, and she testified that Johnny Brewer approached her and asked her to call the police shortly after the man ducked into the theater.

But not only does Burroughs's later testimony contradict Brewer and Postal, it also contradicts his earlier testimony before the Warren Commission. Asked flatly by the Warren Commission counsel, "Did you see that man come in the theater?" Burroughs answered, "No, sir, I didn't." He went on to explain: "I had a lot of stock candy to count and put in the candy case for the coming night. . . . I think he sneaked up the stairs real fast."

Burroughs added that when the police came and asked him whether a man had come in without a ticket, he told them, "I haven't seen him myself. He might have, but I didn't see him when he came in. He must have sneaked in and run on upstairs before I saw him."[19]

So it seems that Burroughs was one of the many witnesses whose memory got "better" with time. There is no particular reason to think he was a liar. As noted previously, discrepancies of this magnitude creep into the testimony of even the most apparently honest witnesses, even witnesses who have never sought the limelight and sometimes have insisted that there was no conspiracy. Memory, quite simply, plays tricks.

MANGLED MEDICAL TESTIMONY

If witnesses who were in Dealey Plaza are unreliable, witnesses to other traumatic events that occurred that day are as well. The president's autopsy at Bethesda Naval Hospital in Maryland (near Washington) produced some additional suspect testimony.

Consider, for example, Capt. David Osborne (USN) who was in the autopsy room when Kennedy's body was brought in. In 1978 the HSCA on Assassinations interviewed him and described his testimony this way:

> Osborne said that the President was fully dressed when the coffin was opened. Upon raising his shoulders to remove the coat, Osborne said that a slug rolled out of his clothing and onto the table. Osborne said that the slug was copper-clad and that the Secret Service or FBI took possession of this. Upon further inquiry, Osborne emphasized that the slug was a fully intact missile and not a fragment.[20]

Conspiracy theorists have jumped all over the this so-called slug account, since it implies both an "extra" bullet, which is inconsistent with the Warren Commission account, and a cover-up since no such bullet appeared in evidence. Unfortunately, none of the other witnesses who were there corroborate this story.[21]

What neither conspiracy authors nor in fact anybody else will mention is Osborne's claim that "the President was fully dressed when the coffin was opened." In reality, Kennedy's nude body was wrapped in sheets at Parkland Hospital and placed in the casket from which it was removed at Bethesda.[22]

Then autopsy radiologist Dr. John Ebersole testified before the HSCA and mostly said sensible things. But he also claimed that when Kennedy's body arrived at Bethesda, it showed "a neatly sutured transverse surgical wound across the low neck."[23] Not only does no other witness remember any such thing, but also the autopsy photos of Kennedy's body show a large gash in the throat that Dr. Malcolm Perry at Parkland Hospital made so that the doctors could get a tracheotomy tube into Kennedy's airway. The wound is not sutured.

The medical evidence, in fact, is a treasure trove of unreliable observations. White House photographer Robert Knudsen, for example, claimed to have photographed the autopsy,[24] but he did not. He also told the committee that he had seen photos of Kennedy's body with metal probes in Kennedy's torso. One he said was in the neck (consistent with the path of the single bullet) and another "six, seven inches" below that, or (alternatively) "midway between the neck and the waist."[25] Not only do extant photos and X-rays show no probes and no other witness remembers probes, but also the supposed lower probe does not fit any plausible bullet's trajectory unless an assassin in the trunk fired through the backseat and into Kennedy's torso.

The Assassination Records Review Board (ARRB), which took a considerable amount of witness testimony in the 1990s, received even wilder reports. One witness, Saundra Spencer, was a photo lab technician who remembered processing photos of Kennedy's body. But she remembered photos that showed a body much less bloody and mangled than what's shown in the extant photos from Kennedy's autopsy.[26] Why any conspiracy would want a nicer looking version of his autopsy photos is a great mystery.

Several of the witnesses interviewed by the ARRB were shown the Kennedy autopsy photos, and the response was often that the images did not correspond with what they remembered from November 22, 1963. This fact has provided more grist for the conspiracy mill in challenging the authenticity of the autopsy photos.

John Stringer, who unlike Knudsen *did* photograph the autopsy, said the photos of Kennedy's brain, supposedly from the autopsy, were not from the angles he remembered shooting. Conspiracist (and ARRB staffer) Doug Horne apparently reported that "John Stringer under oath completely disavowed these photographs saying he did not take them, that he could not have taken them."[27]

Of course, Stringer had signed a statement in 1966 confirming he had examined all the photos and that they were the ones he took.[28]

And yet another witness challenged the authenticity of the brain's photos, former FBI agent Francis X. O'Neill Jr., who had been at the autopsy. He believed the brain shown in the photos was too large to be that of JFK. "I did not recall it [the brain] being that large," he said when shown the photos.[29] He further said, "I can't say that it looks like the brain that I saw." When asked, "Can you identify that in any reasonable way as to appearing to be the—what the brain looked like of President Kennedy?" His reply: "It appears to be too much."[30]

So here are two witnesses questioning the autopsy photos, except for one problem. Stringer never questions the *size* of the brain in the photos, only the angles from which they were photographed.

Stringer and O'Neill also provide testimony questioning the famous photo of the back of Kennedy's head, and particularly the area of the occipital bone, intact.

Conspiracists insist that this part was blown out, proving a shot from the grassy knoll. Stringer examined the photo and said that he remembered the entrance wound in a different place. When O'Neill reviewed the photo, he thought it had been "doctored in some way." He said he thought there was a "larger opening in the back . . . in the back of the head" and "more of a massive wound."[31] Yet Stringer said that, except for the location of the entrance wound, the photo showed the back of the head as he remembered it and that the large defect was "above the ear" in the parietal bone, not in the very back of the head in the occipital bone. He said that the occipital bone was intact at the time of the autopsy.[32]

Thus two witnesses gave testimony that contradicts the extant autopsy photos. Unfortunately, the two witnesses also contradict each other.

Dr. Jeremy Gunn, who was executive director and general counsel of the ARRB, took much of this testimony. Gunn told an audience at Stanford University about what he called "the profound, underscore, profound unreliability of eyewitness testimony. You just cannot believe it. And I can tell you something else that is even worse than eyewitness testimony and that is 35 year old eyewitness testimony."[33]

FITTING THE MODEL TO THE NOISE

Much of the testimony, in other words, is "noise" and not "signal." But what happens when you try to fit a theory to the noise? The answer is you come up with a vastly implausible theory. Author David Lifton latched on to three bits of data and drew the conclusion that Kennedy's body, rather than being flown from Dallas to Andrews Air Force Base and then taken directly to Bethesda Naval Hospital for the autopsy, was stolen from Air Force One at Love Field in Dallas, surgically altered, and then sent to Bethesda. The reason, supposedly, was that all the shots that hit Kennedy had been fired from the front; thus, the wounds had to be altered to make them appear as if the shots had come from the rear, or consistent with shots from the sniper's nest in the depository.[34]

What data did Lifton use? One piece was the testimony of laboratory technologist Paul O'Connor, who remembered Kennedy's body arriving at the autopsy in a body bag and not in the sheets in which it was wrapped in Dallas.[35] Another witness, Dennis David, claimed to have seen Kennedy's body being brought into the Bethesda autopsy in a plain, gray metal shipping casket and not the fancy casket in which it was placed at Parkland Hospital.[36] Finally, an FBI report by James W. Sibert and Francis X. O'Neill Jr. (yes, the FBI agent already mentioned) says that Kennedy's body, on arrival, showed there had been "surgery of the head area."[37] But no surgery had been done in Dallas. So Lifton draws the obvious conclusion that the body had been snatched, mutilated, and put into a body bag that was then put in a plain shipping coffin to be delivered to the autopsy.

Coming to this conclusion requires Lifton to ignore the vast majority of witnesses who said the body had arrived at the autopsy in the same fancy Elgin Britannia casket in which it had left Dallas. And a majority of witnesses likewise said the body arrived in sheets (although some of the descriptions of the wrapping varied a bit).[38] Nobody else said the body was in a body bag. As for the "surgery of the head area," both Sibert and O'Neill told the ARRB that the autopsy doctors— Sibert named Dr. James Humes—had used that phrase.[39] This idea was apparently an initial impression developed early in the autopsy, which became enshrined in the FBI report and then became a "fact" upon which an entire theory could be built.

Lifton's theory is vastly implausible on many counts. For one, the timing he suggests for the body snatching at Love Field in Dallas simply doesn't work.[40] Adm. George G. Burkley, the president's personal physician, certified in an affidavit that he had "traveled from the hospital to the Air Force One in the ambulance with the President's body in the casket and also on the plane; the casket was neither opened nor disturbed in any way."[41] Likewise, Brig. Gen. Godfrey McHugh told *Time* magazine that he at no time left the body unattended except for a few minutes when he went forward in Air Force One to talk to the pilot. McHugh also insists that loyal aides Larry O'Brien and Dave Powers, as well as Mrs. Kennedy, were with the casket while he was gone.[42] Kenneth O'Donnell appears to confirm this, with the proviso that Jackie left for a short time to go to her compartment to freshen up.[43] William Manchester records that McHugh actually made *five* trips through the length of the plane in an effort to get the pilot to take off, but Manchester also notes that, when Jackie and other staffers left the compartment to attend the swearing-in ceremony of Lyndon Johnson, McHugh stood at attention beside the coffin.[44]

Given the unreliability of witness testimony, one can choose a bit here and a smidgeon there and come up with a wholly novel theory. That's what Lifton has done. But if you ignore the weight of the evidence, it's likely to be an absurd theory.

COULD ALL OF THESE WITNESSES BE WRONG?

Of course, if you have a theory to prove and witnesses differ a lot, you can readily back up your theory by quoting those witnesses who happen to support it. Thus in the documentary film *Plot to Kill JFK: Rush to Judgment*, Mark Lane interviews seven witnesses who thought they had heard shots from the grassy knoll.[45] He also interviewed the witness Charles Brehm, who had told the FBI that the shots came (as detailed in chapter 1) from "one of the two buildings back at the corner of Elm and Houston Streets."[46] But apparently knowing what his testimony would be, Lane doesn't ask Brehm from what direction the shots came.[47]

Thus, is it common for conspiracy theorists to parade a bunch of witnesses, all of whom give testimony supporting a conspiracy, and then ask, could all of these witnesses be wrong? Indeed, if you pick a random sample from among (say) all the witnesses in Dealey Plaza or pick the best witnesses (perhaps defined as those with the best view), it's highly unlikely that they will all be wrong. But what if the witnesses were chosen because they support a particular theory? If the theory is wrong, the witnesses are all wrong since they have been *chosen* for their wrong testimony.

A similar way of manipulating evidence involves selecting particular *elements* from the entire testimony of a witness. Quite a large number of witnesses said some things that would imply a conspiracy, and yet other things they said would imply a lone shooter. Bill Newman, standing on the grass near Elm Street and close to the motorcade, thought the shots came from "the garden directly behind me"—the grassy knoll (more or less).[48] Yet he saw the head wound "in the side of the head" and even thought that "the ear went,"[49] flatly contradicting the view (almost universal among conspiracy authors) that the back of Kennedy's head was blown out. He is thus both a conspiracy witness and a lone assassin witness, depending on which part of his testimony is used.

Since there are often different elements to the testimony of any witness, the odds are pretty good that most witnesses will be wrong about *something*. Thus even if you select random witnesses or the best witnesses, you can get a majority that support some wrong conclusion if you pick and choose among the elements of their testimony.

Just What Did the Witnesses Say?

The tour de force of selectively using testimony to reach a particular conclusion can be found in an essay by Gary Aguilar, who claims to have examined the testimony of forty-six witnesses to Kennedy's wounds at Parkland Hospital and Bethesda Naval Hospital. Aguilar found that forty-four of them saw a wound to the "back of the head," contradicting the autopsy photos and X-rays and suggesting a shot from the grassy knoll.[50]

To reach this number, however, Aguilar has to be massively selective in the testimony he uses and quite tendentious in how he interprets it. Some examples follow.[51]

Clint Hill was the Secret Service agent who ran to the presidential limo after the shooting started and huddled over John and Jackie Kennedy on the wild ride to Parkland Hospital. Aguilar quotes him (correctly) as telling the Warren Commission that he saw a "large gaping wound in the right rear portion of the [president's] head." Aguilar interprets this statement as supporting his position despite its vagueness. But Hill told *National Geographic*, in a TV special titled *Inside the U.S. Secret Service*, that there was "a gaping hole above his right ear about the size of my palm."[52] "Above his right ear" implies parietal bone and is consistent with the autopsy photos and X-rays.

Aguilar quotes Doris Nelson, a Parkland nurse, as having been asked by conspiracy authors Robert Groden and Harry Livingstone whether the autopsy photo showing the back of the president's head as being intact was accurate. She had replied, "No. It's not true. Because there was no hair back there. There wasn't even hair back there. It was blown away." Yet when a *Life* magazine photographer asked her to show where the wound was, she put her hand squarely on the top of the head, above the right ear.[53]

Jerrol Custer, a Bethesda X-ray technician, told David Lifton that he had processed X-rays showing "the rear of the President's head was blown off." He apparently repeated at press conferences in the early 1990s his conclusion that the extant X-rays are faked. Yet when the ARRB asked him to draw the head wound, he drew one on the right side of Kennedy's head, explicitly excluding occipital bone.[54]

William Greer, driver of the presidential limo, when testifying before the Warren Commission, put his hand on his head and said the wound was on the "upper right side." Counsel Arlen Specter summarized, "Upper right side, going toward the rear." Specter's statement "going toward the rear" is the apparent basis of Aguilar's claim that Greer is a "back of the head" witness.

Aguilar quoted Charles Carrico, a Parkland doctor, as saying that the wound "was a large gaping wound, located in the right occipitoparietal area" and was a "defect in the posterior skull, the occipital region." Aguilar doesn't tell readers that Carrico also told the HSCA that the wound was "above and posterior to the ear, almost to the crown of the head."[55] Further, Carrico drew the wound for a *Boston Globe* investigative story in 1981, and his drawing shows the wound above the ear, entirely in the parietal bone.[56]

More Problems Interpreting Testimony

Aguilar's essay is rife with this sort of selective use of witness testimony and with questionable interpretations. For example, Aguilar interprets any wound described by a witness as occipital or occipitoparietal as extending into the occipital bone. Yet one of Aguilar's witnesses, Parkland doctor Robert Grossman, explained to the *Boston Globe* that "many doctors loosely use the term to refer to 'the back fifth of the head.' . . . There is the ambiguity about what constitutes the occipital and parietal area. . . . It's very imprecise."[57] If one is inclined to think that Grossman's claim is somewhat quirky, one might check out the report of the HSCA's Forensic Pathology Panel. In two different places the panel says the entrance wound in the back of the head is in the "occipital region" and in two additional places says it is an "occipital defect."[58] But the HSCA panel, consisting of nine of the nation's top forensic pathologists, explicitly placed the entrance defect *in the cowlick area in parietal bone.*

The Ramsey Clark Panel, meeting in 1968, likewise described the entrance wound as in "the occipital region" and put it firmly in parietal bone.[59]

There are other problems with Aguilar's analysis. One in particular involves the fact that several of the doctors he lists as back-of-the-head witnesses could not have seen a wound that extended into the occipital bone since Kennedy was lying face up on a gurney, and the back of his head, or the area of occipital bone, would not have been visible.[60] Add the fact that the wound was obscured by (in the words of Dr. Charles Baxter) "just one mass of blood and hair."[61] One good indicator of how unreliable this sort of witness testimony can be is that Parkland Hospital doctors Marion Jenkins, Robert McClelland, Adolph Giesecke, and David Stewart, as well as Father Oscar Huber (who administered the last rites to Kennedy), said there was a wound on the *left* side of Kennedy's head.[62]

And Aguilar wants to use this sort of testimony to impeach the autopsy photos and X-rays.

THE OSWALD SIGHTINGS

If the witnesses are believable, Lee Oswald was popping up all over the place in the days and weeks before the assassination. There were scores, if not hundreds, of such reports. Only a few examples are explored here.

The Rifle's Scope

A witness working in the Irving (Texas) Sporting Goods Store claimed that he had encountered Oswald when he came in and had a telescopic sight mounted on his rifle. The witness, one Dial D. Ryder, produced an undated repair tag with the name Oswald on it. However, on numerous occasions between November 22 and November 28, Ryder had discussed with his boss, Charles W. Greener, the possibility that

Oswald had been in the store. But although Ryder claimed that he had discovered the tag with Oswald on it on November 23, he neither produced the tag for Greener nor positively claimed to Greener that he had actually seen Oswald. He only came forward with that information after the story broke in the local media. Meanwhile, Oswald had received his Mannlicher-Carcano rifle from Klein's Sporting Goods with the scope already mounted.[63]

The Furniture Mart

Two women working in the Furniture Mart just one and a half blocks from the Irving Sporting Goods Store reported seeing a man they believed was Oswald come into their store and ask to purchase a part for a gun in early November of 1963. He had driven up in a two-tone, blue and white 1957 Ford. Upon being told that the part was not available, he supposedly went to the car; returned with a woman who they later identified as Marina Oswald, his wife, and two young children; and looked at furniture for about thirty-five or forty minutes. When Marina was taken by the Warren Commission on a rather unusual field trip to inspect the premises of the Furniture Mart, she insisted she had never seen the place before.[64] Further, Lee Oswald could not drive. A friend of Marina's, Mrs. Ruth Paine, had been giving him driving lessons, but she was adamant that he had not achieved proficiency. "He couldn't even make a right-angle turn. He'd pull around too far," she told a reporter.[65] Further, he had been unable to obtain a learner's permit.[66] Finally, it's not clear where he could have gotten a car of that description. The coup de grâce for this sighting occurred when one of the women, Mrs. Gertrude Hunter, testified that she remembered the automobile's description because she was expecting the arrival of a friend from Houston who owned a similar car. The FBI contacted the friend, a woman named Mrs. Doris Dominey. She explained that Hunter had "a strange obsession for attempting to inject herself into any big event which comes to her attention," and should a tornado "strike out of a clear sky, Mrs. Hunter would claim that she had known the day before that the event was to occur." Moreover, she "is likely to claim some personal knowledge of any major crime which receives much publicity." Finally, since her family members were aware of her tall tales, "they normally pay no attention to her."[67]

Selective Service Office

After the assassination, Mrs. Lee Dannelly came forward, stating that she was sure that Lee Oswald had come into the Austin, Texas, offices of the Selective Service

System about six or eight weeks prior to the weekend of the assassination. Oswald wanted to change his undesirable discharge from the Marine Corps Reserve. Dannelly claimed she talked to Oswald for thirty minutes and later became specific about the date on which this talk occurred, September 25.[68] Neither her fellow employees nor any written records confirmed Oswald's interview. Although the FBI, unlike the case with Gertrude Hunter, found no derogatory information on Dannelly, and there is no reason to believe she lied, Oswald was not in Austin on September 25. As the Warren Commission observed, "All the information which she furnished with respect to Oswald's appearance and conversation could have been derived from the news media, consciously or unconsciously, by the time she told the FBI her story."[69] So here apparently is an honest witness who had an encounter with someone who, in some way or ways, resembled Oswald. Memory being what it is, this event became an appointment with the famous assassin.

Car Shopping

In the wake of the assassination Albert Guy Bogard, a car salesman in a Lincoln-Mercury dealership in Dallas, claimed that on November 9, 1963, Lee Harvey Oswald came into the dealership and expressed interest in buying a car. Oswald then test-drove a car at high speed on the Stemmons Freeway. Bogard's account received partial corroboration from some of his coworkers. Both Frank Pizzo and Eugene Wilson remembered the instance when Bogard's customer was in the showroom, although neither offered any sort of positive identification of Oswald. Bogard said the customer had given the name Lee Oswald, and he (Bogard) had written that on the back of a business card. Another salesman, Oran Brown, remembered the name Oswald being on a paper in his possession prior to the assassination. Unfortunately, neither the paper nor the business card was ever recovered.[70] This particular incident has some juicy bits associated with it. Bogard remembered the customer saying that he wasn't ready to buy but might be "in a couple or 3 weeks, that he had some money coming in."[71] This recollection is an absolutely explosive piece of evidence, if one believes that Oswald shot Kennedy as a paid assassin.

This incident also has the normal number of inconsistencies among the witnesses. Bogard said the customer wanted to purchase a car with cash, while Pizzo and Wilson both said the customer wanted credit. Indeed, Wilson stated that when the customer was informed about the requirements for getting credit, he responded, "Maybe I'm going to have to go back to Russia to buy a car." Wilson also stated that Bogard's customer was only five feet tall.[72]

But Oswald, as Mrs. Paine indicated, could not drive—at least not well enough to own a car—and lacked even a learner's permit, much less a license. Although Marina had urged Lee to buy a car, Lee had insisted that he simply could not afford one—something that is obvious to anyone who knows about the penury of the Oswalds' existence.[73] Worse, both Marina Oswald and Ruth Paine testified to Lee Oswald's whereabouts on November 9: he had been in Irving and then had gone to Oak Cliff (a Dallas neighborhood across the Trinity River from downtown Dallas) with his family and Mrs. Paine. They had tried to get Lee a learner's permit at the Automobile Driver's License Bureau, but the office was closed. Then they had gone shopping. He could not possibly have been in Dallas trying to buy a car.[74]

Auto Insurance

Edward A. Brand operated an insurance office on Zang Boulevard in the Oak Cliff section of Dallas. He reported to the FBI that a man who identified himself as O. H. Lee had come into his office about two weeks before Kennedy was assassinated and asked for a quote on auto liability insurance. The man said he lived across the street at a rooming house owned by A. C. Johnson. Brand said he thought that the man produced a Texas driver's license with the name Lee on it, but he didn't know whether the initials O and H were included.

Brand was not able to supply a quote, since the man said he did not own a car but planned on buying one in the near future. Brand identified the man as Lee Harvey Oswald, but according to the FBI report,

> BRAND concluded by saying that he did not immediately recognize LEE HARVEY OSWALD'S photograph in the Dallas newspapers, or on television, until after reading OSWALD in the past used the name LEE, at which time he did recognize OSWALD'S photograph as being the individual who contacted him.[75]

Enough rings true here in Brand's account to be rather tantalizing, including the location near Oswald's rooming house, which A. C. Johnson did indeed own, and the fact that, if Oswald were trying to buy a car, it was about the time he might have been shopping for insurance. But again, Oswald never had a driver's license, and it's unlikely he was planning to buy a car. Perhaps the most significant aspect of this sighting, however, is that Brand did not recognize that he had seen Oswald (in spite of having apparently seen his picture multiple times) until he found out that sometimes Oswald used the alias O. H. Lee. There is clearly huge room for suggestibility here. Indeed, by the time Brand read that Oswald had used that alias, Brand had almost certainly also read about the Johnson rooming house on Beckley Avenue, where Oswald used that alias.

Thus, while some might be inclined to take this sighting seriously because certain details match, it's likely that this sighting was the *result* of certain details matching. In other words, somebody who at least vaguely looked like Oswald went to an office in Oak Cliff, may (or may not) have used the name Lee, and may (or may not) have mentioned the Johnson rooming house, and enough things clicked to produce a memory (almost certainly an honest one) of Lee shopping for auto insurance.

The Shooting Range

One of the most interesting sightings—actually a related set of sightings—occurred at the Sports Drome Rifle Range in Dallas, where several witnesses believed they had seen Oswald on various occasions during September, October, and November 1963. Four witnesses—Malcolm H. Price Jr., Garland Slack, Sterling C. Wood, and Dr. Homer Wood—all confidently claimed they had seen Oswald there. These witnesses had variable but significant contact with Oswald: Price adjusted Oswald's scope; Slack had a run-in with the man, who was shooting at Slack's target; and the man spoke briefly with Sterling Wood and his father, Homer, about the man's rifle.

As is usual with these sightings, some of the details don't fit Oswald at all. Price, for example, said the man wore a "Bulldogger Texas style" hat and further that he had bubble gum or chewing tobacco in his cheek. Slack said the individual had blond hair.[76] Slack claimed to "know rifles" and to have gotten a good look at the man's rifle. He insisted it was not the Mannlicher-Carcano shown in published photos of the rifle after the assassination.[77]

As is often the case, the dates throw considerable doubt on these sightings. Price thought Oswald had been at the Sports Drome on September 28, but Oswald—as we will see in chapter 11—was in Mexico City on that day. Garland Slack believed that Oswald had been at the range on November 10.[78] But the same testimony from Mrs. Paine and Marina Oswald that ruled out Oswald having been at the downtown Lincoln-Mercury dealership also ruled out Oswald having been at the Sports Drome the following day. Both women testified that Oswald was in Irving on November 10.[79]

While many of these alleged sightings seem to have a modicum of credibility, others are just random. For example, one report from a witness named Joseph E. Field has Oswald, Jack Ruby (the Dallas strip club owner who later shot Oswald), Marina, and Lee's brother Robert in a bar in Los Angeles in late April 1963, shooting pool and drinking beer.[80] Another tip has both Oswald and Ruby in Tupelo, Mississippi, at the 1963 Mississippi-Alabama Fair and Dairy Show. The informant claimed that at the event's rodeo, Ruby masqueraded as a clown while Oswald served as the master of ceremonies.[81]

Analyzing the Sightings

In all these cases, there is plenty of reason to doubt that the witnesses actually saw Oswald. However, the most interesting sightings involve multiple witnesses who testified to seeing Oswald in a particular location. Somebody who suspected that something interesting was going on might ask whether all these witnesses could have been wrong. The phenomenon of "false corroboration" will be discussed in chapter 13. For now, note that in virtually all these cases, the witnesses had talked to each other. There is no need to posit a conspiracy among witnesses to lie; instead, the simple power of suggestion could account for a great deal.

Also, the witnesses saw a man do something or say something that would have reminded them of Oswald later: he could have mentioned guns or Russia or an undesirable discharge from the military. But what of the inconsistencies among the witnesses who encountered the same Oswald? One possibility is that all witnesses saw a single individual—be it Oswald or an impostor or somebody who just vaguely looked like Oswald—and their variations are just errors of memory. That is, the noise slightly obscured the signal of a single man doing things that reminded people of Oswald. Or do the inconsistencies indicate that the memories of different people were all assimilated to a memory of an "Oswald" after the assassination?

Before reaching any definite conclusions, the most important Oswald sightings must be examined.

ODIO: THE MOTHER OF ALL OSWALD SIGHTINGS

Space precludes a discussion of perhaps the most important Oswald sighting, reported by Sylvia Odio. A Cuban exile living in Dallas, she was visited on September 25, 1963, by three men: two Cubans and one Anglo. The following day, one of the Cubans told her in a phone call that the Anglo was "kind of nuts" and had said, "Kennedy should have been assassinated after the Bay of Pigs." After the assassination, Odio inferred that the Anglo might have been the shooter, remembered his name as "Leon Oswald," and (when she saw Lee Oswald on TV) identified him as the Anglo. However, it couldn't have been Oswald, because solid evidence puts him in Houston on the night when this would have happened.[82]

TWIFORD: OSWALD'S ALIBI

So far, I have merely argued that it's plausible that Odio reconstructed, in the wake of the assassination, a memory of Oswald and two other guys at the door. But is there any evidence that it was not Oswald?

Yes, there is.

But first, one detail needs to be explained: if the man at Odio's doorway was Oswald, the visit had to have occurred on Wednesday, September 25, 1963. Records indicate Oswald left Houston at 2:35 a.m. on September 26 on Continental Trailways bus number 5133 headed for Laredo, Texas.[83] As we will see, Oswald had to have been in New Orleans the morning of September 25. With some help from someone with a car, he could have made it from New Orleans to Odio's apartment in Dallas and then to Houston, but he could not have been in two places on the evening of September 25.

In the wake of the assassination, the FBI discovered the Houston address and phone numbers of a fellow named Horace Twiford in Oswald's address book. Contacting the Twiford household, they found that Mrs. Estelle Twiford remembered Oswald having called her one night. He had wanted to contact her husband, an activist in the Socialist Labor Party. Oswald had sent a request for literature to the Socialist Labor Party in New York, which forwarded it to Twiford in Houston. He had duly mailed a copy of the *Weekly People*, a party newspaper, to Oswald. When he called, Oswald told Mrs. Twiford that he was flying to Mexico and mentioned his membership in the Fair Play for Cuba Committee.[84] Mrs. Twiford explained that her husband, a merchant seaman, was at sea.

Mrs. Twiford's story has some untidy elements to it. She thought Oswald had called in late October or early November.[85] Later, her husband remembered Estelle telling him about Oswald's call when he returned to Houston on September 26.[86] Mrs. Twiford thought the call came "not in the late evening," and the "best she could do" to fix the time of the call was between 7:00 p.m. and 9:00 p.m., and then later between 7:00 p.m. and 10:00 p.m.[87] Yet the only bus Oswald could have taken from New Orleans to Houston on the afternoon of September 25 was scheduled to arrive at 10:50 p.m.[88] So if Oswald was in Houston when he called for her husband, Mrs. Twiford must have been wrong about the time.

Of course, of the three men's visit to her apartment, Sylvia Odio had insisted, "It either was a Thursday or a Friday. It must have been either one of those days, in the last days of September."[89] Indeed, she remembered that it had to be Thursday or Friday because her sister Annie, who was visiting, came on these days to babysit Sylvia's children.[90] So if uncertainty about the date is a problem for Twiford's testimony, it's an even bigger one for Odio, given the latter's apparent certainty.

Mrs. Twiford said that she thought the call was a local one because no operator was involved. Further, Oswald had stated that he only had a few hours to spend in Houston and that he wanted to contact her husband.[91]

Is Twiford's Call Just Another "Sighting"?

If witnesses can think that they saw Oswald at a shooting range (even though he could not have been there) or getting a scope put on his rifle (even though it came with a scope already mounted), could it be that Mrs. Twiford merely *thought* she received a telephone call from Oswald?

Unlike the Odio case, there are three pieces of hard evidence that link Oswald to the Twifords. First, the Twifords produced an envelope with the return address L. H. Oswald, Box 2915, Dallas, Texas.[92] Second, Mrs. Twiford also had a note she said she wrote with the notation "Lee Oswald, Dallas (P.O. Box 2915), Fair Play for Cuba."[93] And finally, as mentioned, Horace Twiford's name, address, and phone numbers were in Oswald's address book.[94]

So the evidence linking Oswald to the Twifords is essentially ironclad.

But does it link Oswald to the Twifords on the evening of September 25? That evening is the only time Oswald was known to have been in Houston (see time line). One can assume, ad hoc, that he had been in Houston some other time, but Horace Twiford's testimony rules out any date after September 25. Because Twiford had mailed the Socialist Labor Party paper to Oswald on September 11,[95] it's hard to see how Oswald would have known Twiford even existed before that date. The impecunious Oswald was not given to gallivanting about the country, although one could posit that conspirators were driving or flying him around. One could also posit that Oswald was not in Houston at all when he called the Twiford residence, although his statement that he had only a few hours and wanted to talk with Mr. Twiford clearly implies he was in town.

So if Oswald attempted to visit either Twiford or Odio, the hard evidence trumps. It was Twiford.

Could He Have Visited Both Twiford and Odio?

If Oswald was in Houston on the evening of September 25, could he possibly have visited Odio the evening of the twenty-fourth? The Warren Commission thought not, since Oswald apparently (as we shall see) picked up his unemployment check at the Lafayette Street Post Office on Wednesday, September 25, no earlier than 5:00 a.m. If he was in New Orleans on the twenty-fifth, he could not have been at the Odio place in Dallas on the twenty-fourth, so the argument goes.

Of course, all this supposition goes out the window if we posit someone (not necessarily conspirators) drove Oswald around.

The most cogent and best-argued defense of the Odio testimony comes from author Jean Davison, who challenges the Warren Commission's logic in several ways. First, she notes that no eyewitnesses established Oswald's presence anywhere from the afternoon of September 24 until he boarded the bus in Houston in the early morning hours of September 26.[96] Nor did investigators find any documents to place him on the bus he presumably took from New Orleans to Houston. He supposedly cashed his unemployment check at a Winn-Dixie supermarket in New Orleans on the morning of September 25, but no solid evidence rules out his having done so on the twenty-fourth. No later than 11:00 a.m. on the twenty-fifth, Oswald mailed a change of address form and closed out his New Orleans post office box; however, he could have mailed it on the afternoon of the twenty-fourth from a mailbox in an outlying area.[97]

So establishing his whereabouts comes down to the unemployment check. The check was cut on September 23 and picked up from the mailroom at the Texas Employment Commission in Austin at 5:15 p.m.[98] The FBI meticulously traced the route it traveled from Austin to New Orleans. First, the mail superintendent in Austin explained that mail to New Orleans was dispatched to Houston by truck on Star Route 48703-T at 10:00 p.m. on September 23. He went on to say that this route was "the only way regular mail could be dispatched from Austin, unless it were delayed or missent." He added that "regular mail is never diverted to airmail or to any other means than stated above."[99]

In Houston, records showed that the mail truck from Austin arrived at 2:40 a.m. on September 24. The mail was placed on Southern Pacific train number 2, which the Houston officials said would arrive in New Orleans at about 6:00 p.m., but the train actually left Houston at 9:45 a.m., or twenty minutes late.[100] Postal officials in New Orleans established that the train did arrive in New Orleans on time on September 24. Mail was then taken off the train and transferred to the branch post offices. The mail to the Lafayette Street Post Office (where Oswald retrieved it from his box) was dispatched at 4:55 a.m. No employees were on duty at the Lafayette Street station during the evening (between 5:45 p.m. and 5:00 a.m.), so the earliest the check could possibly have been put in Oswald's box was a bit after 5:00 a.m. on the morning of September 25.[101]

The New Orleans postal inspector also confirmed what the mail superintendent in Austin told the FBI: his records showed that there had never been any airlift of mail from Austin to New Orleans.[102]

Then what is the evidence that the check arrived on September 24? Davison points out that in an interview just a week after the assassination, Marina had said that Oswald "went every Tuesday to pick up his unemployment check."[103] Davison also points out that the *Warren Commission Report* asserts that Oswald cashed an unemployment check on Tuesday, September 17.[104] Unfortunately, the Warren Commission provided no citation for this transaction, and the FBI report tracing Oswald's check-cashing activities shows no evidence that agents ever established the exact date on which Oswald cashed any check.[105] Davison rather airily suggests that "the postal authorities had for once underestimated the efficiency of the U.S. mails."[106] Unfortunately, Marina's testimony can't outweigh the meticulous reconstruction of the check's journey from Austin to the Lafayette Street station in New Orleans.

Oswald picked up the check on September 25.

True Proof of the Plot?

In judging that Oswald left New Orleans by bus on September 25, called Mrs. Twiford late that night, and then left Houston by bus very early the next morning, the Warren Commission was "connecting the dots" in the most straightforward way—without any trips by means unknown or with people unknown—to Sylvia Odio's apartment in Dallas. Thus the conclusion has the virtue of parsimony. But it omits the Odio sighting. Is Odio an outlier that can be excluded, or does a more elaborate theory have to be adopted that can accommodate her testimony?

The sheer number of Oswald sightings argues for Odio being just another outlier that can be excluded. Knowing that scores, even hundreds, of false Oswald sightings popped up after the assassination, the notion that this sighting is just another one is plausible. Another problem with conspiracy theories that accept the Odio testimony is that it is hard to see what its point would be. Of course, having Oswald (or perhaps an impostor Oswald) talk about shooting Kennedy appears to be a dandy way to set him up. Unfortunately, if Oswald were being set up as a leftist (and the vast majority of conspiracy theorists believe this assertion), it makes no sense to have him running around with a bunch of anti-Castro Cubans. He should have been running around with pro-Castro Cubans or some other variety of left-wingers.[107]

The most straightforward theory puts Oswald in New Orleans, then in Houston, and then on a bus to Mexico City. This itinerary is based on hard evidence of a contact with Twiford and his receipt of the check no sooner than 5:00 a.m. on September 25.

In an "Odio plus Twiford" scenario, however, Oswald was in New Orleans, then in Dallas, then again in New Orleans (to pick up the unemployment check), then in Houston, and then on the bus to Mexico City. But suppose the reader really wants to accept the Odio testimony? What would have been the point of Oswald visiting Odio? The only sensible theory comes from Davison, who suggests that Oswald was infiltrating the anti-Castro movement. On August 5, Oswald showed up at a store in New Orleans called the Casa Roca run by anti-Castro activist Carlos Bringuier. Oswald told Bringuier that he wanted to serve the anti-Castro movement, that he had been a Marine, that he had been trained in guerrilla warfare, and that he was willing both to train fighters and to fight himself.[108] He left Bringuier his *Guidebook for Marines*, which showed how to make bombs and booby traps and how to mount sabotage operations.

Oswald revealed the purpose of this little tableau in his "Revolutionary Resumé," which he presented to the Cuban embassy in Mexico City to establish his credentials as a friend of the revolution when he visited seeking a visa to enter Cuba. Oswald said he "infiltrated the Cuban Student Directorate and then harassed them with information I gained."[109] Davison suggests that the Odio visit was yet another infiltration of the anti-Castro activist community.[110] Thus, if accepting the Odio testimony, the most parsimonious theory is that Oswald was doing something he was known to have done before (infiltrating a group) and did not require him to have been sincerely anti-Castro.

AD HOC REASONING AND THE OSWALD SIGHTINGS

If conspiracy theorists make ad hoc assumptions, non-conspiracy theorists have to make such assumptions, too. In discussing a number of Oswald sightings, I have pretty much dismissed all of them.

Of course, not all ad hoc assumptions are equally implausible. For example, the Warren Commission debunked many of the Oswald sightings mentioned thus far based on the testimony of Ruth Paine and Marina Oswald. If Ruth and Marina said Lee was in Irving and a few guys at the Sports Drome in Dallas who didn't know Oswald said he was there, it's not a hard call deciding who is more reliable. Thus one has to decide to assume, ad hoc, whether Marina Oswald and Ruth Paine were lying or else other witnesses were mistaken. Given what is known in general about witness testimony, this decision is not difficult.

Of interest here is that there were also Oswald sightings *after* the assassination. James Douglass, for example, gives a lengthy account of the testimony of one Robert G. Vinson. Supposedly a sergeant in the U.S. Air Force, Vinson was in Washington, D.C., and went to Andrews Air Force Base to hop a plane back to Colorado, where he was stationed. He was put on a C-54 transport, which headed west with him as the only passenger. When an announcement came over the intercom that Kennedy had been shot, the plane turned south and landed in Dallas in a rough area alongside the Trinity River. Two men got on the plane, one of whom Vinson later recognized as Lee Harvey Oswald. The plane took off, and instead of Colorado it then landed in Roswell, New Mexico. All three men (Oswald, his companion, and Vinson) got off.

Yes, *that* Roswell.

Vinson's later military career took him to "Site 51" (presumably, Area 51) at Nellis Air Force Base, Nevada. He learned that CIA projects based there included aircraft shaped like flying saucers.[111] At least he didn't claim to have seen any aliens.

So what to make of such instances when an Oswald showed up where the real Lee Oswald could not have been? The simplest answer is that people were mistaken. But this conclusion is in many ways unsatisfying, so a theorist might want to see these cases as signal and not noise. Indeed, one theory can fit a scenario to these observations—that is, the existence of *two* Oswalds. According to the theory, there was a real Lee Harvey Oswald and another Oswald (actually an impostor), whose job was to go around and leave a trail of witness testimony involving guns and shootings and of saying nasty things about John Kennedy, all for the purpose of setting up the real Lee Oswald. As conspiracy author James Douglass puts it, "An Oswald other than the man working at the Texas School Book Depository and visiting his family at Ruth Paine's home was simultaneously laying down an overly obvious, false trail of assassination evidence elsewhere."[112] The Oswald sightings after the assassination would have involved a second Oswald, perhaps the fellow who had been running around setting up the real Oswald, who then had to disappear when the real Oswald fell into custody.

This theory originated with a philosophy professor named Richard Popkin who wrote a book titled *The Second Oswald* in 1966, but it has echoed through the years and even appeared in Oliver Stone's 1991 movie *JFK*. Obviously, the theory has logical problems. It would be an incompetent conspiracy indeed that would have a fake Oswald running around when the real one was someplace where multiple reliable witnesses—in some cases, his own wife—could provide an alibi for him. In fact, to account for all the Oswald sightings, a second Oswald alone would not suffice. A whole crew would be necessary account for them all. Douglass, fully aware of the problem, admits that there were "too many Oswalds in view, with too many smuggled rifles, retelling a familiar story to too many witnesses." He attributes this predicament to "the bungling redundancy of cover stories" and explains that "in an overambitious plot, the scapegoat wound up being in too many places at the same time."[113] So these otherwise brilliant plotters sent out way too many Oswalds to do way too many things that were designed to frame the real Oswald. That assumption is entirely ad hoc on Douglass's part. And pursuing such a tactic would be monumentally stupid on the conspirators' part.

Then there is the fact that, according to conspiracy books, Oswald had already been thoroughly established as a malcontent leftist. He had defected to the Soviet Union, participated in demonstrations for the Fair Play for Cuba Committee, left a long trail of correspondence with Communists in New York, defended Castro on WDSU radio in New Orleans, espoused strong leftist views to Russian émigrés in Dallas, gone to Mexico City to get into Cuba,[114] been photographed in his backyard with a rifle and a pistol and two communist newspapers,[115] and was linked by a paper trail to the rifle used to shoot Kennedy and the pistol used to shoot Tippit. Further, he had a spotty work record and had left in his wake an easy dozen witnesses who were willing to say that he was a misfit.

So after conducting such a brilliant and sustained campaign to portray Oswald as a leftist loner, why risk messing it up by having bogus Oswalds run all over the country?

But surely the fact that most of these Oswald sightings involved guns or shooting or a Marine or the discussion of Kennedy would support the idea that Oswald was being framed, would it not?

Actually, it would not. Understanding that memory is a reconstruction, it becomes plausible that if a witness saw a male—one who at least vaguely looked like

Oswald—engage in behavior that was reminiscent of the post-assassination stereotype of Lee Oswald, then an honest witness could become convinced that he or she had had an encounter with the famous assassin.

This observation might sound like an ad hoc assumption, but it is rendered plausible by the fact that false sightings of famous people and especially famous miscreants are common. When prisoners escape from a prison, attempts to catch them are likely to be impeded by false sightings.[116] In one murder case in Australia, a reward of $50,000 was offered for information leading to the arrest of a suspect named Malcolm Naden, and in the following fifteen months the police logged about 460 reports. None led to an arrest.[117]

In early 1993, a suspected serial killer named Leroy Martin was featured twice on the Fox TV show *America's Most Wanted*. It resulted in dozens of tips that the cops chased down but found to be false sightings.[118] Sightings can continue for decades, as was the case with mass murderer Belle Gunness, who apparently faked her own death in a fire in 1908. There were numerous sightings of her over the years, from all over the country, including one as late as 1931.[119] In the wake of Abraham Lincoln's assassination, wild rumors and false sightings of John Wilkes Booth proliferated.[120]

Particularly poignant are sightings of children who have been abducted. American television networks covered the disappearance of a ten-year-old girl named Lindsey Baum in 2009, with reports on *America's Most Wanted*, *Nancy Grace*, and *The Oprah Winfrey Show*. As a consequence, Rick Scott, an investigator on the case, reported that the cops had worked through thousands of leads and tips and false sightings all over.[121]

Thus the urge to fit a theory to the Oswald sightings' data points usually reflects an ignorance of just how unreliable witness perception and especially witness memories are. The "sightings" testimony is, from the perspective of the historian, "noise" and not "signal," but from another angle, that of the psychologist, it is indeed "signal." It's the result of systematic processes in which the image of Lee Harvey Oswald—as conveyed by the media in the wake of the assassination—gets fused with an experience that reminds the witness of the man Oswald. Repeat this process dozens and scores of times, and we get tons of fodder for really interesting theories. But as evidence, it's frail stuff indeed.

Chapter Three

Creating False Memories

When Clay Shaw was on trial in New Orleans in 1969, charged by District Attorney Jim Garrison with having conspired in the assassination of John Kennedy, the key witness was a fellow named Perry Raymond Russo. A friend of David Ferrie's, he testified that he was at Ferrie's apartment at 3330 Louisiana Avenue Parkway on numerous occasions during 1963. On one occasion in September, he recalled, at Ferrie's apartment was a man named Leon Oswald who was introduced as Ferrie's roommate. Russo later identified this man as Lee Harvey Oswald.

Also there "were three or four Latins or Cubans, there were a couple of young guys and there was one well-dressed man." Russo identified the well-dressed man as the defendant, Clay Shaw. Russo said that as the hour got late people started to drift off, and was asked about what happened then.

Q: Perry, do you ever recall a conversation during the course of that meeting in which the Defendant participated?

A: Yes, sir.

Q: Now, approximately how long was that after you arrived at the apartment?

A: Approximately three, four hours; I am not real sure of how much time elapsed.

Q: And, Perry, who was present at the time that the Defendant participated in a conversation that you heard?

A: It was Dave Ferrie, Oswald, and the Defendant and myself.

After further questions, attention turned back to the conversation.

Q: All right, Perry. Now, what conversation took place at this time?

A: This was after everyone had left?

Q: Between the Defendant—

A: —Oswald?

Q: —Oswald, yourself and Ferrie.

A: Yes. Well, Ferrie seemed to me just a continuation of a conversation that he had had before.

Q: Now, what was that conversation?

A: Well, he had said on several occasions about killing Kennedy, how easy it would be to do it or to accomplish it.

Russo went on to describe how Ferrie "was walking up and down telling how the projected assassination could be pulled off," which would involve a "triangulation of crossfire," and how there would be three shooters and "one of them would have to be the scapegoat." Ferrie then said that the shooters (other than the patsy) could fly to Mexico or Brazil or Cuba.

At this point Shaw supposedly objected, saying that "that wouldn't be possible" because of the need to refuel and the fact that "police would be everywhere." Ferrie then outlined an alternative plan, saying that it would be necessary that all the plotters have "alibis and . . . [be] in the public eye at the time of the assassination." Shaw then "said that he could go on business for his company," on "the Coast."

Returning to the need for three shooters, Ferrie said that "one of them would fire a diversionary shot and two of them would shoot to kill the President."[1]

On the face of it, this testimony does not seem to be much more than a recounting of a bull session and only barely resembles a cabal plotting an assassination. Yet the "triangulation of crossfire" business along with the "scapegoat" notion accorded with the conspiracy theory that Garrison's office had been trying to sell to the jury. And in fact Clay Shaw did go to San Francisco and was there at the time of the assassination.

But if the Russo testimony seems tantalizing, and maybe even evidence of an assassination conspiracy, one needs to know where it originated.

RUSSO IN BATON ROUGE

In *On the Trail of the Assassins*, Jim Garrison's 1988 memoir, the former district attorney from New Orleans claimed that Russo had talked to a reporter for the

Baton Rouge State-Times and "in an interview the morning of Friday, February 24, told him about a meeting he had attended at Ferrie's apartment at which the assassination of President Kennedy had been discussed. The story appeared in the *State-Times* that afternoon."[2] Garrison explained that the meeting included "Clay Bertrand" (Shaw's supposed alias) and Lee Oswald.

One might view Garrison's assertion as gutsy, since in making it he had to assume that nobody would actually bother to check the February 24, 1967, *State-Times's* piece. In reality, the paper reported the following:

> A Baton Rouge man today reported to the *State-Times* that David W. Ferrie told him about a month before the assassination of President Kennedy: "We will get him, and it won't be long."
>
> Perry Raymond Russo, 25, 311 East State St., said he has also sent a letter to Orleans Dist. Atty. Jim Garrison about his contacts with Ferrie in the summer and early fall of 1963.
>
> Russo described Ferrie as "screwy but sharp in a brainy way." Russo said he had known Ferrie about 18 months when the statement was made.
>
> On another occasion about the same time, Russo said Ferrie told him, "you know we can get Kennedy if we want him."
>
> The ease with which a president could be assassinated was discussed several times previous to the statements but with no mention of Kennedy.
>
> "It was just general conversation," Russo said.

The "we will get him" statement certainly sounds like a threat, but Ferrie was mostly engaged in a freewheeling discussion of presidential assassination. A similar story published in the *Baton Rouge Morning Advocate* the following day quotes Russo as asserting that "he did not take any of Ferrie's statements seriously until he saw Ferrie's picture in connection with Garrison's probe."[3] In other words, he didn't take Ferrie's statements seriously until early 1967, more than three years after the assassination.

What's missing here? Russo did not make any mention of an "assassination party" or of Oswald or of Clay Shaw (or "Clay Bertrand"). Indeed, in three different broadcast interviews that day, Russo never indicated knowing Oswald or seeing Oswald anywhere near Ferrie, and in one he asserted that "he had never heard of Lee Harvey Oswald until he was linked with the presidential assassination." Further,

Russo insisted, "I never heard of Oswald until on television (after) the assassination," and that Ferrie had never mentioned Oswald's name.[4] Obviously, there was no mention of Shaw or "Bertrand," either.

Russo's testimony clearly needed a great deal of work to make it usable in the Clay Shaw trial.

IMPROVING RUSSO'S TESTIMONY

Garrison then sent Assistant District Attorney Andrew Sciambra to Baton Rouge to interview Russo. Sciambra filed a written report on the interview, and in it Russo's testimony had not gotten much better. Sciambra, for instance, had shown Russo a variety of photos:

> The next picture that he identified was that of CLAY SHAW. He said that he saw this man twice. The first time was when he pulled into FERRIE's service station to get his car fixed. SHAW was the person who was sitting in the compact car talking with FERRIE. He remembers seeing him again at the Nashville Street Wharf when he went to see J.F.K. speak. He said he particularly remembers this guy because he was apparently a queer. It seems that instead of looking at J.F.K. speak, SHAW kept turning around and looking at all the young boys in the crowd. He said that SHAW eventually struck up a conversation with a young kid not too far from him. It was perfectly obvious to him that SHAW stared at his penis several times. He said that SHAW eventually left with a friend. He said that SHAW had on dark pants that day which fit very tightly and was the kind of pants that a lot of queers in the French Quarter wear.

Note that he claims to have seen Shaw *two* times, and neither is at any assassination party. His description of Shaw doesn't ring true. Although Shaw was certainly gay, he was also a decorous gentleman.

Sciambra then showed Russo a photo of Oswald.

> The third picture that RUSSO identified was that of LEE HARVEY OSWALD. When he looked at the picture, he began shaking his head and said that he doesn't know if he should say what he's thinking. I told him to go on and tell me what was on his mind and that we would accept this in relation-

ship to all the information we had, and it may not be as wild as he thinks it is. He then said that the picture of LEE HARVEY OSWALD was the person that FERRIE had introduced to him as his roommate. He said the only thing that doesn't make him stand up and say that he is sure beyond the shadow of any doubt is the fact that the roommate was always so cruddy and had a bushy beard. He then drew a beard on the picture of OSWALD and said this was FERRIE's roommate.[5]

Of course, Oswald was never Ferrie's roommate. Nor did Oswald ever have a "bushy beard," for his personal hygiene habits were good, and he seldom looked "cruddy." Indeed, earlier in the same interview, Russo had described the roommate.

[He had] sort of dirty blond hair and a husky beard which appeared to be a little darker than his hair. . . . a typical beatnik, extremely dirty, with his hair all messed up, his beard unkept [sic], a dirty T-shirt on, and either blue jeans or khaki pants on. He . . . wore white tennis shoes which were cruddy and had on no socks.

Russo's testimony clearly needed more work.

Mercy Hospital

Russo was then taken to Mercy Hospital in New Orleans and questioned under the influence of Sodium Pentothal, a so-called truth serum. Under the influence of the drug, Russo's testimony improved.

Russo denied knowing Clay Shaw, but when asked if he knew "Clay Bertrand," Russo said—apparently for the first time—that he did indeed know a "Bertrand" and that he had met him at Ferrie's apartment. He described Bertrand as a "queer" and "a tall man with white kinky hair, sort of slender." Then he said that Bertrand was the man he'd seen once at Ferrie's service station and at the Nashville Street Wharf. So now Garrison had the same two identifications of Shaw as in the Sciambra memo, plus one that was not found in any previous version of his story.

When Sciambra asked him "if he could remember any of the details about Clay Bertrand being up in Ferrie's apartment," Russo described being in Ferrie's apartment with Bertrand and a Leon Oswald. Ferrie had told him, he said, "We are going to kill John F. Kennedy," and "It won't be long." Sciambra asked whom Ferrie had meant when he used the term "we." Russo replied, "I guess he was referring to the people in the room."[6]

So, from Garrison's perspective, this version of Russo's testimony was substantially improved. It had Ferrie, Oswald, and Bertrand at an assassination party. It had talk about killing JFK. But it did not show Bertrand talking about killing JFK or any planning for an assassination attempt. Indeed, Russo had to guess who besides Ferrie (who said "we") was going to kill Kennedy. In other words, it didn't have Clay Shaw involved in any conspiracy.

The testimony needed more improvement.

Using Hypnosis

If the truth serum failed to do the job, how about hypnosis? Russo was hypnotized three times, although only two of the sessions' transcripts survive. They show the final necessary improvement in the testimony but only after some effort. The hypnotist was Dr. Esmond Fatter, a physician without credentials or expertise in the forensic use of hypnosis.

In the first hypnosis session, on March 1, Russo at first fails to describe anything but himself and "Dave Ferrie just sitting around," until Fatter narrows the subject down. Using the visual device of an imaginary television screen, Fatter tells Russo, "Continue looking at that television picture and notice the news cast—the president, President Kennedy is coming to New Orleans and as you look, describe it to us. . . . Who is that white haired gentleman that is over there looking at President Kennedy?" At this point Russo describes a man he'd seen at the Nashville Street Wharf, but says he was "either with the New Orleans Police Department or government" and fails to mention anything about his having tight pants or leering at a young boy.

"How about this white haired gentleman?" Fatter asks again.

"That was him."

"Do you know his name?"

Russo replies, "No."

Not good. So Fatter continues: "Who else is in the apartment?"

"Nobody," Russo says, "just me and him."

"Just you and—Ferrie?" asks Fatter.

"And Oswald," Russo replies.

After a brief discussion of Ferrie and Leon, Fatter instructs him, "That's right, continue to go deeper and deeper—Now, picture that television screen again, Perry, and it is a picture of Ferrie's apartment and there are several people in there and there is a white haired man."

Thus it is Fatter, and not Russo, who introduces the "white haired man" into the scene. Fatter is certainly persistent. Of course, if this sort of persistence is necessary to elicit the desired testimony, especially in the highly suggestive state of hypnosis, the testimony is not much good.

After some rambling on Russo's part, Fatter takes control of the session again. "Let your mind go completely blank, Perry," he says. He directs Perry to look at the television screen again and notice its picture: "There will be Bertrand, Ferrie and Oswald, and they are going to discuss a very important matter and there is another man and girl there and they are talking about assassinating somebody. Look at it and describe it to me."

Again, Fatter and not Russo introduces the key element—that is, "assassinating somebody"—into the session.

Russo then describes a scene in which "they planned to assassinate President Kennedy." And now, Russo reports Shaw (as "Clem Bertrand") as contributing to the conversation. Shaw discussed how going to Mexico and Brazil would not be possible, given the "gas expense" and the need to have "the cooperation of Mexican authorities."[7] Dr. Fatter had thus succeeded in making Shaw a participant in an assassination plot.

The second hypnosis session added to the scenario. Fatter instructs, "And now, Perry, I'd like for you to go back and listen to Clem Bertrand talking and as you listen to Clem Bertrand talking, relay to me what Clem Bertrand says." So Russo describes "Bertrand" arguing with Ferrie over some of the details of the plot and Ferrie discussing the need for everybody to have an alibi. For the day of the assassination, "Bertrand" mentions that he will be going to "the coast."[8]

And now, Garrison thought, Russo's testimony had been improved to the point that it could be used to convict Shaw.

Interpreting Russo

The radical changes in Russo's testimony, as well as the implausible elements (Oswald as Ferrie's slovenly beatnik roommate, Shaw as a flaming queen leering at young boys), make it unbelievable on its face. But what if you didn't know how it changed over time? Happily, the defense at Clay Shaw's trial had access to early versions of Russo's testimony and used it to impeach his trial testimony. Shaw was acquitted in short order.

But a key element here is the prosecution's use of drugs and hypnosis.

During the time of the trial, Dr. Edwin A. Weinstein of the Washington School of Psychiatry explained the problem associated with using drugs in a letter to the *Washington Post*: "Under the influence of Sodium Pentothal, subjects may give highly fictional accounts of past events and describe incidents that never happened. The drug is not a 'truth serum.'"[9]

The situation with hypnosis is as bad, if not worse. The American Medical Association's *Encyclopedia of Medicine* defines hypnosis as "a trancelike state of altered awareness that is characterized by extreme suggestibility."[10] George H. Estabrooks, in a textbook (*Hypnotism*) that would have been standard at the time of the Shaw trial, explains,

> The first concept we get of hypnotism is that curious picture of an unconscious mind controlled by the conscious mind of the operator. The subject will accept any suggestion the operator gives, within certain limits. . . . In fact, suggestion appears to be the key of hypnotism. It is the method by which the hypnotist first gains his control and unseats the normal conscious mind.[11]

One might assume that even if the subject is highly suggestible under hypnosis, it would have no implications for the truth of testimony given after the subject is awakened. But the opposite is so. A standard work on the subject explains,

> The extreme case in terms of risk of miscarriage of justice is that in which hypnosis is used to "refresh" a witness's or victim's memory about aspects of a crime that are presumed or known to the authorities, the media, or the hypnotist. In such cases, a "memory" can be created in hypnosis where none existed before, and the witness's memory may be irreversibly contaminated. The hypnotic subject may obtain information about the event from the media, from comments made prior to, during, or after an interrogation, or during the hypnotic session itself. . . . There is a significant likelihood that this information will form the basis of confabulation and will become inextricably intertwined with the witness's or victim's own memories of the event.[12]

Russo told journalist James Phelan he had "picked up a lot of information from Garrison's people just from the way they asked questions. I'm a pretty perceptive guy, and besides, when they got through asking me questions, I asked them a lot of questions—like 'Why is this man important,' and so on."[13]

Other cases of recovered memory appear to be the result of suggestion given by an insufficiently careful therapist. Even memories of abuse may be produced in this way. According to the American Medical Association, recovered memories are "of uncertain authenticity which should be subject to external verification. The use of recovered memories is fraught with problems of potential misapplication."[14]

Another interesting set of cases involves memories of abduction by aliens. It's easy to write off all of these reports as lies from attention seekers, but some have been elicited under hypnosis; when the subjects are awakened, they may remember the "memories" they recovered while hypnotized and will sincerely believe them to be real.[15] The same is true of people who, under the influence of hypnosis, remember their "past lives."[16] Thus Russo may have come to "remember" things that were simply the result of suggestion. He wasn't necessarily a bald-faced liar.

Another element to Russo's testimony was that he was simply too pliant. He was the way-too-willing witness who tried hard to be cooperative when the Garrison investigation approached him. The Garrison staff had told him that it had "a closed case against this man."[17] Russo apparently assumed that since the staff must have had plenty of evidence against Shaw, it would do no harm to help the prosecution. But having once told his assassination party story, he could not back out, knowing full well that an indictment for perjury would await him if he failed to tell the required story on the stand.

As recounted by author James Kirkwood,

> [Russo] told me that he was caught in the middle of this thing, that if he stuck to his story, Shaw and his friends and lawyers would clobber him. If he changed his story, then Garrison would charge him with perjury and chuck!—there would go his job with Equitable Life. He told me all he was concerned about was his own position, that he wished he'd never opened his mouth about it, wished he could go back to the day before he shot off his mouth up in Baton Rouge.[18]

In spite of the hypnotic suggestion, Russo was never entirely certain of his testimony. But he appeared to be when he testified in court against Clay Shaw. It's hard to feel sorry for him.

OTHER FALSE MEMORIES IN THE GARRISON CASE

Garrison's case against Shaw was awash in false memories, and most of them did not involve hypnosis or drugs. Particularly important are the Clinton witnesses, who took the stand at the Clay Shaw trial and swore they had seen Lee Oswald, along with Clay Shaw and David Ferrie, drive into the town of Clinton, Louisiana, in the fall of 1963 in a big, expensive-looking black car. Oswald, they claimed, got out of the car and joined a voter registration line. (The Congress of Racial Equality was conducting a drive to get black citizens registered to vote.) If reliable, this testimony would clearly link Oswald to Shaw and Ferrie.

But in fact the testimony at the Shaw trial differed (as did Russo's) from the first accounts elicited by Garrison's investigators.[19] Consider, for example, the case of one Corrie Collins, a witness from Clinton. Collins was interviewed by Sciambra on January 31, 1968, and told the story of the big black car and the man leaving the car and getting in the voter registration line. Shown a photo of Oswald, Collins identified him as the man who got in the line. Sciambra then showed him a photo of Ferrie, and (according to Sciambra) Collins "said that he remembers seeing this man around Clinton somewhere but can't be sure where or when." When shown a photo of Shaw, he (again in Sciambra's words) "said the face was familiar but can't say for sure where he saw the man."

But at the Clay Shaw trial, Collins confidently identified both Ferrie and Shaw as fellow passengers in the big black car.[20]

Quite simply, investigators can produce testimony out of virtually nothing. When witnesses are repeatedly questioned, repeatedly shown photos, and led (perhaps not intentionally) in a particular direction, they can end up giving pretty much the testimony investigators want. And they don't need to be lying to do so.

Chapter Four

Witnesses Who Are Just Too Good

While most witnesses in most criminal investigations are fallible, can be led to give certain sorts of testimony by investigators, and can have their testimony misinterpreted if taken out of context, other witnesses are just too good. Their testimony so clearly implies a conspiracy and so perfectly corroborates what conspiracy-oriented researchers think that to believe these witnesses is to absolutely believe in a conspiracy.

There are many of these kinds of witnesses associated with President Kennedy's assassination, and in this chapter we'll look at a few of them.

JEAN HILL

Perhaps the most colorful of the JFK assassination witnesses present in Dealey Plaza was Jean Hill. The term "colorful" is used literally: she is visible in dozens of photos of Dealey Plaza wearing a red raincoat and standing next to her friend Mary Moorman on the infield, a couple of yards from the south curb of Elm Street.[1] For many years Hill carried a business card identifying herself as the "closest witness" to JFK when he was shot.[2] *That's* not exactly true, but she was among a handful of the closest witnesses when Kennedy's head exploded.

People who have seen her character in the movie *JFK* or have read her book, *JFK: The Last Dissenting Witness*, which she coauthored with Bill Sloan, or have seen her in the video *Beyond JFK: The Question of Conspiracy* (issued in 1992 to promote the film *JFK*) will know that she was an interesting witness indeed.[3] She claimed that in her enthusiasm, she actually stepped onto Elm Street and was so close to the presidential limo that she almost touched the front fender. She shouted,

"Hey, Mr. President . . . look over here. We want to take your picture."[4] Mary Moorman did indeed have a Polaroid camera and took a photo of the shooting.

Hill also claimed to have actually seen the shooter on the grassy knoll and to have seen a man she later identified as Jack Ruby running from the Texas School Book Depository into the rail yard behind the stockade fence. In the wake of the shooting she declared she ran across Elm Street, trying to apprehend the shooter. In her Warren Commission testimony, she said she did not see Jackie Kennedy climb out on the trunk of the presidential limo because she was running across the street at the time,[5] and in her book she writes that she "narrowly avoided being hit" by "Marshall's" motorcycle ("Marshall" being a cop with whom she was having an affair) as she crossed,[6] in spite of Moorman telling her to "get down." Once she got up on the knoll, she was waylaid by a couple of government agents who took her off to the Criminal Courts Building (which is on Dealey Plaza, at the northeast corner of Houston and Main) and tried to intimidate her.

Hill's book includes much contextual detail for her story. She claimed to have been having an affair with a motorcycle officer, one "J. B. Marshall," and she describes Marshall and his position near the limo, but the officer described is actually B. J. Martin.[7] Through the man she calls Marshall, she learned of several sinister happenings that day, including the fact that the parade route, originally planned to proceed down Main Street to the Stemmons Freeway, was changed by the staff of Vice President Lyndon Baines Johnson (LBJ) and made to turn onto Houston and Elm Streets. Conspiracy lore has long held that the purpose of this change was to slow the limo down and bring it into a "kill zone," where shooters in the depository, in the Dal-Tex Building, and on the grassy knoll could catch Kennedy in a crossfire. According to Hill, Marshall also informed her that Johnson had ducked down in the vice presidential limo (two cars behind the presidential limo) before the shooting even started.

Hill's opus is rounded out by her account of how she was harassed by the FBI, endured several attempts on her life, and finally (in the early 1990s) was vindicated by her role in the making of the movie *JFK*. Oliver Stone came to dinner at her house. She baked cookies for the movie's cast and crew.

The Early Jean Hill

Jean Hill's early testimony wasn't nearly as colorful as the version that emerged in the 1980s and 1990s, but it was plenty colorful enough. When interviewed by WBAP-TV less than an hour after the shooting, she said the shots came from the grassy knoll. She heard four to six shots and "saw a man running."[8] She also claimed that she saw a little dog in the limo between Jack and Jackie Kennedy. Her affidavit for the Dallas County Sheriff's Department differs only slightly from this report: she heard five or six shots and added that she thought she saw men in plainclothes shooting back.[9]

The "little dog" statement seems ditzy, but in fact a bouquet of flowers was between Jack and Jackie on the limo's seat. She might have easily mistaken it for a small dog—a poodle, perhaps. As noted earlier, witness misperceptions of this magnitude are common. Her claim to have heard four to six shots is also almost certainly sincere, given that it was in her earliest testimony. Of course, this number puts her in the minority of witnesses who heard more than three shots.

Finally, there is no reason to doubt that she saw a man running and came to believe that he was Jack Ruby. Just as there were numerous bogus Oswald sightings after the assassination, there is no reason to doubt that an honest witness would connect the face of another assassination character to somebody seen fleetingly in an intense situation. Fairly extensive Warren Commission testimony, however, puts Jack Ruby in the offices of the *Dallas Morning News* at the time of the shooting.[10]

Perhaps the most important fact about her early testimony, which includes at least two interviews on WBAP-TV, one interview on WFAA-TV, a sheriff's affidavit, and her Warren Commission testimony, is its consistency. This point is important because Hill later claimed in her book that she never gave her testimony in the sheriff's department affidavit but rather just signed a blank form.[11] She also insisted that her Warren Commission testimony, taken by a hostile Arlen Specter, was tampered with and mangled by the time it appeared in the Warren Commission volumes.[12]

If such tampering with the testimony really happened, one might wonder whether conspirators obtained all the copies of her video interviews and tampered with them too. Did they do a masterful job of creating a consistent record of early testimony that would conflict with her later testimony? And if so, why did they retain elements in the early testimony that implied conspiracy: hearing more than three shots, hearing the shots from the grassy knoll, and seeing Jack Ruby running in the plaza?

The Later Jean Hill

As with many witnesses' stories, the especially interesting parts of Hill's came along later. While in her Warren Commission testimony she said she was merely at the "edge" of Elm Street as the presidential limo approached, in later testimony she was out in the street so close she was "almost touching the front fender of the limousine."[13] In reality, photos of the motorcade in Dealey Plaza show her standing still on the infield and a few feet from the curb.

Further, she did not run across Elm Street and up to the grassy knoll nearly as quickly as she claimed. Wilma Bond's photo, taken a few seconds after the shooting, shows Hill seated next to Moorman in the same location where they had previously been standing. Another Bond photo, taken perhaps a minute later, shows Hill standing in approximately the same location. By this time several people are running up the grassy slope, following motorcycle officer Clyde Haygood, but Hill is motionless.[14]

There is no doubt that she did eventually cross Elm and go up the steps on the knoll. Her November 22 affidavit claims she did this, and film footage shows a woman in a red raincoat going up the steps.[15]

But her original affidavit says nothing about having been waylaid by sinister government agents. Rather, it says that "as I came back down the hill Mr. Featherstone [sic] of the Times Herald had gotten to Mary and ask her for her picture [sic] she had taken of the president, and he brought us to the press room down at the Sheriff's office and ask [sic] us to stay."

Of course, given her claim that the affidavit was fabricated, one might want to know what Mary Moorman and Jim Featherston have to say. Moorman has not gone public on the issue, but it is well known to Dallas-area researchers that she does not support Hill's version. Indeed, this point is conceded in *JFK: The Last Dissenting Witness*, which admits, "It should be noted, and Jean readily admits, that Mary's recollections of the period immediately after the shooting do not necessarily coincide with Jean's own. Differences exist in their recollections of when and where they were reunited following Jean's run to the knoll."[16]

In other words, Jean claims to have been waylaid by agents and then reunited with Mary in the sheriff's department pressroom. Mary disagrees.

Featherston has been quite outspoken. He has insisted on numerous occasions that he did go with Hill and Moorman to the pressroom at the sheriff's office, just as Hill's original affidavit says.[17] Featherston does "admit" to having argued with Hill about some aspects of her testimony:

Mrs. Hill told her story over and over again for television and radio. Each time, she would embellish it a bit until her version began to sound like

Dodge City at high noon. . . . In the meantime, I had talked to other witnesses and at one point I told Mrs. Hill she shouldn't be saying some of the things she was telling television and radio reporters. I was merely trying to save her later embarrassment but she apparently attached intrigue to my warning.[18]

Thus Hill was indeed hassled, but not by government agents intent on a cover-up.

What Marshall Told Her

If some of the things Hill claimed she had seen and heard lack credibility, the stories she attributed to her boyfriend "Marshall" don't fare any better. The claim that Vice President Johnson was ducking before the shooting even started, for instance, is flatly contradicted by the testimony of Rufus Youngblood, the Secret Service agent assigned to guard him.

As we were beginning to go down this incline, all of a sudden there was an explosive noise. I quickly observed unnatural movement of crowds, like ducking or scattering, and quick movements in the Presidential followup car. So I turned around and hit the Vice President on the shoulder and hollered, get down, and then looked around again and saw more of this movement, and so I proceeded to go to the back seat and get on top of him.[19]

Hurchel Jacks, who was driving the vice presidential car, confirms that version of events.[20]

One can, ad hoc, assume that both men—and Johnson himself, who corroborated Youngblood's version of events—were lying.[21] But it's much harder to explain away the "changed parade route" gaffe.

The notion that the parade route was changed at the last minute to bring Kennedy into a kill zone goes back to one of the first assassination conspiracy books, Joachim Joesten's *Oswald: Assassin or Fall Guy?*, which came out in 1964, even before the *Warren Commission Report*.[22] Joesten's "evidence" for a changed parade route was a map published in the *Dallas Morning News* the day of the assassination that showed the motorcade route, which appeared to go down Main Street directly onto the Stemmons Freeway without turning on Houston and Elm Streets. He inferred that sometime after that issue of the *Dallas Morning News* went to press (late the night before) somebody changed the parade route, adding the turns onto Houston and Elm in order to bring Kennedy into the kill zone.

This scenario has multiple problems, the first of which is that the *Dallas Times Herald* of November 21 printed a map of the route that did show turns onto Houston and Elm. (See this book's photo insert for the newspaper's map.) Further, both Dallas newspapers printed descriptions of the route on November 19, and they included the turns onto Houston and Elm. Apparently, the *Dallas Morning News's* map, which spanned two columns of an eight-column front page, was of too small a scale to show those turns. Quite simply, what is true of computer maps today was true of cruder technology in 1963: you cannot show all the details on a small map.

Since Joesten's book was published in 1964, the Warren Commission devoted a bit of space to debunking this factoid. Not only did it include the testimony of the officials who had planned the motorcade route, the commission printed photos of the street signs that clearly directed traffic down Main Street to turn onto Houston and Elm in order to get to the Stemmons Freeway.[23] If a vehicle proceeds down Main, it can get to the Stemmons Freeway only by driving over a divider separating Main and Elm. This maneuver would be easy enough in a Jeep, questionable in the presidential limo (which would probably have bottomed out on the divider), and nearly impossible for the three buses in the motorcade—not to mention being utterly incompatible with any notion of presidential dignity.[24]

Jean Hill's boyfriend allegedly reported something that simply did not happen in the real world, and it is now a staple of conspiracy books. This point is a classic "gotcha." While quite impressive to people who have read a conspiracy book or two, it's the poison pill that makes the testimony impossible to swallow for anybody who's well informed.

Even if Marshall had told her some things that turn out to be factoids—or more likely, Hill or her coauthor inserted conspiracy book factoids into her memoir—what of her testimony of having actually seen the grassy knoll shooter? By now, the reader will not be surprised to find that this detail is a rather late addition to her story. Within an hour or so after the assassination, in the pressroom of the Dallas County Sheriff's Office, WBAP-TV reporter Jimmy Darnell filmed an interview with Hill and Moorman, which included the following exchange:

Jimmy Darnell: Did you see the person who fired the . . .
Jean Hill: No . . . I didn't see any person fire the weapon. . . .
Jimmy Darnell: You only heard it?
Jean Hill: I only heard it.[25]

This interview was not only broadcast on the day of the assassination, it was also rebroadcast on the twenty-fifth anniversary of the assassination (1988) as part of the show *As It Happened* by the Arts & Entertainment network. Nevertheless, this admission did not prevent Oliver Stone from treating Hill as a perfectly reliable witness.

ROGER CRAIG

Roger Craig was everywhere in the wake of the assassination. A Dallas County sheriff's deputy, at the time of the shooting he was standing with fellow deputies in front of the Sheriff's Department headquarters on Main Street just a few yards from Houston Street and Dealey Plaza.

Just like the other deputies, he heard three shots and rushed into Dealey Plaza. Photos show him there. Film footage from WFAA-TV photographer Tom Alyea shows him on the sixth floor of the Texas School Book Depository while the cops were recovering evidence. Photos and film footage show him in the hallways of the third floor of the Dallas Police Department among the throng watching Oswald being hustled from office to office. And photos show him in the Homicide and Robbery Bureau of the Dallas Police Department.

He had many chances to see things, and if one believes his testimony, he saw quite a lot.

As early as the evening of the assassination, Craig gave testimony that contradicted what later became the Warren Commission's official version of events. On November 22, 1963, he swore out an affidavit saying that about fifteen minutes after the shooting, he had seen Lee Oswald come running down the grassy knoll and get into a Rambler station wagon driven by a dark-complexioned man.[26] The Warren Commission concluded that at that time, 12:45 p.m., Lee Oswald was fleeing on a Dallas city bus.

Craig also told of later entering the office of Dallas Police captain Will Fritz, where Oswald was being questioned. In a dramatic moment in the interrogation, Fritz asked Oswald, "What about the car?" Oswald responded, according to Craig, "That station wagon belongs to Mrs. Paine. Don't try to drag her into this."[27]

Including Mrs. Ruth Paine in the story pushes all kinds of buttons with conspiracists, since they suspect her of being deeply involved in an assassination plot. After all, she took in Oswald's wife, Marina, and the couple's young daughter, June, and was instrumental in getting Oswald his job at the School Book Depository.

In an autobiographical essay titled "When They Kill a President" (first distributed in 1971) and in a TV interview with Lincoln Carle in 1974, Craig added several conspiratorial elements to his story. He claimed that he and Sheriff's Deputy Luke Mooney discovered the sniper's nest in the depository and that he saw on the floor there three spent cartridges neatly lined up in a row, about an inch apart, and all pointing in the same direction.

It has long been a staple of conspiracy writing that the police discovered a Mauser rifle and not Oswald's 6.5mm Mannlicher-Carcano when they first searched the depository. Since a Mannlicher-Carcano became a part of the chain of evidence, conspiracists infer that a rifle that could be linked to Oswald was substituted for a Mauser whose provenance would have undercut the case against the "patsy" Oswald. Usually offered as evidence are the statements of some of the cops who searched the sixth floor and got a fleeting look at the rifle, but Craig makes the case even better. He testified that Captain Fritz held the rifle up, and from a distance of six or eight inches, he saw the inscription: 7.65 Mauser.

If Craig mentioned a rifle that didn't fit into the Warren Commission's scenario, he also testified to a bullet that did not either. In the interview with Lincoln Carle, he tells of seeing a .45-caliber slug on the Dealey Plaza infield just a yard or two from the south curb of Elm Street. It was lying in a patch of gore (presumably Kennedy's brain matter and hair).[28] Supposedly a government agent of some sort picked it up and made off with it.

In his essay, Craig also offered testimony that radically challenged the Warren Commission's account of the Tippit shooting.

> At that exact moment [of the discovery of the rifle] an unknown Dallas police officer came running up the stairs and advised Capt. Fritz that a Dallas policeman had been shot in the Oak Cliff area. I instinctively looked at my watch. The time was 1:06 p.m. A token force of uniformed officers was left to keep the sixth floor secure and Fritz, [J. C.] Day, [Eugene] Boone, Mooney, Weitzman and I left the building.[29]

The Warren Commission had concluded that Oswald shot Tippit at 1:15 p.m. Since Oswald left his rooming house at about 1:00 p.m., he would have had time to walk the nine-tenths of a mile to the corner of Tenth and Patton, where Tippit was shot. But if Tippit was shot by 1:06 p.m., Oswald could not have done it.

The Rambler Man

The Rambler station wagon story and the confrontation in Fritz's office form a coherent, connected piece of the Craig account. If the Rambler story is not true, then it becomes quite implausible that Oswald would say, "That's Mrs. Paine's station wagon." Of course, Capt. Will Fritz denied the confrontation ever happened, which is why the Warren Commission dismissed Craig's story.[30] But conspiracists will cheerfully call Fritz a liar when he contradicts a witness like Craig.

There is some corroboration for the Rambler story. A photo of traffic jammed up on Elm Street in the minutes following the shooting does indeed show a Rambler.[31] And two witnesses, Marvin Robinson and Roy Cooper, reported seeing a man run down the slope in front of the depository and get into a Rambler.[32] Unfortunately for Craig, neither witness identified the passenger as Oswald, and these interviews were conducted the day after the assassination, when they would have known who Lee Oswald was and most likely would have seen images of him.

A major problem for Craig's Rambler story is a bus transfer found in Oswald's pocket after his arrest. It shows the time Oswald got on the bus and the route it took, and has the distinctive mark of driver Cecil McWatters.[33] Further, Oswald's former landlady Mary Bledsoe was on the bus and came forward after the assassination to testify that she had seen Oswald. If Oswald was on the bus fifteen minutes after the shooting, he could not have run and gotten into the Rambler.[34] That's two strikes against Craig's Rambler story.

But did Mrs. Paine own a station wagon? Yes, she did. Unfortunately for Craig, she testified it was a Chevrolet and not an AMC Rambler before the Warren Commission. What's more, both the FBI and the Dallas Police confirmed that she owned a Chevrolet, license number NK 4041.[35]

Given previous discussions regarding witness testimony, Craig's claim to have seen Oswald run down the grassy slope and get into the Rambler could easily be an honest misperception. After all, false Oswald sightings are commonplace in this case. And Craig may have believed that the station wagon belonged to Mrs. Paine, since his fellow deputy Buddy Walthers told him that Mrs. Paine had a station wagon with a luggage rack on top (as the Rambler did).[36] Thus Craig may have put two and two together but come up with the mistaken conclusion. It's much harder, however, to come up with an excuse for the supposed confrontation with Oswald in Fritz's office.

Craig supporters claim corroboration from the fact that a photo, shot through the glass panel in the door of the Homicide and Robbery Bureau, shows

Craig inside the room. This photo is usually described as confirmation that Craig was in Fritz's office.[37] But in fact the photo shows the general office of the bureau and not Fritz's inner office, where Oswald was being questioned. Other pictures of the same scene show officers sitting around, chatting, and a secretary eating a sandwich. Fritz is not visible in any of the photos, and neither is Oswald.[38]

On the Sixth Floor

There is no doubt that Craig was on the sixth floor of the Texas School Book Depository with other officers who were searching the building and collecting evidence. But other parts of his testimony are questionable. In the 1974 interview, Craig claimed that he and Deputy Luke Mooney together discovered the sniper's nest.[39] Mooney certainly did, but there is no confirmation for the claim that Craig was with him at the time. Moreover, Mooney had to squeeze between boxes to make it into the sniper's nest, and there is no way Craig could have been with him in that area.

Indeed, Craig's testimony has changed on this point. Before the Warren Commission, he mentioned the spent cartridges, but he made no claim to have been with Mooney when they were discovered.

> **David Belin:** Why did you go up on the sixth floor?
> **Roger Craig:** Well, someone said that's where the shots came from. One of the city officers, if I'm not mistaken.
> **David Belin:** All right.
> **Roger Craig:** So, we went to the sixth floor where—uh—some empty cartridges were found.
> **David Belin:** Did you see the empty cartridges when they were found?
> **Roger Craig:** I didn't see them when they were found. I saw them laying on the floor.
> **David Belin:** About how soon after they were found did you see them, laying on the floor?
> **Roger Craig:** Oh, a couple of minutes. I went right on over there. I was at the far north end of the building. The cartridges were on the southeast corner.
> **David Belin:** Well, how did you know they had been found there? Did someone yell—or what?

Roger Craig: Yes; someone yelled across the room that "here's the shells."

David Belin: Do you remember who that was?

Roger Craig: No; I couldn't recognize the voice.[40]

So Craig makes it clear that he was not with Mooney when the shells were discovered; rather, he went over to see them after they had been discovered.

But this point is a minor issue compared to Craig's claim that he saw three spent cartridges, all lined up in a row about an inch apart, and all pointing in the same direction. That evidence screams, "Planted!" But there is, unfortunately for Craig, no confirmation for this assertion. The spent cartridges were photographed in place by Detective Robert Studebaker, who was working under the direction of J. C. Day, head of the Identification Bureau. The photos show the hulls scattered randomly in the sniper's nest.[41] But a nettlesome issue surrounds these photos. Newsreel photographer Tom Alyea tells of how Capt. Will Fritz, before the cartridges were photographed in place, picked them up and held them so that Alyea could photograph them.[42] If Alyea is correct, Fritz essentially tampered with crime scene evidence.

But Alyea is almost certainly wrong. In the first place, he has produced no film footage of the spent hulls, in spite of the huge news value such footage would have. Further, his testimony has already proven unreliable on the issue of whether a paper sack with the remains of a chicken dinner was found on the sixth floor or on the fifth.

If Fritz held the hulls up for Alyea to photograph, it had to be during a narrow time frame. Mooney discovered the hulls at about 1:00 p.m. and certainly prior to 1:05 p.m.[43] Officers Richard Sims and Elmer Boyd, who had rushed to the depository with Fritz, stayed with the hulls to "preserve the scene." Day and Studebaker arrived shortly afterward and started to take photographs. At 1:22 p.m. the rifle was discovered in the other corner of the depository, and Fritz, Sims, and several other officers went over to where it had been found. Sims then returned and helped Day and Studebaker process the hulls as evidence, putting them into an envelope.[44] Sims took possession of it, and that was the end of any opportunity for anybody to show the hulls to Alyea. At that point Day went across to where the rifle had been found.[45]

As much as certain cultural biases might incline some people to think of Captain Fritz as a hick who might cavalierly disturb a crime scene, the Dallas cops were scrupulous about securing the scene until Day could properly collect the evidence. Detective L. D. Montgomery, for example, testified that when he arrived at the depository, Fritz assigned him to "protect the part of the scene where the window was where the shooting took place."[46] Not only was Fritz never alone with Alyea and the spent cartridges, Alyea's own film shows a whole crowd of officers around the sniper's nest.[47] It's implausible that Fritz would have done something that all of these officers would have recognized as a major breach of procedure. Thus the Alyea account lacks credibility, and the photo of the spent cartridges in the sniper's nest almost certainly shows the undisturbed hulls.

What Did Craig First Say?

Before the Warren Commission, Craig mentioned seeing the spent cartridges, but when asked whether he looked closely at the area where the shells were found, he responded, "Uh—no, because the identification men hadn't arrived, and we didn't want to stir up anything."[48]

He made no mention at all of any shells lined up in a row.[49] So it seems, here as elsewhere, he added this element to his account years later.

What Was the Point?

If one still has any doubt about whether to believe Craig's testimony on the three cartridges, one needs simply to ask, what would be the point of arranging them that way? One can try to imagine a conspirator on his hands and knees in the sniper's nest carefully lining up empty cartridges. But why make it *look* as if they were planted when it would be so much easier to just toss them down and let them bounce around, exactly as they would have if they had been ejected from a bolt action rifle?

What kind of conspirators would go to this trouble? Only anal-retentive conspirators. They blew Kennedy's brains all over Dealey Plaza, but they didn't want to leave an untidy mess in the sniper's nest.

The Mauser Story

Craig's story of the recovery of a Mauser rifle would seem to be more plausible, because early reports did say a Mauser had been recovered. Indeed, Sheriff's Deputy Seymour Weitzman signed an affidavit saying the recovered rifle was a Mauser, and his fellow deputy Eugene Boone reported that it "appeared to be" a Mauser.[50] District Attorney Henry Wade also told reporters, "It's a Mauser, I believe."[51] However, since he was not on the sixth floor, Wade must have been repeating a claim he had heard.

When questioned by the Warren Commission, Weitzman explained that the rifle looked like a Mauser "in a glance."[52] He had not examined the rifle but merely secured the area where it was found jammed into a stack of boxes and waited for Fritz and J. C. Day of the Identification Bureau. This action, of course, was simply "by the book" police work. Day would today be called a criminalist, or a specialist in retrieving and processing evidence.

Conspiracy theorist Josiah Thompson, in his book *Six Seconds in Dallas*, printed a photo panel showing a Mauser and a Mannlicher-Carcano together, and it would appear quite easy to confuse them.[53] (See also this book's photo insert.) Indeed, a panel of firearms experts studied this issue for the HSCA and concluded that "a Mannlicher-Carcano rifle could very easily be mistaken for other military rifles of its general type, including the 7.65-millimeter caliber German and other model Mausers."[54]

So far, some testimony supports Craig's version of events, and some offers a reasonable basis for doubting him. But there are further grounds for doubting Craig.

Tom Alyea photographed the recovery of the rifle, and his film appeared on WFAA-TV at about 3:30 p.m.[55] Clear, 16mm black-and-white footage shows the configuration of the weapon. Also, Officer Studebaker photographed the rifle in its place in the stack of boxes before it was removed. Finally, numerous newspaper photographers recorded J. C. Day exiting the depository with the weapon.

The HSCA had its photographic experts examine all these photos along with the backyard photos of Oswald holding the rifle and contemporary photos of the supposed murder weapon as it existed in the National Archives in the late 1970s. All the photos showed a Mannlicher-Carcano. Indeed, distinctive marks on the weapon indicated that all the photos were of the *same* Mannlicher-Carcano.[56]

The story of seeing the inscription 7.65 Mauser on the rifle was a late addition to Craig's story. It is neither in his early statements nor in his Warren Commission testimony. And as late as 1968, he was telling a rather different story. During the Garrison investigation, the *Los Angeles Free Press* interviewed Craig and assassination researcher Penn Jones (famed for writing of the "mysterious deaths" associated with the JFK assassination case).

Free Press: Did you handle that rifle [the Mannlicher-Carcano]?

Roger Craig: Yes, I did. I couldn't give its name because I don't know foreign rifles, I know it was foreign made, and you loaded it downward into a built-in clip. The ID man took it and ejected one live round from it. The scope was facing north, the bolt facing upwards and the trigger south.

But there was another rifle, a Mauser, found up on the roof of the depository that afternoon.

Free Press: A Mauser on the roof? Who found it?

Penn Jones: I don't know who found it, but I do know that a police officer verified its existence.[57]

So here Craig does not mention a Mauser being on the sixth floor. Rather, it was on the roof.

The Slug on the Dealey Plaza Infield

As was the case with the Mauser, Craig was not the first person to talk about a .45-caliber slug being found on the Dealey Plaza infield. In the December 21, 1963, issue of the *New Republic*, Richard Dudman reported,

On the day the President was shot, I happened to learn of a possible fifth [bullet]. A group of police officers were examining the area at the side of the street where the President was hit, and a police inspector told me they had just found another bullet in the grass.[58]

The *New Republic* would seem to be a reliable enough source, but if one takes this report absolutely at face value, it's mere hearsay.

Craig, in his 1974 interview, upped the ante and claimed to have actually seen a .45-caliber slug lying in gore (presumably from Kennedy's shattered head). Two identifiable officers—Sheriff's Deputy Buddy Walthers (in plainclothes) and Patrolman J. W. Foster—are visible in the photos that are alleged to show the bullet on the ground and then being picked up by a mysterious "agent." Both men appeared to believe a bullet hit near that spot, but neither claimed to have actually *seen* a bullet. Indeed, both Walthers and Foster explicitly said they had not.[59] Foster did declare to the Warren Commission that he had seen where a bullet hit the turf and ricocheted out.[60] But when asked point-blank by researcher Mark Oakes whether he had seen a bullet, Foster flatly denied that he had.[61] The photographers who were shooting the scene, Jim Murray and William Allen, both denied seeing any bullet. Indeed, Murray made blow-up prints to examine for a slug. He found none.[62]

There is one final witness who denied seeing a slug. Testifying before the Warren Commission in 1964, Craig recounted how a fellow officer ("Either Lemmy Lewis or Buddy Walthers," he said) told him about a bullet that had ricocheted off the south curb of Elm Street. Asked by Warren Commission counsel if he had found anything there to indicate the ricocheted bullet, Craig responded, "No; we didn't find anything at that time."[63]

The Time of the Tippit Shooting

One final element completes the cornucopia of conspiracy evidence in Craig's testimony. Craig, as previously noted, claims to have looked at his watch immediately upon hearing about the Tippit shooting and saw that the time was 1:06 p.m. This point, remember, was also "the exact moment" when the rifle was discovered. But according to Seymour Weitzman, the rifle was discovered at 1:22 p.m., although he insisted he couldn't be precise about the time.[64] His fellow officer, Eugene Boone, said it was discovered at 1:22 p.m. and that he knew the time precisely because he had looked at his watch.[65]

This point of 1:22 p.m., interestingly, would be reasonably consistent with the news of the Tippit shooting coming at the exact time the rifle was discovered. But it was not consistent with Craig's testimony about the time being 1:06 p.m.

Even if the shooting was before 1:06 p.m., how would anybody in the depository have known that? The first report of the Tippit shooting went out over Dallas Police radio at 1:16 p.m. or 1:17 p.m. People didn't have cell phones in 1963, and even if they did, it's absurdly unlikely that somebody on the scene of the Tippit murder would have called an officer who was searching the depository rather than the police dispatcher, who would immediately broadcast it.

Here, as before, one might wonder what Craig had said earlier than 1971. Again, the *Los Angeles Free Press* provides the answer in the March 1968 interview.

Roger Craig: Tippit went to Oak Cliff, and subsequently was killed. Why he went to Oak Cliff I can't tell you; I can only make an observation. He was going to meet somebody.

Free Press: Do you know what time he was killed?

Roger Craig: It was about 1:40—

Penn Jones: No, I think it was a little before 1:15.

Roger Craig: Was it?

Penn Jones: Yes, Bill Alexander—

Roger Craig: Oh, that's right. The broadcast was put out shortly after 1:15 on Tippit's killer, and it had not been put out yet on Oswald as the assassin of President Kennedy.[66]

So Craig in 1968 thought that Tippit was shot at about 1:40 p.m. (which was the approximate time Oswald entered the Texas Theatre), and he accepted Penn Jones's correction of the time to 1:15 p.m. But in 1971 Craig claimed that news of the shooting came to him at precisely 1:06 p.m.

CHARLES CRENSHAW

Charles Crenshaw was one of the many doctors in Emergency Room (ER) 1 at Parkland Hospital who worked to save John Kennedy's life. Although a junior and a bit player, he was indeed there. Thus, especially if one believes that physicians are particularly sober and reliable people, he should have been a good witness.

In his 1992 book, *JFK: Conspiracy of Silence*,[67] Crenshaw makes a batch of rather explosive claims. For example, he asserts that Kennedy's head wound was in the back, and thus "there was no doubt in my mind that the bullet had entered his head through the front."[68] Crenshaw alleges, as the book title implies, that

> every doctor who was in Trauma Room 1 had his own reasons for not publicly refuting the "official line." . . . I believe there was a common denominator in our silence—a fearful perception that to come forward with what we believed to be the medical truth would be asking for trouble.[69]

So Crenshaw presents himself as a fearless truth teller in contrast to all the other doctors, who were cowards. Unfortunately, by the time Crenshaw published his book, many of the Parkland doctors had been talking their heads off for decades to conspiracy authors such as Robert Groden, David Lifton, and Harry Livingstone. Their statements, usually interpreted as supporting a conspiracy, can be found in such books as *Six Seconds in Dallas*, *High Treason*, *High Treason II*, and *Best Evidence*. They can be seen in videos such as Nigel Turner's *The Men Who Killed Kennedy*, Bob Groden's *The Case for Conspiracy*, and NOVA's *Who Shot JFK?* and in a major investigative piece the *Boston Globe* published in 1981.[70]

Crenshaw claimed to have seen the wound in Kennedy's throat, saying that he had "identified a small opening about the diameter of a pencil at the midline of his throat to be an entry bullet hole,"[71] which would imply a shot from the front fired by somebody besides Lee Oswald. Crenshaw also gave a vivid account of entering the ER with Dr. Robert McClelland, which McClelland confirmed.[72] But McClelland also testified that he had entered the ER after the throat wound had been obliterated by a tracheotomy (intended to allow a breathing tube to be put in Kennedy's throat).[73] Dr. Malcolm Perry confirmed in his testimony that McClelland was not present when he began the tracheotomy, that McClelland arrived "shortly after" he had entered the neck, and that he (Perry) and Carrico were the only people who saw the unaltered wound.[74] So Crenshaw provided a vivid first-person description of something he could not have seen.

LBJ Wanting a Confession

Perhaps the most arresting claim Crenshaw makes in his book involves not the attempt to save Kennedy but the attempt to save Oswald's life two days later. According to Crenshaw, while Oswald was in the operating room (OR) and desperate efforts to save him were under way, Lyndon Johnson called Parkland and was put through to the OR. The nurse who answered the call then handed the phone to Crenshaw, who heard the voice on the other end say, "This is President Lyndon B. Johnson. Dr. Crenshaw, how is the accused assassin?" After a short discussion, LBJ demanded, "Dr. Crenshaw, I want a deathbed confession from the accused assassin."[75]

Unfortunately for Crenshaw, LBJ could not have made the call. According to researcher Gary Mack,

> LBJ was in his limo at the very moment Crenshaw's book indicates the call came in. There is no record of any such radiotelephone call which, according to the procedures in place, would have to have been routed to Dallas through the White House switchboard where all calls were logged. Nor is there an account from any of the people in the car that LBJ said, "Excuse me, I have to call the hospital."[76]

And indeed, William Manchester confirms Mack's chronology. The Johnsons had met the Kennedy family in the East Room of the White House at 11:55 a.m. central daylight time and then proceeded to the ceremonies involved with moving Kennedy's body from the White House to the Capitol.[77] According to Crenshaw's own time line, LBJ's call to the OR would have had to come a little less than fifty minutes later.[78]

But It Gets Worse

The claim that LBJ had called the OR to demand a confession from Oswald was not the first version of Crenshaw's story. The first version had LBJ demanding that Oswald be killed! This story is in Harry Livingstone's *Killing the Truth*, a book that takes a rather favorable view of Crenshaw's testimony.[79] A more reliable source than Livingstone would be the author Gus Russo, who recounted an experience from the early 1990s.

> When Oliver Stone was in Dallas prepping for *JFK*, a number of us were around as "technical advisors," which was a bit of a joke, since Stone only listened to people with crazy conspiracy info.
>
> One night at the Stoneleigh [Hotel], Stone was having a slew of top secret meetings in his suite with people like Ricky White, whom Stone paid $80,000 for his fraudulent story, and the positively goofy Beverly Oliver. That night, Stone ushered Gary Shaw, [Robert] Groden and Crenshaw into his room; I was not invited, but I pressed Shaw (Crenshaw's and Oliver's advisor) for info in the lobby. He was the first to tell me that LBJ ordered Oswald killed. Later, Crenshaw came down, and we happened to be in the Stoneleigh men's room at the same time, standing at adjacent urinals. It was there that he told me that Johnson had ordered the Parkland staff to "kill the son-of-a-bitch." It was decided to "drown Oswald in his own blood," i.e. transfuse him until his lungs collapsed.[80]

So apparently, if a story is just too outrageous, it can be watered down a bit to be tolerably palatable.

THE "INTERESTING" WITNESSES

Charles Crenshaw, just as Roger Craig, Jean Hill, Beverly Oliver, Madeleine Brown, and similar witnesses to aspects of the case, didn't just start telling tall tales in a vacuum.[81] As with Hill and Craig, he was actually present and saw some interesting things. Jean Hill almost certainly did believe she heard four to six shots and that the shots had come from the grassy knoll (but she also believed she had seen a little dog with Jack and Jackie in the limo). Roger Craig may have honestly thought he saw Lee Oswald get into a Rambler station wagon. And when fellow deputy Buddy Walthers told Craig that Ruth Paine had a station wagon, he may have made an honest, if unwarranted, connection. Furthermore, honest witnesses in Alice, Texas, and at the Sports Drome Rifle Range reported similar Oswald sightings (discussed in chapter 10 and chapter 2, respectively).

But then the stories took on a life of their own. Things were added.

The additions were not random. Rather, conspiracy factoids were added. Craig added two factoids—finding a .45-caliber slug on the Dealey Plaza infield and saying the recovered rifle was a Mauser—and implicated Ruth Paine. Jean Hill added two factoids—the motorcade route changed and LBJ ducked—and government agents tried to intimidate her. She even fortified the grassy knoll part of her story, claiming to have actually *seen* a shooter. Both she and Craig appropriated the "mysterious deaths" factoid, which, since they themselves were still alive, had to be changed to the "attempts on my life" factoid. Dr. Crenshaw adopted the "back of the head was blown out" factoid and implicated LBJ. Madeleine Brown, who claimed to have been LBJ's mistress, accepted a story about an alleged "assassination party" at the home of Dallas millionaire Clint Murchison in November 1963. She upped the ante by placing a large cast of powerful people there and by claiming LBJ said something incriminating during the party. Another person claiming to be a witness, Beverly Oliver, started her story with the facts: she sang at the Colony Club (a venue that competed with Jack Ruby's Carousel Club) and that there was a real "Babushka Lady" in Dealey Plaza (a woman wearing a head scarf, or babushka, as she apparently photographed the motorcade). Then she built into her story real characters like Jada (a stripper at Ruby's club), an almost certainly bogus friendship with Jack Ruby, and hoary suspicions that Oswald worked for the CIA and that the FBI articulated a wide-ranging cover-up.

Thus these interesting witnesses have pursued an effective strategy for gaining acceptance, although they may not have been consciously shrewd and calculating in doing so. To a degree, they may have been manipulated by conspiracy researchers who asked leading questions and gave subtle clues as to what sort of testimony worked in gaining credibility and further interest. To maintain that interest, of course, it's desirable to give better and better testimony.

Thus they added elements that are staples of conspiracy folklore and that seem both to corroborate their testimony and in turn to corroborate the folklore.

It's a self-reinforcing cycle and highly seductive for those researchers who believe in a conspiracy.

But typically these witnesses push their factoids too far and add something to their stories that simply could not have happened.

Judyth Baker

A classic case of pushing the limits of plausibility too far comes from one Judyth Vary Baker, a woman who claims to have had an adulterous affair with Lee Oswald in New Orleans during the summer of 1963. Baker's story is laced with grossly implausible elements. It centers around a supposed CIA bioweapons project in New Orleans during that summer. Baker claims that she was working with other researchers to produce a drug "cocktail" to be injected into Fidel Castro. It consisted of something akin to the AIDS virus to suppress his immune system mixed with cancer cells to kill him. This high-powered team of researchers included Dr. Mary Sherman, a reputable orthopedic surgeon; David Ferrie, who had a mail order PhD from an Italian "university"; high school dropout Oswald; and Baker herself, who had at most one year of college science courses. The research was conducted in Ferrie's and Sherman's apartments.[82]

Putting aside the inherent implausibility of the story and the Byzantine twists and turns in her ever-changing account, the coup de grâce was administered to her tall tale when skeptical researchers leaked a draft chapter of her manuscript. The text included a heart-rending phone conversation between Baker and Oswald, who had become an unwilling participant in the Kennedy assassination plot and feared he would be killed by other plotters. It supposedly took place on the Wednesday before the Friday assassination.

> Because time was so short now, Lee told me there wouldn't be another call from him unless he reached Laredo.
>
> "Lee," I said slowly, "you didn't say until. You said 'unless.'"
>
> "I apologize," he answered. I heard him suck up his breath. We were both very close to tears. Outside, it was sunset.
>
> "You'll go to Cancun," Lee said. "You'll stay in a fine hotel. I'll be there—if they—"
>
> We were both speechless.
>
> "You know," he said then, "if I don't make it out—you have to go on with everything."

"Oh, sure!" I said, bitterly. I told him that I would never allow anyone to replace him in my heart.[83]

Unfortunately, there were no fine hotels in Cancún in 1963. The location was a series of deserted sandbars. Development of the site didn't begin until years later.

The Paul Hoch Ratio Test

Baker's narrative also provides an example of how a key analytical tool can be used to sort the wild and woolly stories from the moderately plausible ones among JFK assassination witnesses' claims. Respected researcher Paul Hoch has developed an informal but powerful test to assess the plausibility of any supposed witness offering new or explosive testimony. Quite simply, he asks how many names appear that are familiar to assassination researchers. As Hoch put it at a 1993 assassination conference, "I suspect that a useful measure of the plausibility of an allegation could be derived from the percentage of well-known names. If a source claims to have met with David Ferrie, Allen Dulles, and Fidel Castro in Jack Ruby's nightclub, I'll go on to the next document."[84]

The ratio test makes sense if you believe that the vast majority of suspects fingered in JFK conspiracy books must be innocent; otherwise, a literal cast of thousands killed JFK. Further, it's unlikely that more than a tiny handful of the real plotters have been identified. If, say, some rogue faction in the CIA assassinated Kennedy, then one or two men whose names loom large in conspiracy literature might have led it. It must have also included several foot soldiers who are and will always remain anonymous. Moreover, the more diverse the story's cast of plotters, the less plausible the plot. For a cast derived from New Orleans, including Guy Banister (former FBI agent and down-on-his-luck private detective), David Ferrie (oddball character who worked for Banister), and Jack Martin (another Banister employee) might not be too terrible, since they did know one another. Adding New Orleans figures such as Dr. Alton Ochsner and Clay Shaw, who ran in different social circles, makes things less plausible. But you've gone too far if you then toss in a bunch of people from Texas (Jack Ruby, Oswald's petroleum geologist friend George De Mohrenschildt, political operative Bobby Baker, LBJ crony Billie Sol Estes, Ruby stripper Janet Conforto [aka Jada], and Dallas Police officer Roscoe White), a mobster in Tampa (Santos Trafficante), a CIA operative who was in Mexico City during all of 1963 (David Atlee Phillips), plus FBI director J. Edgar Hoover. Judyth Baker, however, does include all of them and another two dozen people or so familiar in conspiracy literature. It's hard to avoid the conclusion that this motley crew of assassins and conspirators was drawn from conspiracy books and not real life.[85]

WHY DOES ANYBODY BELIEVE THESE PEOPLE?

It might seem that nobody would believe any of these witnesses, but what sort of deluded person would accept such stories? In the first place, some people dearly *want* to believe. They are capable of coming up with a seemingly endless string of excuses. In the case of Judyth Baker, her supporters on the Internet claimed she didn't write the passage about Cancún; rather, an associate of hers named Howard Platzman, who "misunderstood" her story, wrote it. Then they said it was written by Judyth's first agent, who got it wrong. When this explanation didn't convince anybody, they declared that the passage meant that Judyth and Lee were planning to go to Cancún but were going to stay in a fine hotel somewhere else. Chichén Itzá was suggested, but Judyth herself, in the TV documentary *The Men Who Killed Kennedy*, said their destination was Mérida, a town on the Yucatán Peninsula (a two-hundred-mile drive from present-day Cancún), because it "had CIA contacts located there." Each new excuse, contradicting the previous excuse, eroded her credibility even further.[86]

The more seasoned and knowledgeable assassination buffs generally disbelieve these interesting witnesses. Not only do lone assassin theorists discount them (which is true almost by definition), but even many conspiracy-believing researchers reject them. Judyth's critics include conspiracists such as Debra Conway, a proprietor of the JFK Lancer website; the late Mary Ferrell, an icon among conspiracy researchers; and David Lifton, who, as noted earlier, believes a conspiracy waylaid Kennedy's body on the way to the autopsy and altered his wounds.

When witness Beverly Oliver testified before the Assassination Records Review Board in 1994, conspiracist researcher Gary Mack appeared and testified that her claims were nonsense. Mack has also been instrumental in debunking the claims of Charles Crenshaw and Madeleine Brown. Conspiracy researcher David Perry wrote the definitive debunking of Brown's revelations ("Texas in the Imagination") and a fine critical piece on Craig ("The Rambler Man").

But the majority of people who watch movies like *JFK*, read conspiracy books available at chain bookstores, or view purported documentaries such as *The Men Who Killed Kennedy* on television are not seasoned and knowledgeable researchers.

Thus they are exposed to these bogus accounts but not to their debunking. And increasingly, sober and knowledgeable conspiracy-oriented researchers find themselves allied with lone assassin theorists in unmasking such witnesses to both the hard-core true believers, who will accept them, and the innocent neophytes.

NOT JUST A JFK THING

Someone too engrossed in the Kennedy assassination might assume that bogus tales are somehow uncommon. But false and fictionalized memoirs are not, in fact, that rare. In 2008, for example, a book called *Love and Consequences* told the story of a "Margaret B. Jones," who claimed to be a half-white, half–Native American foster child who grew up in South-Central Los Angeles and ran drugs for a gang called the Bloods.[87] Another tale of personal redemption came from James Frey, a supposed ex-criminal and drug addict whose book *A Million Little Pieces* was puffed by Oprah Winfrey.[88]

The Holocaust has produced some heartrending stories of hardship and heroism. Indeed, a book called *Misha: A Memoir of the Holocaust Years* tells the story of how the title character lived in the woods with a pack of wolves after the Nazis took her parents away.[89] And Holocaust survivor Herman Rosenblat wrote a compelling account of how the woman who later became his wife had passed him food through the fence of the concentration camp in which he was imprisoned. Oprah embraced this book too.[90]

What do all these accounts have in common? All are fabricated. It seems that human nature enjoys a juicy conspiracy story on the one hand and a heartwarming story of triumph over adversity on the other hand, creating a market that a fair number of people will cater to and exploit.

Unfortunately, the truth is often much less entertaining than fiction. If that principle applies to the Holocaust and the trials of inner-city youth, it applies to the JFK assassination too.

Chapter Five

Bogus Quoting: Stripping Context, Misleading Readers

If it is sometimes difficult to figure out what a witness actually meant when a full and accurate version of testimony is available, then it's obviously more difficult to know what a witness meant when a quote is ripped out of context.

Everybody knows and pretty much accepts that advocates selectively present information that serves their purposes, but it's all too easy to forget that book authors and video producers are advocates too. And it is sometimes hard to grasp how radically selective advocates are prone to be. An author would not present the testimony of a witness and willfully omit parts that show the witness to be insane, would he? A director of a documentary would not produce something that puffs witness accounts she knows to be contradicted by reliable evidence, would she?

Yes, he or she would.

Nobody entirely avoids selectivity, since reviewing all the primary source documents, photos, and videos would be too tedious for all but hard-core buffs to bear. Every author, even the most sensible, is an advocate to a degree. But some are much worse than others. The following are some examples.

JACK RUBY'S PLEA

Testifying before the Warren Commission, Jack Ruby famously begged the commission to take him to Washington. Many authors quote his appeal entirely out of context to imply that Ruby wanted to reveal his part in a conspiracy. But they engage in massive selectivity and spin to support this notion. Typical is David Scheim's *Contract on America*, a book whose treatment of Ruby's testimony is stunningly tendentious.[1] Scheim tells of Ruby's pleas to be taken to Washington, his claims that he "can't tell the truth" in Dallas, and his assertion that "my life is in danger here."[2] Indeed, he reports that Ruby said, "I tell you, gentlemen, my whole family is in jeopardy. My sisters, as to their lives."[3] All of this pleading, of course, is consistent with the notion that Ruby was a conspirator, that he was tasked to silence Oswald, and that he feared retribution on himself and his family if he "spilled the beans."

But what does one find when looking at his entire testimony?[4] Rather than wanting to describe a conspiracy he was allegedly a part of, Ruby wanted to take a lie detector test to prove his innocence. But there was another thing he wanted to do, as evidenced in his Warren Commission testimony:

> I am in a tough spot, and I don't know what the solution can be to save me.
>
> And I know our wonderful President, Lyndon Johnson, as soon as he was the President of his country, he appointed you as head of this group. But through certain falsehoods that have been said about me to other people, the John Birch Society, I am as good as guilty as the accused assassin of President Kennedy.
>
> How can you remedy that, Mr. [Earl] Warren? Do any of you men have any ways of remedying that?

Rather than admitting to being part of a conspiracy, Ruby saw himself as the victim of a conspiracy that rendered him "as good as guilty" in Kennedy's murder. Ruby was looking for help in clearing his name, something that neither the Warren Commission nor anybody else could really give him.

Then, in regard to the John Birch Society, Chief Justice Warren responded:

> **Earl Warren:** I think it is powerful, yes I do. Of course, I don't have all the information that you feel you have on that subject.
>
> **Jack Ruby:** Unfortunately, you don't have, because it is too late. And I wish that our beloved President, Lyndon Johnson, would have delved deeper into the situation, hear me, not to accept just circumstantial facts about my guilt or innocence, and would have questioned to find out the truth about me before he relinquished certain powers to these certain people.

The latter statement appears to be a complaint that Ruby was having to talk to men he considered the president's representatives rather than getting to talk to the president himself. Then, he made yet another desperate entreaty to be taken to

Washington, by saying, "There is only one thing. If you don't take me back to Washington tonight to give me a chance to prove to the President that I am not guilty, then you will see the most tragic thing that will ever happen."

Then Ruby explained the nature of the conspiracy he thought was arrayed against him:

> All I know is maybe something can be saved. Because right now, I want to tell you this, I am used as a scapegoat, and there is no greater weapon that you can use to create some falsehood about some of the Jewish faith, especially at the terrible heinous crime such as the killing of President Kennedy.
>
> Now maybe something can be saved. It may not be too late, whatever happens, if our President, Lyndon Johnson, knew the truth from me. But if I am eliminated, there won't be any way of knowing.
>
> Right now, when I leave your presence now, I am the only one that can bring out the truth to our President, who believes in righteousness and justice.
>
> But he has been told, I am certain, that I was part of a plot to assassinate the President.

Ruby's addled brain seemed to go from obsession to obsession. In this portion of his lengthy testimony, he expressed his desire to go to Washington and convince Lyndon Johnson that he was not part of any conspiracy to kill "our beloved President" (Kennedy).

Ruby clearly believed he might be "eliminated." Indeed, earlier in his testimony he claimed that "the Jewish people are being exterminated at this moment. Consequently, a whole new form of government is going to take over our country, and I know I won't live to see you another time."[5]

Scheim, just as other conspiracy authors generally do, entirely sanitized Ruby's fears about "the Jewish people" from the testimony he reported. And he did so for a reason. Ruby believed that there was a plot, all right, a plot by anti-Semites to blame him for killing Kennedy and to scapegoat the Jews. In his early testimony is a statement of his belief that a new holocaust was being mounted, and Jews, including himself and his family, would be killed. This idea dogged him until his death, a paranoid delusion that raged out of control. Conspiracy authors like Scheim know this belief would sound far-fetched, so they report only the testimony that's consistent with standard conspiracy theories.

Ruby also wanted to prove his innocence to President Johnson, and this desire likewise had to be sanitized out of conspiracy books. It's inconsistent both with the claim that Ruby wanted to confess to being part of a conspiracy and with the notion that LBJ was part of the same conspiracy Ruby was. Why try to prove your innocence to the chief conspirator if you are one of his minions?

Rather than wanting to confess his role as coconspirator, Ruby told the Warren Commission, "No subversive organization gave me any idea. No underworld person made any effort to contact me. It all happened that Sunday morning." Conspiracy authors, of course, could claim that Ruby was lying in all his statements; instead, they mislead readers about what Ruby actually said.

THE KATZENBACH MEMO: RECIPE FOR A COVER-UP?

Those who believe that the U.S. government (in league with, obviously, Dallas law enforcement) covered up a conspiracy love to quote a memo Assistant Attorney General Nicholas Katzenbach wrote to Bill Moyers of the White House staff on November 25, 1963. The portions that are typically quoted follow:

> The public must be satisfied that Oswald was the assassin; that he did not have confederates who are still at large; and that evidence was such that he would have been convicted at trial.
>
> Speculation about Oswald's motivation ought to be cut off, and we should have some basis for rebutting thought that this was a Communist conspiracy or (as the Iron Curtain press is saying) a right-wing conspiracy to blame it on the Communists.[6]

The conspiracy-oriented website of the Mary Ferrell Foundation notes, "To many observers, the Katzenbach memo provides the blueprint for the cover-up which followed."[7] And author Gerald McKnight mentions the memo in eleven different places in his book *Breach of Trust*, always treating it as the establishment of a government cover-up.[8]

But what parts of the memo do conspiracy books seldom quote? The following passages:

> It is important that all of the facts surrounding President Kennedy's Assassination be made public in a way which will satisfy people in the United States and abroad that all the facts have been told and a statement to this effect be made now.

And further:

> I think this objective may be satisfied by making public as soon as possible a complete and thorough FBI report on Oswald and the assassination.

And finally:

> I think, however, that a statement that all the facts will be made public property in an orderly and responsible way should be made now.[9]

Katzenbach does worry about "Congressional hearings of the wrong sort." Given that his generation vividly remembered Joe McCarthy (and McCarthy was neither the first nor the last irresponsible congressional demagogue), this concern is perfectly understandable. Katzenbach also called for "a Presidential Commission of unimpeachable personnel to review and examine the evidence and announce its conclusions." This panel, of course, is what became the Warren Commission, and conspiracists who believe the Warren Commission was a "cover-up" also believe that proposing such a commission was part of a cover-up plan.

Begging the Question

So just how is the Katzenbach memo sinister? If one *begins with the assumption* that there was a conspiracy, that the evidence of conspiracy was obvious on the Monday after the Friday assassination, and that Katzenbach knew (or somehow suspected) a conspiracy was afoot, then the memo is certainly nefarious. But you have to begin with that assumption. If Katzenbach believed that Oswald was the lone assassin—as the Dallas Police Department said and as the FBI believed and told Katzenbach as of November 24—it's entirely different.[10] And if you believe that rumors and speculation can be harmful—for example, they could fan a war with Russia by implying Communist involvement or hurt the international reputation of the United States if right-wingers could pull off the murder of a president—then a public-spirited person would advocate doing exactly what Katzenbach did. Today such action is called transparency.

WHY DID RUBY KILL OSWALD?

Another rather explosive claim involves Jack Ruby's motive for shooting Oswald. Ruby told the Warren Commission that he shot Oswald so that Jackie Kennedy would not be forced to return to Dallas and testify at a trial of Lee Oswald. So quite a few eyebrows were raised in 1967 when one of Ruby's former attorneys, Joe Tonahill, announced that Ruby had passed a note to him saying, "Joe, you should know this. Tom Howard told me to say that I shot Oswald so that Caroline and Mrs. Kennedy wouldn't have to come to Dallas to testify, OK?"[11] Tom Howard was Ruby's first lawyer, and conspiracists were quick to draw conclusions. Jim Marrs claimed that the note showed that Ruby was "propelled by motives not his own," and Noel Twyman said the note exposed Ruby's explanation as a "fabricated legal ploy."[12]

What are conspiracy books failing to tell their readers? After he shot Oswald but long before he ever talked to Tom Howard, Ruby told several people he did it for Jackie. These people included Secret Service agent Forest Sorrels, Detective T. D. McMillon, Detective Barnard Clardy, and Assistant District Attorney Bill Alexander.[13] All of these conversations occurred before 1:55 p.m. on November 24, 1963, which is the time Howard was issued a permit to visit Ruby.[14]

Officer Ray Hall, who also talked to Ruby before 1:55 p.m., reported,

> He [Ruby] read in the newspaper about OSWALD having a trial, and he thought that President KENNEDY's wife would have to return to Dallas for the trial and he did not think she should have to undergo that ordeal. . . . RUBY said he thought about these things, and had become very emotional.[15]

Finally, reporter Wes Wise recounted how Ruby approached him in Dealey Plaza the day *before* he shot Oswald, saying that it would be terrible if Jackie had to return to Dallas to testify.[16] And indeed, a photo of Ruby's bedroom, taken by police on the afternoon that he shot Oswald, shows a copy of the *Dallas Times Herald* on the floor.[17] On page 5A of that paper was an article speculating that Mrs. Kennedy would have to return to Dallas and testify at Oswald's trial.

But if Ruby was sharing this concern for Mrs. Kennedy before he even talked to Tom Howard, how do we explain the note to Tonahill? We have to remember that many thoughts were going through Jack Ruby's addled brain. As researcher Dave Reitzes put it,

> People don't seem to understand that if Ruby's act was an impulsive one, as he claimed, then all his later explanations are, to some extent, after-the-fact rationalizations. Thus, "I did it for Mrs. Kennedy" may be no more or less accurate than "I did it to show the world that Jews have guts," or "That rat killed my President!" or "You guys [the Dallas police] couldn't do it!" or "I

only wanted to be a hero"—all of which (and more) he reportedly said soon after the shooting, and all of which, to some extent, may well be true.[18]

And Jean Davison explained the note succinctly:

> If a defendant tells his lawyer, "I robbed the bank because I had a grudge against the bank president, and I like the excitement, and my mother needs an operation," the lawyer might tell him to say he did it because his mother needs an operation. Ruby had mentioned several motives, and Howard may have felt that this one would gain more sympathy from a jury than "to prove that Jews do have guts" or "you [cops] couldn't do it, and somebody had to."[19]

So the story was, in a sense, a legal ploy. But it was not a lie and certainly not evidence of a conspiracy.

E. HOWARD HUNT: ASSASSINATION CONSPIRATOR?

If you read and believe Mark Lane's book *Plausible Denial*, you would think a Miami jury convicted E. Howard Hunt as a conspirator in this case.

The book is about a legal case that Hunt, the ex-CIA operative and Watergate burglar, brought against a journal called the *Spotlight* for saying that he had had a role in the Kennedy assassination. In 1981 Hunt won a libel judgment, but the Liberty Lobby, which published the *Spotlight*, appealed and got the earlier verdict thrown out. The case was retried in Miami in 1985.

The jury in Miami sided with the *Spotlight* and refused to find it guilty of libel. According to Lane, this finding showed that Hunt was guilty of conspiring to kill Kennedy. Lane tells his readers he was "prosecuting a murder case [the JFK assassination] within a civil action [the Hunt libel case]." Explaining that the jury found for the *Spotlight*, Lane claims that "the evidence was clear" and that "the CIA had killed President Kennedy, [and] Hunt had been part of it."[20]

Using Marita Lorenz

Lane argued in court that Hunt was in Dallas on the day of the assassination, and Lane used the testimony of a woman named Marita Lorenz to attempt to implicate Hunt in a conspiracy. Lorenz wasn't at the trial in person, but she gave a deposition that was read in court. She told the story of several conspirators driving a two-car caravan from Miami to Dallas and arriving the day before the assassination. When the assassins arrived in Dallas, Hunt, under the pseudonym Eduardo, met with them at a motel and gave them a sum of money.

Lane's case for Hunt being involved in an assassination conspiracy thus hangs on the credibility of Lorenz, and Lane never tells his readers anything that would lead them to question her credibility. But Lorenz's story about an assassination conspiracy had come out years before the trial, had been thoroughly investigated, and had been found to be fabricated.

The HSCA investigated her claims extensively in 1977 and 1978. According to Chief Counsel Robert Blakey,

> We also rejected the story of Marita Lorenz, who told us she had driven from Miami to Dallas on November 15, 1963, with Oswald and several anti-Castro activists, including Gerry Patrick Hemming, Orlando Bosch, a terrorist, . . . Pedro Diaz-Lanz, the former Cuban Air Force chief, and Frank Sturgis, who was arrested in the Watergate break-in in 1972. All four men denied Lorenz's charge emphatically, and we could find no evidence to refute them. Lorenz, who claimed to have been Fidel Castro's mistress as well as the instrument of an attempt by the CIA to poison Castro . . . did not help her credibility by telling us that when she arrived in Dallas with Oswald and the anti-Castro activists, they were contacted at their motel by Jack Ruby.[21]

A classic bugaboo for witnesses who make up wild stories is their tendency to place iconic assassination characters where they could not have been and when ironclad evidence places them elsewhere. In this case it is true of Ruby, whose movements on the day before the assassination where methodically established by the Warren Commission. He could not have been at any motel with Lorenz and her merry band of assassins.[22] The situation is even worse regarding Oswald, for she claimed he was actually *in* the car caravan from Miami. But during these several days, he is known to have been in Dallas.[23]

One might think that Lorenz would know that her story was problematic by the time she gave the deposition for the Liberty Lobby trial, but in the deposition she *still* includes Oswald in the caravan, in the "back up car."[24] Lane handles this problem in *Plausible Denial* by simply editing out that part of her testimony.[25]

Other parts of Lorenz's testimony were absurd, and Lane, of course, edits those out too. Lorenz, for example, claimed to have met Lee Oswald while she was with a group of people training in the "Everglades [and] Central American countries" for the Bay of Pigs invasion and that "he wanted to be part of the invasion."[26] The Bay of Pigs invasion happened in April 1961, but Oswald was in the Soviet Union between September 1959 and June 1962.[27]

At the Liberty Lobby trial, Hunt's fellow CIA employees Walter Kuzmuk, Connie Mazerov, and Elizabeth (Betty) McIntosh all testified that Hunt had been in Washington on November 22, 1963. Lane attacks the credibility of Kuzmuk and Mazerov with ad hominem arguments, but then he evades talking about McIntosh by exploiting an apparent error in the trial transcript.[28] Lane writes, "When [Walter] Kuzmuk was asked who might have seen Hunt that day if he had been in the office [at the CIA], he replied Betty McDonald. The plaintiff did not call McDonald; Hunt explained that she had been absent that day."[29] But in reality, Betty McIntosh did appear and did testify she had seen Hunt.[30]

The possibility that Hunt and Sturgis might have been doing some dirty deeds in Dallas in November 1963 had come up years earlier, in connection with the photos of the so-called three tramps in Dealey Plaza taken after the assassination.[31] The men were arrested in the railroad yards near Dealey Plaza, and marched through the plaza. For almost thirty years, there were no available records of their identity or what happened to them, so speculation that they were part of some assassination conspiracy was rife. The Rockefeller Commission had investigated the whereabouts of Hunt and Sturgis on the day of the assassination. Two of Hunt's children and a domestic employee testified that Hunt had been in Washington on November 22, 1963, and Sturgis's wife and her nephew (who was living with them) confirmed that he had been in Miami.[32]

One can, of course, claim that the men's relatives were lying and that Blakey was biased against finding a CIA conspiracy. One can also maintain that the CIA employees were lying, which is an easy sell for conspiracists. But two HSCA staffers, who were happy to blame the CIA, came to the conclusion that Lorenz was telling tall tales. HSCA investigator Gaeton Fonzi, who wrote an entire chapter about her in his book *The Last Investigation*, said that she turned into a mere "diversion" and "injected a dose of slapstick" into the HSCA's work.[33] His colleague Ed Lopez was more direct. He told Gerald Posner,

> Oh God, we spent a lot of time with Marita. . . . It was hard to ignore her because she gave us so much crap, and we tried to verify it, but let me tell you—she is full of shit. Between her and Frank Sturgis, we must have spent over one hundred hours. They were dead ends. . . . Marita is not credible.[34]

Reading the Jury's Conclusion

Just as Lane conceals information about what happened during the trial, he uses the same tactic when he describes the jury verdict. As noted, the jury found for the *Spotlight* and against Hunt. Lane interprets this decision as a judgment that Hunt was indeed an assassination conspirator. To support this claim, he puffs the statements of jury foreperson Leslie Armstrong. Lane summarizes her opinion as: "The evidence was clear, she said. The CIA had killed President Kennedy. Hunt had been part of it, and that evidence, so painstakingly presented should now be examined by the relevant institutions of the United States government so that those responsible for the assassination might be brought to justice."[35]

But what of the five other jurors?[36] Lane doesn't mention them. Most didn't see the case the way Armstrong did.

Juror Suzanne Reach told the *Miami Herald*, "We were very disgusted and felt it was trash. . . . The paper published material that was sloppy—but it wasn't malicious." Reach added, "We were worried that our verdict might give the wrong impression to the public" and insisted that Lane's conspiracy theories were "absolutely not" the reason for the verdict.[37]

The *Miami Herald* also quoted another juror, who did not want to be named, saying that Hunt had failed to show that the article was printed with "reckless disregard for the truth" and that Lane's theories about conspiracy were "so much extraneous matter."[38] Likewise, the Associated Press reported that an unidentified juror said (in the words of the reporter) that "no evidence was presented showing malice toward Hunt by the publication."[39] Finally, the United Press reported that juror L. L. Cobb insisted the jury was only concerned about whether the article was damaging to Hunt and not whether he was an assassination conspirator. "What we looked at was the article and whether there was any instances [sic] of malice," she said. "We did not find any because there had been many stories written about the issue."[40]

The jurors' concern with malice reflects what they were told about the law by the judge. A Supreme Court decision called *New York Times Co. v. Sullivan* (1964) had made it extremely hard for a public figure to successfully sue for libel. A story about a public figure, such as Hunt, could be untrue, could make scurrilous accusations, could be lousy journalism, and, indeed, could be absurd, but if it was not published with "actual malice," the public figure could not collect a libel judgment.

The judge explicitly instructed the jury about this issue,[41] and posttrial news reports show it abided by the law. Indeed, while it was deliberating, the jury asked to review the testimony of author Victor Marchetti, who wrote the story that precipitated the suit; *Spotlight* publisher Willis Carto; and *Spotlight* managing editor James Tucker.[42] The testimony of those witnesses had nothing to do with whether there was a conspiracy involving Hunt, but it would have been relevant to whether there was actual malice.

How does Lane deal with all this information? He puffed the one juror who believed in a conspiracy and ignored the three or four (depending on whether the anonymous juror in the two different stories was the same person) who either didn't believe Hunt was a conspirator or based their verdict on the issue of actual malice rather than any conspiracy theory. Lane explains the *Sullivan* decision to his readers,[43] but he insists it had nothing to do with the verdict. Then he fails to mention that the judge's charge to the jury explicitly said that Hunt was a public figure and that they must find actual malice.[44]

RUBY THE FBI INFORMANT

If one regards the FBI as sinister, then anybody who gives information to the FBI is sinister too, and being an FBI informant makes one especially sinister. Therefore, conspiracy books have a field day with the fact that Jack Ruby was an FBI informant. Henry Hurt, for example, reports that "Ruby was approached by the FBI and agreed to work as a potential criminal informant. He was so listed in bureau files, a matter that has never been adequately explained."[45]

In fact, however, it has been explained: because Ruby was a nightclub owner, the FBI thought he "might have knowledge of the criminal element in Dallas." When the FBI first visited him in 1959, Ruby agreed to help. The FBI came to him eight more times during that year, but he did not furnish the bureau with any useful information.[46] The bureau insisted that he was not an informant, since he was not paid, but merely a "potential informant."[47] This distinction, of course, is a semantic quibble (although semantics are often important to bureaucrats). The bald fact is that Ruby, a huge sycophant, would have loved to have been an important FBI informant, but he didn't know anything worthwhile. Call him an informant "wannabe."

Conspiracy books usually fail to tell their readers that Jack Ruby had no useful information. Doing so would suggest that he was just the hapless schlub he seemed to be.

It's not uncommon, of course, for advocates to present only one side of an issue. That's typical of pundits with a point to make, activists with a cause to promote, or politicians with an agenda to push. But sometimes, withholding facts can be used to make a situation appear to be quite different from what it really is. That's way too common in books about the Kennedy assassination.

Chapter Six

Probability:
Things that Defy the Odds

Sometimes, things happen that just seem too strange. They seem to defy the odds. Indeed, if something really does defy the odds of happening in a nonconspiratorial way, one should think seriously about conspiracy at work.

THE 544 CAMP STREET MYSTERY

This artful kind of logic makes the New Orleans address of 544 Camp Street look sinister indeed. When Lee Oswald was in New Orleans, handing out leaflets for the Fair Play for Cuba Committee, there were three different addresses placed on the different batches of the leaflets he handed out. One was for his Magazine Street apartment. Another was his post office box with two digits reversed (Oswald was dyslexic). The final one said 544 Camp Street.[1]

As any good assassination buff knows, 544 Camp was the address of the Newman Building, and in the Newman Building was the office of Guy Banister, a suspect in the assassination. Often found in that office was another suspect, David Ferrie. (If you've seen the movie *JFK* and read a few conspiracy books, you likely view them as two of the most sinister characters in all of New Orleans.) This setup allows conspiracy authors Ray La Fontaine and Mary La Fontaine to claim "Oswald and Banister shared the same 'space,' not in some sterile high rise, but a shabby three-story wooden building, the sort of unpretentious cozy quarters where other tenants were likely to know something about your business."[2]

The odds against that happening innocently are huge, wouldn't one think?

To figure out just how unlikely an innocent connection really is, one has to take some factoids off the table. The address of Banister's office was not 544 Camp

Street. One entered the Newman Building from Lafayette Street to access Banister's first-floor office, so the address was 531 Lafayette Street. If one entered at 544 Camp Street, one faced a stairway that led up to the Newman Building's second floor. Just as you couldn't get to Banister's office by entering 544 Camp, you couldn't get to any offices at 544 Camp by entering Banister's office. Building owner Sam Newman himself explained this configuration to the HSCA.[3] Private detective Joe Newbrough, who once worked with Banister, told *Frontline* in 1993,

> Absolutely, you could not find yourself in Banister's office if you went through the entrance at 544 Camp. It went strictly to the second floor of the building. There was no stairwell down. You had to exit the second floor to the sidewalk, walk around the corner and go into Banister's office. . . . Totally separate entrances, and probably 60 steps apart.[4]

So for all practical purposes, Oswald might as well have used the address of the building next door to Banister's office.

A second point to remember is that the Newman Building was on Lafayette Square, and just a short stroll from the Reily Coffee Company, at 640 Magazine Street, where Oswald worked (or rather "was employed," since he reportedly did little work). A casual walk to Lafayette Square during his lunch hour could have easily taken Oswald past 544 Camp, which was two short blocks from Reily. Oswald was apparently thinking of getting (or *pretending* to have) an office, since he had written to V. T. Lee, then the national president of the Fair Play for Cuba Committee, and told him he had gotten one.[5] If Oswald wanted to come up with an address to give his fictional New Orleans chapter of the Fair Play for Cuba Committee legitimacy, 544 Camp was handy enough.

The Probability Issue

These observations don't directly address the probability issue of how Oswald came to use the 544 Camp Street address, although they do put it in perspective. What are the odds that if Oswald picked out a random building in the city, it would connect him to the two most sinister characters in New Orleans who were suspects in the JFK assassination?

The answer depends on a key issue. Could anyone say, a priori, that Banister and Ferrie were "the two most sinister characters in New Orleans" and "suspects in the assassination"? The answer is no. One only sees them as such precisely because Oswald used the address of their building on his leaflets.

No doubt, the men seem extremely sinister to people steeped in the conspiracy literature and to people who have seen the movie *JFK* or documentaries like *The Men Who Killed Kennedy*. But how the men have been portrayed stems from their (rather slight) connection with Oswald and his use of their address.

So, the real probability question to consider is this: suppose Oswald picked out a random building in New Orleans in order to use its address on his pamphlets. It would likely have been in the area where he worked and not some fancy high-rise building that a big corporation or top law firm would occupy, because those locations weren't plausible for the Fair Play for Cuba Committee. What were the odds that he would have chosen a random building that would have connected with it two people who could be considered sinister? Even a building as small as the Newman Building would have had a few dozen people associated with it. But what is necessary, in the conspiracy literature, to be portrayed as sinister? Being connected to the anti-Castro exiles. Or having a job with the federal government. Perhaps expressing strong anti-Communist views (and just how many people in New Orleans in 1963 were not strongly anti-Communist?). Or being part of the rich civic elite (which overlapped with being anti-Communist). Being gay (a big factor in Garrison's belief that Clay Shaw was a conspirator). And even engaging in cancer research.[6]

So it's likely that if Oswald had picked, more or less at random, another address, then a generation of assiduous researchers would have found linked with it at least a couple of people whom they also could have made to sound quite sinister and who would have met the qualifications to be considered suspects.

Banister and Ferrie were not, in fact, terribly sinister people. At one time, Banister had been the special agent in charge of the Chicago office of the FBI, an extremely important law enforcement position. Then he went to New Orleans to clean up local law enforcement, but he had had run-ins with the local elite and was, by 1963, a broken-down has-been with a drinking problem. Ferrie had been a reputable pilot for Eastern Airlines, but given his predilection for having sex with young teenage boys, he got in deep trouble, lost his airline position, and was reduced to doing odd jobs for some occasional cash. Ferrie once had ties with the anti-Castro Cuban movement, but his sex scandal destroyed those.[7] It's true that Ferrie did investigative work for G. Wray Gill, the lawyer for New Orleans Mafia boss Carlos Marcello, but that job made him about as "connected" to the mob as Marcello's barber was. For this relationship to be sinister, one would have to assume that Marcello let his lawyer, Gill, in on the details of the Kennedy assassination and that Gill in turn shared them with Ferrie.

Conspiracy literature is rife with claims that Banister and Ferrie were involved with U.S. intelligence, but they are all based on bogus notions. The movie *JFK*, for example, posits that Banister was with the Office of Naval Intelligence (ONI) in World War II and that "once ONI, always ONI." Both assertions are silly. Banister was with the FBI throughout World War II. A secret internal CIA memorandum prepared during the Garrison investigation (when Garrison made wild charges about spooks everywhere) says Guy Banister was not associated with the CIA. Further, the same memo indicates there was no relationship between the CIA and David Ferrie, and the agency did not even have a file on Ferrie before the assassination.[8] The HSCA reviewed Guy Banister's CIA file and cited a document showing only that the agency "considered contacting him for use as a foreign intelligence source and for possible use of his firm for cover purposes. However, security investigation revealed derogatory information about his professional conduct, and he was not contacted."[9]

So by 1963 Banister's unprofessional conduct had ruled out using him as an intelligence asset. The same document said of David Ferrie that "agency files indicated that CIA never considered contacting him for any purpose at any time."[10] Banister could not pay the rent for his office in the Newman Building, and in early 1964 he had to move out. He died of a heart attack while in the process of moving.

Another secret internal CIA document confirmed that "there have [*sic*] been no documented Agency utilization of . . . [Gordon] Novel, Ferrie or [Sergio] Arcacha Smith."[11] (Novel was an attention seeker who claimed to be a CIA operative, and Arcacha was a hapless suspect caught up in the chaos that was the Garrison investigation. We'll run across Arcacha again in chapter 8.)

There are fairly extensive FBI files on Banister from the early 1960s, but none show Banister to have been any sort of asset or informant. Rather, the FBI was surveilling right-wing extremist groups, and Banister's politics made Joe McCarthy appear to be a rather mellow fellow by comparison.

In sum, while both Banister and Ferrie were strongly anti-Communist and had ties with the anti-Castro Cubans (although Ferrie's had been severed), neither man was acting as any sort of government spook during the time of Oswald's visit to New Orleans. They were considered too low class to be government spooks.

Of course, if any hard evidence surfaced that Oswald actually associated with Ferrie and Banister in 1963, then that information would have been significant indeed. There were, in fact, a fairly large number of Ferrie-Oswald and Ferrie-Banister sightings, but they all lacked credibility. Jack Martin, who was often in Banister's office, eventually claimed that Oswald was there frequently as well. Unfortunately, he had made numerous phone calls to authorities and journalists on the weekend of the assassination, trying to link Oswald and Ferrie and saying that Ferrie might have taught Oswald to fire foreign weapons. This talk was mere speculation. Martin then piled on additional claims, such as that Ferrie was an amateur hypnotist who may have hypnotized Oswald and that Ferrie had once told him about a "crime against nature" that he had engaged in with a young man who later joined the Marines. Martin *suspected* that this Marine might have been Oswald.[12]

All these reports are certainly interesting enough, but early on Martin had said nothing about Oswald ever being in Banister's office. But his story got better over time.

In the late 1970s Delphine Roberts testified to conspiracy author Anthony Summers and to the HSCA that she had seen Oswald in Banister's office frequently.[13] Unfortunately, she had made no such claims when the Garrison staff interviewed her in 1967, and she also said she had not seen Oswald in Banister's office in her initial interview with the HSCA.[14] The HSCA found several witnesses who had spent considerable time in Banister's office during the summer of 1963, and all denied seeing Oswald there.[15] The committee thus decided that Roberts and Martin were unreliable.

Ferrie, Oswald, and the Civil Air Patrol

There is, however, one other coincidence to deal with: when Oswald was fifteen years old, he apparently was in David Ferrie's Civil Air Patrol (CAP) squadron at the Moisant Airport. The HSCA found several witnesses who put Oswald in the CAP at the time Ferrie was a leader, and if there was any doubt at all, a photo surfaced in 1993 that shows both Oswald and Ferrie at a CAP bivouac. Oswald is on one side of a group of cadets and leaders, and Ferrie is on the other side. The photo doesn't prove that they ever met or talked to each other, but only that they were in the organization at the same time.

The HSCA considered the testimony of Oswald's cohorts from Ferrie's CAP unit, including his friend Edward Voebel, Fred O'Sullivan, Collin Hamer, John Irion, Anthony Atzenhoffer, George Boesch, and Jerry Paradis.[16]

Their stories differed slightly in detail, but all of them confirmed that Oswald had indeed been in Ferrie's CAP unit and that he had been a cadet for only a brief time. None of them reported any sort of relationship between Ferrie and Oswald, and indeed Voebel said, in a revealing comment, that "Oswald had a knack for being there and not being noticed."[17]

While it's hard to prove a negative, the fact that there were so many such witnesses—including Oswald's good buddy Voebel—strongly argues that had there been such a relationship, someone would have known about it.

Coincidence or Conspiracy?

In sum, the coincidence of Oswald putting the 544 Camp address on his leaflets is not particularly far-fetched. Further, at least hundreds and probably thousands of people in New Orleans in 1963 were as "sinister" as Banister and Ferrie were, and if Oswald had picked some other building, then a generation of conspiracy researchers would have found evidence and told us that some other hapless fellows were "connected" to mob types, to the CIA, to the FBI, to the gay underground, or such. And many silly factoids about them would have been invented, such as the claim that Ferrie flew missions for the CIA over Cuba or that Banister was in the Office of Naval Intelligence.

If we take into account the fact that Oswald was in Ferrie's CAP unit, that might seem to render it less likely that their connection was innocent. However, Oswald had lived in New Orleans both as a small child and a teenager, and would have come in contact with a fair number of other people—teachers, friends, bosses, family friends—who could have turned up in some nefarious context later. One has to ask the question: was Oswald at age fifteen somehow recruited by David Ferrie into a sinister cabal? Admittedly, it could not have focused on killing Kennedy, for it was way too early for that. But could a youth who considered himself a Marxist be recruited into a right-wing, anti-Communist cabal?

If not, Oswald's time in the CAP means nothing in terms of a conspiracy.

RUBY'S CONNECTION TO DAVID FERRIE: A PHONE CALL?

Once one starts looking for connections and one is assiduous enough, it's possible to link just about anybody to anybody else. How this process works is demonstrated by a "finding" of New Orleans district attorney Jim Garrison, who managed to tie David Ferrie with Jack Ruby.

How did this association turn up? First, in January 1967, Garrison obtained the phone records of G. Wray Gill, the attorney of Mafia chief Carlos Marcello. The district attorney found a call placed from Gill's office to a phone number in Chicago (WH 4-4970) that was mentioned in Warren Commission documents.[18] It was the phone number of one Miss Jean Aase (aka Jean West), a woman who accompanied Lawrence Meyers, a friend of Jack Ruby's, on a trip to Dallas on November 20, 1963. The following evening, Meyers and Aase hung around with Ruby for a while at Ruby's Carousel Club and then at the Cabana Hotel, where Ruby briefly joined Meyers and Aase for a drink before returning to his club.

The call from Gill's office was made on September 24, two days before Kennedy's trip to Dallas was announced on September 26.[19] Garrison, in *On the Trail of the Assassins*, suggests why the phone call was disquieting. He asks rhetorically, "Was Ferrie calling, perhaps, to report to some intermediary that the sheep dipping job had been completed or that 'the kid is leaving New Orleans' or something of the sort?"[20] "The kid," of course, would be Oswald, and by "sheep dipping" Garrison means setting Oswald up with a history of connections and actions that will make him the appropriate patsy.

But did the call really come from David Ferrie? At the time, Ferrie was working for Gill, so perhaps it was he who made the call. But as researcher Dave Reitzes has pointed out, that's far from clear.[21] The phone bills languished for over three years before Gill's secretary Alice Guidroz went over them to determine which of the calls had been made "by the office."[22] As researcher David Blackburst has noted, people working in Gill's office at the time included a secretary in addition to Guidroz, G. Wray Gill Sr., Gilbert Bernstein, Gerard H. Schreiber, George W. Gill Jr., Regina Francovich, David W. Ferrie, Morris L. Brownlee, plus two additional investigators.[23] Sorting out who made what calls must have been an iffy proposition indeed.

Richard Billings, a *Life* magazine reporter who worked closely with District Attorney Garrison and kept a journal, notes in an entry from January 22, 1967: "Giant [Garrison] has from Gill 1962 and 1963 phone bills and thinks he knows . . . calls made by Ferrie."[24] He "thinks he knows"? His knowledge appears to have been driven by his suspicion of Ferrie rather than based on any solid information.

Furthermore, the Chicago phone number (WH 4-4970) didn't ring in Aase's room. It was in fact the main number of the Delaware Towers, an apartment building. Researcher Russ Burr, who phoned the building (now the Talbott Hotel) in 1999, reported that "it is a 16 story building with 146 rooms, ten to a floor. I wasn't able to talk to any of the old timers . . . but the hotel manager told me that the numbers of rooms are approximately the same as in 1963."[25] So whoever called the Delaware Towers talked to *somebody* who lived in the approximately 146 rooms or to one of the employees.

Aase denies any connection with Ferrie. According to researcher Peter Whitmey, who interviewed Aase in 1998, "Ms. Aase did not know David Ferrie, did not recall receiving a 15-minute phone call originating in New Orleans from Ferrie on September 24, 1963, and did not know Jack Ruby before meeting him with Lawrence Meyers shortly before the assassination."[26] Given the weakness of the evidence that Ferrie ever actually called her, it would be grossly unfair to call her a liar.

Probability

So is this phone call a "strange" or "spooky" event that would be improbable in the absence of any plot? As with the case of the 544 Camp Street address, it depends on one's a priori expectations. With 544 Camp, if one can establish a priori that Banister and Ferrie were the two people in all of New Orleans most likely to plot to kill JFK, then the odds against Oswald, out of mere coincidence, picking the address of the Newman Building to put on his leaflets are remote. But if one could have had no such a priori expectation, then Banister and Ferrie become just two scruffy, rather disreputable New Orleanians out of hundreds or thousands who might, after the fact, be seen as likely conspirators, and the logic breaks down.

The same principle applies with Ferrie's connection to Ruby. If one starts with the assumption that Ferrie was a coconspirator, would his calling Jean Aase and having her go to Dallas with Meyers to contact Ruby be *the* one sensible way to send a message? If so, the phone call would be vastly improbable merely by chance.

But if one can't start with that assumption, then the question becomes, what are the odds that Ferrie would call some phone number associated with somebody who would know somebody else who would make a trip to Dallas and talk to Jack Ruby? That probability is fairly high. Suppose, for instance, Ferrie made twenty calls from Gill's office. Some calls would go to individual residences, but others would go to businesses or hotels or other institutions that would have several hundred people associated with those numbers Ferrie called. And how many other people would be linked in some way with one of those several hundred people who were associated with those phone numbers? The result has to be quite large. Given that Ruby knew a lot of people, the probability of *some* link is pretty good.

And, of course, Ferrie was not the only person in New Orleans with a claimed connection to Oswald. Had Guy Banister or Carlos Bringuier or Carlos Quiroga or Dean Andrews or Clay Shaw or Kerry Thornley—all New Orleans characters suspected of being conspirators—made a phone call to a number that was "associated with" a person who was also "associated with" a person who knew Jack Ruby, he would have established the same sort of link.

Think Scenario

But let's step back and look at this issue in context. Aase insisted that she did not even know Meyers on September 24 and that she had met him only a few weeks before the assassination.[27] And Meyers told the HSCA that he had met her "probably a week or a maximum of two weeks prior to the trip [to Dallas]."[28] But, of course, some will cheerfully say both are lying.

But why assign such significance to a call placed on September 24, when Meyers was not going to Dallas until November 20? Whatever information was conveyed would have been pretty stale by November. And why bring Aase, who Meyers described as a "rather dumb, but accommodating broad" and a "semi-professional hooker," into the assassination conspiracy of the century?[29] But if one asks why the conspirators involved Aase, one could also ask why Meyers, who worked for the Ero Manufacturing Company as the sales manager of the sporting goods division, was qualified to be a coconspirator. The HSCA concluded that "there is no indication that Meyers had engaged in criminal activities, had a criminal record or had been the subject of any criminal or related investigations (besides the assassination investigation). He did not appear to have any political or law enforcement connections."[30] He was, simply, an adulterer who wanted to "get some on the side" during a trip to Dallas and had no qualifications whatsoever to be part of an assassination plot.

But worse, if Ferrie did have a message for Ruby, why did he have Aase relay it through Meyers? Why didn't Ferrie just call Meyers directly, if necessary using an untraceable public phone? Indeed, why didn't Ferrie simply call Ruby? Why employ an elaborate scheme to do something that could be accomplished with a pocketful of quarters and a stroll to the pay phone at the corner?

The whole business is so silly that the reader might think that nobody but Garrison could take it seriously, but it has appeared in Bernard Fensterwald's *As-*

sassination of JFK by Coincidence or Conspiracy?, in Harrison Edward Livingstone and Robert J. Groden's book *High Treason*, and in Anthony Summers's *Conspiracy*.[31] Henry Hurt, in *Reasonable Doubt*, claims that the whole business "heightens the interlocking connections that seem to link David Ferrie with various figures, including Marcello, Jack Ruby, and Lee Harvey Oswald."[32] George Michael Evica, in *And We Are All Mortal*, repeats the whole scenario, and Noel Twyman's *Bloody Treason* buys it entirely.[33] And, of course, Jim Marrs's *Crossfire* repeats the whole phone factoid.[34] So this is not just an arcane theory from some obscure conspiracy book. It has gone mainstream.

Chapter Seven

More on Defying the Odds: The Mysterious Deaths

One of the most intriguing arguments for an assassination conspiracy is the supposedly large number of assassination witnesses, investigators, journalists, and their associates who died under "suspicious" circumstances. The clear implication is that some sort of cleanup squad has gone around the country, killing those people who might reveal what they know about the conspiracy.

MYSTERIOUS DEATHS: HOW MANY ARE CONNECTED?

Penn Jones, the late conspiracy curmudgeon and editor of a weekly newspaper in Midlothian, Texas, first popularized the notion of "mysterious deaths" surrounding the assassination. Jones's newspaper columns, later collected into a series of volumes titled *Forgive My Grief*, listed fifteen persons. The *London Sunday Times* reported that it had a statistician consider this issue, and the odds against all these people dying by chance by February 1976 were one hundred thousand trillion to one.[1]

The Stakhanovite theorist of mysterious deaths is Jim Marrs, whose book *Crossfire* has a list of 103 persons who died mysteriously. Well, actually, it's only 101 people. He lists the same woman twice, and she's not known to be dead.[2]

Still, 101 corpses are quite a lot, aren't they?[3]

Well, it all depends. The first issue is the size of the population in which the 101 deaths occurred. Suppose we could identify the 101 people who were closest to the case by some objective criterion—for example, the people who interacted most closely with Lee Oswald. If 101 (or even half) of them were dead within a couple of decades after the assassination, that finding would be significant. But as of this writing, his wife, Marina, is still alive. So are both Ruth Paine and her estranged husband, Michael Paine (in whose house Marina was staying at the time of the assassination and from whose garage Lee supposedly recovered the assassination rifle). So is Wesley Frazier, with whom Oswald caught a ride to work on the morning of the assassination. Going further afield one can find plenty of people who once associated with Oswald and have since died, but how far afield does one have to go?

Alternatively, suppose 101 of the 400–500 witnesses to the assassination in Dealey Plaza died within, say, ten years of the shooting. Leaving aside for the moment the facts that most of these witnesses were on Houston Street and not positioned to see much and that few of them gave testimony that either implicated or exculpated Oswald, this number would seem rather large.

But if considering only the closest witnesses, as of this writing, all are either still alive or have died rather recently. Assassination witness Jean Hill (see chapter 4) died in 2000 after giving vivid stories of conspiratorial goings-on since the day of the assassination. Standing next to her as she viewed the presidential motorcade was Mary Moorman, who is still alive. Visible near the limo at the time of the head shot are Jack and Joan Franzen and their son Jeff. All three are still alive. Charles Brehm and his son Joe are visible in multiple photos on the south side of Elm Street, positioned between the place where the first shot hit Kennedy and the place where the head shot exploded his skull. Brehm died in 1996, and Joe is still alive. Malcolm Summers, positioned on the south side of Elm near where Kennedy was hit in the head, died on October 8, 2004, and Associated Press photographer James Altgens (along with his wife) died as the result of a defective furnace in his home in 1995.[4] Bill and Gayle Newman, the closest witnesses on the north side of Elm Street during much of the shooting, are still alive. So being among the closest witnesses does not guarantee immortality, but these people did have long lives.

The mysterious deaths list does not contain any Dealey Plaza witnesses and certainly not the closest Dealey Plaza witnesses. To see what it takes to be considered connected to the assassination, the following are just some of the people who made the list.

Hank Suydam was a *Life* magazine editor who worked on two JFK assassination articles. So being a journalist who covered the case is sufficient to get on the list. Conspiracists also point to an article by *Life* reporter **Paul Mandel** (who is on the list too) as an example of a cover-up, since his article gave an inaccurate account of Kennedy's actions during the shooting sequence—an account that supported the idea of a shooter being on the depository's sixth floor. But errors were rife in the coverage of the shooting.

C. D. Jackson was a *Life* magazine executive who authorized the purchase of Abraham Zapruder's film of the assassination. Since *Life* made it difficult for researchers to access the film for years (although anybody could go to the National Archives and view high-quality color slides of individual frames), Jackson is considered a suspect in the cover-up. In 1966 *Life* asked Governor John Connally and his wife, Nellie Connally, who were riding in the limo with the Kennedys, to examine the film. The Connallys reported that John was hit too late for him to have been struck by the same bullet that hit JFK. Rather than hush it up, *Life* called for the case to be reopened.[5] Conspiracists, however, accuse the media generally of articulating a cover-up and name the *New York Times* and CBS News in particular. But oddly, no executives from either of those outlets make the list.

Mrs. Earl Smith, as she was designated on the list, was a newspaper columnist and a friend of Dorothy Kilgallen's. While Kilgallen herself was not an assassination witness, she did use her column in the *New York Journal-American* to promote conspiracy theories, mostly using material that conspiracists like Mark Lane fed to her. So it seems that the pool of people connected to the assassination includes friends of writers who wrote conspiracy columns.

Judge Joe Brown presided over the murder trial of Jack Ruby. What he might have known about the case that was not revealed in open court, or in the briefs of the prosecution and defense counsels, is unclear. If he is considered as being connected to the assassination, then every judge involved in the case (including the judges who heard Ruby's appeals) as well as all the prosecutors and defense lawyers were likewise linked. Brown had suffered four heart attacks before the Ruby trial; in 1968 a final one killed him.[6]

Hiram Ingram was a friend of conspiracy witness Roger Craig (see discussion in chapter 4). Without any other connection to the case, it seems that his merely being a friend of a conspiracy witness put him into the at-risk population.

Charles Mentesana, an amateur photographer, shot footage of a supposed second rifle (besides the Mannlicher-Carcano) being examined in Dealey Plaza after the assassination. His footage actually shows a shotgun on the shoulder of a police officer. Although his film does survive, Mentesana saw nothing of importance and is not on record as having given any testimony whatsoever. He was, in other words, merely one of scores and perhaps hundreds of spectators who took their 8mm cameras to film JFK on that day in Dallas.

Dr. Charles Francis Gregory, a Parkland Hospital doctor, operated on John Connally. None of the doctors who worked to save Kennedy's life are on the list, and all of the key medical witnesses lived into the 1990s, with several still alive. Why would conspirators kill off a witness to the Connally surgery while leaving all the witnesses to the attempts to save Kennedy's life alone?

Marilyn "Delilah" Walle was a former employee of Jack Ruby's. So now everybody who worked for Ruby is connected.

DeLesseps Morrison was the former mayor of New Orleans. His only link to the assassination was his being mayor of a city in which Oswald once lived.

Karyn Kupcinet, a TV actress in Hollywood, was the daughter of Chicago columnist Irv Kupcinet who knew Jack Ruby in the 1930s and 1940s when he lived in Chicago. Penn Jones claims that Karyn had phoned a telephone operator before the assassination and said that Kennedy was going to be killed. A woman did indeed do that, but Kupcinet lived in Hollywood, and the caller (whose name is unknown) was in Pomona, fifty miles away. So now relatives of Jack Ruby's former buddies are also in the pool.

Mona Saenz worked at the Texas Employment Commission and tried to help Oswald get a job. It seems that every government bureaucrat with whom Oswald interacted is deemed connected.

Lou Staples was a former Dallas talk radio personality who promoted conspiracy theories. He had moved to Oklahoma and was working there before he (supposedly) committed suicide. So radio or TV personalities who promoted conspiracy ideas are in danger.

As these examples clarify, the criteria for linking an individual to the case are lax. Indeed, the connection often more closely resembles a reaction to a Rorschach test than the application of some objective criterion. Thousands of people must be associated with the case if one thinks in this manner.

Further, the people who are considered connected with the assassination are not a random cross section of the population. The list is liberally laced with people whose odds of dying are higher than average: cops, Mafia types, and people on the fringes of the underworld (such as strippers). It also includes people who were mentally unstable and appear to have been telling conspiracy stories *because* they were unstable. See the case of Gary Underhill, who appears later in this chapter.

Begging the Question

Much of the logic of "connection" actually begs a question. If one assumes that there was a media cover-up of a conspiracy, then people in the media such as Suydam and Mandel and Jackson are connected. If one assumes that the FBI covered up a conspiracy, then people such as William Sullivan, a high FBI official under Hoover, are connected—and he is indeed on the list. If one assumes that the Mafia was part of a conspiracy, then perhaps the Mafia figures Sam Giancana, Johnny Roselli, and Salvatore Granello are connected and thus deserve their place on the list. If one assumes that Ruby was part of a JFK assassination plot, then his lawyers, employees, and friends are all "connected," although one would also have to believe he blabbed the details of the conspiracy quite promiscuously.

But in establishing all these associations, note the circular logic. How does one know there was a conspiracy? Because so many people connected with the assassination died. But who was actually connected with the case? Of course, members of the groups who killed Kennedy and then covered up the murder were. But how does one know these groups were involved in killing Kennedy? Because so many of those connected people died.

LOGICAL PROBLEMS

This kind of begging the question is just the first of numerous logical problems with the notion of a "cleanup squad" running around the country and killing off people who had dangerous knowledge.

In the first place, it is difficult to see why any conspiracy would want many of these people eliminated. The list is rife with people who maintained that Oswald was guilty or gave testimony indicating his guilt. Even FBI head J. Edgar Hoover is on the list. As one of my students once asked, "Wasn't he running the cover-up? Who killed him?"

The list also includes William Whaley, a cabdriver who drove Oswald from downtown Dallas to a point near his rooming house in Oak Cliff. Likewise, Earlene Roberts, the housekeeper at Oswald's rooming house, added another link to the chain that connected Oswald with the murder of Officer J. D. Tippit in Oak Cliff at about 1:15 p.m.[7] She's on the list, as is Nicholas Chetta, the coroner in New Orleans who ruled that David Ferrie died because of a berry aneurysm and not of a suicide (as Garrison claimed) or the result of thugs forcing pills down his throat (also a claim of Garrison's, enshrined in the movie JFK).[8] James Cadigan, an FBI documents expert whose testimony to the Warren Commission put in place a key element in the case against Oswald, died in 1977 and was put on the list.

Of course, one can posit that each of these people had some sinister knowledge that they had failed to reveal in previous testimony. Maybe Whaley failed to tell the Dallas cops that Oswald said, "I've got to go meet E. Howard Hunt," or maybe Hoover told Cadigan, "Tie those documents to Oswald, and you needn't be picky about how you do it!"[9] There is, of course, no evidence to support such an assumption; indeed, it's purely ad hoc. And one has to make it quite often to link all these people who died "mysteriously."

But then what about the people whose testimony seemed to support the idea of a conspiracy? Since they were already on record with their testimony, killing them would not wipe out what they had said and might draw attention to it in the wake of a mysterious death. One can get around this problem by positing, again ad hoc, that there were some really dangerous things to which they had yet to testify. But since they had already willingly given testimony that contradicted the official version of the case, why wouldn't they tell everything? Doing so would seem to offer protection against getting killed, because they would have no more secrets that were dangerous to a conspiracy.

Among those witnesses whose testimony is pregnant with conspiracy implications, Jean Hill died in 2001. Her supporters at the JFK Lancer website make no claims that her death was mysterious. Beverly Oliver, who claims to be the Babushka Lady visible in multiple photos of Dealey Plaza at the time of the shooting, is still alive. Ed Hoffman, who testified to a shooter behind the stockade fence on the grassy knoll (see chapter 1) died in March 2010.

It's also interesting that being a high-profile conspiracy supporter or author seems to guarantee a long life. Most of the first generation of conspiracy authors are still alive, including Mark Lane, Josiah Thompson, and Edward Jay Epstein. Sylvia Meagher died in 1989, at the age of sixty-seven, but nobody has claimed the circumstances of her death were sinister.[10] Likewise, pioneer conspiracy researcher Harold Weisberg died in February 2002 after a long period of failing health. The list's inventor, Penn Jones, died of Alzheimer's disease in a nursing home in January 1998.

Meanwhile, all the most important conspiracy authors from the 1970s and 1980s are still alive, including David Lifton, Henry Hurt, Robert Groden, Anthony Summers, and Harry Livingstone.

Still More Logical Problems

The most fundamental problem with notion of a cleanup squad is, quite simply, that it doesn't actually make the conspirators any safer. If a group needs to kill a bunch of people with "dangerous knowledge," it can only do so by recruiting a bunch of assassins; however, each of them then has dangerous knowledge. It could be the case that after Cleanup Squad 1 kills off all the dangerous witnesses, the group would need to recruit Cleanup Squad 2 to eliminate Cleanup Squad 1. Unfortunately, this action leads to an infinite, vicious regress. Recruitment for Cleanup Squad 2 might be extremely difficult, however, with potential recruits easily envisioning Cleanup Squad 3.

Then another problem is that most of the supposed mysterious deaths don't in fact look like murder. Slightly more than half of the people on Marrs's list died of natural causes, but as Marrs assures his readers, the CIA knows how to kill people and make their deaths look natural. Even among those who died an unnatural death, only a minority were apparently murdered. The rest died in accidents, were killed in bar brawls, were killed in the line of police duty, committed suicide, and so on. Of course, maybe a cleanup squad managed to convincingly fake all of these deaths too. If so, its members show a degree of competence not otherwise seen in American life.

Why Take So Long?

Another problem with the mysterious deaths list is that it extends over so many years. The last death noted by Marrs is that of Secret Service agent Roy Kellerman, who died of heart failure in 1984. It would seem that a cleanup squad would have wanted to kill off witnesses as quickly as possible, because the longer they were allowed to run free, the more likely they were to divulge secrets.

What about the report in the *London Sunday Times* saying that the odds against this many people dying were one hundred thousand trillion to one? The HSCA challenged the paper to explain its analysis, and it backed down, writing,

> Our piece about the odds against the deaths of the Kennedy witnesses was, I regret to say, based on a careless journalistic mistake and should not have been published.
>
> . . . There was no question of our actuary having got his answer wrong. It was simply that we asked him the wrong question. He was asked what were

the odds against 15 named people out of the population of the United States dying within a short period of time to which he replied—correctly—that they were very high. However, if one asks what are the odds against 15 of those included in the Warren Commission index dying within a given period, the answer is, of course, that they are much lower.[11]

Conspiracy books, including, for example, Marrs's *Crossfire* and Hurt's *Reasonable Doubt,* have accepted that this supposed statistic is bogus. But why didn't more people challenge the statistic when it first began to circulate?

REALLY SUSPICIOUS?

If the sheer number of dead people doesn't seem out of line—which it doesn't if one knows how easy it is to get on the list—then perhaps the nature of at least some of these deaths suggests conspiracy. Perhaps a detailed examination of particular deaths will reveal telltale evidence of the cleanup squad.

I can't cover all 101 deaths here, and in many instances, little information is available about them. But while there often isn't sufficient information to absolutely establish that a death was ordinary, neither does the available evidence show that the death had anything to do with the JFK assassination.

The toughest cases, of course, are the five Mafia-related deaths. In virtually all of them, the victim really was murdered, and the murderer hasn't been caught and convicted. Mafia types getting killed, however, is not a particularly rare or surprising occurrence.

But what of the cases about which some detailed information is available? Invariably, conspiracists try to make something sinister out of tragic but entirely normal deaths.

Dorothy Kilgallen

A newspaper columnist, she wrote frequently about the assassination, and she supposedly claimed, "I'm going to break the real story and have the biggest scoop of the century."[12] The reality, as historian Eric Paddon has shown, is that Kilgallen did little if any real reporting or research and merely wrote about material that conspiracy-oriented sources fed to her.[13] Her big claim to having some real knowledge was based on a supposed exclusive interview she did with Jack Ruby. In reality, she merely had a brief conversation with him while leaning over the railing in the courtroom where he was being tried.[14] Further, her death happened twenty months after the Ruby interview. If she learned any explosive new information, she certainly kept it quiet for a long time. She never, in fact, claimed she had "broken" the case; instead, she merely said she was going to do so.

Nothing about the circumstances of her death suggests any foul play. Her maid and hairdresser found her dead in her New York City residence. Both her husband and son were sleeping in other rooms when she presumably died.[15] The medical examiner's report, which came out a week later, said that moderate quantities of alcohol and barbiturates, unfortunately combined, killed her.[16] The examination of the body at the scene found "no trauma" and "no signs violence [sic]." The autopsy found no injuries to her body or any evidence of a struggle.[17] Some sources suggest she was depressed and killed herself with sleeping pills, but the moderate to high levels of both barbiturates and alcohol shown in the toxicology report seem to rule out this idea as well as the suspicion that some thugs entered her apartment and forced pills down her throat.

Florence Pritchett

Identified in all the "mysterious deaths" lists as Mrs. Earl Smith, she is described by Marrs as follows: "close friend to Dorothy Kilgallen, died two days after columnist, may have kept Kilgallen's notes."[18] In fact, nobody has produced evidence the two women were close friends, although as fellow columnists for the *Journal-American*, it's quite likely they were acquainted. Nor is there the slightest proof that Pritchett had any of Kilgallen's notes or even that Kilgallen told her anything about the assassination.

Of course, if Kilgallen's death was not suspicious, Pritchett's isn't, either. At the absolute most, she knew what Kilgallen knew, which apparently wasn't much. Further, the circumstances of Pritchett's death do not seem peculiar. According to the *Journal-American*,

> Mrs. Earl E.T. Smith, wife of the former U.S. Ambassador to Cuba and columnist of *The Journal-American*, died today in her apartment at 1120 5th Ave. She was 45.
>
> Mrs. Smith, the former Florence Pritchett, died of a cerebral hemorrhage. She had been in ill health since mid-August, and only recently had been discharged from Roosevelt Hospital.[19]

So if the women were targets, it would seem that the conspirators somehow decided to attack Pritchett before going after Kilgallen. But they just made the former sick and let her linger for a couple of months.

David Ferrie

As mentioned, there are two distinct conspiracy interpretations of his death. One, proffered by Jim Garrison shortly after Ferrie was discovered dead on February 22, 1967, was that he committed suicide to avoid being prosecuted for conspiracy to murder Kennedy. Garrison said he expected more suspects would commit suicide as his investigation progressed. The other explanation is that goons murdered him by forcing pills down his throat. Both theories involve the thyroid medication Proloid, which, according to Garrison, could radically increase blood pressure and cause a stroke.

However, Proloid is too slow acting to have killed Ferrie. *Washington Post* journalist George Lardner Jr. interviewed Ferrie late the night before he died (Lardner left at about 2:30 a.m.), and even a massive dose after that point would not have caused Ferrie's death almost eleven hours later, or by 1:00 p.m., which was the estimated time of death.[20] Additionally, a bottle of Proloid was found in Ferrie's apartment after this death that still contained seven tablets.[21] Wouldn't somebody intent on suicide take the whole bottle?

Two supposed suicide notes were found in his apartment.[22] But one of them doesn't read as if it was a suicide note at all; rather, it reads more like a political manifesto. Among other things, it says, "Daily we are propagandized more and more about a rising crime rate. But how do we know it is true? We don't, for we Americans have little or no access to the truth."

The other message does sound like a suicide note. Ferrie wrote to his ex-roommate Al Beauboeuf,

> When you read this I will be quite dead and no answer will be possible. I wonder how you are going to justify things. . . . All I can say is that I offered you love, and the best I could. All I got in return in the end was a kick in the teeth. Thus I die alone and unloved.

While the tone certainly suggests it's a suicide note, witnesses say that in the days before he was found dead, Ferrie was in the mood to fight Garrison's charges.

No witness recounts him talking about killing himself. One possibility is that Ferrie at some point (perhaps months earlier) had considered suicide and then repented of the notion after writing the note. Another possibility is that he wrote it in response to his own failing health. Ferrie had been complaining about headaches (as well as various other problems) in the days before he died.[23]

In this instance, as in other issues, the hard medical evidence trumps. Ferrie died of a berry aneurysm, just as the pathologist said.[24]

Clay Shaw

Jim Marrs says that Clay Shaw was a "prime suspect in [the] Garrison case, reportedly a CIA contact with Ferrie and E. Howard Hunt."[25] The "prime suspect" part, at least, is true. Marrs goes on to list the cause of death as "possible cancer."

In reality, there is no doubt that Shaw died of cancer. The New Orleans Department of Police Hospitalization Case Report tracks the progress of the disease through an interview with Shaw's attending physician, Dr. Hugh Batson. The doctor started treating Shaw in May 1973 for an ulcer and quickly found that Shaw had lung cancer. The cancer metastasized to his brain and liver (at least), and Shaw's health went downhill. Shaw discontinued radiation treatments in April 1974, developed seizures, and finally died on August 15, 1974. Don Doody, a longtime friend of Shaw's who cared for him during the last months, confirmed the tragic trajectory of his illness.[26]

Gary Underhill

Marrs says Underhill was a "CIA agent who claimed [the] Agency was involved" and that he died of a "gunshot in head" that was ruled a suicide.[27] Jim Garrison supporter James DiEugenio provides much more detail in his book *Destiny Betrayed*:

> On that evening of November 22, 1963, Gary Underhill was a deeply troubled man. What he had learned, and the fact that *they knew* he had learned it, were too much for him. He had to escape. Once he was out of Washington, he could regain his equilibrium. Then he would decide what to do. He had friends in New York he could talk to without fear of the word getting back to Washington.[28]

DiEugenio recounts that Underhill also said, "Oswald is a patsy. They set him up. It's too much. The bastards have done something outrageous. They've killed the

President! I've been listening and hearing things. I couldn't believe they'd get away with it, but they did! . . . They're so stupid. . . . They can't even get the right man."[29] One could interpret this statement as showing some sort of inside knowledge, except for one fact. A classified CIA document, drafted during the Garrison investigation in response to the Justice Department's queries about many of Garrison's wild charges, specifically deals with Underhill.

> 15. Who is the J. Garrett UNDERHILL referred to in Garrison's Playboy interview as a former CIA agent? UNDERHILL was born 7 August 1915 in Brooklyn, was graduated from Harvard in 1937, and committed suicide on 8 May 1964. He served with the Military Intelligence Service from 6 July 1943 to May 1946 as an expert in photography, enemy weapons, and related technical specialties. He was in infrequent contact with the New York office of the Domestic Contact Service, of CIA from late 1949 to the mid-'50s. The contact was routine. Mr. UNDERHILL was not an employee of CIA.[30]

The Domestic Contact Service (DCS) was the division of the CIA that debriefed rather ordinary tourists, businessmen, and journalists on what they had seen and heard after visiting foreign countries. The DCS didn't run covert agents. And, as indicated, even Underhill's contact with the DCS had ended long before the assassination. If Underhill had no connection with the CIA, he could hardly have had any insider knowledge of the assassination. He was, quite simply, a mentally unstable fellow who thought there was a JFK conspiracy, just as many other (stable and unstable) Americans did. Thus, there is no reason to doubt his death certificate, which says he "shot self in head with automatic pistol."[31]

William Whaley

On the day of the assassination, Whaley was the cab driver who drove a fleeing Lee Oswald from the cab stand in front of the Greyhound bus station to an intersection near Oswald's rooming house in Oak Cliff. Whaley died in an accident in December 1965. The *Dallas Morning News* described the accident as follows: "Whaley, of Lewisville, driving his cab, and John Henry Wells, 83 year old driver of the other car, were found dead in the wreckage after their cars crashed head-on at Hampton Road Viaduct shortly after 8 a.m." The article added that "a drizzling rain was falling when the cars collided Saturday."[32]

As is typical in these cases, there is absolutely no evidence that Whaley had any dangerous knowledge he had been withholding in the thirteen months since the assassination. Whaley insisted that Oswald had been "tight lipped" during his ride, and it's vastly implausible that Oswald would have blurted out some details of a conspiracy to a cabbie he didn't know.

But what is worse is the idea that the conspirators would have recruited an eighty-three-year-old kamikaze to smash headlong into Whaley.

Albert Guy Bogard

Bogard, as seen in chapter 2, was a car salesman who reported that Lee Oswald came into his dealership shortly before the assassination. In all probability, this account was one of scores of Oswald sightings that were reported after the assassination, and there is no evidence that he had any knowledge threatening to conspirators or at least none that he had not already relayed. In 1966 Bogard committed suicide in his hometown of Coushatta, Louisiana. Of course, conspiracy authors always put the term "suicide" in quotes, so one might ask how solid the evidence of suicide is. The local paper, the *Coushatta Citizen*, published the details:

> Albert G. Bogard, 41, was found dead in his car near the Mt. Zion cemetery about 7:00 a.m. Tuesday morning. Dr. L.E. L'Herisson, parish coroner, ruled cause of death as carbon monoxide poisoning, self-inflicted.
>
> The coroner's report said Bogard was found in his late model car, doors locked, and a white piece of garden hose extending from the exhaust to the left rear window, the switch on.
>
> Dr. L'Herisson said Bogard's parents, Mr. and Mrs. A.T. Bogard, said their son had been ill with flu some few days before and had been despondent. On Monday night he had come to his parents' home to ask them if he could borrow a piece of garden hose.[33]

Jimmy Harper, who is the husband of Bogard's first cousin, discovered Bogard's body. In an interview, Harper reported that there was no sign of a struggle or any violence at the scene. In the trunk of Bogard's car was a stack of newspapers with headlines about the Kennedy assassination, and Bogard's shoes. The car was an overdue rental unit, and the gas tank was empty. Harper confirmed that Bogard had been depressed before his death. Bogard's mother had been worried about him, and Harper thought it was a combination of "woman" problems and financial problems.[34]

OTHER LISTS OF MYSTERIOUS DEATHS

There are many more cases, but the point is most of the deaths are in fact not mysterious. For most of the people on the list, there is no clear reason, and usually not even a slightly plausible reason, that conspirators would want to kill them.

But if the list of JFK assassination–related mysterious deaths is so bogus, one might ask why there aren't such lists for other high-profile public events or highly visible public figures. The answer is simple: they exist.

The most famous concerns former president Bill Clinton. The Clinton Body Count is featured in a video that was promoted by conservatives such as Pat Robertson, Rush Limbaugh, and the late Jerry Falwell.[35]

Using the Clinton Body Count as an example, Barbara Mikkelson, of the invaluable debunking website Snopes.com, explains how to construct such a list. She points out that one need have only the most tangential connection with the event or person to qualify for the list, and that "the longer the list, the more impressive it is and the less likely anyone is to challenge it."

You can, she notes, get a lot of mileage by playing word games. If the victim committed a suicide, say it was "ruled a suicide" to imply it was really a murder. Use "allegedly" or "supposedly" when recounting things that might imply a rather ordinary death, and throw in every strange or odd detail, even if it's quite irrelevant to the actual cause of death. After all, if something "can't be explained," that adds to the sinister ambience.

And finally, "don't let facts get in your way," because "it's not like anybody is going to check up on this stuff."[36]

Of course, if the Clintons have had partisan enemies who were none too scrupulous about the facts, the Bushes have too. Yes, there is a Bush Body Count list.[37] There is also an anthrax mysterious deaths list, produced in the wake of infected letters sent to certain news organizations and government offices in 2001. Apparently, five scientists associated with the case either have since died or gone missing.[38] If five dead or missing microbiologists don't sound impressive enough, another website ups the ante. It says that "as many as 14 world-class microbiologists died."[39]

There is a "Star Wars" mystery deaths site that lists dead scientists who had worked on the Strategic Defense Initiative.[40] And further, there is even a list of deaths associated with the religion of Scientology.[41]

In principle, anybody with time on their hands and a conspiracy theory or a grudge against some public figure can concoct a list of mysterious deaths with as much validity as the JFK list has. In the forty-seven years since the shooting, JFK assassination buffs have generated a very long list, for these lists only grow over time. Mikkelson explains that the first version of the Clinton Body Count tabulation, in 1994, listed 24 people. By 1998, when Mikkelson examined it in detail, the list had grown to 44 names. And a check of the Internet found a list from 2001 with 107 names.[42] Perhaps, since Hillary Clinton failed to win the presidency in 2008, the list won't expand much further.

If the 2008 presidential election had turned out differently, a "McCain's Mysterious Murders" list might have been generated by now.[43] One might think that an "Obama Obituaries" list would not appear, because the people who might put it together have been trying to prove that Obama was born in Kenya. But alas, there is an "Obama Death List."[44] One must pick one's poison, we suppose.

Chapter Eight

Did People Know It Was Going to Happen?

If anybody had actually described the Kennedy assassination before it happened, that would have been dynamite evidence. It would have implied a plot that had somehow lost control and leaked key details. Many people have come forward after the fact and claimed to have known about and been part of an assassination conspiracy (as we will see in chapter 12). However, it's not hard to concoct a tale that resembles what really happened, or what some conspiracy theorists think happened, after the fact.

THE MIAMI PROPHET

Conspiracy author Jim Marrs called Joseph Milteer the Miami prophet because of his supposed "foreknowledge" of the assassination. The claim is that Milteer, a fellow from Quitman, Georgia, who ran in extreme right-wing and racist circles, had gotten wind of the real plot to kill Kennedy.

His supposed foreknowledge is revealed in a conversation he had with one William Somersett in Miami, Florida, on November 9, 1963. Somersett, who claimed to be an ideological cohort of Milteer's but was in fact a police informant, recorded the conversation. The following exchange, from Anthony Summers's book *Conspiracy*, is typical of what conspiracy books show readers.

> **William Somersett:** I think Kennedy is coming here on the 18th, or something like that to make some kind of speech . . .
>
> **Joseph Milteer:** You can bet your bottom dollar he is going to have a lot to say about the Cubans. There are so many of them here.

William Somersett: Yeah. Well, he will have a thousand bodyguards, don't worry about that.

Joseph Milteer: The more bodyguards he has the easier it is to get him.

William Somersett: Well, how in the hell do you figure would be the best way to get him?

Joseph Milteer: From an office building with a high-powered rifle. . . . He knows he's a marked man. . . .

William Somersett: They are really going to try to kill him?

Joseph Milteer: Oh yeah, it is in the working. . . .

William Somersett: Boy, if that Kennedy gets shot, we have to know where we are at. Because you know that will be a real shake if they do that.

Joseph Milteer: They wouldn't leave any stone unturned there, no way. They will pick somebody up within hours afterwards, if anything like that would happen. Just to throw the public off.[1]

It sounds as if Milteer knew something. Even at this point, though, the critical reader might ask some questions. For example, the context is Miami and not Dallas. Next, the scenario described involves a lone gunman (who, of course, might be part of a conspiracy). There is nothing about an "insurance shot from the front" or a "triangulation of crossfire." So if conspiracists want to say this conversation demonstrates foreknowledge, they have to junk all the shooters but one.

When faced with such witness quotes, the reader should ask what was left out. The transcript is quite long, but a more complete version appears in *Miami Magazine*'s September 1976[2] issue:

William Somersett: . . . I think Kennedy is coming here on the 18th . . . to make some kind of speech. . . . I imagine it will be on TV.

Joseph Milteer: You can bet your bottom dollar he is going to have a lot to say about the Cubans. There are so many of them here.

William Somersett: Yeah, well, he will have a thousand bodyguards. Don't worry about that.

Joseph Milteer: The more bodyguards he has the easier it is to get him.

William Somersett: Well, how in the hell do you figure would be the best way to get him?

Joseph Milteer: From an office building with a high-powered rifle. How many people does he have going around who look just like him? Do you know about that?

William Somersett: No, I never heard he had anybody.

Joseph Milteer: He has about fifteen. Whenever he goes anyplace, he knows he is a marked man.

William Somersett: You think he knows he is a marked man?

Joseph Milteer: Sure he does.

William Somersett: They are really going to try to kill him?

Joseph Milteer: Oh yeah, it is in the working. Brown himself, [Jack] Brown is just as likely to get him as anybody in the world. He hasn't said so, but he tried to get Martin Luther King.

The conversation veered off in another direction for a while, but then it returned to the subject of assassination.

William Somersett: Hitting this Kennedy is going to be a hard proposition, I tell you. I believe you may have figured out a way to get him, the office building and all that. I don't know how the Secret Service agents cover all them office buildings everywhere he is going. Do you know whether they do that or not?

Joseph Milteer: Well, if they have any suspicion they do that, of course. But without suspicion, chances are that they wouldn't. You take there in Washington. This is the wrong time of the year, but in pleasant weather, he comes out on the veranda and somebody could be in a hotel room across the way and pick him off just like that.

William Somersett: Is that right?

Joseph Milteer: Sure, disassemble a gun. You don't have to take a gun up there, you can take it up in pieces. All those guns come knock down. You can take them apart.

A little later, Milteer adds the comment pregnant with conspiratorial import: "They wouldn't leave any stone unturned there. No way. They will pick somebody within hours afterwards, if anything like that would happen, just to throw the public off."

The more complete version, quite obviously, gives a rather different impression. Milteer mentions the "about fifteen" look-alikes that Kennedy has traveling around with him. While it might seem plausible, it just wasn't true. Then there is the fact that Milteer names the fellow who will kill Kennedy, and he doesn't appear on any list of suspects.[3] The business about carrying a disassembled rifle up into a tall building might sound as if he had foreknowledge too, until one notices that the precise context is using it to shoot Kennedy on the veranda of the White House in the summer.

The Milteer story becomes more complicated from here, including an account of Milteer calling Somersett from Dallas on the morning of the assassination and implying that Kennedy would be killed there. For example, Henry Hurt, in *Reasonable Doubt*, asserted, "On November 22, Milteer telephoned his 'friend,' the informant and told him he was in Dallas. Prior to the midday events, Milteer told the informant that Kennedy was expected in Dallas that day and would probably never again visit Miami."[4]

However, not until the Garrison investigation, years after the assassination, did Somersett mention the "Milteer in Dallas" details. When the Miami police interviewed Somersett on November 26, 1963, he was asked, "Do you think maybe Milteer could have been in Dallas, Texas, in the last two weeks?" He answered, "Yes, he could have been there, I am satisfied that he could have been most anywhere he wanted; he has two cars ready to move at anytime." When the questioner asked, "You have seen no evidence that he was there?" Somersett replied, "No. He didn't say that he was, the only thing he said that he had been in Texas." Somersett then said that Milteer "didn't say" when he had been in Texas.[5]

Researcher Bernard Fensterwald interviewed Somersett four and a half years later and got the "Milteer in Dallas" story. Many authors cheerfully use it while ignoring other information that Fensterwald obtained. For example, Somersett told Fensterwald,

> Milterr's [sic] account of the shooting in Dallas is that Ruby shot from the Mall and that Tippett [sic] shot from the top of a building. A good guess is that this was the Daltex [sic] Building. Milterr [sic] was not clear about Oswald's role although he thought he was downstairs in the book depository rather than on an upper floor. Somersett guesses that it might have been Milterr [sic] himself that fired the shots from the windows of the book depository.[6]

One can see why conspiracy authors use Somersett's statements selectively. Interestingly, the FBI, which was carefully monitoring hate groups, determined that Milteer was in his hometown of Quitman, Georgia, on the day of the assassination.[7] By the time Fensterwald was receiving his wild account from Somersett, federal authorities had decided that the latter was unreliable, having "been described as overenthusiastic, prone to exaggeration, and mentally unstable."[8] They also determined he had "furnished information bordering on the fantastic, which investigation failed to corroborate."[9]

But the information was good enough, apparently, for private researchers.

ROSE CHERAMI

Rose Cherami was a prostitute with a long arrest record. In Louisiana a few days before the assassination, two white males apparently threw her out of a car on Highway 190.[10] Lt. Francis Frugé of the Louisiana State Police picked her up and took her to the Moosa Hospital in Eunice and then to the Eunice jail (because narcotics withdrawal was suspected). Because of her erratic behavior she was transferred to the state hospital, a mental institution, in Jackson. There she supposedly told the attending physician, Dr. Victor Weiss, that Kennedy and Texas officials would be killed during Kennedy's visit to Dallas.[11] She later said that the men she was riding with were going to kill Kennedy.

Conspiracists, of course, have treated Cherami as quite reliable. A supporter of District Attorney Jim Garrison, James DiEugenio, asks rhetorically, "How reliable a witness was Cheramie [sic]?" He answers, "Extremely."[12] Few if any conspiracy books suggest that she has any credibility problems.

But her credibility problems, in fact, are massive.

In the first place, she made a series of ridiculous statements. She claimed, for example, to have worked as a stripper for Jack Ruby. No evidence has come to light of any such employment. She maintained that Ruby was a homosexual and that his homosexual name was Pinky. She also said that Oswald was gay and that he and Ruby "had been shacking up for years."[13] As Dave Reitzes explains,

> It also should be noted that in her short life, Rose Cherami was arrested over 50 times in ten different states for charges including larceny, auto theft, possession of narcotics, driving under the influence of narcotics, driving while intoxicated, prostitution, arson, vagrancy, drunk and disorderly behavior, and still other charges. She is documented as having used over 30 different names and claiming at least six different dates of birth. She committed at least one documented suicide attempt, in 1947, was "believed to be insane" at that time, and was ruled "criminally insane" in 1961. She was institutionalized several times, with "psychotic" and "psychopathic" behavior noted.[14]

Cherami had a history of giving "information" to various law enforcement agencies. One tip about a supposed drug dealer operating from a ship in New Orleans appeared to be accurate, but in another case she gave a detailed account of a drug transaction in Texas that investigators found to be "erroneous in all respects." She had also given the FBI false information.[15]

THE REAL DEAL?

So did Cherami or Milteer or both have any actual foreknowledge of the assassination? Interestingly, some conspiracy books will repeat both accounts, apparently without noticing that they seem to contradict each other. Cherami said the men who talked of killing Kennedy and then threw her out of the car were "Italians or resembled Italians."[16] But when the investigator, Lt. Francis Frugé, gave a pile of mug shots to the owner of the bar where Cherami had fought with the two men, the owner supposedly identified Sergio Arcacha Smith as one of the men.[17] So was she with Italian assassins or Hispanic assassins? It's doubtful that either group would have been tight with Milteer's racist buddies. Indeed, no details of the Milteer account and the Cherami account overlap.

This issue, of course, resolves into a matter of probabilities. Were the Milteer and the Cherami accounts grossly improbable under the "null hypothesis"? The null hypothesis is that neither informant really knew anything about the assassination before it happened. Where Milteer is concerned, he described the most generic assassination scenario possible: "From an office building with a high-powered rifle." Interestingly, Dallas Secret Service chief Forest Sorrels told the Warren Commission that

> during the time that we were making this survey with the [Dallas] police, I made the remark that if someone wanted to get the President of the United States, he could do it with a high-powered rifle and a telescopic sight from some building or some hillside, because that has always been a concern to us, about the buildings.[18]

And presidential aide Kenneth O'Donnell told the Warren Commission,

> [Kennedy] said that if anybody really wanted to shoot the President of the United States, it was not a very difficult job—all one had to do was get a high building some day with a telescopic rifle, and there was nothing anybody could do to defend against such an attempt on the President's life.[19]

So did Kennedy have foreknowledge of his own death?

Of course, actual, precise details of an assassination plot would change the probabilities. Suppose Milteer had said that the shooter would be somebody who looks like a communist and would shoot Kennedy with a foreign-made rifle. That description sounds more as if he knows something. That's not utterly generic, although with over 189 million Americans in 1963,[20] it's not absurd that somebody would come up with that idea without any foreknowledge. But suppose somebody said, "A fellow named Oswald is going to shoot Kennedy with a Mannlicher-Carcano rifle"? That declaration would be wildly unlikely under the null hypothesis.

Cherami's allegation has similar problems. She gave no details of any actual plot but rather reported (apparently) two guys talking about killing Kennedy.[21] Just how uncommon was making this threat?

The HSCA looked at the computerized files of the Protective Research Section of the Secret Service and discovered that between March and December 1963 over four hundred possible threats to the president had come to their attention.[22] This reported information has to represent a drop in the bucket. Across the country, the number of inebriated guys sitting at a bar and bloviating about how the president should be killed has to run into the thousands every month. Thus, if Kennedy had been killed at another time, there would still have been dozens or scores of cases of "foreknowledge" from people who engaged in loose talk.

One final issue concerns the kind of people who supposedly had foreknowledge of this case. In the Milteer account it's racists. Doubtless such folks had guns and knew how to shoot, but could they have mounted an elaborate plot to frame Oswald and cover up the conspiracy? Could they have engineered a plot that would have required the cooperation of Dallas Police, the FBI, the CIA, and the Warren Commission? Or (alternatively) a plot that would have fooled all those officials? Had they been sophisticated enough to do that, they wouldn't have been in organizations like the Dixie Klan. Also, while the Washington establishment was afraid of blaming communists for the assassination (and of the dangerous consequences that would entail) and might have been protective of the CIA or the FBI, executing a few Klansmen for conspiracy to murder Kennedy would have suited it just fine.

The Cherami account did not feature sophisticated assassins either. Indeed, what kind of men would pal around with an unstable prostitute like Cherami, blab about a Kennedy assassination plot in front of her, get into a fight with her, and then toss her out on the highway? If they were cold-blooded enough to kill Kennedy, they would hardly scruple in eliminating her as well. If they had had the professionalism to be part of a sophisticated plot, then they probably would have kept their mouths shut.

The same logic applies to yet a third character who supposedly had foreknowledge, one Richard Case Nagell. Space precludes a detailed treatment of his testimony, but he claimed to have ties to Oswald, the FBI, the CIA, the KGB, and Cuban intelligence, among others. A secret internal CIA document described him as "a crank because he is mentally deranged" and noted he never worked for the agency.[23]

GENERIC OBSERVATIONS AS EVIDENCE OF CONSPIRACY

If Joseph Milteer offered an unspecific scenario by which a president might be assassinated, similarly generic observations have often been the basis of other conspiracy theories. Theorists who believe that the U.S. government was behind the 9/11 attacks, for instance, often point to a document titled *Rebuilding America's Defenses: Strategy, Forces and Resources for a New Century*.[24] Issued in September 2000, the report was a product of the Project for the New American Century, a hawkish, neoconservative think tank. The document points to the need for a transformation of America's defense establishment to "preserve American military preeminence" and goes on to say, "Further, the process of transformation, even if it brings revolutionary change, is likely to be a long one, absent some catastrophic and catalyzing event—like a new Pearl Harbor."[25]

So theorists claim 9/11 was the "new Pearl Harbor" that the neoconservatives (prominent in the George W. Bush administration) wanted; so they must have arranged it.[26] But the notion that a catastrophic and catalyzing event would radically change things is hardly evidence of inside knowledge. Somewhere in the files of a pro–gun control lobby group is probably a memo saying that, barring another massacre similar to the one at Columbine High School in 1999, getting significant gun control legislation is going to be difficult or impossible. If such a massacre happens, however, it won't be because the lobby group arranged it.

Thus, before accepting any claims of foreknowledge, one has to determine how likely it is that somebody in this vast nation who actually knew nothing about a plot would make such claims. If the statements are just generic observations, the answer is pretty likely. If the statements are mostly incoherent babbling, but mention killing the president, the answer is still pretty likely. Real foreknowledge means the person knows something that he or she couldn't know without a pipeline to the real conspiracy.

Chapter Nine

Signal and Noise:
Seeing Things in Photos

It's a truism of cognitive psychology: present people with an ambiguous stimulus, and they will interpret it in different ways. And the way they will interpret it will depend on their psychological needs, their predispositions, and their biases. One standard psychology text discusses how perceptions are selective, how they are contextual, and creative:

> Our perceptual systems . . . help us fill in incomplete information, whether this information prevents us from having a visual blind spot or completes an unresolved chord in our auditory imagination. In total, these characteristics contribute to the development of a perceptual set, expectations that influence how perceptual elements will be interpreted. Perceptual sets act as filters in how we process information about the environment.[1]

Thus it has long been that conspiracy researchers, looking diligently at photos relevant to the assassination, have been able to see evidence of conspiracy in ambiguous, blurred, and grainy images. Following are some examples.

QUESTIONABLE EVIDENCE
Shooters in Dealey Plaza

For assassination researchers, it would be a coup of galactic proportions to find evidence of a second shooter in Dealey Plaza. And not surprisingly, several of them have claimed to have found such a shooter in photos. In his pioneering 1967 book, *Six Seconds in Dallas*, Josiah Thompson maintains he found a shooter in the

Moorman Polaroid, a photo that shows the grassy knoll and the stockade fence within a second of the shot that hit Kennedy in the head. Thompson thought he saw a shooter behind a tree along the northeast–southwest leg of the fence a few yards from the corner. To fortify his case, Thompson selectively uses tendentious quotes from witnesses. For example, he uses quotes from an FBI interview with Emmett Hudson, who said that he thought the shots came from "behind him, . . . above him, and . . . to his left."[2] Thompson ignores the fact that this description also fits the Texas School Book Depository and that Hudson explicitly told the FBI in that same interview that the shots sounded as if they were coming from the depository (see chapter 1).[3] Thompson also quotes Bill Newman, who was standing on the grass in front of the pergola near Elm Street, as saying, "I thought the shot was fired from directly behind where we were standing."[4] Of course, directly behind Bill Newman (who was standing with his wife, Gayle, and their two children) was the pergola, not the stockade fence. Indeed, Newman explicitly said he thought the shots came from "that mall up there."[5]

Obviously, seeing a shooter in the photo was quite subjective. Thompson showed it to witness Sam Holland (who was a railroad supervisor and not any kind of photo expert). Holland examined it "for a long time" and then declared, "Well do you know I think that you're looking right down the barrel of that gun right now!"[6] But the biggest problem with Thompson's "find" is that this particular area behind the stockade fence is visible in the last seconds of the Zapruder film, and nobody is there.

The "Classic Gunman"

A fellow named Orville Nix was standing in Dealey Plaza, up near the corner of Main and Houston Streets (see photo insert), filming the presidential limo as it drove down Elm Street, and he captured an important part of the shooting.[7] Researcher Jones Harris, in 1965, first noticed an apparent human figure on the grassy knoll.[8] As the HSCA described it,

> As Nix panned his camera from right to left following the motion of the Presidential limousine, the background of the grassy knoll came into view. In it, beyond the retaining wall and running along the crest of the knoll, is a region of deep shadow that is broken by patches of light. For a number of frames there appears to be a brightly lit object whose shape some have

interpreted to be that of a man sighting a rifle toward the Presidential limousine. The right "arm" of this object is rigidly extended outward from the "body," with the left "arm" tucked in more tightly, as if supporting a rifle stock. There is, between and above these arms, a shape that looks like a "head." That object has been interpreted to be a rifleman in the classic military posture for firing a rifle.[9]

No doubt, it does look like a shooter, but the HSCA's photo experts decided it could not be one. The Nix film shows clear flesh tones in the persons visible in the frames, but the "classic gunman" showed no such flesh tones. Instead, his image was the same color as patches of light on the wall of the pergola. Further, Nix was moving as he shot his film, which made it possible to use photogrammetry to determine the distance of the image from Nix's camera. It turned out that the image was at the location of the wall of the pergola. The rifle, if it were a rifle, would have to be nine feet above ground level. But nobody noticed a giant with a rifle in Dealey Plaza, and nobody saw a platform that would allow a man of normal height to shoot from nine feet above ground level. Finally, one of the figure's arms disappeared in one frame, only to appear in the next frame. While this movement would be inconsistent with a person, it was quite plausibly from tree branches casting a shadow on the pergola wall.[10]

In spite of the HSCA and Josiah Thompson himself debunking it, the classic gunman image was treated as genuine in Harry Livingstone and Robert Groden's *High Treason*.[11] Jim Marrs's *Crossfire* notes that the the Itek Corporation debunked the image in 1966, but he insists that Itek "handles government contracts and is closely tied to the CIA."[12] Since Itek is one of the top (and maybe *the* top) photo analysis firms in the country, one would hope that the CIA used its services.

The Black Dog Man

Phil Willis was a witness (see chapter 2) and took a photo of the motorcade on Elm Street at about Zapruder frame 202.[13] Seen in the photo is the area of the grassy knoll and the nearby retaining wall, and a figure that appears to be a black dog sitting on its haunches is visible on top of the retaining wall. A linear feature that somewhat resembles a gun is visible in a position suggesting that the "black dog man" might be holding it. Robert Groden insists that the figure is "a man crouching behind the retaining wall, perhaps to fire upon the President."[14]

The HSCA examined the photo and determined that the figure was indeed a man because of the flesh tones in the figure's face. As for the rifle, the committee determined that the supposed weapon was consistent with motion blur. The direction of motion blur in that part of the photo is such that it would stretch a short object along a five o'clock–eleven o'clock axis, which is the exact orientation of the rifle.[15]

Of course, being consistent with motion blur is not the same as showing that the image of the supposed rifle was indeed the result of motion blur. So the HSCA's analysis doesn't rule out a shooter. However, a shooter at the corner of the retaining wall would have been right out in plain sight, visible to everybody in Dealey Plaza. He would have needed to wear body armor, since if he had shot from that position, an easy dozen cops and Secret Service agents would have fired back at him.

The Torn-out License Plate

Conspiracists like to talk endlessly about evidence tampering on the part of authorities, and proven examples of real evidence tampering would indeed strongly suggest a conspiracy. One related case involves a photo that the police seized from Lee Oswald's possessions at the Paine house after the assassination. The photo shows the back of Gen. Edwin Walker's house and a parked car, a 1957 Chevrolet. The license plate of the car had been torn out of the photo.

Things got interesting when Dallas Police chief Jesse Curry published a book in 1969 that included a photo, taken by the Dallas cops shortly after the assassination, of various evidence laid out on the floor of police headquarters. The photo of the Walkers' backyard is there among other artifacts, but the license plate seems to be intact. The obvious inference is that somebody in the Dallas Police Department tore it out after the evidence was photographed but before it was turned over to federal authorities. Author Anthony Summers asks, "Did somebody tamper with vital evidence after the assassination? If so, why?"[16] And Robert Groden asks, "How and why was the photo damaged before its submission to the Warren Commission?"[17]

But this evidence tampering business is based on the fact that, in the low-resolution version shown in Curry's book, the photo is on a white sheet of paper. Thus the hole appears to be white and not black as it does in the Warren Commission exhibit. The Texas State Archives has an original print of the evidence photo, and a blowup of the area of the license plate shows that it has already been torn out (see photo insert). How the license plate got torn out is still a mystery—Marina insisted that it had not been torn out when Lee showed her the photo[18]—but this allegation of supposed photographic evidence tampering turns out to be bogus.

Jack Ruby in Dealey Plaza

The official story, as outlined by the Warren Commission, has Jack Ruby at the offices of the *Dallas Morning News* at 12:30 p.m., the time of the shooting. But some people say they can certainly see Ruby in various photos shot in Dealey Plaza. Witness Phil Willis took one such photo, and it's labeled "Willis #8," or the eighth slide he shot. A figure appears at the far right-hand side of the frame who looks like Jack Ruby (see photo insert). Mark Lane puffed the Ruby identification in his 1966 book, quoting Willis himself as saying, "It looks so much like him [Ruby], it's pitiful. When I saw him in the court-room and all, my God, it looked just like him."[19] By 1978, Willis was even more convinced, saying flatly that "I also got a photo . . . that shows Ruby standing in front of the Depository building. He was the only one wearing dark glasses. He was identified by people who knew him and no one else has been able to say it was someone else."[20] Other conspiracy books have followed suit, claiming or implying the photo showed Ruby.[21]

But unfortunately for this theory, other film footage and still photos exist of this man, with his dark glasses, receding hairline, and open collar. These images include photos by freelance photographer Jim Murray, "Cooper film" footage shot by Don Cook for KTVT (in Fort Worth), and in footage shot by a photographer for WFAA-TV in Dallas. The man is not Ruby.[22]

Who Were the Three Tramps?

Unlike some other figures that people think they see in Dealey Plaza photos, the three tramps were most certainly there, being marched by the cops through the plaza after the assassination. But who were they and what were they doing there? Since no arrest records were available for decades, their identities were unknown. And because they were "mysterious," conspiracists quickly came to believe they had some role in the assassination.

By the late 1970s, conspiracists looking at the tramps' photos had developed a list of suspects, identifying at least five possible candidates. Key suspects were Watergate conspirators E. Howard Hunt and Frank Sturgis. Also included were less celebrated figures: Thomas Vallee, Daniel Carswell, and Fred Chrisman.[23] As the years passed, even more were identified. By the early 1990s three additional tramps had been named: Charles Harrelson, father of actor Woody Harrelson, was imprisoned in Texas for the murder of a judge and claimed to be the tall tramp; Chauncey Holt, the oldest of the group, who "confessed" to being the last tramp in line; and Charles Frederick Rogers, who was "positively identified" as the first tramp, generally called "Frenchy," in the line. Rogers is still wanted by Texas authorities for the 1965 murder of his parents.[24]

HOW TO APPROACH THIS ISSUE

When people perceive stimuli, and especially ambiguous stimuli, all sorts of distortions enter into the process. As discussed, one of the best documented issues is that people "see" what they expect to see and what they want to see. Thus people who believe that Hunt and Sturgis had to be two of the tramps can certainly see a resemblance in the photos. Alan J. Weberman and Michael Canfield, in the book *Coup d'État in America*, included numerous carefully selected photos of Hunt and Sturgis and even went so far as to include acetate overlays of Hunt, Sturgis, and Daniel Carswell superimposed over the respective tramps.[25]

But we researchers would like to adopt a more serious way of examining this kind of evidence. Happily, there is a class of people in the world who, most of the time, exist in comfortable obscurity and do this kind of work—forensic anthropologists. They specialize in studying the human body and especially those features, particularly the face, that can distinctively identify individuals. They use both metric and morphological features.

Morphological and Metric Features

The human face has many distinctive features. As the HSCA's experts explained,

(548) An example of such a [morphological] trait is the lowly ear lobe which, aside from providing a convenient place to hang earrings, seems to have no discernible purpose except to provide physical anthropologists with something to classify. Accordingly, a threefold classification of ear lobes as either free, attached, or soldered has been devised. Free lobes are those that are to some degree pendulous; in attached lobes the outside margins of the ears connect more or less directly to the side of the face. The soldered lobe is an extreme form of the attached type in which union of ear margin and cheek is so direct that there is no

discernible lobe at all. Since ear lobe type can frequently be determined from photographs, the trait can be useful in identification.

(550) Along with ears, the human face possesses an array of morphological features that, while difficult to measure, can be readily classified. The nasal tip can be elevated ("snub-nosed") or depressed, pointed or bulbous: the bridge of the nose, in profile, can be straight, convex or concave. Lips can be thick or thin: hair—straight, wavy, curly, or kinky, and so on. Also within this category are traits that are acquired by accident or age (or as Shakespeare put it ". . . through chance or nature's changing course untrimmed"). Among traits acquired during life may be included warts, moles, and other random blemishes, scars from accidents or surgery, broken noses, cauliflower ears, and other more or less permanent disfigurements. The inevitable loss of skin elasticity with age produces wrinkles and these networks of creases and furrows form patterns that uniquely characterize each human face. The comparison of traits that cannot be measured but only classified (as the ear lobe) or described as "present" or "absent" (such as a scar) constitutes the morphological analysis of the photographs question.[26]

In addition to observing morphological characteristics, metric characteristics of the human face can, as the term implies, be measured. (See this book's photo insert.) The measurements can then be combined into an index of the degree of difference between an individual shown in one photo and an individual (purported to be the same individual) shown in another photo. If the difference index is too large, it isn't the same person.

This process is obviously miles beyond what folks with acetate overlays can determine.

Early on, soon after Sturgis and Hunt were "identified" as two of the three tramps, the President's Commission on CIA Activities within the United States, also known as the Rockefeller Commission, asked the FBI to investigate this issue. The bureau's experts not only compared the morphological characteristics of the tramps, they also went to Dealey Plaza and used the same cameras that had been used to shoot the original tramps' photos to re-create them and determine the relative heights of the "Sturgis" tramp and the "Hunt" tramp. They found that while the difference in height of the two tramps in the Dealey Plaza photos was about seven inches, the difference in heights between the real E. Howard Hunt and the real Frank Sturgis was two inches. It wasn't Hunt and Sturgis.[27]

As one can imagine, an FBI analysis done for a commission with Rockefeller in the name was pretty much blown off by conspiracy theorists, since both the Rockefellers and the FBI are thought to be part of all sorts of conspiracies.

The HSCA tackled the issue in the late 1970s, and by that time the ever-expanding cast of tramp suspects included Vallee, Carswell, and Chrisman. The HSCA experts debunked some of the various factoids surrounding the tramps, particularly the claim that the tramps were suspiciously well dressed, wearing shoes of good leather.

> (675) All three men are shabbily dressed, befitting their apparent status as vagrants. Tramp A, however, is the better attired, wearing well-fitting jeans and a tweed-like sports jacket, although this, judged by 1963 styles, was several years out of date. Tramp B is wearing ill-fitting slacks and a double-breasted suit coat. Tramp C, from his battered fedora to his worn-out shoes, has managed to achieve a sartorial effect similar to what one would expect had he been fired from a cannon through a Salvation Army thrift shop.
>
> (676) While such clothing might be a disguise, their footwear seems consistent with their classification as vagrants. All three men are shod in worn, low-cut oxfords that appear to be leather-soled. Tramp C's shoes seem to be several sizes too large for him.

What about their identities? None of the tramps were Sturgis, Hunt, Vallee, or Carswell. One of the tramps *could* have been Fred Chrisman, so far as the experts could determine.[28] But HSCA staffers discovered that he had been teaching in an Oregon high school on the day of the assassination in 1963, with three of his fellow teachers vouching for that fact.[29]

Sometimes somebody out there is your dead ringer. In such cases, it's good to have an alibi.

Thus the committee eliminated many suspects, but plenty of conspiracy theorists rejected or simply ignored the HSCA's conclusions. As noted, more suspects kept getting added to the brew.

And then came a huge break in 1992 when archivist Cindy Smolovik handed a list of documents to researcher Mary La Fontaine at the Dallas Municipal Archives.

On the list was an entry reading "Arrests, November 22, 1963." Sure enough, this file included the tramps' long-missing arrest records, which showed them to be Harold Doyle, John Forrester Gedney, and Gus W. Abrams.[30]

These names meant nothing, and just looking at the records, one could question whether these really were "the three tramps." Mary La Fontaine and her husband, Ray, found one useful clue on the arrest sheets. Doyle was from Red Jacket, West Virginia. Following a trail from Red Jacket through Amarillo, Texas, to Klamath Falls, Oregon, they found Doyle, who admitted to being one of the tramps.[31] The FBI followed close behind and interviewed Doyle, and then it located and interviewed Gedney. Gedney also admitted to being one of the tramps, and both he and Doyle explained their relatively clean appearance. According to Dallas FBI special agent Oliver (Buck) Revell, "Both commented that they had gotten fresh clothes, showered, shaved and had a meal. They headed back to the railroad yard when they heard all the commotion and sirens and everything, and they asked what happened. They were told the president had been shot."[32]

Abrams, unfortunately, was dead. But researcher Kenneth Formet found his sister, with whom he had lived the last fifteen years of his life. Shown a photo of the tramps from Dealey Plaza, she exclaimed, "Yep, that's my Bill!" She knew of his hobo life and explained, "He was always on the go hopping trains and drinking wine."[33]

So it seems the mystery was solved. But not to everybody's satisfaction. The book *Murder in Dealey Plaza*, published in 2000 and edited by James Fetzer, treats the Chauncey Holt story as accurate. Chauncey Holt's daughter spoke at the Dallas Research Conference in November 2000, claiming that her father was one of the tramps. Indeed, Holt was the subject of an entire panel.[34] And what about authors Weberman and Canfield? They dismissed the discovery of the tramps' identities as "the intricate disinformation the CIA has come up with."[35]

After decades of demanding that the government "tell the truth," some folks seem unable to accept the truth.

Scientific Testing

Perhaps the most compelling evidence of a grassy knoll shooter in Dealey Plaza is seen in the Zapruder film when John Kennedy's head (and indeed his entire body) goes back and to the left after a shot explodes his skull. The issue here is not exactly what one "sees" in the Zapruder film, for there is no doubt that Kennedy is thrown backward and to the left. The issue is how one interprets what is shown. The film certainly seems to reflect the transfer of momentum from a bullet to Kennedy's head.

In fact, this incorrect notion is an example of Hollywood ballistics. Everybody has seen movies in which the bad guy, shot by the hero, is thrown bodily backward by the force of the shot. That's not the way it happens in real life. The medical panels of both the Rockefeller Commission and the HSCA addressed this issue. First, the Rockefeller Commission's panel said,

> [Members] were . . . unanimous in finding that the violent backward and leftward motion of the President's upper body following the head shot was not caused by the impact of a bullet coming from the front or right front.
>
> Drs. [Werner] Spitz, [Richard] Lindenberg and [Fred] Hodges reported that such a motion would be caused by a violent straightening and stiffening of the entire body as a result of a seizure-like neuromuscular reaction to major damage inflicted to nerve centers in the brain.
>
> Dr. [Alfred] Olivier reported that the violent motions of the President's body following the head shot could not possibly have been caused by the impact of the bullet. He attributed the popular misconception on this subject to the dramatic effects employed in television and motion picture productions. The *impact* of such a bullet, he explained, can cause some immediate movement of the *head* in the direction of the bullet, but it would not produce any significant movement of the *body*.[36]

In 1978, before what must have been one of the most bizarre congressional hearings ever held, scientist Larry Sturdivan, from the Aberdeen Proving Ground Vulnerability Laboratory, showed members of the HSCA a slow-motion film of a goat being shot in the head. He described what happened:

> Four one-hundredths of a second after that impact then the neuromuscular reaction that I describe begins to happen; the back legs go out, under the influence of the powerful muscles of the back legs, the front legs go upward and outward, that back arches, as the powerful back muscles overcome those of the abdomen.[37]

Sturdivan went on to explain that

> the momentum of the bullet could not have thrown him in any direction violently. The neuromuscular reaction in which the heavy back muscles

predominate over the lighter abdominal muscles would have thrown him backward no matter where the bullet came from, whether it entered the front, the side or the back of the head.[38]

Cyril Wecht, a forensic pathologist who is one of the very few (and perhaps the only) bona fide forensic pathologists who believes in a conspiracy, can be seen in various videos appearing to suggest that Kennedy might have been thrown backward by the force of the bullet.[39] But put Wecht under oath, in a context where he has to render a sober professional opinion, and he usually sounds much less the conspiracist.[40] For example, when Wecht was put on the stand in the retrial of the notorious Menendez brothers in California, counsel asked him whether it is a "matter of physics" that a body will move in the same direction as a bullet that hits it. His response was that "some of the [Newtonian] concepts, indeed are applicable and relevant, but you have to then factor in the biological element, the entire neuromuscular system and so on, all of the voluntary and involuntary reflexive aspects of it." And further, "Sir Newton and others just never dealt with those things. . . . That's just a very different situation."[41]

The TV show *MythBusters* dealt with this issue, shooting a dummy with a .50-caliber sniper's rifle, a weapon far more powerful than any rifle likely to have been used in Dealey Plaza. The dummy was blown backward by only a couple of inches, and it merely fell to the ground.[42]

Thus it seems that any movement "back and to the left" actually proves nothing.

Other Images

The total number of conspiratorial claims based on seeing something in rather ambiguous photos is large. James Altgens's photo, for instance, shows a man who resembles Oswald standing in the doorway of the Texas School Book Depository during the shooting in Dealey Plaza. If the man was Oswald, he could not have been upstairs shooting at Kennedy. Both extensive witness testimony and the analysis of forensic anthropologists, however, have showed that the man was one Billy Lovelady, a coworker of Oswald's who somewhat resembled him.[43]

Conspiracist Robert Groden has tried to tie Oswald to the Garrison investigation's suspect, Clay Shaw, on the basis of a grainy frame from a television news film of Oswald leafleting in front of the International Trade Mart, where Shaw worked as the director. Supposedly, the frame "shows Clay Shaw, wearing a white suit, walking toward Oswald . . . who is handing out leaflets. Shaw looks over at Oswald, then enters his office building."[44] This footage wouldn't prove much, even if true, but it turns out it's not true. Cameraman Johann Rush, who shot the film footage, knew Shaw well and was indeed looking for Shaw, wanting to get his reaction to Oswald's leafleting. He insists the man in the film was not Shaw.[45]

Groden also claims that a sequence from amateur film footage that Charles Mentesana shot in Dealey Plaza some minutes after the assassination shows a "rifle" that was "handed down . . . from the roof [of the depository] to the seventh floor fire escape" and "examined." The rifle is not a Mannlicher-Carcano and "had never been placed into evidence," which might raise suspicions about a second shooter.[46] But in reality, it's not a rifle; in fact, it's a Remington 870 shotgun, a policeman's weapon.[47] Numerous Dallas cops can be seen holding the same weapon in numerous Dealey Plaza photos. Further, the cops in the Mentesana film are not examining the rifle; rather, they are having a discussion while the shotgun rests on the shoulder of one policeman.

Non-JFK Examples

Seeing things in photos that aren't there or at least misinterpreting what one sees is extremely common. The evergreen, if by now quite jejune, accounts come from the literature about unidentified flying objects (UFOs).[48] But theorists behind other conspiracy theories have their "photographic evidence" as well. For example, moon landing conspiracy theorists point to a famous photo of the American flag on the moon. After American astronauts planted it on the moon in 1969, the flag is unfurled and waving. Since there is no atmosphere on the moon, the flag supposedly can't wave, so the inference is that the photo was shot on a movie set here on earth. In reality, the flag was held out from the flagpole by a horizontal crossbar. The flag is waving because when the astronaut moved the pole, it transferred momentum to the flag. Given the lack of an atmosphere to damp the waving, the flag would wave for quite a while, no wind needed.[49]

Likewise, members of the 9/11 Truth movement—Truthers, or those theorists who think the U.S. government was behind the attacks—point to "concrete clouds shooting out of the buildings [that] are not possible from a mere collapse. They do occur from explosions." Indeed, in film footage of the 9/11 attacks in New York City, in particular, as each floor of the damaged buildings is crushed by the weight of the pancaking floors above, debris does shoot out in a way that looks as if an explosive charge was set off inside. But in reality, the air inside the offices on each floor was compressed and forced to the sides.[50] (See also chapter 10.)

Seeing Things in Photos

Considered broadly, this business of seeing things in photos is no different from the issue faced in addressing the Oswald sightings or the perceptions of Dealey Plaza earwitnesses as to the source of the shots. It's a matter of signal and noise, and it is especially affected by the human mind's tendency to make sense out of ambiguous stimuli. And of course, random processes can produce apparent signal, as anybody who has spent any time looking at clouds in a blue sky can attest. Such was also the case with the classic gunman in the Nix film.

Scientists can sometimes filter out noise, leaving signal. When the HSCA analyzed the classic gunman theory, its experts digitized and averaged the image across several frames.[51] Averaging tends to let signal cumulate and noise cancel. Likewise, the work of forensic anthropologists focuses on facial features that don't change over time and are not based on lighting conditions, on camera angles (assuming one can actually see the feature), or on whether the anthropologist believes in conspiracy theories or has had a bad day.

But lacking such a disciplined approach, what one sees depends both on one's preexisting dispositions and one's technical competence in evaluating what's present in the visual stimuli. Where the former are strong and the latter is lacking, intellectual havoc can ensue.

Chapter Ten

Think Scenario

Conspiracy books like to throw at the reader a large number of events (or claimed events) that strike one as odd or peculiar or out of line. The intention is to create a spooky ambience. So much is unexplained. Just why did this event happen? Was something going on here? The cumulative effect of this uncertainty is to make the reader think there *must* have been a conspiracy. After all, there was just so much strange stuff going on.

There is a simple rule to follow when faced with these odd or strange happenings. Ask, what exactly does this information mean? Or ask, if this information is true, then what scenario does it imply? Quite frequently, it implies some scenario that would seem downright silly. Following are some examples.

THE MAN IN THE SNIPER'S NEST

Under the Warren Commission scenario, Oswald had to leave the sniper's nest immediately—within at most a few seconds—to get downstairs and confront Dallas Police officer Marrion Baker between seventy-five and ninety seconds after the shots rang out at 12:30 p.m.[1] Yet no cops made it up to the sniper's nest until about 1:00 p.m., or thirty minutes after the shooting.[2]

So what then is one to make of the testimony of Lillian Mooneyham, cited by Jim Marrs as evidence of something sinister going on?

Mrs. MOONEYHAM and Mrs. CLARK left Judge KING's courtroom and went to the office of Judge JULIEN C. MYER to observe the happenings from Judge MYER's window. . . . Mrs. MOONEYHAM estimated that it was about 4½ to 5 minutes following the shots fired by the assassin, that she looked up towards the sixth floor of the TSBD [Texas School Book Depository] and observed the figure of a man standing in the sixth floor window behind some cardboard boxes. This man appeared to Mrs. MOONEYHAM to be looking out of the window, however, the man was not close up to the window but was standing slightly back from it, so that Mrs. MOONEY-HAM could not make out his features.[3]

Four and a half minutes to five minutes after the shooting, Oswald was gone from the depository and headed up Elm Street to catch a bus.[4] So if it wasn't Oswald she saw and it wasn't the cops, it had to be a conspirator. But what was the conspirator doing? Why didn't he flee?

The answer is that it's absurdly implausible that any conspirator would simply hang around in the sniper's nest after shooting the president. He would have to assume that cops would quickly be all over the building, that the building would be closed off, or that some extremely brave (or perhaps merely reckless) employees would come looking for a shooter. Given what we have seen about eyewitness testimony (chapters 1 and 2), the most plausible explanation is that Mooneyham was simply confused—perhaps about the time at which she saw the figure in the window, or perhaps about the window in which she saw the man.[5]

THE PICKUP TRUCK

The testimony of Julia Ann Mercer is a "twofer." Not only does it link Jack Ruby to a JFK assassination plot (and not merely to a plot to silence Oswald), it provides a juicy scene of conspiratorial shenanigans in the area of the grassy knoll.

The most famous version of Mercer's testimony is the one presented in the movie *JFK*. Supposedly, Mercer was driving through Dealey Plaza, but the flow of traffic was blocked by a pickup truck that was parked partly in Elm Street, with its right wheels pulled off the street. Jack Ruby was at the wheel of the truck, and another man took a gun case out of the back of the truck and walked up the grassy slope toward the Grassy Knoll.

There is considerable corroboration for some parts of Mercer's story although not for the juicy parts. At about 11:07 a.m. on the day of the assassination, a Dallas cop called the dispatcher and asked, "Could you send a City wrecker to the Triple Underpass, just west of the underpass on Elm to clear a stalled truck from the route of the escort?" Then, eight minutes later, the cop called in saying, "Disregard the wrecker at the Triple Underpass. We got a truck to push him out of there."[6]

That Mercer saw a stalled truck is also supported by the testimony of Secret Service agent Forest Sorrels, who told the Warren Commission,

> There was another witness there that I started talking to—I don't recall the name now, because I told him to go in—somebody that saw a truck down there—this is before the parade ever got there—that apparently had stalled down there on Elm Street. And I later checked on that, and found out that the car had gone dead, apparently belonged to some construction company, and that a police officer had come down there, and they had gone to the construction company and gotten somebody to come down and get the car out of the way.
>
> Apparently it was just a car stalled down there.
>
> But this lady said she thought she saw somebody that looked like they had a guncase. But then I didn't pursue that any further—because then I had gotten the information that the rifle had been found in the building and shells and so forth.[7]

So far so good for Mercer, who not only immediately reported what she had seen but also gave a statement to the Dallas County Sheriff's Office on the day of the assassination. She was also interviewed multiple times by the FBI.

Various elements of Mercer's account do raise suspicion, however. As conspiracy author Henry Hurt notes,

> At four o'clock the following [Saturday] morning, men came to her apartment and showed FBI identification. She accompanied them back to the sheriff's office, where they showed her a dozen or so photographs, asking her to pick out any she thought might be of the men she saw Friday morning. She selected two pictures. Miss Mercer had no idea of the men's identities.
>
> On Sunday morning, the day after Miss Mercer made the identification; she was watching the assassination coverage on television with friends and saw Ruby shoot Oswald. Instantly, she shouted that they were the two men she had seen on Friday and had identified for the FBI. Ruby, she said, was the driver and Oswald the man with the rifle.

If true, Julia Mercer's identification of Jack Ruby preceding his murder of Oswald would have introduced a new twist to the official FBI version of the assassination. The revelation not only would have suggested a rifleman on the grassy knoll, but would have shown an FBI interest in Ruby in connection with the killing of Kennedy.

It is not surprising that Miss Mercer's claim is not backed up by any official reports of the incident.

Some years later, when Miss Mercer saw the official reports, she was aghast. The FBI, in its report of the Mercer interview, omitted her asserted identification of Jack Ruby as the driver of the truck. It also reported that even though Miss Mercer was shown pictures of Oswald, she was unable to identify him. The sheriff's department report included a statement attributed to Miss Mercer to the effect that she did not see the driver clearly enough to be able to identify him. Miss Mercer adamantly denounces the reports as corruptions and fabrications by the FBI and the sheriff's department of her actual experiences. Miss Mercer is one of many other witnesses who claim discrepancies between what was told to the authorities and what later appeared in the official reports.[8]

To anybody who is skeptical of witness testimony, this claim of massive fabrication of official reports will seem suspicious. As previously noted, such claims tend to come from witnesses who have been telling wild tales. Indeed, some of what Hurt reports her saying is clearly untrue. Mercer's statement to the sheriff's department, for example, actually says, "The man who remained in the truck had light brown hair and I believe I could identify him also if I were to see him again."[9] Why Hurt didn't bother to check the affidavit Mercer signed on the day of the assassination is a mystery.

At any rate, authorities took the Mercer sighting quite seriously, and the FBI finally produced a report on it. That report says:

JOE MURPHY, Patrolman, Traffic Division, Police Department, Dallas, Texas, advised that on November 22, 1963, he was stationed at the Triple Underpass on Elm Street to assist in handling traffic. At approximately 10:30–10:40 AM, a pickup truck stalled on Elm Street between Houston Street and the underpass. He was unable to recall the name of the company to whom this truck belonged but stated it is the property of the company working on the First National Bank Building at Elm and Akard in Dallas.

There were three construction men in this truck, and he took one to the bank building to obtain another truck in order to assist in moving the stalled one. The other two men remained with the pickup truck along with two other officers. Shortly prior to the arrival of the motorcade, the man he had taken to the bank building returned with a second truck, and all three of the men left with the two trucks, one pushing the other.[10]

Of course, anybody who believes in a massive government cover-up will cheerfully label the FBI report a fake and a fabrication. So can we get beyond merely deciding whether we trust Mercer or trust the FBI?

To evaluate the plausibility of Mercer's story, one has to start with the notion that any conspirators needed to get a shooter and a gun onto the grassy knoll. So far so good for Mercer. How did they try to do it? They parked a pickup truck on Elm Street in plain sight of three cops (who were charged with keeping the motorcade route clear) and heaven knows how many irate, badly inconvenienced drivers.[11] And then the grassy knoll shooter took out a gun case in front of everyone and sauntered up the slope to the knoll.

Meanwhile, the testimony of Lee Bowers, a signalman who was in the train yard's signal tower behind the stockade fence atop the knoll, makes it clear that anyone could have simply driven down the Old Elm Extension and around the parking lot behind the fence to access the knoll. In chapter 1, he described three cars doing exactly that on the morning of the assassination.[12] But to believe Mercer, one has to believe that the conspirators ignored the simple, easy way of getting a shooter behind the fence atop the knoll and chose a plan designed to draw the maximum possible attention to themselves.[13]

THE "TOO QUICK" VISA

Conspiracists specialize in scrutinizing, in excruciating detail, Oswald's life in an attempt to find some suspicious event that might be the tip-off that a cabal had moved him around the landscape for some sinister purpose. And in principle, there is nothing wrong with this sort of research. Real intelligence agencies catch real spies exactly this way; paying minute attention to the spies' actions turns up telltale evidence of their treason.

But when attempting this kind of research, one needs to exercise judgment about what information really is suspicious. Take, for example, Oswald's defection to the Soviet Union in October 1959. Oswald traveled to Moscow via Helsinki and obtained a visa from the Helsinki Soviet embassy in just two days.[14] To conspiracy theorists, this transaction was too quick and thus raises suspicion. Even the Warren Commission admitted that his request was processed quicker than normal, although it had evidence of wide variation in the speed of issuing visas in Helsinki.[15]

But the visa's processing time raises suspicion of what exactly? It was the Soviets who gave Oswald the visa so quickly. Did the CIA ask the Soviet embassy to issue his visa on the double?

Was he working for Soviet intelligence, the KGB? Assassination buffs who want to tie Oswald to an American intelligence agency don't care for this notion. It is true, however, that the KGB would obviously have been able to swiftly get a visa for Oswald, had it wanted to do so.

Perhaps the CIA could have too. Perhaps the CIA had an operative or two strategically positioned in the Helsinki embassy. Might that operative have been able to procure a visa quickly for Oswald? Perhaps, but it would have been dangerous. If any covert CIA operative had acted suspiciously, he or she could have been detected and ceased being a usable intelligence asset (not to mention possibly getting killed).

More generally, any suspicious or out of the ordinary treatment of Oswald would have been poor spy craft. Conspiracy authors fancy themselves experts on all kinds of things relating to intelligence. But if Oswald was of any serious intelligence interest, his movements would have been evaluated by intelligence agencies. Who is better qualified to know what sorts of movements really are suspicious, conspiracy authors or the KGB and the CIA? Not a hard call. Thus if the KGB rapidly obtained a visa for Oswald, the CIA would have deemed it suspicious. And likewise, the KGB would have thought so if the two agencies' roles were reversed.

Next, why would either agency need to get Oswald into the Soviet Union so quickly? After his arrival on October 16, 1959, he toured Moscow, told his tour guide Rima Shirokova that he wanted to defect to the Soviet Union, and then cooled his heals in the Hotel Berlin. After being told that he had to leave the country since his visa would not be extended, he attempted suicide (or perhaps, staged a bogus attempt) and spent three days in the psychiatric ward of Botkin Hospital. Then he moved to the Hotel Metropole, where he waited to find out whether he would be allowed to stay in the country. As the Warren Commission noted,

For the rest of the year, Oswald seldom left his hotel room where he had arranged to take his meals, except perhaps for a few trips to museums. He spent most of his time studying Russian, "8 hours a day" his diary records. The routine was broken only by another interview at the passport office; occasional visits from Rima Shirokova; lessons in Russian from her and other Intourist guides; and a New Year's visit from [Intourist Guide] Roza Agafonova.

On January 4, he was summoned to the Soviet Passport Office and told he would be allowed to remain in the country.[16]

So one wonders, what exactly was the point of rushing Oswald to Moscow just so that he could spend five or eight or ten extra days at the Hotel Metropole? Why not just let him endure the normal wait in Helsinki?[17]

GUIDING OSWALD TO THE DEPOSITORY

One major problem that conspiracists face is explaining what appears to be a far-fetched coincidence—Lee Oswald had a job in the Texas School Book Depository, a building that overlooked the motorcade route and provided a perfect perch for an assassin. How did he get there? One theory is that, to use Jim Garrison's term, the "guiding hands" of a conspiracy put him there.[18]

When Oswald returned from a trip to Mexico City—his dream of getting into Castro's Cuba shattered—he immediately started looking for a job. He took a bus to Dallas, arriving on October 3, 1963, and got a room at the YMCA. The following day he responded to a help wanted newspaper ad placed by the Padgett Printing Company. The plant superintendent, Theodore Gangl, was favorably impressed by Oswald, but unlike everybody else who hired Oswald, he decided to check out the references of this prospective hire.

One of Oswald's references was Robert Stovall of Jaggers-Chiles-Stovall, where Oswald had worked in the spring. Stovall explained to the Warren Commission what happened when Gangl called:

> He called me and asked me and I told him I did not know, but I would check, so I asked John Graef and they said this fellow was kind of an odd-ball, and he was kinda peculiar sometimes and that he had had some knowledge of the Russian language, which—this is all I knew, so I told Ted, I said,

"Ted, I don't know, this guy may be a damn Communist. I can't tell you. If I was you, I wouldn't hire him."[19]

Gangl took Stovall's advice.

The still-unemployed Oswald contacted Marina (who with their daughter June was living with Ruth Paine in Irving), moved out of the YMCA and into a rented room, and took it easy for a few days. When his last unemployment check came in, he roused himself and went to the Texas Employment Commission to seek a job. That agency got him interviews at Solid State Electronics, Harrel and Harrington (architects), Texas Power and Light, and Burton-Dixie. None panned out.[20]

But Oswald's luck took a turn for the better after a coffee klatch that involved the women in his life and some neighbors. On October 14, Marina Oswald, Ruth Paine, and neighbors Dorothy Roberts and Linnie Mae Randle got together over coffee, and the conversation turned to Lee's employment problems. Randle mentioned that her brother, Wesley Frazier, had gotten a job at the Texas School Book Depository. Later, at Marina's urging, Mrs. Paine called the depository's superintendent, Roy Truly, who said that there indeed might be a job available.

That evening Mrs. Paine talked to Oswald (who called from his rooming house) and told him about the possible job. The next day, Oswald went to the depository and talked to Truly, who found him respectful and well mannered. Impressed that Oswald was quiet and needed a job to support his family, Truly hired him.[21]

Just how many sets of "guiding hands" would have been necessary to ensconce Oswald in his "patsy position" in the depository, and what would they have had to do to set up Oswald? First, instead of just hiring Oswald, Theodore Gangl had to put him off by calling Oswald's former employer Stovall, who, in turn, needed to give him a bad recommendation. The Texas Employment Commission then had to send Oswald only to businesses that likewise had been properly briefed not to hire him. Then Marina Oswald, Ruth Paine, Dorothy Roberts, and Linnie Mae Randle all had to steer Oswald into pursuing a job at the depository.[22] Finally, Roy Truly had to hire Oswald. If any link in the chain had broken, the plot would have fallen apart.

But it's even more complicated. Randle did not make a random suggestion about a possible job somewhere in the Dallas metropolitan area. Her brother worked at the depository. Thus another set of guiding hands had to put Wesley Frazier into his job.

But how would anybody know that of all the employers listing jobs in the paper on October 2, Oswald would call the Padgett Printing Company, which had presumably been informed not to hire him? The only way to get around this problem is to posit that Oswald himself was part of the plot. And if Oswald was a coconspirator, it adds another person to the already bloated cast engaged in an elaborate charade, going through the motions of having a frustrated Oswald finally landing a job at the perfect place to shoot the president. And more important, all of them had to lie about it after the assassination.

Once Oswald is made a part of the conspiracy, one has to wonder what the purpose of the elaborate charade was. Oswald could simply have gone directly to the depository. At most, some conspirator leaning on Truly is all that the conspirators would have needed to get Oswald in the building.

Of course, if one set of guiding hands positioned Oswald in the depository, then another set of guiding hands had to route Kennedy down Houston and Elm Streets and into the kill zone. It's true that for maximum visibility in Dallas, a motorcade has to proceed on Main Street. But there was a vigorous debate between two powerful Texas Democrats—Governor John Connally and Senator Ralph Yarborough—as to whether the luncheon for Kennedy would be at the Trade Mart (which would result in the motorcade proceeding from northeast to southwest on Main) or at the Women's Building at the State Fairgrounds (which would have resulted in the motorcade traveling from southwest to northeast). The latter route would have presented a depository sniper with a difficult shot. The target would have been moving from right to left, he would have been halfway across the plaza, and Jackie Kennedy and Nellie Connally would have blocked the sniper's view of Kennedy for much of the time.

So a "guiding hands" theory putting Kennedy within yards of the depository would have involved an easy dozen Texas and White House political figures, operatives, and staffers, all staging a convoluted tableau. They would have had to pretend to debate the location of the luncheon when in fact the conspirators had already determined where it had to be.[23]

LOST LUGGAGE: A TELLTALE SIGN?

Anthony Summers, in his book *Conspiracy*, reports an anomaly in the historical record that, he strongly implies, might be of great significance:

The Oswalds, it seems, flew to Texas the day after their arrival in the United States. As they were preparing to leave, one of the officials helping them noticed something that was to recur—the Oswalds had two suitcases fewer than the seven they had been carrying when they arrived. Oswald said he had sent them ahead by rail, but the baggage was to shrink even more before the family reached Texas. When Oswald's brother met them at Dallas airport, he observed that there were only two suitcases.[24]

Summers notices something else. The Oswalds flew through Atlanta on Delta Flight 821, "although there were direct routes available." And this route causes him alarm because "an Atlanta name and address were found in Oswald's address book after the assassination. It was that of Natasha Davison, the mother of Captain Davison, the American attaché with intelligence connections who had talked to the Oswalds at the Moscow Embassy."

So he has a real find here.

But what sort of plot has Summers uncovered? Apparently he believes that Lee and Marina had carried some kind of contraband, perhaps documents stolen in the Soviet Union.[25] Summers doesn't say what it was, but Oswald never had any kind of security clearance in the Soviet Union and his work in a radio factory in Minsk involved making routine consumer products. He was also subject to minute scrutiny from the Minsk KGB, which apparently surveilled his every move.[26] When he left the socialist state, he somehow failed to give the contraband to officials at the U.S. embassy (which the Oswalds visited on May 24, 1962, and whose officials could have safely sent it out of the country in a diplomatic pouch). Rather, Oswald carried the goods on the train trip out of the country, taking them right through Customs at Brest and on to the Netherlands. Apparently, nobody from the CIA would take them there, so the Oswalds carried them on the steamer *Maasdam* to New York. There the CIA's documents reception center was open, but it had a two-bag limit. Then Lee remembered that he had the address of a nice lady in Atlanta whose son had intelligence connections. Surely she would take them. And of course, she did.

Meanwhile, there is no evidence that the Oswalds ever made contact with Natasha Davison. But if they didn't, what was the point of going through Atlanta?

Summers, an Irishman, appears to know nothing about the U.S. civil aviation system. He believes that if you fly on Delta Airlines, it's odd to stop in Atlanta. But anybody who has flown Delta has quite likely connected through their massive hub in that Georgia city.

THE OSWALDS IN ALICE, TEXAS

Chapter 2, for instance, discussed some of the witnesses who said they saw Lee Oswald before the assassination, mostly in places he could not have been and doing things he would not have done. As noted, these witnesses came forward after the assassination to describe their supposed contact with Oswald. One extremely interesting set of such sightings supposedly happened in and around Alice, Texas, in early October 1963. Researcher Dave Reitzes sums up the testimony of numerous witnesses who came forward after the assassination:

> To sum up, fourteen witnesses believed they'd seen or spoken to Lee Harvey Oswald in or near Alice, Texas in or around the first week of October 1963, several of them specifying October 3rd, 4th, and 5th. Many of these witnesses believed that Marina Oswald was with him. . . . Some witnesses said he had a car at that time. Several said he did not. Two said he was trying to rent one. The physical descriptions are problematic, though the witnesses seem to have genuinely believed it was Lee and Marina Oswald they had seen, sometimes with one or two very small children.[27]

The Oswalds, of course, could not have been in Alice on those days. As noted, Lee was riding a bus back to Dallas from Mexico City, then applying for a job at the Padgett Printing Company, and visiting Marina at Mrs. Paine's house in Irving. Further, there is plenty of evidence in the witness reports that the person they saw could not have been Oswald. First, the Alice "Oswald" was frequently described as dirty and slovenly. The real Lee Oswald was neat, clean, and well groomed. Some of the Alice accounts mention an "Oswald family," with "Marina" having a babe in arms. Of course, at the time the Oswalds were supposedly in Alice, Marina was in the late stages of pregnancy, and their daughter, June, was a toddler. Finally, Lee did not know how to drive a car in early October (although Ruth Paine would soon give him lessons).

Note that the Alice sightings make sense when considering that memory is a reconstruction. The Alice-based Oswald fit the popular stereotype of the left-winger as unkempt beatnik, the sort of person who might kill the president. Also, this Oswald was heard to speak to his wife in "a foreign language," and Lee, of course, spoke Russian to Marina. In photos and TV coverage of the assassination aftermath, Marina was often seen holding infant Rachel Oswald, with toddler June in tow. So the Alice "Oswald family" corresponded to the image that citizens would have acquired of the Oswald family after the assassination. It didn't correspond to the real Oswald family of early October 1963.

But before taking these sightings even slightly seriously, one needs to answer a single question: what was the point? Not surprising, conspiracists are vague and even evasive about their purpose. Chris W. Courtwright, for example, suggests that the "sum of these documents viewed together raises the intriguing possibility of a second Oswald or of Oswald's having been impersonated in southern Texas immediately after his departure from Mexico in early October."[28] What then was the point of the impersonation?

Courtwright goes on to suggest that these events "provide further evidence that Oswald and his identity may have somehow been at the vortex of a complicated web of intersecting and overlapping intelligence operations in the weeks and months leading up to the assassination." This, of course, is no explanation at all.

The Alice sightings, however, are quite varied and inconsistent in terms of what Oswald was doing. In one case, he was applying for a job at a radio station. In another, he filled out an employment application at the Hill Machinery Company. Others have him asking for directions to the bus station, inquiring about work in a café, trying to rent a car at the San Antonio airport, and so on.[29]

Many of the Oswald sightings discussed earlier actually might make sense if a conspiracy was trying to set up a patsy. Oswald getting a scope put on a rifle; Oswald at the Sports Drome Rifle Range, shooting at another customer's target; Oswald with two Cubans at Sylvia Odio's house, having apparently told the two Cubans that Kennedy should be shot—all suggest a violent Oswald with an animus against Kennedy.

But how does Oswald get set up as a patsy by simply having him going around Alice looking for a job, trying to get a bus to Dallas, and attempting to rent a car? Moreover, having an Oswald impersonator in one place doing one thing is terribly risky when there might be good witnesses who can place the real Oswald somewhere else and doing something else. Thus, if no conspiracy would have any reason to have Oswald impersonated in Alice, one can conclude that he was not.

No doubt some person (or more likely, several persons) was in Alice and the surrounding area, sometimes with a woman and infant in tow, and in the aftermath of the assassination the good citizens of the area dutifully reported their honest but unfortunately quite contaminated recollections. Since the real Oswald could not have been in Alice, these sightings are just noise and more evidence of the fallibility of witness testimony.

THE BUMBLING SPOOK AND THE AUTOPSY PHOTOS

Nothing exudes "spooky" more than the actions of a CIA agent named Regis Blahut. An agency liaison to the HSCA in 1978, he went into a safe and handled the president's autopsy photos. These photos and the associated X-rays were not publicly available in the National Archives; instead, they were under the control of the Kennedy family. The HSCA had taken possession of them since it was both studying their authenticity and using them to determine the nature of Kennedy's wounds.

In late June 1978, a security officer working for the committee noticed something irregular about the materials. Someone had apparently taken them out and looked at them, and one color photo had been taken out of its sleeve. The FBI was called in. After agents fingerprinted the autopsy materials and the people who had access to the safe, it was soon discovered that Blahut was the culprit.

There followed a rather complicated series of events in which Blahut was repeatedly questioned about the matter, and he gave inconsistent answers and apparently lied. The upshot was that the CIA fired Blahut, although Chief Counsel Robert Blakey declined to make a public issue of Blahut's misconduct (which eventually leaked to the *Washington Post*).[30]

This episode was a fiasco, most certainly, but what did it mean?

Conspiracists, of course, are convinced it was sinister, although some are rather vague. Matthew Smith, for example, says, "The incident [was] seemingly attributed to Blahut's curiosity, he was fired and the matter was left at that. Any deeper motives were never brought to light."[31] Others are slightly more pointed. Anthony Summers claims, "One of the pictures that had attracted his [Blahut's] specific interest was the photograph of the late President's head. The pictures of the head are, of course, at the center of controversy over the source of the shot or shots that caused the President's fatal head injury."[32] Robert Groden reports that having "discovered" that the photos of the back of Kennedy's head were forged, he had reported it to Blakey only one week before Blahut examined the photos, "specifically the one of the back of the head."[33]

Given the conspiracists' insistence that the autopsy photos had been tampered with in order to show two shots from behind (consistent with Oswald as the lone shooter), one might wonder whether Blahut was somehow involved in the supposed tampering. Did he have a photo lab in his briefcase that allowed him to make the appropriate modifications and then sneak the photos back into the HSCA safe? Anybody familiar with photo technology of the 1970s will quickly dismiss this idea.

But what are the other possibilities? Conspiracy author Jim DiEugenio offers a different theory. After suggesting that Blahut might be connected with the CIA's Office of Security, he asserts,

> One of the functions of the Office of Security (OS), is to keep tabs on potential enemies of the Agency. It tracks potential threats by surveillance and other means and does its best to neutralize them. If Blahut had an OS file, it could reveal if his function was to monitor the HSCA and ward off any destabilizing acts the Committee would take against the CIA.[34]

It's perfectly plausible that CIA officials working with the committee would report to their bosses what the committee was doing. But why did Blahut have to access (and leave his fingerprints on) the autopsy materials?

If the CIA bosses had been paying any attention at all (and the conspiracists believe they were paying intense attention), they already knew what the photos and X-rays showed. Two blue-ribbon panels of scientists—one appointed by Attorney General Ramsey Clark in 1968 and another working for the Rockefeller Commission in the mid-1970s—concluded that two and only two bullets hit Kennedy, both from behind, and inflicted wounds entirely consistent with a lone shooter in the Texas School Book Depository.[35] In both cases, the conclusions were based on study of the autopsy photos and X-rays. Did they think the photos and X-rays had changed since the last two times they were examined? And why would they assign Blahut to examine the materials, especially given that he had no medical expertise that would allow him to actually understand what he was viewing?

If they did task Blahut to examine the photos and X-rays, he did an absurdly incompetent job, arousing suspicion through his actions and leaving his fingerprints all over the materials. Admittedly, the CIA can seem terribly incompetent at times. Their attempts to kill Fidel Castro remind one more of Wile E. Coyote chasing the Road Runner than the actions of the top intelligence agency in the Free World. But what kind of spook doesn't know how to surreptitiously examine documents without getting his fingerprints on them? Had he not been fired for misconduct, he should have been fired for incompetence.

Conspiracists often seem convinced that the CIA and FBI are, even to this day, intensely concerned with the assassination and constantly scheming to continue the cover-up. In reality, people tasked in either agency to deal with the JFK assassination are going to be people who can be spared from more pressing tasks such as fighting the Cold War (in the 1970s and 1980s) or fighting terrorism (since 9/11).

THE SUPPOSED CIA PHOTOS OF OSWALD IN MEXICO CITY

Lee Oswald's trip to Mexico City in late September 1963, as part of his plan to get a visa to enter Communist Cuba, has been the source of huge controversy in assassination literature. Given that it reinforces a picture of Oswald as a leftist and as a restless dreamer who always schemed to make himself the important person he thought he should be, it's not surprising that a fair number of conspiracy theorists believe he never actually went to Mexico City but rather was impersonated.[36] As Michael Benson's *Who's Who in the JFK Assassination* puts it,

> The problem with this [Warren Commission] scenario is that there is much evidence that it is fake. Photographs, claimed by the CIA to be taken of Oswald in Mexico City show an entirely different man. Sound recordings, now reportedly destroyed, of "Oswald" speaking with a Soviet official are of a man with a rudimentary knowledge of Russian; the real Oswald was fluent. Witnesses in Mexico City who saw Oswald have described a different man from the one who was arrested in Dallas less than two months later.[37]

The evidence that raises "suspicion" is in fact pretty extensive, but nothing is more suspicious than the fact that the CIA initially claimed to have photographed Oswald in Mexico City and even sent photos of Oswald to the United States late on the evening of the assassination. But everything then blew up in the agents' faces. The man in the photos clearly wasn't Oswald.

That the CIA could not produce any photos of Oswald at either the Cuban or the Soviet embassies, in spite of the fact that Oswald had visited the Cuban embassy three times and the Soviet embassy twice, is certainly suspicious. A simple camera malfunction would seem a reasonable enough excuse, but not that many malfunctions.

But what does the photo mishap mean? It most certainly doesn't support the hoary notion that the man in the CIA photographs was in fact an Oswald impostor. In the first place, why would conspirators send somebody who looks nothing like Oswald to impersonate him? And if the CIA had any photos of Oswald, then why wouldn't they produce them? Indeed, that the CIA's Mexico City station sent a photo of a fellow who clearly wasn't Oswald to Dallas reeks of incompetence. If the agency knew the fellow was not Oswald, then why not immediately wheel out the "our cameras were broken" excuse (which it used later)? If the agency *didn't* know the fellow wasn't Oswald, then that absolves the CIA (or at least the Mexico City station) of any conspiratorial machinations surrounding this issue.[38]

Could it be that somebody was with Oswald in the photographs, particularly somebody whom the CIA would not want to be associated with Oswald in the minds of investigators or the public? Could it, perchance, be Oswald's CIA handler? The theory's not very likely, since it would be absurdly bad spy craft for a CIA agent to be seen standing with an asset, out in the open, in front of a Communist embassy. The Cubans and the Russians could have seen them or photographed them too.

Could it have been somebody with Communist or leftist connections? This idea begins to sound a bit more plausible. There are some accounts of Oswald hanging around with local leftists while he was in Mexico City, and it's far from impossible that he might have been photographed with one.[39] Indeed, something as innocuous as Lee asking a KGB agent (whom he may not have even known was a KGB agent) for directions would have set off alarm bells. Given the Cold War atmosphere of the time, what Washington feared most was talk of a Communist plot to kill Kennedy. That scenario risked nuclear war. Other kinds of conspiracy talk did not.

Of course, Oswald made multiple trips to the two Communist embassies. Were there not *some* photos from any of his visits that could have been safely released and showed that Oswald was in Mexico City without raising the specter of a Communist plot? And the photos that were actually released of the anonymous embassy visitor were tightly cropped (see photo insert), with the background and any other person who might have been in the photos cut out.[40] Couldn't whoever was suspicious have simply been cropped out so that some photos could be released?

Sherlock Holmes once said, "Once you eliminate the impossible, whatever remains, no matter how improbable, must be the truth." As detailed in chapter 11, Lee Oswald was clearly in Mexico City and did visit the Cuban and Soviet embassies. Eliminating the impossible—that Lee Oswald never went to Mexico City— leaves the improbable reality that the CIA simply failed to photograph him while he was there.

THE BAG TO NOWHERE

A key artifact in the assassination (see chapter 11) was the brown paper bag that Lee Oswald apparently used to bring the Mannlicher-Carcano rifle to work on November 22. According to Oswald's coworker Wesley Frazier, Oswald said the bag contained curtain rods, but it almost certainly contained Oswald's rifle.

Given the centrality of the paper bag in the assassination, it certainly sounds suspicious that another paper bag, addressed to Lee Oswald, turned up in a dead-letter bin at a post office near Oswald's rooming house in the Oak Cliff section of Dallas. But it did happen. According to conspiracy author Anthony Summers,

> On December 4, 1963, an undeliverable package addressed to "Lee Harvey Oswald" was retrieved from the dead-letter section of a post office in a Dallas suburb. It was wrongly addressed to 601 W. Nassaus Street, which could approximate Neches Street, which was near where Oswald had lived. When opened, it turned out to contain a "brown paper bag made of fairly heavy brown paper which was open at both ends." Since it seems unlikely that a postal worker would have tossed aside a package addressed to "Lee Oswald" *after* the name became world-famous on November 22, it is reasonable to suppose the parcel arrived before the assassination. Who sent it to Oswald, and why, are questions that appear especially pertinent with the knowledge that another paper bag became key evidence.[41]

But just how is it "especially pertinent"? In the first place, is it really certain that the bag arrived at the post office before November 22? One can easily imagine a rather harried postal worker looking at the address after the assassination, seeing the name Lee Oswald, and thinking, "Some joker we have here." Then, instead of bothering to raise a ruckus, he might have simply put it in a bin with other misaddressed mail.

But if the bag is pertinent, just what does it mean? Perhaps a coconspirator of Oswald's was assigned to make the bag and then mail it to him so he could use it to bring the Mannlicher-Carcano to the depository. To posit this idea is to admit that Oswald was a conspirator and that at least the original plan was to use a brown paper bag to bring a rifle to the depository. This possibility is way more than most conspiracists are willing to concede.

But then the coconspirator, instead of mailing the bag to Oswald's correct address or even mailing it to a correct previous address, mailed it to an address that had nothing to do with Oswald, except having been in the neighborhood of a former apartment shared by Lee and Marina on Beckley Street. And the coconspirator misspelled that street name. A pretty sloppy conspiracy.

So, if this bag didn't get to Lee, what bag did Lee use? Presumably, Lee fabricated the bag that Wesley Frazier saw in Lee's hands the morning of the assassination, since both the paper and the tape used to hold it together matched the paper and tape in the depository's mail room.[42] The alternative to believing that Oswald fabricated the bag is that some conspirator snuck into the depository and did it. But, remember, to take the second bag—mailed to Oswald at a nowhere address—seriously as part of the assassination plot, we must believe Oswald was a coconspirator. And if he were, then why not just have him fabricate the bag himself?

Just as much of the "evidence" in this case, the misaddressed bag exudes a strong conspiratorial aura, but it can't pass the test of asking, what was its point?

MARXIST MARINE

Conspiracy books find it odd indeed that Lee Oswald, a member of the U.S. Marine Corps, spouted Marxist doctrine and yet was not punished or kicked out of the corps for doing so. According to the *Warren Commission Report*,

> Oswald's interest in Russia and developing ideological attachment to theoretical communism apparently dominated his stay at El Toro. He was still withdrawn from most of his fellows, although his special interests appear to have made him stand out more there than he had at other posts and to have given him a source for conversation which he had hitherto lacked. . . . His reading acquired direction; books like "Das Kapital" and Orwell's "Animal Farm" and "1984" are mentioned in the testimony concerning this period. He played chess; according to one of his opponents he chose the red pieces, expressing a preference for the "Red Army."[43]

And further:

> Oswald studied Marxism after he joined the Marines and his sympathies in that direction and for the Soviet Union appear to have been widely known, at least in the unit to which he was assigned after his return from the Far East. His interest in Russia led some of his associates to call him "comrade"

or "Oswaldskovitch." . . . He studied the Russian language, read a Russian language newspaper and seemed interested in what was going on in the Soviet Union.[44]

None of this behavior reflects the way one would expect an American Marine to act. That Oswald did, and without facing any official consequences, raises the question of whether some intelligence agency was "running" him as an agent or asset.

How Bureaucrats Behave

So why didn't Oswald's superiors in the Marine Corps toss him out? Even if he could not be court-martialed, his superiors had all sorts of possible means of giving him a discharge. One tempting explanation is that they were just incompetent. HSCA chief counsel Blakey told *Frontline*,

> In retrospect, I think that what this indicates—and this was the judgment of the committee—is that our own people aren't as efficient as we might think they ought to be, that more often than not, it's Keystone Cops you know, and not stainless-steel efficiency, and that we drew, ultimately, no sinister inference from our own people's failure to take action, or even to investigate Oswald in any way.[45]

It's always tempting to accuse bureaucrats of incompetence, but is that actually necessary here? Oswald had a security clearance, but it was only "confidential": the lowest level of clearance.[46] Perhaps more important, he was relegated to duties far from anything sensitive. His buddy Kerry Thornley described Lee's time at the Marine Corps Air Station El Toro: "At that time his assignments and activities were primary [*sic*] janitorial. He was—he had lost his clearance previously, and if I remember, he was assigned to make the coffee, mow the lawn, swab down decks, and things of this nature."[47]

So maybe Oswald's superior officers had better things to do than get on the case of a sad-sack Marine who had no access to classified materials and was at most a minor irritant to his fellow soldiers.

Think Scenario

Before coming to a conclusion, one needs to ask: If some intelligence agency were protecting Oswald, what was the point? If Oswald were spying for somebody—say, the KGB—then drawing attention to himself would seem utterly irrational. But suppose Oswald was being run as an agent, and his handlers were creating a "legend" of Oswald as a troublemaker, malcontent, and left-wing radical? Since that's the way his life *looks*, either he really was that sort or somebody wanted him to look like one.

But what would better serve to create that legend than to have him drummed out of the corps as undesirable on the basis of his leftist beliefs? Why protect him from something that would help build the perfect paper trail for some later time when conspirators needed a likely looking fellow to frame?

Conspiracists have actually claimed that Oswald was sent to spy on his fellow Marines and spouted Marxist rhetoric as a provocateur to coax out any disloyal Marines. But in 1959? And in the Marine Corps? Sending provocateurs to the University of California–Berkeley campus in 1968 might have made sense—indeed the FBI did so as part of its notorious counterintelligence program (COINTELPRO)—but Oswald's Marine unit could hardly have been a hotbed of subversives. There was only one, and the Marines seemed to find him too insignificant to bother with.

FILCHED PHOTO

The Dallas Police, in the wake of the assassination, turned over to federal authorities two different photos of Oswald in his backyard. They ultimately ended up in the Warren Commission's possession. Designated as Commission Exhibits 133-A and 133-B, they have iconic status as evidence showing that Oswald was a left wing-radical who was "ready for anything."

But then it was a bit shocking when a different pose, designated (anachronistically) 133-C, turned up in 1976 during the Schweiker-Hart investigation (which was part of the Church Committee).[48] It was in the possession of Mrs. Geneva Ruth Dees, the widow of Roscoe White. A Dallas cop at the time of the assassination, White had apparently appropriated a copy of the print.

It turns out that Dallas cops who made copies of evidence photos and kept them as souvenirs were not at all rare. R. L. Studebaker of the Dallas Police Department told the HSCA that he had made numerous copies of evidence photos for his fellow officers, and the committee got another copy of 133-C from Officer Stovall.[49] There is, in fact, an entire book based on evidence photos that a Dallas cop named Rusty Livingston took and then stored in a briefcase for thirty years.[50]

But finding extra copies is not nearly so disturbing as the fact that no one gave copies of photo 133-C to the Warren Commission during the initial investigation. Is this an example of "suppression of evidence"? To consider this idea, first one needs to answer that simple question: what would be the point of suppressing this evidence? Photo 133-C shows exactly what the other two photos do—that is, Oswald with a rifle in his hands and a revolver in a holster, holding two left-wing newspapers in his other hand, and wearing an all-black outfit. It contains absolutely zero evidence of any conspiracy, although it's more (but entirely redundant) evidence of Oswald's left-wing fantasies.

NON-JFK EXAMPLE: WORLD TRADE CENTER 7

On September 11, 2001, a terrorist attack destroyed the Twin Towers of the World Trade Center (WTC) in New York and damaged the Pentagon in Arlington, Virginia. Damage to another target in Washington, D.C., was prevented when heroic passengers on United Flight 93 fought terrorists for control of the jetliner, bringing the plane down in Pennsylvania. Little noticed at the time but now looming large in conspiracy literature was the collapse of WTC Building 7, which occurred seven hours after the Twin Towers fell. The 9/11 Truthers believe the Twin Towers were brought down by a controlled demolition and that they have the "smoking gun" that proves that WTC 7 was also destroyed by a controlled demolition, contrary to the claims of government officials.

Real estate magnate Larry Silverstein, who owned the lease on the building, told the Public Broadcasting Service,

> I remember getting a call from the fire department commander, telling me that they were not sure they were gonna be able to contain the fire, and I said, "We've had such terrible loss of life, maybe the smartest thing to do is pull it." And they made that decision to pull and we watched the building collapse.[51]

The Truthers then go on to explain that "pull it" means to bring a building down in a controlled demolition. So, in their view, the government lied. The building was brought down intentionally, presumably as part of a plot to mobilize the American people to fight a war on terrorism that would profit all the usual suspects.

With this issue, as with all claimed conspiracies, there are plenty of untidy elements. Via a public relations staffer, Silverstein claimed that there was a contingent of firefighters in the building, and he was giving instructions to pull that group out. But it appears there were no firefighters in the building at the time.[52] Before deciding that Silverstein was lying, however, one should ask how plausible it is that the demolition of WTC 7 was part of some 9/11 conspiracy.

First, one should determine whether Silverstein himself was part of the conspiracy. If he was not, why would conspirators bother to ask his permission to destroy his building? That is, if he was not, he was one of the people they were conspiring *against*. And if he was, why would he admit that he ordered the building demolished? And wasn't the demolition of WTC 7 planned by the conspirators from the beginning? Why did they need to consult him about it? And if it wasn't planned from the beginning, was the demolition just a brilliant improvisation, with the conspirators seeing that they had an opportunity to bring another building down and then planting explosives on the spur of the moment?

The more fundamental question is, given the mayhem that had already happened, why bring down one more building, which would barely be noticed? A Lexis/Nexis search of "major world publications" for September 11–14, 2001, shows 1,964 mentions of the various terms used for the Twin Towers buildings.[53] Meanwhile, a search of the same sources over the same period shows only 91 mentions of "Seven World Trade Center" or "World Trade Center 7" or "World Trade Center Seven."[54] The destruction of WTC 7 simply was swamped, in public perceptions, by the mayhem elsewhere. After the destruction of the iconic Twin Towers, it was a sideshow. If some conspiracy wanted to convince Americans of the need for a war on terrorism, the collapse of WTC 7 added nothing significant to the horror of that day.

ASKING THE "SCENARIO" QUESTION

When any piece of conspiracy evidence implies an absurd scenario, a researcher can pretty much disregard it. Admittedly, all kinds of different problems could lead to this sort of evidence. Much of the conspiracy evidence discussed in this chapter is simply noise and not signal. There is little reason to doubt that Lillian Mooneyham saw somebody on the depository's sixth floor (or even actually in the sniper's nest) after the shooting. It's just that given her time frame, the sighting of an assassin isn't plausible. Witnesses are fallible. The anomalies surrounding the Oswalds' luggage probably fit this category too. Simple inattention or confusion on the part of the witnesses could easily account for the Oswalds' lost bags.

But the "noise" is seldom pure noise. The Alice, Texas, sightings of Lee seem to result from a systematic process wherein the image of the Oswald family seen after the assassination (Oswald, wife who spoke no English, babe in arms) and the stereotype of an unkempt, slovenly, radical beatnik seem to have (more or less) matched some real people who were seen in southern Texas. These images then merged in the memories of sincere but mistaken witnesses. These sightings fit very well a scenario involving "memory as a reconstruction," in which different elements become conflated to produce a memory that, while sincerely believed, is bogus.

Likewise, Roger Craig's story about the three spent cartridges all lined up in a row facing in the same direction (discussed in chapter 4) is hardly noise. It fits a theory of a witness continually embroidering his testimony to make it more and more interesting and more and more conspiratorial. Julia Ann Mercer is similar to Craig. She immediately came to believe that the little tableau involving the stalled truck was part of a conspiracy, and she probably later came to believe that she had really seen Jack Ruby at the wheel. But her story, like Craig's, got better over time. In the 1980s, she told Henry Hurt that the man she saw taking the gun case out of the back of the truck was Lee Oswald, yet this observation was not part of her story in the 1960s. Not only do FBI reports fail to show her fingering Oswald, but also the account she gave the Garrison investigation does not involve Oswald. Garrison, in *Heritage of Stone*, ridicules the notion that she might have identified Oswald.[55]

It is true that in the presence of data known to be reliable, people might re- vise their opinion about what is plausible. Authentic photos of Lee Oswald in Alice, Texas, would require everyone to radically rethink his movements in the weeks before the assassination. A CIA document outlining a plan to send Oswald to the Soviet Union might make folks reconsider whether something really was amiss with his receiving a visa that was issued quicker than usual. And a photograph of a worker planting demolition charges in WTC 7 would make Americans question the official explanation of what occurred on 9/11.

But the evidence cited in the ordinary conspiracy book can't override com- monsense ideas about how the world works. Conspiratorial machinations have a purpose. If after canvassing all the possibilities, one can't see any conspiratorial pur- pose, it's not conspiracy evidence. If you can't imagine why a conspiracy would want to do a particular thing, it probably didn't.

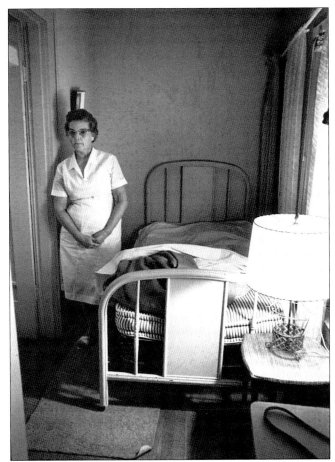

Oswald's landlady, Mrs. Gladys Johnson, in a photo of Oswald's room taken on the afternoon of the assassination.
ALLAN GRANT/*LIFE*

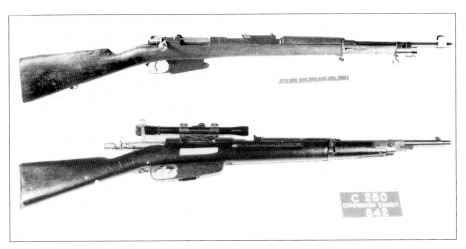

Bolt action rifles: Mauser (top) and Oswald's Mannlicher-Carcano (with bolt open). COURTESY OF JOSIAH THOMPSON

This rendering from a three-dimensional model of the single bullet trajectory by Dale Myers shows the view from a scope on a rifle in the sniper's nest at the moment the single bullet was fired—as seen in Zapruder film, frame 223. © 1995–2010 DALE K. MYERS. ALL RIGHTS RESERVED.

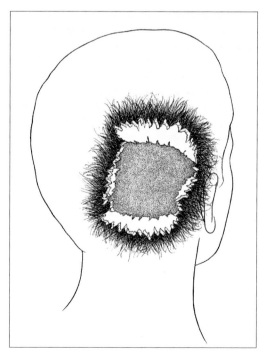

The "McClelland drawing" from Josiah Thompson's book *Six Seconds in Dallas*, illustrating a common conspiracy theory interpretation of Kennedy's head wound. The image, in fact, was not drawn or approved by Dr. Robert McClelland, but rather drawn by an artist based on McClelland's verbal description. COURTESY OF JOSIAH THOMPSON

Scene from Dealey Plaza shortly after the shooting. A figure in a suit, known as Agent (real identity unknown), supposedly picked up a bullet. © Corbis

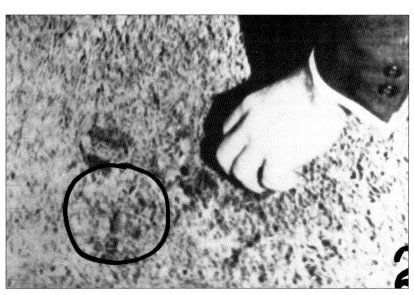

Blowup of the Dealey Plaza photo. The circled object is supposedly a slug. © Corbis

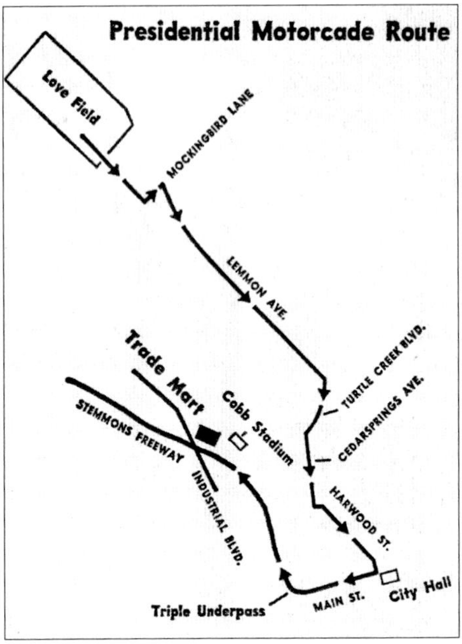

Map of the motorcade route, which appeared in the November 22, 1963, edition of the *Dallas Morning News*, fails to show the turn on Houston and Elm Streets. © 1963 DALLAS MORNING NEWS

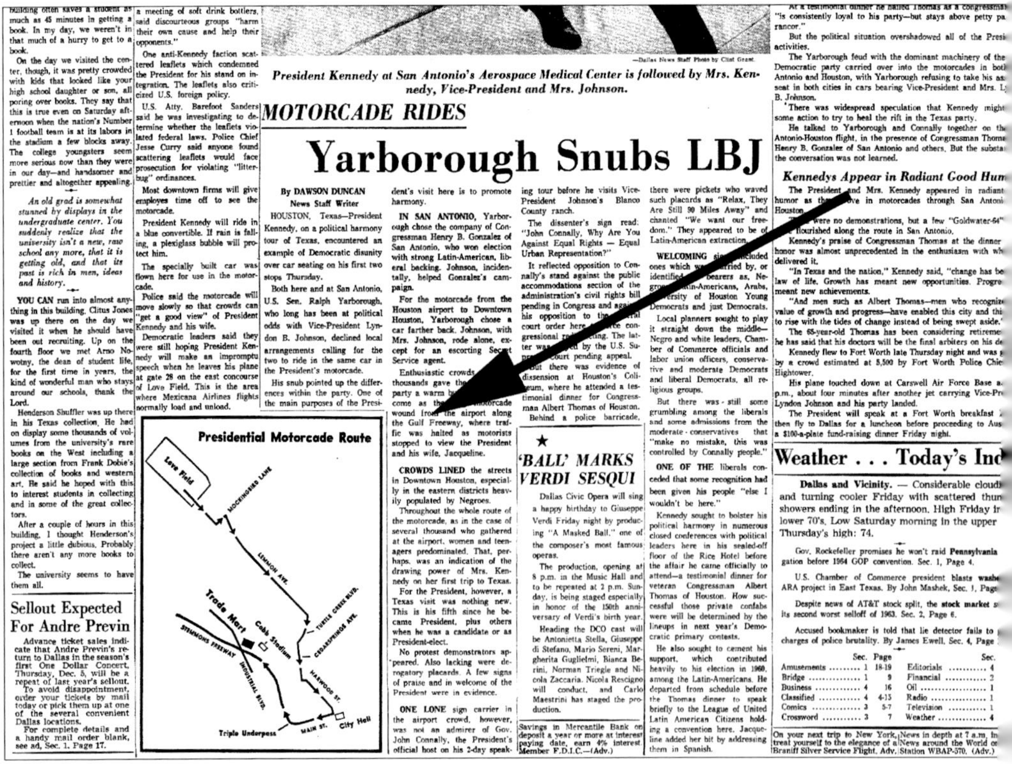

building often saves a student as much as 45 minutes in getting a book. In my day, we weren't in that much of a hurry to get to a book.

On the day we visited the center, though, it was pretty crowded with kids that looked like your high school daughter or son, all poring over books. They say that this is true even on Saturday afternoon when the nation's Number 1 football team is at its labors in the stadium a few blocks away. The college youngsters seem more serious now than they were in our day—and handsomer and prettier and altogether appealing.

An old grad is somewhat stunned by displays in the undergraduate center. You suddenly realize that the university isn't a new, raw school any more, that it is getting old, and that its past is rich in men, ideas and history.

YOU CAN run into almost anything in this building. Clitus Jones was up there on the day we visited it when he should have been out recruiting. Up on the fourth floor we met Arno Nowotny, the dean of student life, for the first time in years, the kind of wonderful man who stays around our schools, thank the Lord.

Henderson Shuffler was up there in his Texas collection. He had on display some thousands of volumes from the university's rare books on the West including a large section from Frank Dobie's collection of books and western art. He said he hoped with this to interest students in collecting and in some of the great collectors.

After a couple of hours in this building, I thought Henderson's project a little dubious. Probably there aren't any more books to collect.

The university seems to have them all.

Sellout Expected For Andre Previn

Advance ticket sales indicate that Andre Previn's return to Dallas in the season's first One Dollar Concert, Thursday, Dec. 5, will be a repeat of last year's sellout.

To avoid disappointment, order your tickets by mail today or pick them up at one of the several convenient Dallas locations.

For complete details and a handy mail order blank, see ad, Sec. 1, Page 17.

a meeting of soft drink bottlers, said discourteous groups "harm their own cause and help their opponents."

One anti-Kennedy faction scattered leaflets which condemned the President for his stand on integration. The leaflets also criticized U.S. foreign policy.

U.S. Atty. Barefoot Sanders said he was investigating to determine whether the leaflets violated federal laws. Police Chief Jesse Curry said anyone found scattering leaflets would face prosecution for violating "litterbug" ordinances.

Most downtown firms will give employes time off to see the motorcade.

President Kennedy will ride in a blue convertible. If rain is falling, a plexiglass bubble will protect him.

The specially built car was flown here for use in the motorcade.

Police said the motorcade will move slowly so that crowds can "get a good view" of President Kennedy and his wife.

Democratic leaders said they were still hoping President Kennedy will make an impromptu speech when he leaves his plane at gate 28 on the east concourse of Love Field. This is the area where Mexicana Airlines flights normally load and unload.

Presidential Motorcade Route

—Dallas News Staff Photo by Clint Grant.

President Kennedy at San Antonio's Aerospace Medical Center is followed by Mrs. Kennedy, Vice-President and Mrs. Johnson.

MOTORCADE RIDES

Yarborough Snubs LBJ

By DAWSON DUNCAN
News Staff Writer

HOUSTON, Texas—President Kennedy, on a political harmony tour of Texas, encountered an example of Democratic disunity over car seating on his first two stops Thursday.

Both here and at San Antonio, U.S. Sen. Ralph Yarborough, who long has been at political odds with Vice-President Lyndon B. Johnson, declined local arrangements calling for the two to ride in the same car in the President's motorcade.

His snub pointed up the differences within the party. One of the main purposes of the President's visit here is to promote harmony.

IN SAN ANTONIO, Yarborough chose the company of Congressman Henry B. Gonzalez of San Antonio, who won election with strong Latin-American, liberal backing. Johnson, incidentally, helped Gonzalez's campaign.

For the motorcade from the Houston airport to Downtown Houston, Yarborough chose a car farther back. Johnson, with Mrs. Johnson, rode alone, except for an escorting Secret Service agent.

Enthusiastic crowds thousands gave th party a warm b come as th motorcade wound fro the airport along the Gulf Freeway, where traffic was halted as motorists stopped to view the President and his wife, Jacqueline.

CROWDS LINED the streets in Downtown Houston, especially in the eastern districts heavily populated by Negroes.

Throughout the whole route of the motorcade, as in the case of several thousand who gathered at the airport, women and teenagers predominated. That, perhaps, was an indication of the drawing power of Mrs. Kennedy on her first trip to Texas.

For the President, however, a Texas visit was nothing new. This is his fifth since he became President, plus others when he was a candidate or as President-elect.

No protest demonstrators appeared. Also lacking were derogatory placards. A few signs of praise and in welcome of the President were in evidence.

ONE LONE sign carrier in the airport crowd, however, was not an admirer of Gov. John Connally, the President's official host on his 2-day speaking tour before he visits Vice-President Johnson's Blanco County ranch.

The dissenter's sign read: "John Connally, Why Are You Against Equal Rights — Equal Urban Representation?"

It reflected opposition to Connally's stand against the public accommodations section of the administration's civil rights bill pending in Congress and aga his opposition to the ral court order here ce congressional re ting. The latter wa d by the U.S. Supr ourt pending appeal.

ut there was evidence of dissension at Houston's Coli eum, where he attended a testimonial dinner for Congressman Albert Thomas of Houston.

Behind a police barricade, there were pickets who waved such placards as "Relax, They Are Still 90 Miles Away" and chanted "We want our freedom." They appeared to be of Latin-American extraction.

WELCOMING si cluded ones which w rried by, or identifie bearers as, Negro in-Americans, Arabs, ersity of Houston Young Democrats and just Democrats.

Local planners sought to play it straight down the middle—Negro and white leaders, Chamber of Commerce officials and labor union officers, conservative and moderate Democrats and liberal Democrats, all religious groups.

But there was still some grumbling among the liberals and some admissions from the moderate-conservatives that "make no mistake, this was controlled by Connally people."

ONE OF THE liberals conceded that some recognition had been given his people "else I wouldn't be here."

Kennedy sought to bolster his political harmony in numerous closed conferences with political leaders here in his sealed-off floor of the Rice Hotel before the affair he came officially to attend—a testimonial dinner for veteran Congressman Albert Thomas of Houston. How successful those private confabs were will be determined by the lineups in next year's Democratic primary contests.

He also sought to cement his support, which contributed heavily to his election in 1960, among the Latin-Americans. He departed from schedule before the Thomas dinner to speak briefly to the League of United Latin American Citizens holding a convention here. Jacqueline added her bit by addressing them in Spanish.

★

'BALL' MARKS VERDI SESQUI

Dallas Civic Opera will sing a happy birthday to Giuseppe Verdi Friday night by producing "A Masked Ball," one of the composer's most famous operas.

The production, opening at 8 p.m. in the Music Hall and to be repeated at 2 p.m. Sunday, is being staged especially in honor of the 150th anniversary of Verdi's birth year.

Heading the DCO cast will be Antonietta Stella, Giuseppe di Stefano, Mario Sereni, Margherita Guglielmi, Bianca Berini, Norman Triegle and Nicola Zaccaria. Nicola Rescigno will conduct, and Carlo Maestrini has staged the production.

Savings in Mercantile Bank on deposit a year or more at interest paying date, earn 4% interest. Member F.D.I.C.—(Adv.)

At a testimonial dinner he hailed Thomas as a congressma "is consistently loyal to his party—but stays above petty pa rancor."

But the political situation overshadowed all of the Presi activities.

The Yarborough feud with the dominant machinery of the Democratic party carried over into the motorcades in both Antonio and Houston, with Yarborough refusing to take his as seat in both cities in cars bearing Vice-President and Mrs. Ly B. Johnson.

There was widespread speculation that Kennedy might some action to try to heal the rift in the Texas party.

He talked to Yarborough and Connally together on the Antonio-Houston flight, in the presence of Congressman Thoma Henry B. Gonzalez of San Antonio and others. But the substa the conversation was not learned.

Kennedys Appear in Radiant Good Hum

The President and Mrs. Kennedy appeared in radiant humor as th ve in motorcades through San Antoni Houston.

ere no demonstrations, but a few "Goldwater-64" flourished along the route in San Antonio.

Kennedy's praise of Congressman Thomas at the dinner honor was almost unprecedented in the enthusiasm with wh delivered it.

"In Texas and the nation," Kennedy said, "change has be law of life. Growth has meant new opportunities. Progre meant new achievements.

"And men such as Albert Thomas—men who recogniz value of growth and progress—have enabled this city and thi to rise with the tides of change instead of being swept aside."

The 65-year-old Thomas has been considering retireme he has said that his doctors will be the final arbiters on his de

Kennedy flew to Fort Worth late Thursday night and was by a crowd estimated at 5,500 by Fort Worth Police Chie Hightower.

His plane touched down at Carswell Air Force Base a p.m., about four minutes after another jet carrying Vice-Pr Lyndon Johnson and his party landed.

The President will speak at a Fort Worth breakfast then fly to Dallas for a luncheon before proceeding to Aus a $100-a-plate fund-raising dinner Friday night.

Weather . . . Today's Ind

Dallas and Vicinity. — Considerable cloudi and turning cooler Friday with scattered thun showers ending in the afternoon. High Friday ir lower 70's. Low Saturday morning in the upper Thursday's high: 74.

Gov. Rockefeller promises he won't raid **Pennsylvania** gation before 1964 GOP convention. Sec. 1, Page 4.

U.S. Chamber of Commerce president blasts **washe** ARA project in East Texas. By John Mashek, Sec. 1, Page

Despite news of AT&T stock split, the **stock market** s its second worst selloff of 1963. Sec. 2, Page 6.

Accused bookmaker is told that lie detector fails to charges of police brutality. By James Ewell, Sec. 4, Page

	Sec.	Page		Sec.
Amusements	1	18-19	Editorials	4
Bridge	1	9	Financial	2
Business	4	16	Oil	1
Classified	4	4-15	Radio	1
Comics	3	5-7	Television	1
Crossword	3	7	Weather	4

On your next trip to New York, treat yourself to the elegance of a Braniff Silver Service Flight. Adv.

News in depth at 7 a.m. In News around the World o Station WBAP-570. (Adv.)

Bottom half of front page, November 22, 1963, edition of the *Dallas Morning News*, showing the motorcade route map in context. © 1963 DALLAS MORNING NEWS

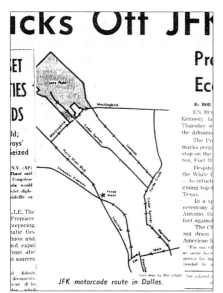

icks Off JFK

From November 21 issue of the *Dallas Times Herald*, map of the motorcade route showing the turn onto Houston and Elm Streets. © 1963 *DALLAS MORNING NEWS*

JFK motorcade route in Dallas.

Phil Willis's slide 8 shows a man with a receding hairline, thought by some to be Jack Ruby, standing near the Texas School Book Depository shortly after the shooting. © 1964 THE SIXTH FLOOR MUSEUM AT DEALEY PLAZA

Dallas Police Department photograph showing evidence collected from the Paine residence on November 22, 1963, including Minox light meter and empty Minox case (highlighted). COURTESY OF THE SIXTH FLOOR MUSEUM AT DEALEY PLAZA/R. W. "RUSTY" LIVINGSTON COLLECTION

Blowup of the evidence photo, showing empty Minox camera case. Courtesy of the Sixth Floor Museum at Dealey Plaza/R. W. "Rusty" Livingston Collection

Another blowup showing the Minox light meter. Courtesy of the Sixth Floor Museum at Dealey Plaza/R. W. "Rusty" Livingston Collection

Warren Commission Exhibit 5: a photo, found among Oswald's possessions, of the back of Gen. Edwin Walker's house. The license plate of a parked car has been torn out. Courtesy of the Mary Ferrell Archives

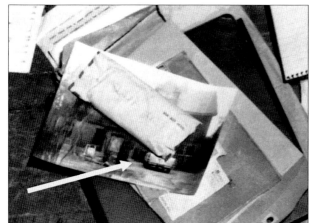

A photo of evidence spread out on the floor at the Dallas Police Department. The license plate appears intact, suggesting police or FBI tampering after this photo was taken. COURTESY OF TEXAS STATE LIBRARY AND ARCHIVES COMMISSION

Blowup of evidence photo shows that the license plate is indeed missing. NATIONAL ARCHIVES PHOTO, SCAN COURTESY OF JOHN HUNT

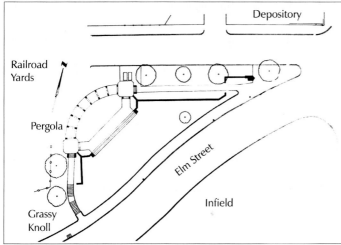

Map of Dealey Plaza. Adapted by the author from a drawing for the House Select Committee on Assassinations. HSCA DRAWING COURTESY OF THE NATIONAL ARCHIVES

The "Mystery Man" in Mexico City, briefly thought by the CIA to have been Lee Oswald. COURTESY OF THE MARY FERRELL ARCHIVES

Comm. Exh. 237

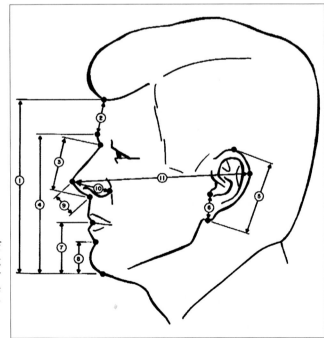

Metric characteristics of the human face, showing measurements used by House Select Committee scientists. 6 HSCA 237

Chapter Eleven

Not All Evidence Is Equal: Using Reliable Evidence

It sounds like a truism: base your conclusions on the most reliable evidence, not the least reliable. But why is that so often ignored?

One reason is that reliable evidence is pretty sparse, buried in a great mass of testimony from mistaken or lying witnesses, documents from clueless bureaucrats, people "confessing" that they killed Kennedy, photo "experts" who see things in photos that aren't there, and so forth. Focusing on the most reliable evidence violates the collector's instinct of conspiracy theorists. They collect evidence assiduously, and whoever has the biggest collection is the best researcher—just as the best stamp collector is one who has the largest number and the rarest stamps.

If you pride yourself on having discovered a particularly rare and arcane bit of "evidence," the temptation to build a theory around it is strong. Thus author Dick Russell, having access to a fellow named Richard Case Nagell, writes an 824-page book around the tales of a man who was certifiably insane.[1] And Ray and Mary La Fontaine, having discovered the testimony of one John Elrod, who claimed to have been a cell mate of Oswald's in the Dallas City Jail, built an entire theory around his claims. In reality, it's quite clear that Oswald—the prisoner of the century—never had a cell mate, and Elrod must have been lying.[2]

Once an unreliable piece of evidence is accepted, it is likely to conflict with the reliable evidence in the case, which is why conspiracy books are rife with claims of evidence tampering, faked documents and photos, witnesses pressured by authorities, and so on.

We have already considered some examples of hard evidence settling an issue. The Alyea film destroys the notion that the rifle discovered in the Texas School

Book Depository was a Mauser. And analyses by photo experts trump any notion that two of the three tramps were Hunt and Sturgis, or that a gunman taking aim at Kennedy can be seen in the Nix film. But let's turn to some other issues.

DID OSWALD OWN THE RIFLE?

One central issue in the case is whether Lee Harvey Oswald owned a Mannlicher-Carcano rifle, serial number C2766, Warren Commission Exhibit 139, now housed at the National Archives. The evidence linking him to the weapon is overwhelming. First, there is the paper trail. Klein's Sporting Goods in Chicago received on March 13, 1963, an order coupon for a Mannlicher-Carcano rifle from an "A. Hidell, P.O. Box 2915, Dallas, Texas." It came in an envelope with a handwritten return address identical to the one on the coupon.[3] In the envelope with the order coupon was a money order for $21.45, with the "From" notation "A. Hidell, P.O. Box 2915, Dallas, Texas."[4]

Hidell was an alias Oswald used with some frequency. Found in Oswald's wallet after his arrest were a bogus Selective Service system notice of classification and a bogus certificate of service in the U.S. Marine Corps, both listing "Alek James Hidell." Then there was a bogus smallpox vaccination certificate, supposedly issued by "Dr. A. J. Hideel, P.O. Box 30016, New Orleans, La.," which was found among Oswald's possessions at his rooming house. Finally, when Oswald started a rump chapter of the Fair Play for Cuba Committee in New Orleans, he had Marina sign membership cards with "A. J. Hidell" as chapter president.[5]

The Warren Commission had two documents experts, Alwyn Cole of the Treasury Department and James Cadigan of the FBI, examine the rifle order coupon, the return address on the envelope, and the money order. Both unequivocally stated that the writing was Oswald's.[6] The HSCA, going over the same ground, conducted an informal survey and identified three of the top questioned documents experts in the country: Joseph P. McNally, David Purtell, and Charles C. Scott.[7] McNally unequivocally identified the three handwriting samples as Oswald's.[8] Scott unequivocally identified the handwriting on the money order as Oswald's but quibbled about the writing on the coupon and envelope, pointing out the poor quality of the copy from microfilm. But he did say that "so far as the pictorial aspects of form or design, proportion, alignment, slant and connecting strokes are concerned," the writing corresponded to Oswald's.[9]

Klein's produced a record showing that a Mannlicher-Carcano rifle, serial number C2766, had been shipped to P.O. Box 2915 at the Dallas Post Office, on

March 20, 1963.[10] But what about that box? It was rented to "Lee H. Oswald" on November 9, 1962. The same Treasury and FBI experts examined the handwriting on the application for the box, and found it to be Lee Oswald's, as was the handwriting on a "change of address" form Oswald filed on May 12, 1963, when he moved to New Orleans.[11] HSCA experts McNally, Purtell, and Scott all unequivocally stated that the handwriting on the application for the post office box was that of Oswald.[12] None of the HSCA experts was asked to examine the change of address form.

Conspiracists huff and puff about the fact that there is no evidence that Oswald picked up the rifle at the post office. As Anthony Summers has written, "It was never established that it was he who picked up the package containing the rifle at the post office."[13] A key question was whether any "A. Hidell" was listed as a person allowed to receive mail on the application for the box. Postal Inspector Harry Holmes told the Warren Commission that the part of the application listing the persons entitled to receive mail at the box was, according to postal regulations, thrown away when the box was closed since "it has no more purpose." The main part of the application was endorsed and kept to show that the box was closed.[14] And indeed, the Dallas Post Office was not able to produce the portion of the application showing who was entitled to receive mail.

Conspiracists have jumped all over this. Mark Lane produced postal regulations indicating that "box rental applications and control cards showing payment" should have been kept for two years after the box was closed.[15] Lane also produced a letter from the Special Services Branch of the Post Office Department saying that the "portion of the box rental application, identifying persons other than the applicant authorized to receive mail, must be retained for two years after the box is closed."[16] However, the section of the regulations cited, 846.53h, says nothing about different "parts" of the application, simply saying that "applications" should be kept.[17] Interestingly, the post office in New Orleans kept the portion of Oswald's application that listed the people entitled to receive mail at that address, and "A. J. Hidell" was listed.[18] This fact could be interpreted to show that Holmes was wrong about postal regulations, but since Oswald listed "Hidell" on his New Orleans application, and since he regularly used it as an alias, it's quite plausible that he put it on his Dallas application.

But does any of this matter? In the first place, we might note that conspiracists are happy to claim that authorities faked and forged all the evidence against Oswald. But if so, why didn't they forge this very convenient piece of evidence? Further, did "Hidell" have to be on the list in order for the rifle to be handed over at the Dallas Post Office? Holmes claimed that if a package arrived, a notice was put in the box "regardless of whose name was associated with the box."[19] Holmes gave an example: if his cousin comes to visit him, it would be desirable for the cousin to be able to get mail. Whoever presented the notice at the window was assumed to be a person with a right to the package (they obviously had access to the box, since they had the notice).[20]

Holmes's picture of post office employees doing things the quick and dirty (but also reasonable) way, minimizing hassle for themselves and their customers, rings true.

Conspiracists are capable of quibbling endlessly about the rifle. They even carp about the fact that Klein's apparently sent Oswald a rifle slightly different from the one he ordered.[21] Is this the tip-off to a conspiracy? Is there one sort of "lone assassin" Mannlicher-Carcano, and another sort of "conspiracy assassin" Mannlicher-Carcano, and Klein's gave the entire plot away by sending Oswald the "conspiracy assassin" Mannlicher-Carcano?

LINKING THE RIFLE TO THE CRIME

Several pieces of ballistic evidence link the C2766 rifle to the crime. The first is Commission Exhibit 399, dubbed by conspiracists the "magic bullet." It's extremely controversial, and we'll get back to it when we talk about the Single Bullet Theory.

Also, two fragments, apparently from the head shot, were found in the front seat of the limo after the shooting. Both matched C2766 to the exclusion of all other weapons.[22] Finally, three spent cartridges were found in the sniper's nest in the depository, and all three could be matched to Oswald's rifle to the exclusion of all other weapons.[23]

Fingerprints

On the day of the assassination, J. C. Day of the Dallas Police Identification Bureau lifted a palm print from the barrel of the rifle, from a location that would be underneath the stock and had to have been put on the rifle while it was disassembled. The rifle was abruptly taken out of Day's possession on the evening of the assassination and was spirited away to the FBI in Washington. The FBI failed to find the print, apparently because Day had "lifted" it off.

This, of course, has created the claim that Oswald's palm print was never on the rifle, and is responsible for the scene in the movie *JFK* where the barrel of the rifle is pressed into the dead hand of Oswald as he lies in the morgue. This piece of evidence fakery would have had to happen on Sunday night or Monday morning, but in fact several police officers—including Rusty Livingston, Peter Barnes, H. R. Williams, and Bobby Brown—were around the Dallas Police Identification Bureau before the FBI returned the rifle to Dallas, and testified they saw the print that Day claimed to have lifted.[24]

The Dallas Police also found and photographed some faint ridge formations (very partial fingerprints) on the magazine housing of the Mannlicher-Carcano. The FBI did not consider these prints sufficient to identify the person who made them. But in 1993 the book *First Day Evidence* came out, and with it a cache of evidence, some of which had not been previously fully analyzed. As we have seen with regard to the "third backyard photo" (chapter 10), Dallas cops made copies of various evidence photos, and kept them as souvenirs. One such cop was Rusty Livingston, and he kept a briefcase full of these photos, apparently not knowing that some of them were of evidentiary value, for thirty years.[25] Livingston's briefcase had a set of photos of these ridge formations more complete than the FBI (or anybody else) had seen.[26] In 1993 *Frontline* asked fingerprint expert Vincent Scalice (who had examined the fingerprint evidence for the HSCA) to look at the photos—four in all. He found that they were made at different exposures, lighter exposures picking up some detail and darker exposures picking up other detail. He concluded,

> Using all of the photographs at different contrasts, I was able to find in the neighborhood of about 18 points of identity between the two prints. Well, I feel that this is a major breakthrough in this investigation because we're able for the first time to actually say that these are definitely the fingerprints of Lee Harvey Oswald and that they are on the rifle. There is no doubt about it.[27]

The Backyard Photos

If Oswald ordered the rifle, and if that rifle was the one that shot Kennedy, can we document that the rifle was in Oswald's possession during the intervening months?

I will skip quickly over witness testimony about Oswald owning the Mannlicher-Carcano. In fact, I view as reliable Marina's testimony that Oswald owned at least a bolt-action rifle that looked much like the Mannlicher-Carcano[28]—she could hardly give reliable testimony that it was the precise rifle that Lee ordered.

The next piece of evidence, however, is the backyard photos. These celebrated snapshots show Oswald holding two left-wing newspapers, *The Militant* and *The Worker*, along with the Mannlicher-Carcano. On his hip is a revolver, presumably the one he used to shoot Tippit. He is dressed entirely in black.

The photos are widely, indeed almost universally, denounced as fakes by conspiracists. Jim Marrs, for example, notes that Oswald himself claimed the photos were faked and adds, "Various researchers have spent years studying this incriminating evidence, and today almost all are convinced Oswald was truthful about the pictures being fabricated."[29] And Robert Groden declares that the photos "were subjected to careful analysis by photography experts . . . and were found to be composite pictures: photos of Oswald's head pasted atop someone else's body."[30]

Any theory that the photos were faked has to explain away the witnesses who saw the photos well before the assassination. First there is Marina, who has consistently said that she took the pictures—although over the years her testimony as to where she was standing and how many photos she took has varied.[31] Oswald told her he was going to send a photo to *The Militant* to show that he was "ready for anything."[32] And indeed, he did so. Gus Russo interviewed the woman on *The Militant* staff who opened the envelope that contained Oswald's photo—one Sylvia Weinstein—and she thought the photo "kookie." The fact that Oswald held both Stalinist and Trotskyist papers made her conclude that the fellow was "really dumb and totally naïve," not knowing that the two groups hated each other.[33] This was four months before Oswald's August arrest for handing out leaflets on Canal Street in New Orleans. Conspiracy-oriented researcher Hal Verb also talked to a (male) staffer of *The Militant* who confirmed the receipt of the odd photo of a man with a rifle.[34] The extreme-left-wing paper, fearing some sort of provocation, disposed of the photo and for decades concealed the fact that it had been received by staff.[35]

But what of the supposed evidence of fakery in the photos themselves? Conspiracists have pointed to what they believe to be evidence of tampering. They see inconsistencies in the shadows, and especially in shadows under Oswald's nose. They claim that the backgrounds in the photos are identical, notwithstanding that if Marina moved the camera at all between shots there should be at least minor differences. They claim that all the photos show the exact same expression on Oswald's face, suggesting that a single photo of his face was inserted on somebody else's torso, with the torso in different positions.[36]

The Warren Commission had FBI photo expert Lyndal Sheneyfelt examine the photos, and he authenticated them to the satisfaction of any reasonably minded person.[37] But of course, *that's* not adequate in a case like this, so the HSCA decided on the nuclear option: they had the top photographic experts in the country run every imaginable test. The results, which were devastating to alteration theories, have largely been ignored by conspiracists.

Conspiracists, for example, have argued that the backgrounds in the three photos are identical, which would be extremely unlikely in three genuine photos shot with a hand-held camera, since the person who shot them would move at least slightly. If the backgrounds are in fact identical, it would be evidence for the argument that different "Oswald" bodies had been inserted into the single background to make three supposedly different photos. But the two best photos of the three, designated 133-A and 133-B, constituted a "stereo pair." When a stereo pair is viewed in a stereoscope (much like the Viewmaster that kids all over America used to have), a three-dimensional image is created, because the brain processes the two images in the same way it would if a person were looking at a scene with both eyes. (Two identical images will not produce a stereo effect.) The two backyard images do produce a three-dimensional effect, proving they are authentic, since it's essentially impossible to fake a convincing 3-D image.[38]

Conspiracists have also argued that in some of the photos, a dark line across Oswald's chin, just below the lower lip, indicates that Oswald's face was posted on somebody else's body. In fact Oswald used the so-called chin transplant argument during his interrogation. The HSCA had the original negative of 133-B, and they scanned it at high resolution and enhanced the grain pattern. No inconsistency of grain structure above or below the horizontal chin cleft was found. The line is found only in photos that have been copied through multiple generations, a process that increases contrast.[39]

As for shadows, there is a scientific method to check their consistency: vanishing point analysis. Things that are parallel in the real world (railroad tracks, for example) do not generally look parallel in photos but will instead point toward a "vanishing point," which might or might not be in the photograph. Thus if one draws lines connecting points in a photo (say, the muzzle of Oswald's rifle) through the shadow thrown by each point, all the lines should converge at a single vanishing point. In the backyard photos, they do.[40]

In addition to establishing that the photos show no evidence of fakery, we can also match them to Oswald's Imperial Reflex camera. Cameras, particularly cheap cameras, tend to have imperfections in the film plane aperture. These imperfections will show up on the edge of the negatives they produce, and may also scratch the film as it is wound through. This amounts to a kind of "fingerprint" of a particular device. The HSCA had both the original negative of 133-B and a print of 133-A that was uncropped and showed the very edge of the negative. They perfectly matched test negatives shot with Oswald's Imperial Reflex—indeed there were eleven distinctive marks. Where the scratches on the film were concerned, they were visible on all seven of the prints the HSCA had, and "established that the Oswald backyard photos had been exposed in Oswald's Imperial Reflex camera." [41]

Some conspiracists have argued that fake composite photos were produced and then photographically copied with the Imperial Reflex, thus leaving the distinctive marks of that camera. HSCA scientists tried copying photos with Oswald's camera and found that the copies would be easily detectable, due to a severe drop-off in illumination at the corners and exaggerated pincushion distortion. [42] Very high-quality optics would be required to make convincing copies.

Here, as is frequently the case, some of the best evidence is logical, and not strictly scientific. The Photographic Experts Panel asked why, if the photos were faked, the conspirators would fake three of them, opening up opportunities for the fakery to be discovered. But the most damning argument is that one of the prints, obtained from George De Mohrenschildt, was signed with an inscription "to my friend George from Lee Oswald 5/IV/63." [43] All three HSCA-questioned documents experts—Scott, Purtell, and McNally—unequivocally stated that the signature was Oswald's. [44]

Do the Photos Show the Rifle Used in the Assassination?

HSCA scientists noted that the configuration of the rifle in the backyard photos exactly matches the Mannlicher-Carcano recovered in the Texas School Book Depository. But if it were indeed a Mannlicher-Carcano like Oswald's, was it the same rifle (C2766, produced at the armory in Terni, Italy)? While looking at the photos, the HSCA noted a distinctive mark: a gouge on the forestock of the rifle. This matched the C2766 rifle in the National Archives and was judged to be a "random patterning" and "sufficient to warrant a positive identification." [45]

To connect the dots: Oswald was shipped C2766, and that rifle was recovered in the depository. Either the rifle pictured in Oswald's hands is C2766, or it is another Mannlicher-Carcano that just happens to have an identical gouge in the forestock. So we can go with a simple theory, or we can go with a very complicated one, involving the disappearance of the rifle shipped to Oswald, its replacement with a virtually identical Mannlicher-Carcano for the backyard photos, and then another switcheroo putting C2766 back into the chain of evidence at the depository. That's a lot of ad hoc assumptions, and they get us nowhere in terms of better explaining the evidence.

In Summary

So here we have hard evidence linking Oswald to the rifle, and the rifle to the shooting. Of course, it proves only what it proves, and nothing we have discussed here proves that Oswald shot at Kennedy, nor even that he took the rifle in to work on the morning of the assassination (we'll discuss that later). But the connection between Oswald and the rifle is beyond questioning by reasonable people.

DID LEE OSWALD SHOOT AT GENERAL WALKER?

One prominent citizen of Dallas in 1963 was Edwin Walker, a retired army general, political activist, and right-wing rabble-rouser. According to the Warren Commission, on the evening of April 10 Lee Oswald shot at Walker from the alley behind the general's house. Oswald missed, and then left the scene on foot.[46] If Oswald shot at Walker, it's extremely easy to believe he shot at Kennedy seven months later. Although Kennedy was hardly a right-winger, Oswald may well have believed that the Kennedy administration was engaged in plots on Castro's life (which it was),[47] and if Oswald was motivated by a desire to be a historically important figure, killing Kennedy would trump killing Walker any day.

Needless to say, conspiracists deny that Oswald shot at Walker. The volume *Who's Who in the JFK Assassination* concludes that "the balance of the evidence indicates that Oswald probably had nothing to do with the Walker incident,"[48] and author Gerald McKnight fusses and fumes about every aspect of the issue in fourteen pages of his book *Breach of Trust*.[49] McKnight actually implies that the FBI did not think that Oswald shot at the general, despite the FBI report on the assassination, submitted on December 5, which clearly concluded that Oswald did shoot at Walker.[50]

There are three kinds of evidence here. The first is the testimony of Marina, who told the Warren Commission that Oswald came back very late one night, pale, and told her he had shot at General Walker.[51] Of course, conspiracists routinely say that Marina's testimony was coerced by threats of deportation from the FBI. But note that Marina, long after any such threat would have lost any credibility, continued to say that Lee told her he shot at Walker. She told this to author Priscilla McMillan, to the HSCA,[52] and even Oprah Winfrey on her November 22, 1996, show.[53]

The second sort of evidence is a set of three photos of Walker's house found among Oswald's possessions. The photos were taken with Oswald's Imperial Reflex camera.[54] Anybody who wants to claim that Oswald was not planning to shoot at

Walker needs to come up with an adequate explanation of these photos. The most plausible explanation for the photos is that Oswald was casing the premises, planning a shooting position and an escape route.

But the "killer" piece of evidence is a note that Lee left for Marina. On the night of the Walker shooting, Marina became disturbed that Lee was out so late, and went into his "private office"—a room in the Neely Street apartment where Marina had been forbidden to go. There she found the following note, written in Russian.

1. This is the key to the mailbox which is located in the main post office in the city on Ervay Street. This is the same street where the drugstore, in which you always waited, is located. You will find the mailbox in the post office which is located 4 blocks from the drugstore on that street. I paid for the box last month so don't worry about it.

2. Send the information as to what has happened to me to the Embassy and include newspaper clippings (should there be anything about me in the newspapers). I believe that the Embassy will come quickly to your assistance on learning everything.

3. I paid the house rent on the 2d so don't worry about it.

4. Recently I also paid for water and gas.

5. The money from work will possibly be coming. The money will be sent to our post office box. Go to the bank and cash the check.

6. You can either throw out or give my clothing, etc. away. Do not keep these. However, I prefer that you hold on to my personal papers (military, civil, etc.).

7. Certain of my documents are in the small blue valise.

8. The address book can be found on my table in the study should need same.

9. We have friends here. The Red Cross also will help you [Red Cross in English].

10. I left you as much money as I could, $60 on the second of the month. You and the baby [apparently] can live for another 2 months using $10 per week.

11. If I am alive and taken prisoner, the city jail is located at the end of the bridge through which we always passed on going to the city (right in the beginning of the city after crossing the bridge).[55]

The note is not dated, but the Warren Commission established that all of the references that imply a date (rent, gas, and water paid, and so on) are consistent with the date of the Walker shooting. The note is not signed, but Cadigan testified that it was written by Lee Oswald.[56] HSCA experts reached the same conclusion.[57]

Conspiracists belabor trivia surrounding the Walker shooting, such as the fact that the note was not turned over to police by Mrs. Paine until December 2, or the fact that a witness (Walter Kirk Coleman) saw two men in the parking lot of a Mormon church next door to the Walker house. One of them got in a car and left at a normal rate of speed. Nothing even slightly suggests they were assassins, but Coleman's testimony is enough, in some minds, to "raise questions."[58]

On the other hand, the hard physical evidence—the photos and the note to Marina—leave little doubt. If Oswald wasn't shooting at Walker that night, he was doing something likely to get him locked up or killed.

DID OSWALD BRING HIS RIFLE TO WORK ON THE MORNING OF THE ASSASSINATION?

The night before the assassination, Oswald had stayed over with his wife, Marina, at Ruth Paine's house in Irving, Texas. Paine was a neighbor of Oswald's coworker Wes Frazier and his sister Linnie Mae Randle. The following morning, Oswald caught a ride to work with Frazier.

Both Frazier and Randle testified that Oswald was carrying, on the morning of November 22, a long package that contained something wrapped in brown paper. Randle saw Oswald holding the package and approaching her house as she looked out her kitchen window.[59] Frazier saw Oswald put the package in the backseat of his car as he and Oswald got into the vehicle. Oswald told Frazier the bag contained "curtain rods."[60] The Warren Commission concluded that the bag in fact contained Oswald's Mannlicher-Carcano rifle. That is, the bag is a critical and damning piece of the assassination puzzle.

Problems with the Evidence

Things seldom add up perfectly in any complex criminal case, and this one is no exception. Some of the claimed anomalies are just bogus. An FBI document—a letter over the signature of J. Edgar Hoover—is quoted to the effect that the rifle was "well oiled." Yet, conspiracists point out, no oil was found on the inside of the bag. Author Sylvia Meagher asserts, "It is difficult to understand why a well-oiled rifle carried in separate parts would not have left distinct traces of oil on the paper bag, easily detected in laboratory tests if not with the naked eye." And further: "Equally significant, there were no oil stains or traces on the blanket in which a well-oiled rifle ostensibly had been stored—not for hours but for months."[61]

But in fact only part of the letter—a passage referring to the "current well-oiled condition" of the rifle—is usually quoted. Yet a passage earlier in the letter says that "the firing pin and spring of this weapon are well oiled."[62] There is no implication here that the entire weapon was dripping oil. Indeed, no "well-oiled" weapon would be. What "well-oiled" would mean can be found in the Army's *Operator's Manual for the M16 and M4*. It instructs soldiers to "lightly lubricate the firing pin."[63] The definition of light lubrication is "a film of lubricant barely visible to the eye."[64] Thus the notion that Oswald's rifle would have been dripping oil is yet another of the numerous firearms factoids in the case.

How Long Was the Bag?

A more serious anomaly is the fact that the two witnesses to Oswald holding the bag, Frazier and Randle, estimated the length of the bag that Oswald was carrying, and their estimates, if correct, preclude Oswald having his Mannlicher-Carcano in that bag. Although there was some variation in their testimony, both thought the bag was about 27 inches long. The longest part of Oswald's rifle when disassembled was 34.8 inches in length. The bag recovered from the depository and entered into evidence is 38 inches long. As witness testimony goes, Frazier's and Randle's are pretty good. Neither appears to be any sort of crackpot or attention seeker. Further, the FBI ran careful simulations to ascertain exactly what each had seen. It had an agent simulate Oswald's approach to the Randle house carrying an exemplar bag rolled up to various lengths, with Randle looking out the window as she had that morning. In the case of Frazier, FBI agents asked him to indicate on the backseat of his car the point reached by the end of the package.[65]

Such care, of course, flatly contradicts the claim of conspiracists that the FBI was engaged in some wide-ranging cover-up.

So why in the world should we reject their testimony?

Tying the Bag to Oswald

The evidence that ties Oswald to the bag discovered in the depository is strong indeed. In the first place, fibers found in the depository bag matched fibers from a blanket on the floor of the Paine garage, which Marina testified held Oswald's rifle. FBI fiber expert Paul Stombaugh noted that the bag contained "1 brown viscose fiber, and 2 or 3 light green cotton fibers." This was well short of a definitive match, and Stombaugh was only willing to say that the "the possibility exists, these fibers could have come from this blanket."[66] So the fibers were consistent with the blanket in the Paine garage, although some other blanket (or other wrapping) made from similar material could be responsible for the fibers in the bag.

Much stronger evidence is the one fingerprint and one palm print, both conclusively matched to Oswald, found on the bag. Two Dallas police officers—Lt. Joseph Mooney and Officer Arthur Mandella—matched the prints to Oswald.[67] So did the FBI fingerprint expert Sebastian Latona. Latona remarked that the clarity of the palm print found on the bag was typical of cases in which something heavy was being carried in the bag, thus leaving an especially clear impression.[68] Finally, for people who don't want to believe either the Dallas cops or the FBI, the HSCA employed Vincent J. Scalice to review the evidence, and he stated flatly that the palm print and the fingerprint were those of Oswald.[69]

Could the bag have been forged? If so, it was a brilliantly quick job, since Detective L. D. Montgomery was photographed bringing the bag out of the depository at 2:19 p.m.[70] So, if Dallas cops forged the bag, they had little more than an hour to do it. And how did they get Oswald's prints on the bag? Oswald was nowhere near the depository during the time that Dallas cops would have had to forge the bag. If it were forged in advance of the assassination, it would still require Oswald's cooperation to forge it.

Was It Curtain Rods?

There are multiple problems with Oswald's "curtain rods" story. On the morning of November 21 (the day before the assassination), Oswald asked Frazier for a ride to Irving that night. According to Frazier, Oswald said he had to pick up some curtain rods.[71] Where he could have bought curtain rods is a mystery, since he didn't go shopping in Irving. There were some curtain rods in the Paine garage, but both Ruth Paine and her estranged husband, Michael Paine, testified they were all accounted for after the assassination.[72]

Worse, for anybody who takes the curtain rod story seriously, is the fact that Oswald had no use for curtain rods. His landlady, Mrs. Gladys Johnson, testified that Oswald's room at the rooming house at 1026 North Beckley had curtain rods and that he was not allowed to redecorate without permission. Oswald had not asked for permission.[73]

Numerous news photographers shot pictures of Oswald's room on the afternoon and evening of November 22. Allan Grant of *Life* magazine photographed the room on the afternoon of the assassination, with Mrs. Johnson standing by Oswald's bed, and curtain rods plainly visible in the picture (see photo insert). That evening, a photographer from the *Fort Worth Star-Telegram* photographed the room from two angles, both showing the curtains and rods clearly.[74]

The Rifle in the Depository

We have already discussed how the rifle discovered on the sixth floor of the depository was linked to Oswald. Marina testified that Oswald kept the rifle in a blanket in the garage of the Paine residence. Mrs. Paine, a Quaker, did not know about the rifle and quite likely would have refused to have it in her house had she known about it. Not only did Marina know about it, she knew that Oswald had used it to shoot at General Walker several months before. When Marina heard that Kennedy had been shot, she told the Warren Commission that "my heart dropped. I then went to the garage to see whether the rifle was there, and I saw that the blanket was still there, and I said, 'Thank God.' . . . But I was already rather upset at that time—I don't know why. Perhaps my intuition."[75]

When police came to the Paine home on the afternoon of the assassination, they asked whether Lee owned any guns. Mrs. Paine said no, but Marina (speaking through Ruth as interpreter) told the officers that Lee did indeed have a gun. The police then searched the garage, and according to Marina when they "took the blanket, I thought, 'Well, now, they will find it.' They opened the blanket but there was no rifle there. Then, of course, I already knew that it was Lee."[76]

Homicide detective Gus Rose, one of the cops in the garage, described the scene vividly:

> I stepped out into the garage, walked over and picked it up. I could see what I believed was the imprint of a rifle. Though it may have been partly suggestive, there was something there that made me think a rifle was there. When I picked it up, it fell limp empty across my arm. At that point, Marina let out an audible gasp. I turned and looked at her and noticed that she was wide-eyed and pale. I thought for a moment that she might be about to faint. I now believe that at that point, with the rifle not being there, the full realization had soaked in.[77]

Conspiracy theorists tend to dismiss Marina's testimony on the grounds that it was coerced by federal agents. But Rose's testimony jibes perfectly with Marina's own Warren Commission testimony. Further, Marina, on the afternoon of the assassination, before she was sequestered and questioned by federal agents, swore out an affidavit stating that Lee's rifle, which had been there two weeks before, was now missing from the Paine garage.[78]

Then there is the fact that Marina, who in the decades following the assassination came to believe that her former husband was innocent of killing Kennedy, has never recanted any of the testimony that was key in the Warren Commission case against Oswald. When Gerald Posner interviewed her in the early 1990s, she opined, "There are just too many things, like how he could have fired the shots that fast."[79] But she has never said that Lee did not own a gun, or that no rifle turned up missing from the Paine garage, or that Lee did not shoot at Walker. Indeed Marina, appearing before the HSCA in 1977 (long after she faced no fear whatsoever of deportation) explicitly commended Priscilla McMillan's book *Marina and Lee*, which accepts all the key testimony Marina gave to the Warren Commission.[80]

So how did the rifle get from the Paine garage to the depository, if it was not carried by Oswald in the paper bag that Frazier and Randle saw, and which was later recovered in the depository? One can concoct all sorts of theories about how the rifle was stolen from the Paine garage, but all of these theories involve ad hoc assumptions. We have absolutely no evidence that the rifle was stolen, and if it were, we still have to embrace several other ad hoc assumptions to account for the paper bag found in the depository.

Lee denied bringing any sizable bag to work but claimed that he only brought a sack lunch.[81] Wes Frazier, however, reports that he asked Lee about lunch, and Oswald said he was going to buy his lunch that day.[82] When the cops broached to Oswald the notion that the bag contained curtain rods, he continued to deny he brought any such bag.[83]

Lee Lied

If we find it implausible that Frazier and Randle lied about the package that Oswald took to work, we have to ask why Lee lied about that issue. His statements look for all the world like "guilty knowledge." Guilty knowledge involves a suspect knowing something that only a guilty person would know. An innocent person who had simply brought a bag lunch in to work (or curtain rods, for that matter) would have no reason to lie about it. But, as one writer in the *FBI Law Enforcement Bulletin* put

it, "Many times a defendant will make inconsistent statements or come up with implausible stories. Inconsistent or implausible statements can be circumstantial evidence of guilty knowledge."[84] Such statements were rife in the Oswald interrogation,
in which Lee denied owning the Mannlicher-Carcano rifle, denied that it was he in
the backyard photos, and even denied having lived on Neely Street, the location of
the apartment behind which the backyard photos were shot.

Back to Frazier and Randle

All of this brings us back to the testimony of Wes Frazier and of Linnie Mae Randle
about the length of the bag. Do we accept it or reject it?

We reject it as mistaken. In doing so, we are admittedly making two ad hoc
assumptions—one that Frazier was wrong, and another that Randle was wrong. We
have no reason to do so besides the fact that we must, to make our theory fit all the
other evidence. The most compelling of the other evidence is Oswald's prints on
the bag that was recovered by the Dallas cops in the depository. The photographic
evidence that Oswald's room at 1026 North Beckley did not need curtain rods is
rock-hard too.

We reject Frazier's and Randle's testimony not merely because of what we
know about witness testimony *in general*, but because when closely examined, it's
just not that solid. Randle, on the afternoon of November 22, told Detective Stovall
about the package she had seen Oswald carrying, and (in Stovall's words) "that her
brother had taken Oswald to work that morning and she said that she had seen him
put some kind of a package in the back seat of her brother's car. She told us it could
have been a rifle is what she said."[85] On the day of the assassination, she told the FBI
that the length of the package was "approximately 3 feet by 6 inches." But she further
said that (in the words of the FBI report) "she had only observed the brown package
from her residence window at a distance."[86]

Frazier's testimony is laced with admissions that he wasn't paying attention.
When asked by Warren Commission counsel, "What did he [Oswald] do about the
package in the back seat when he got out of the car?" Frazier answered, "Like I say,
I was watching the gages and watched the car for a few minutes before I cut it off."
And again, in response to another question, "Well, I will be frank with you, I didn't
pay much attention to the package because like I say before and after he told me that
it was curtain rods and I didn't pay any attention to it, and he never had lied to me
before so I never did have any reason to doubt his word." And "I didn't pay much
attention to the package other than I knew he had it under his arm and I didn't pay

too much attention [to] the way he was walking because I was walking along there looking at the railroad cars." Earlier, Frazier had described Lee getting into his car in Irving, saying,

> When I got in the car I have a kind of habit of glancing over my shoulder and so at that time I noticed there was a package laying on the back seat, *I didn't pay too much attention* and I said, "What's the package, Lee?" And he said, "Curtain rods."[87]

Thus, witness testimony can't overrule the more solid physical evidence. And rejecting that physical evidence as faked or forged requires a dizzying array of ad hoc assumptions.

OSWALD IN MEXICO CITY

As we have seen, conspiracy authors often assert (or at least suggest) that Lee Oswald was impersonated in Mexico City. But there is quite a lot of evidence that Oswald was there, including witness testimony and a paper trail of documents. But the most reliable evidence is various samples of his handwriting. First, Oswald signed the register at the Hotel del Comercio when he checked in. The FBI laboratory concluded that the signature was in Lee Oswald's handwriting.[88] Anybody not wanting to believe the FBI on this point might consider the HSCA, which had three separate handwriting experts provide independent reports on the questioned documents in the case. The three basically authenticated it was Oswald's, although two of them raised caveats since they had to work from photographs and not the original document.[89]

At the Cuban embassy, Oswald submitted a visa application, given to Silvia Duran at the Cuban embassy. It was forwarded on to Havana and eventually approved—long after the issue became moot—with the proviso that Oswald had to have a visa to the Soviet Union, which that country was unwilling to grant. The Warren Commission had a photograph of the document and noted that CIA experts had given the opinion that the signature was Oswald's.[90] The commission also noted that the clothes Oswald was wearing in the photo on the application appeared to be identical with those found among Oswald's possessions after the assassination, and the photo matched a negative found among Oswald's effects.[91] The HSCA had two versions of the application. One was the same photograph the Warren Commission had, and the other was a photograph of a carbon copy (that had an original Oswald signature) shown to HSCA staff when they met with Fidel Castro in Havana. Again, the HSCA experts authenticated the signatures, although two of them issued caveats about having to work from photos.[92]

The point is that one version of the Oswald signature on the visa application came from Fidel Castro's government. For it to be forged, Communist Cuba would have had to deal in fake documents at the behest of the CIA.

After Oswald had returned to Dallas, he composed a letter to the Soviet embassy in Washington, mentioning his visit to the Soviet embassy in Mexico City and complaining about the treatment he got. The letter exists in two forms: a handwritten draft with no signature—found among Oswald's possessions after the assassination—and a typed version, signed with Oswald's name. Both now exist as photographs, rather than original documents. Again, the HSCA authenticated the signatures.[93]

One piece of evidence connects Oswald to Silvia Duran, the secretary at the Cuban embassy who is a key witness placing him there. Duran testified that she wrote her name and number on a piece of paper and gave it to Oswald. The name and number were found in Oswald's address book, apparently copied there by Oswald. No handwriting expert examined this precise entry in Oswald's address book, but if he didn't do it, we have to posit a rather elaborate scheme to get control of the book and insert the fake notation.

Finally, Oswald had to sign, in two different locations, the tourist card he obtained from the Mexican Consulate in New Orleans on September 17, 1963. The FBI lab determined that both signatures were his.[94] There is thus essentially no doubt that Oswald was in Mexico City.

THE TIPPIT SHOOTING

Warren Commission counsel David Belin famously called the Tippit killing the Rosetta Stone of the Kennedy assassination.[95] About forty-five minutes after Kennedy was shot, a report came over police radio saying that a cop had been shot in the Oak Cliff section of Dallas. The officer was J. D. Tippit, and he was shot and killed by a pedestrian, later claimed to be Lee Harvey Oswald, near 10th Street and Patton Avenue.

The killing was the Rosetta Stone in the sense that about the time Oswald was being arrested by cops in the Texas Theatre near the scene of the Tippit shooting, officers at the Texas School Book Depository were being told that an employee named Lee Harvey Oswald was missing. The description of the shooter in the depository matched reasonably well the description of the shooter of Tippit. Two murders so close together could not, it seemed, be a mere coincidence. As it turns out, they were not.

But the murder of Tippit is the Rosetta Stone in another sense as well. If Oswald killed Tippit, it becomes very easy to believe he killed Kennedy too. Innocent men don't routinely shoot cops. Vincent Bugliosi goes so far as to say that "the Tippit killing, showing that Oswald was in flight from some awful deed, does *confirm* Oswald's guilt for the murder of Kennedy."[96] As will be discussed in chapter 16, Bugliosi's logic on this point is hardly ironclad, but his shooting of Tippit would be damning.

Using Witness Testimony

Both sides in the conspiracy debate use witness testimony here. Conspiracists comb through the testimony looking for anomalies that might seem strange or that conflict with the Warren Commission version of events. For example, they cite Helen Markham and T. F. Bowley, both of whose testimony about the time of the event would not allow Oswald to get from his rooming house to 10th and Patton in time to kill Tippit.[97] But of course, sometimes people's watches are running slow.

When there is this much noise in the data, it's perfectly possible to find evidence for pairs of scenarios that contradict the Warren Commission version and also contradict each other. Author Mark Lane, for example, claimed to have phoned Helen Markham and gotten her testimony that "the man who she said shot Officer Tippit" was "short, a little on the heavy side, and his hair was somewhat bushy."[98] This, of course, would not fit Oswald. Lane, in fact, engaged in a heroic feat of manipulation to get Markham to say anything even remotely resembling that, and even then had to seriously misrepresent what Markham said.[99] But Lane also invoked the testimony of Acquilla Clemons, who saw two men besides Tippit (presumably in cahoots with each other) at the scene of the shooting, and features both women in his book *Rush to Judgment* and in a companion documentary film.[100] So was it one shooter who wasn't Oswald, or two assassins?

Jim Marrs takes this tactic even further than Lane, first repeating that Markham "initially said that Tippit's killer was short and stocky with bushy hair." But this is after he has informed us that "other witnesses at the scene—William Scoggins, Ted Callaway, and Emory Austin—even today claim they never saw Mrs. Markham in the minutes immediately following the shooting."[101] So not only did Mrs. Markham identify somebody other than Oswald as the shooter, she wasn't even there!

Of course, those who believe that Oswald shot Tippit also use witness testimony. My view is that witness testimony alone would have convicted Oswald, but only after most of the witnesses were heavily discounted. Some were scared (Domingo Benavides, William Scoggins) or downright hysterical (Markham). Some were interviewed days or weeks later, after they had had plenty of time to see Oswald identified as the prime suspect in the media (William Arthur Smith, Warren Reynolds, Harold Russell, Pat Patterson). Two rather cool-headed witnesses who had not seen Oswald in the media (Virginia Davis and Ted Callaway) did pick him out of a lineup.[102]

Still, witness testimony is not the best evidence here. Witness testimony virtually never is.

The Hard Evidence

As with all other aspects of the assassination, the hard physical evidence implicates Oswald. But as usual, conspiracy theorists raise multiple problems and strongly imply (and sometimes state outright) that it was all faked, forged, or tampered with.

In a fair number of criminal cases, bullets in the victim or at the scene can be linked to a gun in the possession of the suspect "to the exclusion of all other weapons." This is about as "hard" as evidence gets. But things are more complicated here. FBI firearms expert Cortlandt Cunningham told the Warren Commission that bullets found in Tippit's body could not be definitively linked to the revolver found on Oswald's person when he was arrested in the Texas Theatre. The reason was that the revolver had been rechambered to fire .38 Special rounds, rather than the .38 rounds for which it was manufactured. Thus a bullet, rather than moving smoothly down the barrel picking up a consistent set of striations, would wobble and the pattern of striations would vary for each bullet fired. Thus test bullets fired from Oswald's revolver did not match the bullets found in Tippit, but multiple test bullets known to have been fired from the Oswald revolver did not match each other either. The bullets found in Tippit, however, were *consistent* with the revolver Oswald had.[103]

The Warren Commission, however, had a firearms expert independent of the FBI: Joseph D. Nicol, superintendent of the Illinois Bureau of Criminal Identification Investigation. He told the Warren Commission that, in his judgment, one of the bullets found in Tippit could be matched to the Oswald revolver "to the exclusion of all other weapons."[104] Interestingly, the FBI, which was supposedly dedicated to convicting Oswald regardless of the evidence, offered a more conservative assessment than an independent expert.

The situation with the spent cartridges—"hulls" to the Dallas cops—was different. All four spent cartridges found at the scene matched Oswald's revolver to the exclusion of all other weapons.[105]

Not surprisingly, conspiracist authors try to impeach this evidence. They point out, for example, that the first report from the scene over the Dallas Police radio said the shooter "was apparently armed with a .32 dark-finish automatic pistol which he had in his right hand." And less than a minute later: "The shells at the scene indicate that the suspect is armed with an automatic .38, rather than a pistol."[106] Of course, Oswald had a revolver on his person when arrested, so if the shooter really had an automatic, the shooter was not him.

However, the discrepancy between a ".32" and a ".38" ought to suggest that we are not dealing with precise data. Indeed, at 12:44 p.m. a Dallas Police radio transmission said the weapon used by the shooter in the depository "looked like a 30-30 rifle or some type of Winchester."[107] This description does not match Oswald's 6.5mm Mannlicher-Carcano, the Mauser that many conspiracists say was found, and indeed anything except perhaps somebody's generic notions about what a high-powered rifle is likely to be. Officer Gerald Hill, one of the cops on the scene and one of the officers responsible for the second report mentioning an "automatic," explained to researcher Dale Myers in an October 30, 1986, interview,

> I assumed it was an automatic simply because we had found all the hulls in one little general area. . . . If you find a cluster of shells—say a foot or foot and a half in diameter on the ground—you have to assume that they were fired from an automatic, because a revolver does not eject shells. You have to remove the shells. And so, that's why I say, when we found the cluster of shells, we assumed we were looking for a man armed with an automatic.[108]

Hill gave essentially the same story to *Frontline*.[109]

We might, of course, dismiss Hill as part of the cover-up, but one more kind of evidence is relevant here. Multiple witnesses—Domingo Benavides, Virginia Davis, Barbara Jeanette Davis, Acquilla Clemons, Helen Markham—saw the shooter manually ejecting spent cartridges from his gun. Automatics kick out the spent cartridge after each shot. Either all these witnesses were mistaken, or the shooter had a revolver.

Chain of Possession on the Cartridge Cases

Another anomaly in the physical evidence is the fact that two of the cartridges were given, at the scene of the shooting, to Officer J. M. Poe. Poe claimed he initialed the cartridges, but he was unable to locate his initials when shown the cartridges by the FBI and later by the Warren Commission.[110] Jim Marrs claims that this "leaves many researchers with the suspicion that the shell cases from Oswald's revolver [were] substituted for the ones marked by Poe."[111] And Mark Lane fulminates about "the [Warren] Commission's abandonment of the chain-of-evidence rule regarding the shells which passed through the hands of the Dallas police."[112] In fact, however, Poe gave the hulls to Pete Barnes of the Identification Bureau. Barnes marked them and was able to identify his marks later.[113]

The "Admissibility" Red Herring

The spent cartridges would therefore have been admissible in a Lee Oswald murder trial. Marking evidence is merely one way of establishing the chain of evidence. Another is to simply have all officers who handled it testify to their place in the chain of possession.[114] Of course, given the willingness of conspiracists to posit that so much evidence was faked or forged, one might ask why somebody didn't take Poe aside and tell him he needed to say his initials were in the hulls? Indeed, why not give him a diamond-tipped pen and tell him to put them there?

It's also the case that another spent cartridge was received by Capt. G. M. Doughty and yet another by Dtv. C. N. Dhority. Both men marked them and identified their marks.[115] These two cartridges would have been quite sufficient to tie Oswald's revolver to the murder scene.

Proof of Ownership

None of this evidence tying the revolver to the Tippit murder matters very much if it isn't Oswald's revolver. Of course, the Dallas cops *said* they found it on him, but perhaps this was all part of a larger plot to frame him. The problem with this notion is that a solid paper trail connects Oswald to the gun. Oswald sent a mail-order coupon to Seaport Traders in Los Angeles for a Smith & Wesson .38 Special sometime after January 27. Seaport Traders shipped him a revolver with serial number V510210.[116] It was shipped, as requested, to Post Office Box 2915, Dallas, Texas. The order was not in Oswald's name but came from an "A.J. Hidell."[117] As we have seen, Hidell was an Oswald alias, having been used to order the Mannlicher-Carcano, used as the name of the president of Oswald's rump chapter of the Fair Play for Cuba in New Orleans, and indeed was the name on a fake Selective Service identification card found on Oswald's person when he was arrested. The reader may recall that P.O. Box 2915 had been rented by Oswald. A document from the Railway Express Agency showed the gun to have been shipped, and another showed that "Hidell" had picked it up and paid the $19.95 (plus $1.27 shipping charges) due.

Handwriting experts James C. Cadigan of the FBI and Alwyn Cole of the Treasury Department both testified to the Warren Commission that the writing on the mail-order coupon was Lee Oswald's. Interestingly, a fellow named "D.F. Drittal" was listed on the coupon as attesting to the fact that "A.J. Hidell" was an American citizen and had not been convicted of a felony. Both handwriting experts testified that, like the "Hidell" signature, the "D.F. Drittal" signature was Oswald's.[118]

This evidence about the ownership of the revolver fits together very neatly, pointing to Oswald as the fellow who shot Tippit. But a conspiracy would want it to fit together quite neatly, would it not? Except, what would a conspiracy have to do to make this happen? Quite a lot. And since a conspiracy would have no way of knowing in advance that Oswald would get clean away from the depository and need to be framed for shooting a cop, it all had to be done on the spur of the moment by Dallas cops.

THE "KILLER EVIDENCE" ON THE HEAD WOUND

An iconic but entirely faceless figure in all JFK conspiracy theories is the grassy knoll gunman. As we have already seen, witness testimony doesn't give much evidence of any such shooter, and the "back and to the left" lurch of Kennedy's head and torso simply proves very little about where the shot came from.

But the best evidence here is the medical evidence and especially the autopsy photos and X-rays. Do they show a hit from the right front? Do they show the back of Kennedy's head blown out, something that would strongly suggest a shot from the right front? Conspiracists will labor mightily to impeach the photos and X-rays, typically by invoking witness testimony that supposedly contradicts them. As we have seen in chapter 2, the witness testimony is not at all like the heavily selected and heroically spun "testimony" that conspiracy books and articles show readers. But even if it were, it would not trump the authenticated X-rays and photos.

The HSCA, coming on the scene in 1977, knew that the landscape was awash in charges of fakery, and they did a stupefyingly thorough authentication of the materials. Much of the analysis was based on premortem X-rays obtained from the JFK Library. Experts examined the dentition (as distinctive as fingerprints) and the nasal sinuses (also as distinctive as fingerprints) and found that the purported autopsy X-rays matched the premortem X-rays. It was the same person in both sets. Anthropologists examined both the purported autopsy X-rays and the premortem X-rays and found that the "turcica, cranial sutures, vascular groves and air cells of the mastoid bone" were sufficient to conclude that both sets of X-rays were of the same person.[119]

Forensic anthropologists—the same people who examined the photos of the three tramps—examined the autopsy photos to see if the man in the autopsy photos was the same man shown in premortem photos known to be JFK. He was. Even the photos of the back of Kennedy's head showed enough distinctive characteristics to conclude they were of JFK.

Contrary to claims of conspiracists, none of the autopsy photos showed evidence of fakery. Indeed, within the set of photos were stereo pairs showing the back of the head, the top of the head, the large skull defect, the head from the right front, the back wound, and the anterior neck wound. As we have discussed, it was essentially impossible, using technology available at the time, to fake or tamper with a stereo pair and not have the fakery detected. None of the stereo pairs showed any evidence of fakery.[120]

Once we establish that the autopsy photos and X-rays are authentic, there ceases to be any real doubt about the nature of the head wound. A bullet hit Kennedy in the back of the head in the cowlick area, shattered, blew out brain matter and parietal bone, and one sizable piece of the bullet exited at the coronal suture.[121] The HSCA Forensic Pathology Panel concluded this, and so did the Ramsey Clark Panel (1968) and the Rockefeller Commission's forensic pathologists (1975).[122] The autopsy photos and X-rays not only show the back of Kennedy's head intact (although the underlying bone is riven with nasty fractures), but there are no bullet fragments in the skull to the left of the centerline. That's virtually unimaginable if a bullet hit Kennedy's head from the right front.

Less arcane than the autopsy photos and X-rays are three amateur movies that show Kennedy getting hit in the head, shot by Zapruder, Nix, and Muchmore. All show the brain matter exploding forward and upward from Kennedy's skull. The Zapruder film has several frames with clear images of the back of Kennedy's head after the fatal shot at frame 313, and they show it intact.[123]

This evidence leaves no substantial doubt as to the nature of Kennedy's head wound. No bullet hit him from the right front.

IS SCIENTIFIC EVIDENCE ALWAYS DECISIVE?

Since science has quite a mystique in the modern world, we might believe that scientific evidence is the decisive evidence on every issue. Often it *is* decisive, but there is science and there is "science." Sometimes scientists have a material interest or a career interest or an ideological interest in a particular branch of inquiry. Some may push their methods beyond what sound methodology allows, and draw conclusions that turn out to be frail when subjected to scrutiny.

The Acoustic Evidence

The HSCA claimed that scientists it hired found evidence of a grassy knoll shooter in an audio recording of Dallas Police radio transmissions made during and shortly after the shooting.[124] The acoustic experts seemed to have all the accoutrements of science in place to support their conclusions—elaborate graphs showing audio waveforms, computer analysis, and a lot of scientific jargon. Unfortunately, when the "acoustic evidence" was subjected to rigorous peer review by a blue ribbon panel under the auspices of the National Academy of Sciences, it was torn to pieces.[125]

Arguments about the acoustic evidence can get extremely arcane, but one need not be a scientist to understand how implausible the HSCA's conclusions were. First, the committee concluded that the grassy knoll shooter missed, since, as we have seen, the medical evidence allows for no bullet strike from that direction. Second, the acoustic evidence seemed to show that a bullet fired from the sniper's nest reached the limo roughly at Zapruder frame 160 and another fired from the same place reached the limo at about frame 190. A shooter (the committee believed it was Oswald) could have gotten off both shots *only if he didn't bother to aim the second shot.*[126] Third, Oswald (or any other shooter) would be trying to fire through the foliage of an oak tree if he fired at frame 190.[127] And, as we shall see, there is strong evidence that Kennedy and Connally were hit at Zapruder frame 223, but the "acoustic evidence" doesn't allow for a hit in that frame.

It's worth pointing out that when the committee's acoustic scientists tried to match sounds in the radio transmissions from the day of the assassination to the acoustic "fingerprint" of rifle test firings in Dealey Plaza, they found fifteen matches. But there was only one motorcycle supposedly picking up the sound of the shots, and certainly not fifteen shots. So the experts began to eliminate matches. In one case, for example, the acoustic evidence indicated a shot "in the opposite direction" from the limo.[128] By eliminating the matches that didn't fit any plausible shooting scenario, they whittled the number down to four.

Which was fine, so long as one can forget that the "acoustic fingerprint"—the scientific match—identified fifteen matches. There were, in short, way too many false positives.

The "Jet Effect"

The "back and to the left" movement of Kennedy's body seemed to imply conspiracy from very early on, and naturally supporters of the lone assassin theory looked for an explanation. As we have seen, the theory of a neuromuscular spasm is the most likely explanation, and hits from bullets simply don't throw people around. But a Warren Commission defender and very eminent physicist produced another explanation: the jet effect. The theory is that brain matter exiting the front of Kennedy's skull pushed his head backward in an "equal and opposite" reaction. The author of this theory, Dr. Luis Alvarez, did indeed show that when you shoot at melons, and you do it just right (high muzzle velocity, expanding soft-nosed bullets), the melons will jump back toward the shooter. Dr. John Lattimer showed that you can get the same retrograde motion with human skulls.[129] The problem is this: a "perfect" jet effect model would impart to the brain matter all the kinetic energy of the bullet. But if a bullet could not throw Kennedy backward through the transfer of momentum, neither could brain matter that (at most) had the amount of kinetic energy of the bullet.

Lattimer was responsible for another bit of pseudoscience related to the case. In the wake of the bullet strike to his torso, Kennedy's arms move sharply upward, toward his throat. He doesn't actually grasp at his throat, and his fists are balled up in what looks like an involuntary reaction. Lattimer found a "golden oldie" (from 1889) of an article in a medical journal and decided that Kennedy had assumed "Thorburn's position"—something documented as happening in the wake of trauma to the spine. Kennedy's arm movements were indeed a neuromuscular reaction, but not the one Thorburn described, since Thorburn's position develops over days or weeks or even months.[130]

So should we accept the evidence of science? Yes, as long as we are talking about well-established forensic science. But if it's some new theory or field that hasn't been around for long, hasn't survived extensive peer review, and comes from people intent on proving something? Not so much.

THE OBAMA BIRTH CERTIFICATE

Of course, sometimes the best evidence is not scientific, and is not arcane in the slightest. Let's set the JFK assassination conspiracies aside and consider the issue of President Barack Obama's birth certificate.

Because the U.S. Constitution requires that the president of the United States be a "natural born" citizen,[131] the political enemies of Barack Obama have made political hay with the claim that Obama was not "natural born." Maybe he was born in Kenya, they have suggested.

The Obama campaign, in June 2008, published an Obama birth certificate on the Internet.[132] The document, printed from a database by officials of the state of Hawaii, was perfectly legal for all purposes. But unfortunately, its provenance didn't make it entirely reliable: anybody with access can change a database (and "with access" could mean the illegal access of a hacker). The issue then became the "vault copy" of the document—the one originally filed when Obama was born in 1961. One might think that the mere fact that such a document exists would be proof that Obama was born in Hawaii, but it isn't, since in Hawaii a foreign-born person may be issued an "amended" birth certificate.[133] Hawaii state officials claim to have examined the "vault copy,"[134] but political officials are political officials, and some have wondered whether they were not "covering" for a politician they very much wanted to win the presidency.

So what is the best evidence here? Both daily newspapers in Honolulu (the *Advertiser* and the *Star-Bulletin*) published birth announcements about a son born to Mr. and Mrs. Barack H. Obama on August 4, 1961.[135] August 4, 1961, is the birth date on the certificate the Obama campaign released. So, while it's conceivable that officials in Hawaii might "cover for" Obama by altering a database or lying about having seen the vault copy, how does one explain the alteration of forty-eight-year-old microfilm copies of two Honolulu newspapers?

Birthers (as the people pushing this issue are called) have suggested that Obama's grandmother put the notices in the two newspapers. But think about the scenario this implies. If Obama was born in Kenya, and at least one parent was a U.S. citizen (Obama's father was not a U.S. citizen, but his mother was), he would be a U.S. citizen.[136] Only if his grandmother foresaw the need to fulfill the rather arcane "natural born citizen" requirement to be president would this make any sense. Did she somehow know that her grandson would be running for president in 2008? In any case, this matter is moot, since in 1790 Congress legislated that people born outside the United States to parents who are U.S. citizens are considered "natural born."[137]

In 2011 the White House finally released what purported to be the vault copy ("long form") of the birth certificate. Almost instantly the Internet was buzzing, with posts on blogs and discussion boards claiming to have found evidence of fakery. As with the backyard photos of Oswald and other photographic evidence in this case, it's easy to find evidence of fakery. And it's especially easy if you know nothing about photography.

HARD EVIDENCE

There are some issues that can be decided by highly reliable evidence: handwriting identification, expert analysis of authenticated photos, ballistics evidence. These sources trump the testimony of mistaken or crackpot witnesses, memories ten or twenty or thirty years old, memos from bureaucrats who are clueless, and this or that anomaly in the written records. Intellectually serious analysis starts with this sort of evidence. Of course, nothing we have discussed in this chapter rules out a conspiracy, although it does limit the kinds of conspiracy theories we can seriously consider.

And the hard evidence does rule out a lot of factoids.

Chapter Twelve

Too Much Evidence of Conspiracy

It might seem counterintuitive to say that there's too *much* evidence of conspiracy, but consider the effect of learning about dozens and scores and hundreds of unexplained circumstances, situations that raise suspicion, and contradictions in the evidence. The psychological impact can leave you reeling and thinking that "there has to be something going on." But in reality, the massive amount of supposed conspiracy evidence researchers have produced suggests just the opposite.

Let's take some examples.

PLOWING THROUGH THE EVIDENCE
Dave Perry's Rashomon List

Researcher David Perry has compiled a list of all the people who have been accused of (or confessed to) being a shooter or accomplice in Dealey Plaza.[1] There are sixty-eight names on the list.

It's a veritable menagerie, from the black dog man to the umbrella man to three guys from Corsica to the three tramps to Frank Sinatra's drummer. Of course, *somebody* shot Kennedy. Lee Oswald is number-one on Perry's list. Is anyone else on the list guilty? Since the vast majority of people on the list must be innocent, it's easy to believe that all but one are.

Shots in Dealey Plaza

The Warren Commission ruled that three shots were fired during the assassination, but some conspiracists have pointed to evidence of many more.[2] Let's make a list:

1.   An envelope that contained a 7.65 mm rifle shell that the FBI discovered in Dealey Plaza. The envelope was empty, but a notation on it said it had contained the shell.[3]

2.   A 30.06 shell casing found by a maintenance man on the roof of the County Records Building.[4]

3.   Dallas cop J. W. Foster saw what he thought was a bullet striking the grass on the Dealey Plaza infield about 350 feet from the depository, close to a manhole cover. (This was discussed in chapter 4.)[5]

4–5.   Two bullets that supposedly produced two mounds of earth on the infield of Dealey Plaza. Wayne and Edna Hartman said they noticed the mounds and were told by a cop that bullets fired from the grassy knoll must have been the cause.[6]

6.   A bullet that supposedly penetrated the windshield of the limo, leaving a through-and-through hole, as reported by Stavis Ellis and H. R. Freeman.[7] This would imply a shot from the front.

7.   The bullet that J. Edgar Hoover told Lyndon Johnson "rolled out of the President's head" on the way to Parkland Hospital. The bullet, according to Hoover, was loosened by heart massage.[8] This might be the same as . . .

8.   The bullet, fired from the grassy knoll, that most conspiracists believe hit Kennedy in the head from the right front.

9.   The bullet that, most critics of the single bullet theory insist, hit Kennedy in the throat from the front.

10.   A bullet that, according to John Connally, fell on the floor and was picked up by a nurse who put it in her pocket as he was rolled off the stretcher and onto the examining table.[9]

11.   The Osborne bullet, an intact slug that Admiral David Osborne said rolled out of JFK's clothing when the body was removed from the casket prior to being autopsied at the Bethesda Naval Hospital.[10]

12.   A "missile removed by Commander James Humes" at the autopsy, as reported by FBI agents Sibert and O'Neill.[11]

13.   A bullet that supposed Dealey Plaza witness James Hicks said hit the Stemmons Freeway sign in Dealey Plaza. The sign was supposedly removed about a half hour after the shooting.[12]

That's a lot of bullets, especially when we add them to the three the Warren Commission said were fired. This number would certainly require more than one shooter in Dealey Plaza; indeed, it would appear to require at least four or five.

Rifles in Dealey Plaza

If so many shots were fired, it makes sense that many rifles were involved. And indeed if one looks at early reports, there seem to be. Let's look at one of the early journalistic treatments of some anomalies in initial reports:

> First press accounts quoted various members of the Dallas police force as saying the assassin's weapon was a .30-caliber Enfield and a 7.65mm Mauser. One Secret Service man said he thought the weapon was an "Army or Japanese rifle" of .25 caliber. The same accounts reported that the rifle was found on the second floor of the building by a window, in the fifth-floor staircase, by an open sixth-floor window, and hidden behind boxes and cases on the second or sixth floors.[13]

Of course, we can add a couple. A report on Dallas Police radio stated the "weapon looked like a 30-30 rifle or some type of Winchester."[14] And NBC reported that "the weapon that was used to kill the President" was a "British .303 rifle with a telescopic sight."[15] All these are in addition to the rifle that was later identified as a 6.5mm Mannlicher-Carcano recovered in the depository. This would seem to be a massive amount of evidence of either additional shooters or evidence tampering, as rifles were made to disappear. Or it could be that, like so much other "evidence," this is just noise: misperceptions, guesses, and rumors about what the murder weapon was. Given that most of these reports must have been mistaken, we can reasonably dismiss all of them and accept the one piece of hard evidence on this issue: the 6.5mm Mannlicher-Carcano that, as we have seen in chapter 4, was photographed, entered into evidence, and resides to this day in the National Archives.

Those Who Have Confessed

If the number of extra bullets doesn't impress you, consider the number of people who have confessed to being part of a conspiracy to kill Kennedy.[16] Take a look at the "People Who Have Confessed to a Role in the Kennedy Assassination" table, which includes people who have confessed their own role in an assassination conspiracy or have claimed personal knowledge of the participation of relatives, boyfriends and girlfriends, and close associates. Some of the so-called confessors claim they played their role inadvertently, aiding the conspirators without knowing that Kennedy was to be killed.

People Who Have Confessed to a Role in the Kennedy Assassination

Confessor	Implicated whom?	Role of person implicated	Source
James Files	Himself	Grassy knoll shooter	James E. Files, *The Murder of JFK: Confession of an Assassin* (Oakland Park, IL: MPI Home Video, 1996), VHS
Loy Factor	Himself, Malcolm Wallace	Depository shooters	Glen Sample and Mark Collom, *The Men on the Sixth Floor* (Garden Grove, CA: Sample Graphics, 2003)
John Martino	Anti-Castro Cubans	Shooters	Anthony Summers, *Not in Your Lifetime* (New York: Marlowe, 1998), 76, 325–28, 372–73
Billie Sol Estes	Himself, LBJ, and Clifton C. Carter	Conspirators	Douglas Caddy, letter to Stephen S. Trott at the U.S. Department of Justice (August 9, 1984), http://www.spartacus.schoolnet.co.uk/JFKestes.htm
	Malcolm Wallace	Shooter	
Barr McClellan	LBJ, Edward Clark, Texas oil millionaires (including Clint Murchison and H. L. Hunt)	Ordered killing	Barr McClellan, *Blood, Money and Power: How LBJ Killed JFK* (New York: Hanover House, 2003)
	Malcolm Wallace	Shooter	
Frank Ragano	Jimmy Hoffa, Santos Trafficante, Carlos Marcello	Ordered killing	Frank Ragano, *Mob Lawyer* (New York: Scribners/Maxwell Macmillan Canada, 1994)
Antoinette Giancana	Sam Giancana	Ordered killing	Antoinette Giancana, *JFK And Sam: The Connection Between the Giancana and Kennedy Assassinations* (Nashville, TN: Cumberland House, 2005)
Chuck Giancana and Sam Giancana	Sam Giancana	Ordered killing	Chuck Giancana and Sam Giancana, *Double Cross: The Explosive, Inside Story of the Mobster Who Controlled America* (New York: Warner Books, 1992)

Confessor	Implicated whom?	Role of person implicated	Source
Ricky Don White and Geneva White	Roscoe White	Shooter	David B. Perry, "Who Speaks for Roscoe White," http://davesjfk.com/roscoew.html; Gary Cartwright, "I Was Mandarin...," *Texas Monthly*, December 1990
Madeleine Brown	LBJ	Coconspirator	Madeleine Brown, *Texas in the Morning: The Love Story of Madeleine Brown and President Lyndon Baines Johnson* (Baltimore: Conservatory Press, 1997)
E. Howard Hunt	LBJ, Cord Meyer, Frank Sturgis, the Corsican Mafia, David Sanchez Morales, William Harvey, Antonio Veciana	Plotters	Erik Hedegaard, "The Last Confessions of E. Howard Hunt," *Rolling Stone*, April 5, 2007
Carlos Marcello	Himself	Ordered killing	Lamar Waldron and Thom Hartmann, *Legacy of Secrecy: The Long Shadow of the JFK Assassination* (Berkley, CA: Counterpoint, 2009)
Chauncey Holt	Charles Nicoletti, James Canty, Leo Moceri, Charles Harrelson, Charles Rogers (aka Richard Montoya)	Tramps who were also Dealey Plaza shooters	Michael Benson, *Who's Who in the JFK Assassination: An A-to-Z Encyclopedia* (New York: Citadel Press, 1993), 194–96
Robert Morrow	Himself	Supplied rifles and communications equipment for killers	Robert Morrow, *First Hand Knowledge: How I Participated in the CIA-Mafia Murder of President Kennedy* (New York: S.P.I. Books, 1992)
David Sanchez Morales	Himself and unnamed associates	"Took care of" Kennedy	Gaeton Fonzi, *The Last Investigation* (New York: Thunder's Mouth Press, 1993), 389–90
"Saul"	Himself	Dealey Plaza shooter	Hugh McDonald, *Appointment in Dallas: The Final Solution to the Assassination of JFK* (New York: H. McDonald, 1975)

People Who Have Confessed to a Role in the Kennedy Assassination (continued)

Confessor	Implicated whom?	Role of person implicated	Source
Robert Easterling	Manuel Rivera, David Ferrie, Lee Harvey Oswald, Clay Shaw *or* Guy Banister, Jack Ruby	Various: Easterling claimed to be coconspirator who deserted plot before Dallas	Henry Hurt, *Reasonable Doubt: An Investigation into the Assassination of John F. Kennedy* (New York: Holt, Rinehart, and Winston, 1985), chapter 12
Marita Lorenz	Herself, Gerry Patrick Hemming, Orlando Bosch, Pedro Diaz-Lanz, Frank Sturgis, E. Howard Hunt, Jack Ruby, Lee Oswald	Plotters and shooters, in Miami-to-Dallas "caravan"	Gaeton Fonzi, *The Last Investigation* (New York: Thunder's Mouth Press, 1993), 83–107
Christian David	Lucien Sarti, Sauveur Pironti, Roger Bocognani	Plotters and shooters in Dealey Plaza	Nigel Turner, *The Men Who Killed Kennedy: The Definitive Account of American History's Most Controversial Mystery*, season 1, episode 2 (TimeLife Video, 1993), VHS
Charles Harrelson	Himself	Shooter in Dealey Plaza	Allen Pusey and Howard Swindle, "Drugs, Gambling Mark Harrelson's Trail," *Dallas Morning News*, March 20, 1981

HOW MUCH IS TOO MUCH?

So how is all this "too much" evidence of conspiracy? Quite simply, the vast majority of Dealey Plaza suspects on Dave Perry's list *must* be innocent; else they had to be shoulder to shoulder in Dealey Plaza, jostling one another. The vast majority of reports of extra bullets and missed shots must be bogus, else there were four or five shooters in Dealey Plaza blasting away with abandon. And the vast majority of confessions must be untrue as well, since the various accounts contradict one another.

And if the vast majority *must* be bogus, it's easy to believe they all are. The large number, in other words, discredits the value of any single JFK assassination confession. Put another way, the bar for what constitutes conspiracy evidence has been set way too low. Way too many reports, sightings, documents, and accusations qualify as conspiracy evidence. Put still another way, there is a lot of noise rather than signal. How is all this conspiracy evidence generated? One culprit is simply misperception, which produces accounts of bullets hitting here and there. Second is odd behavior on the part of certain individuals. For instance, Louie Witt (the umbrella man) was holding an umbrella in Dealey Plaza as the presidential limo passed, in spite of the fact that it was not raining. He was making a political statement, albeit a rather arcane one that few people would understand.[17] So this odd behavior, which in other times and in other places would be dismissed, makes him a suspect. That's what put him on Dave Perry's list.

Another reason for all this evidence is the large number of assiduous researchers who go around looking for "connections" that might be sinister. We have discussed one of these in chapter 6: a phone call that supposedly links David Ferrie to Jack Ruby, but doesn't really. Researchers have turned up all kinds of connections of this sort. For example, the owner of the Texas School Book Depository was a man named D. Harold Byrd, a supposed right-winger and founder of the Civil Air Patrol, of which Oswald was briefly a member. The president of the Book Depository Company was a fellow named Jack Cason, supposedly a longtime member of a Dallas American Legion post.[18] Barr McClellan, for example, says that "the full extent of Byrd and the assassination are not known however he ties directly into Big Oil and the important cover-up."[19]

Likewise, when Lee and Marina Oswald arrived in New York on their return from the Soviet Union, a fellow named Spas Raikin from the Traveler's Aid Society helped them get through customs and sent them to the Welfare Department. Conspiracy books typically note that he was secretary-general of the "American Friends of the Anti-Bolshevik Bloc of Nations."[20] An anti-Communist, in other words, and therefore in the mirror image McCarthyism of too many conspiracy theorists, a suspect.

Of course, there is no evidence at all that Raikin was any sort of conspirator, and neither D. Harold Byrd nor Jack Cason had even the slightest role in hiring Oswald at the depository. But diligent researchers who search can find an unlimited number of "connections" like this.

Add also the fact that there are a certain number of liars and attention seekers in the world, willing to supply a connection between two people by inserting one or both of them into their narrative. We have discussed people like this in chapter 4.

The process isn't pure noise. It's what statisticians call a censored distribution. When researchers look for connections, they ignore those that don't point to somebody *already* suspected. Connections to the Boy Scouts or the League of

Women Voters will be ignored. But any links to the Mafia, anti-Castro Cubans, the CIA, the FBI, rich Texas oil millionaires, and so on will find their way into conspiracy books.

Likewise, when people confess to involvement in the assassination, they are not going to name as coconspirators four guys from Boise City that nobody had ever heard of. They are going to name familiar characters from conspiracy books: CIA types, anti-Castro Cubans, Mafia types, LBJ's Texas cronies. The effect of this is that once some person or group is fingered as suspect, their sinister connections will quickly grow in number as diligent researchers uncover yet more connections. The noise comes in because the connections implicate different CIA agents, anti-Castro Cubans, Mafia types, and so on. And the scenarios contradict one another. So what we see fits a model in which there is no conspiracy but rather random processes (and the biases of researchers) that throw up a massive amount of conspiracy evidence.

TOO MANY FALSE POSITIVES

All these pieces of conspiracy evidence may be compared to a medical test that produces too many positive results. Imagine you and sixty coworkers are tested for some dread disease (leukemia, perhaps) and fifteen of you test positive. Yet you know that, at most, only a few of you might have the disease. You would quickly conclude that there is no real evidence that *any* of you have the disease. If there must be eleven or twelve false positives from the test, it's easy to believe that there could be fifteen. The test, in other words, really proves nothing. This is the exact situation we discussed in chapter 11 with regard to the acoustic fingerprints of supposed shots in Dealey Plaza.

Likewise, the sheer number of extra bullets or confessions or spooky connections is evidence that none of them are strong evidence of anything.

A Non-JFK Example: Evidence of Alien Visitors

Hard on the heels of a spate of UFO reports in the late 1940s, the Air Force commissioned an investigation, called Project Sign, of whether the sightings were evidence of extraterrestrial visitors. Given that UFO reports were initially not very numerous, and came from apparently reliable witnesses, the Project Sign team produced a document called *Estimate of the Situation*, which concluded that the reports indicated real alien visitors.

Gen. Hoyt Vandenburg, who had commissioned the project, would have none of this, and ordered a new study done. The later, revised analysis concluded,

It is hard to believe that any technically accomplished race would come here, flaunt its ability in mysterious ways and then simply go away. . . . The lack of purpose in the various episodes is also puzzling. Only one motive can be assigned; that the space-men are "feeling out" our defenses without wanting to be belligerent. If so, they must have been satisfied long ago that we can't catch them. It seems fruitless for them to keep trying the same experiment.

Thus the revised report asked the "scenario" question and then noted that there had been too many UFO sightings. Four or five *reliable* UFO sightings, in other words, would have constituted better evidence of real extraterrestrial visitors than the dozens that had accumulated.[21]

CAN WE GET BEYOND THE NOISE?

"But," one might reply, "it's still possible that some of these pieces of evidence really prove something, isn't it?" Could it be that underneath all the pieces of suspect evidence there lurks some real evidence of a conspiracy? That could be, but if so, the almost fifty-year enterprise of accumulating conspiracy evidence has been profoundly counterproductive. It has muddied the waters, rather than bringing clarity. As we have discussed, the best conspiracist researchers spend a lot of their time debunking silly conspiracy factoids. For example, a recent article from Barb Junk-karinen, Jerry Logan, and Josiah Thompson destroys the notion that there was a through-and-through hole in the windshield of the presidential limo. Such a hole would, as noted, clearly imply a conspiracy, but the evidence is against it.[22] As noted, David Perry has done signal service by debunking dubious witnesses like James Files and Madeleine Duncan Brown.[23] Conspiracists like Clint Bradford and Tony Marsh have decisively refuted those researchers who think the Zapruder film is forged or tampered with.[24] And Gary Mack, curator of the Sixth Floor Museum in Dallas, has been a voice for sanity in too many ways to list here.

Folks like these typically find themselves siding with lone gunman theorists on any particular issue. Both groups want to debunk the factoids and get the noise out of the data. They only differ on what will be left when the noise is purged. Will it be a select few pieces of reliable evidence of conspiracy, or just one guy with a grudge and a gun? As of today, conspiracists have way too much so-called conspiracy evidence that implicates way too many suspects and supports way too many theories.

Chapter Thirteen

Beware False Corroboration

Sometimes a researcher will run across a source that seems to corroborate something he or she already believes. Multiple sources saying the same thing generally make a historical case stronger. If there is, for example, a 0.3 probability that one source is wrong about something, then the probability that two sources addressing the same issue and saying the same thing are wrong should be .09. Thus there are better than nine chances in ten that the information is accurate. Except that this logic doesn't hold when the second source was *derived from* the first source (or vice versa) or if both accounts were derived from a common source. If some inaccurate piece of information is going around, and multiple people repeat it, the information is only as good as the one source that started the whole thing.

CHANGED PARADE ROUTE

We have already seen some examples of the false corroboration problem among our witnesses. As detailed in chapter 4, Jean Hill described how her boyfriend, whom she identified as J. B. Marshall, learned of a "changed parade route" at Love Field. But as we have seen, the parade route was never changed, and Hill included in her story a factoid that goes back to Joachim Joesten's pioneering conspiracy book, *Oswald: Assassin or Fall Guy?* There is no evidence that Hill ever read that book, but the "changed parade route" story is now a part of conspiracy lore, handy for any witness to add to his or her story.[1]

Another person who used this same factoid was James Files. Files, who in the 1990s begin to claim that he was the grassy knoll shooter, said that on the morning of the assassination he went to a pancake house with mobster Johnny Roselli. Jack

Ruby then came in and gave Roselli an envelope containing Secret Service identification and a map of the motorcade route. The map showed a "change" in the route: a "zig-zag, that little turn they should never have made."[2] Amazingly, Dick Clark Productions took up the Files story, and NBC was seriously considering broadcasting it when they hired a consultant (Edward Jay Epstein) to vet it for accuracy. According to Epstein,

> In brief, NBC retained me as a consultant for their planned story on Files. I hired the detective firm of Jules Kroll. JK established from telephone records Files was in Chicago, not Dallas, on November 22, 1963. We then placed a call to Files from Dick Clark's office (DC was producer), and I interviewed Files about [the] Kroll findings. He said he had a twin brother, who no one knew about, and whom he met shortly before November 22, and who he murdered after November 22. He said it was his twin brother in hospital with his wife, not him. His wife, however, said there was no twin, and Kroll confirmed there was no twin. My view then and now is that Files invented the story for the money it would earn him.[3]

TOO MUCH CORROBORATING EVIDENCE?

A testimony that relies on lots of corroborating detail should probably raise red flags, rather than lend credibility. Author Henry Hurt, recounting the testimony of one Robert Easterling, a fellow who quite obviously (to almost everybody besides Hurt) was insane, says his is a "persuasive version of events."[4] It's persuasive because Easterling includes all the usual suspects and usual factoids in his story.

We have already discussed the testimony of Judyth Baker, a woman who claims to have been Lee Oswald's lover in New Orleans in the summer of 1963. She and her supporters have claimed corroboration from a book called *Mary, Ferrie & the Monkey Virus: The Story of an Underground Medical Laboratory* written by Edward T. Haslam in 1995.[5] In his book, Haslam claims there was a secret bioweapons laboratory, sponsored by the CIA, involving Mary Sherman (a well-known, reputable orthopedic surgeon at the Ochsner Clinic), David Ferrie, and Lee Oswald. Judyth appears to have added herself to this story, since the Haslam book came out before Judyth started telling people about her sinister involvement.[6] Of course,

Judyth claims not to have read the Haslam book. That's something you might believe if you actually find Haslam and Judyth plausible.

In an interesting turn of events, a 2007 revision of Haslam's book mentions a Judyth Baker (who was entirely missing from the earlier edition).[7] So it seems they now corroborate each other.

THE CIA SAID THE RIFLE WAS A MAUSER

We have already discussed, in the context of Roger Craig, the significance of the claim that the rifle discovered on the sixth floor of the depository was a Mauser, and not a Mannlicher-Carcano. In the video *Two Men in Dallas*, conspiracy author Mark Lane, puffing Roger Craig's testimony, shows two pieces of striking evidence: both are CIA documents.

One document states that "the rifle he used was a Mauser which OSWALD had ordered from Klein's Mail Order House, Chicago, Illinois."[8] It's odd that conspiracists would quote this document, since it said Oswald was the shooter. And we know that Klein's shipped a Mannlicher-Carcano to Oswald. And the memo says the assassination took place on September 22.

The other document doesn't exactly say the rifle was a Mauser, but says that "the description of a 'Mannlicher Carcano' Rifle in the Italian and foreign press is in error" and goes on to pontificate at length about the "Model 91."[9] But in Lane's world, that supports Craig's Mauser story.

The CIA *would* know the inside scoop on this, right? It *would* have information that nobody else had, wouldn't it? Unfortunately, as we have detailed in chapter 4, news film shot by Tom Alyea leaves no doubt. The rifle was a Mannlicher-Carcano. Apparently the same bogus reports that circulated in the news media made it into CIA documents.

THE MEXICO CITY TAPES

On the day of the assassination, the CIA station in Mexico City swung into action, putting together the evidence it had of Oswald's visits to the Cuban and Soviet embassies. They quickly dispatched to Dallas photos they thought to be of Oswald (they weren't) and transcripts of phone calls Oswald had made.

But what about the tapes of phone taps that the CIA claimed to have made of Oswald? The CIA insisted that the tapes had been erased, and that only transcripts survived.

Yet for a generation, conspiracists have claimed that the tapes did survive. If so, the unwillingness of the CIA to produce them would be extraordinarily suspicious. And conspiracists have what superficially seems like a lot of evidence that the tapes survived, were sent to Dallas, and were listened to by FBI agents who insisted that the voice on the tapes was not that of Lee Oswald.

For example, we have an FBI letterhead memorandum from J. Edgar Hoover sent the day after the assassination to James Rowley, head of the Secret Service:

> The Central Intelligence Agency advised that on October 1, 1963, an extremely sensitive source had reported that an individual identified himself as Lee Oswald, who contacted the Soviet Embassy in Mexico City inquiring as to any messages. Special Agents of this Bureau, who have conversed with Oswald in Dallas, Tex., have observed photographs of the individual referred to above and have listened to a recording of his voice. These Special Agents are of the opinion that the above-referred-to individual was not Lee Harvey Oswald.[10]

And in a phone conversation with Lyndon Johnson the same day, Hoover told LBJ, "We have up here the tape and the photograph of the man who was at the Soviet Embassy, using Oswald's name. That picture and the tape do not correspond to the man's voice, nor to his appearance." Conspiracy books quote this part of the conversation as though it's gospel truth but ignore other statements Hoover made in the same phone call. The FBI director told the president that the rifle used to kill Kennedy had been shipped from Chicago to a woman named A. Heidel. Authorities had, Hoover said, a whole bullet that had fallen out of the president when his heart was massaged. (As we will see in chapter 15, the bullet came from John Connally.) Oswald's mother, according to Hoover, had told authorities that he kept the rifle in a blanket in the garage. Further, Hoover thought the bullets had been fired from the fifth floor of the depository, and Oswald had gone upstairs to the sixth floor to ditch the rifle. Finally, Oswald then went to a theater where he had a gun battle with a policeman. We shall see more about Hoover's cluelessness in chapter 14, but given that the call to LBJ contained so much misinformation, it's hard to see why one should take Hoover's statements as any sort of solid evidence.[11]

In 1999 Associated Press reporter Deb Riechmann wrote a story trumpeting yet more evidence that Oswald was impersonated at the Soviet embassy, saying that,

"Only now—36 years to the day after the murder—has the government released a flurry of new details about it."[12] In fact, the majority of the material in the Riechmann article was not new, but the story did quote a memo from Alan Belmont, an official at the FBI's Washington headquarters, to Clyde Tolson, Hoover's second in command:

> The Dallas agents who listened to the tape of the conversation allegedly of Oswald from the Cuban Embassy to the Russian Embassy in Mexico and examined the photographs of the visitor to the Embassy in Mexico . . . were of the opinion that neither the tape nor the photograph pertained to Oswald.[13]

There would thus seem to be plenty of sources supporting the idea that Oswald was impersonated in Mexico City. And indeed, there is another memo from Belmont to William Sullivan (another top FBI official) that uses the exact same "pertained to Oswald" language.[14]

But all of the accounts coming from Washington came through Belmont, who phoned Gordon Shanklin, special agent in charge of the Dallas office of the FBI. Once Belmont heard (or thought he heard) that agents had listened to the tapes and said it wasn't Oswald's voice, that was then written in memos and disseminated among Bureau officials. So when we find Hoover writing something to Rowley, or telling LBJ something, those weren't independent accounts. All of them originated with what Belmont thought he heard from Shanklin.

But what did the people in Dallas say? The Church Committee talked to Shanklin and Elbert Rudd (the FBI agent who brought the photographs and transcripts to Dallas from Mexico City by plane) and found that "neither of them recall being aware of a tape recording of Oswald's voice." Further, "Shanklin cannot explain the statements set forth in Belmont's memorandum."[15]

When Rudd delivered the materials from Mexico City to the Dallas FBI office, very early on the morning of September 23, he supplied a memo describing the material. The memo lists as "attached" the photos of a man visiting the embassy (as we have seen, he was not Oswald) and notes that "CIA has advised that these tapes have been erased and are not available for review." Succeeding pages of the memo are transcripts of phone conversations thought to involve Oswald. Of course, there was no mention of tapes. This was before anybody could have known of the need for a cover-up of an Oswald impostor.[16]

The HSCA also took up this issue and questioned Shanklin, James Hosty, John W. Fain, Burnett Tom Carter, and Arnold J. Brown, all Dallas FBI special agents who had conversed with Oswald at one time or another. All testified that they had never heard any tape from Mexico City purporting to be Oswald's voice. "On the basis of an extensive file review and detailed testimony by present and former CIA officials and employees" the HSCA determined that CIA headquarters had never gotten any recording of Oswald's voice.[17]

So the *only* real source of the claim that Dallas agents listened to tapes from Mexico City was Alan Belmont. It's hard to claim he was somehow lying for the purpose of contradicting the CIA or wanting to promote conspiracy theories. But it's easy to believe he confused "tapes" with "transcripts of tapes" and "the photos weren't of Oswald" with "the photos and tapes weren't of Oswald."

OTHER GOVERNMENT ERRORS

Further examples of misinformation from government officials abound. We have seen how multiple witnesses corroborate the claim that a Mauser and not a Mannlicher-Carcano was found on the sixth floor of the depository on the afternoon of the assassination. In reality, Deputy Seymour Weitzman first identified the rifle as a Mauser, and other people merely repeated what turned out to be a mistaken statement.

Likewise, conspiracist Tom Rossley has identified three different documents claiming that the bullet that was shot at General Walker was a "steel jacketed" bullet.[18] That would be impressive if three different ballistics experts examined it and agreed on the description. But much more likely is that a mistaken initial identification simply got repeated as boilerplate text and was copied from one document to the next. When the Dallas Police, in the wake of the JFK assassination, turned the bullet (Warren Commission Exhibit 573) over to the FBI, it was found to be copper jacketed and to match the bullets fired at Kennedy.[19] One could posit a conspiracy to switch bullets. Or one could say that somebody messed up. If Oswald in fact shot at Walker—and as we have seen, the reliable evidence says he did—no conspiracy to switch bullets would have been necessary. Quite simply, the Dallas cops messed up.

EVIDENCE MULTIPLIERS

An "evidence multiplier" is when one piece of bogus evidence begets others, and it's often the case when it comes to JFK assassination conspiracy evidence. We have seen one of these already in chapters 6 and 12. Once someone is identified as a suspect, assiduous researchers can produce all sorts of connections between the newly designated suspect and established assassination figures. In this chapter, we have seen how one official error gets repeated and spread around, parlaying a single mistake into multiple, apparently corroborating documents. Likewise, once a piece of conspiracy evidence becomes widely known among researchers and widely cited in conspiracy books, it begins to appear in the first-person accounts of people like Jean Hill, James Files, and Robert Easterling.

The conclusion here is simple. Two sources are better than one, and three better than two, but only if they are independently derived. Otherwise, one piece of bogus information can generate a towering but ramshackle structure of seemingly corroborating evidence.

Chapter Fourteen

How Bureaucrats Act

How much credibility we give to conspiracy theories necessarily turns on how we view government officials. This is obvious when we are talking about purported government conspiracies related to 9/11, the moon landing, or Pearl Harbor. But even when we are talking about supposed private conspiracies—a Masonic conspiracy, a conspiracy of the Elders of Zion, or a conspiracy by Texas oil millionaires to kill Kennedy—the government is always going to be involved. After all, conspirators did (and typically are thought to still be doing) evil things, and the government is doing nothing to stop them. It must be (so the logic goes) that the government is simply a pawn of powerful conspiratorial forces.

Conspiracy theories necessarily view government as very evil but very competent. Public officials are willing to do dastardly things, and when they do dastardly things, they do them so well that they leave no solid evidence behind—or at least, no hard proof of their evil deeds (although plenty of stuff that creates suspicion).

Of course, out in the real world, bureaucrats don't seem to fit that mold. They are often incompetent and inefficient. Often they do things for bureaucratic reasons that make no particular sense in terms of a wider objective, whether benign or malevolent. And sometimes they are actually benevolent, "cutting some slack" for somebody in a tough situation, or bending the rules for what everybody would agree is the right outcome.

But let's narrow the scope and discuss the government officials who were involved in the Kennedy assassination. The ones who had to articulate the cover-up (if there *was* a cover-up) and the ones who may have actually plotted to kill Kennedy.

BUREAUCRATIC INCOMPETENCE
Hoover Briefs RFK and LBJ

If anybody were instrumental in a cover-up, it had to be J. Edgar Hoover. The long-time director of the FBI, he was one of the greatest bureaucrats of all time (not that "greatest bureaucrat" is necessarily a good thing). The Warren Commission depended heavily on the work of the Bureau's agents. But just how well informed was Hoover in the hours and days following the assassination, the period when a cover-up would have had to be put in place? As noted in chapter 13, Hoover was pretty clueless on the day following the assassination. But his cluelessness started earlier than that, and lasted for quite a while.

A memorandum written by Hoover and dated 4:01 p.m. on the day of the assassination records that Hoover called Robert Kennedy at home and told him that he thought "he had the man who killed the President down in Dallas" and that his name was "Lee Harvey Oswald." Fair enough: Oswald was under arrest and was the chief suspect. Hoover continued that Oswald "left the building and a block or two away ran into two police officers and, thinking they were going to arrest him, shot at them and killed one of them." Not good: Oswald shot and killed one police officer (J. D. Tippit, as we have discussed) in the Oak Cliff neighborhood of Dallas, way across the Trinity River valley. Hoover also told Bobby about Oswald's defection to the Soviet Union and his return, and stated Oswald "went to Cuba on several occasions but would not tell us what he went to Cuba for."[1] The reality: Oswald had *tried* once in Mexico City to get a visa to go to Cuba but failed.

Slightly earlier in the afternoon, Hoover had called James Rowley, chief of the Secret Service. In a memo dated 3:21 p.m., Hoover explained that he had told Rowley that a Secret Service agent had reportedly been killed, that the shots had come from the fourth floor of a building, and that shells had been found in the building and they were Winchester shells, apparently meaning a Winchester rifle was used.[2] Note that Hoover, the supposed evil genius behind the cover-up, was out to lunch on several issues. No Secret Service agent had been killed, the shots came from the sixth floor, and the shells matched Oswald's Mannlicher-Carcano.

In his conversation with Rowley, Hoover was merely reporting what the news media were reporting. But how can you mount an effective cover-up if all you know is what the media are telling the whole wide world?

But of course, everything was confused in the hours after the assassination, so surely Hoover straightened things out eventually. Or so one would think.

A full week after the assassination, on November 29, Lyndon Johnson called Hoover to sound him out on what later became the Warren Commission. Hoover told Johnson quite a few details of the assassination, and much of what he said was simply wrong. Hoover mentioned "the matter of Oswald's getting $6500 from the Cuban embassy and coming back to this country with it," although, he added, "we are not able to prove that fact." He said that the Dallas chief of police "admits he moved Oswald in the morning as a convenience and at the request of motion picture people who wanted daylight."[3] Hoover told LBJ that a whole bullet rolled out of Kennedy's head onto the stretcher during heart massage on the way to the hospital. He said the shots could have been fired in three seconds. According to Hoover, "The President then asked, if Connally had not been in his seat, would the President have been hit by the second shot. I said yes." Hoover apparently believed that Connally had taken a bullet (it would have had to be from the front) intended for JFK. Hoover said the shots had been fired from the fifth floor of the building, and that Oswald "got on a bus; went to his home and got a jacket; then came back downtown."[4] Hoover was doing a bit better on November 29 than on November 22, but he was still a fount of misinformation.[5]

So just how does somebody who is so confused on so many points direct a cover-up? One could claim that Hoover eventually learned all he needed to know, and that the serious cover-up started weeks or months later. But unfortunately, most of the FBI forensic work and many of the witness interviews were done in the hours and days after the assassination. On December 9, 1963, the FBI released a five-volume report on the assassination.[6] By then most of the key issues had been ironed out, largely because virtually all the work was being done by Hoover's subordinates.[7] But it's absurd to claim that he somehow got up to speed between November 29 and December 9 and coordinated a massive project of producing bogus evidence, writing bogus reports (and destroying the genuine ones), and instructing all the forensics experts of the Bureau about the lies they would have to tell, all with the effect of creating a consistent case against Oswald.

Dallas Police and the Minox Camera

After the assassination Dallas cops searched the Paine residence (where Marina and the two Oswald children were staying and where Oswald had visited on weekends), and they turned up what they believed was a Minox camera. As cameras go, this one is redolent with intrigue. According to the official CIA Museum website,

"The Minox subminiature camera, in its various models, was the world's most widely used spy camera."[8]

The Dallas cops supposedly crated up the "Minox camera" (as it was listed on the manifest sent to the FBI), along with the other evidence they collected, and sent it off to the FBI. But two months later the FBI came back to the Dallas cops asking them to change the description on the manifest that listed the seized possessions. The FBI insisted that it had received a Minox *light meter*. The Dallas cops hung tough, insisting that it was a camera, not a light meter. Gus Rose, who said he found the camera in Oswald's old Marine seabag, was adamant it was a camera, and he was supported by Assistant District Attorney Bill Alexander, who saw the seized evidence and claimed to have personally worked the mechanism.[9]

So we have what, for all the world, looks like an FBI cover-up.

However, not everybody in Dallas said it was a camera. FBI agent Vince Drain, who worked with the Dallas cops to itemize the seized evidence, insisted that he didn't see any Minox camera.[10] But then, Drain was FBI, so maybe he was in on the cover-up and lying. Except that in other contexts conspiracists are happy to call the Dallas cops liars. But if they lied about a variety of other issues, all for the purpose of framing Oswald, why would they have an attack of honesty on this issue? And indeed, why would they loudly complain to the local media and embarrass the FBI?

Here we have a piece of very hard evidence that I would call dispositive. The Dallas Police photographed the seized evidence laid out on the floor of police headquarters. Does the photo show a Minox camera? No, it shows an empty Minox camera case and a Minox light meter (see photo insert for a copy of the image).[11]

There is no Minox light meter on the Dallas Police inventory. (Actually, there was both a Dallas Police and a joint DPD/FBI list made in Dallas; both list a Minox camera, and neither a Minox light meter. Both list a Minox case.) So where did the light meter and case come from if there was no camera also? The answer is quite simple. Michael Paine, the estranged husband of Ruth Paine, owned a Minox camera, which he turned over to the FBI at the end of January of 1964. The Dallas Police Property Report G-11193, dated November 26, 1963, lists "two rolls [of] apparently exposed Minox film."[12] The FBI developed the film, and Michael Paine said that he had taken all the photos. None of the photos showed anything one would expect a spy to want to photograph.[13]

But what about the claims that a Minox was taken from Oswald's seabag? Those claims came out fifteen years after the assassination, given to reporter Earl

Golz of the *Dallas Morning News* and to the HSCA. Back on January 31, 1964, FBI agent Bardwell D. Odum took a statement from Michael Paine, who told him (in Odum's words),

> When the police came to his house on November 22, 1963, they took the entire contents of a drawer containing photographic equipment which included the items mentioned above with the exception of the camera. He stated that this camera was in his garage at that time and that although he mentioned the camera to the police, they did not seem interested in it. He stated that he is sure LEE HARVEY OSWALD never used this camera, and he is of the opinion that it is not in working condition at the present time.[14]

So was the "Oswald's seabag" story simply an example of faulty memory? That's entirely plausible.[15] And consider the fact a Minox camera and a Minox light meter look rather similar and might easily be confused.[16]

Let's consider the issue further. We might ask why government spooks would equip Oswald with a Minox camera. Wasn't his role to act like a leftist radical and malcontent in anticipation of his being made a patsy? Why did he need to take spy pictures, and indeed what was there in Dallas to take spy pictures of? Oswald had no security clearance at this point and could photograph nothing beyond what anybody could shoot.

Of course, one could argue that the FBI covered up Oswald's ownership of a Minox merely because it *seemed* spooky, even though it meant nothing.

Michael Russ, who has written the definitive essay on this issue, points out how convoluted an evidence-tampering scenario would be. Conveniently, when the camera "disappears" (in the evidence photo and in the evidence the FBI obtained), the light meter appears. And vice versa. Moreover:

> The other argument against tampering would be the incredible luck that the person who was doing the tampering would have to have had in covering it up. Once it was discovered that Oswald's supposed Minox camera was missing, whoever did the tampering was lucky enough to be able to use the fact that Michael Paine also owned a Minox camera as a diversion from their tampering (just the odds that both Oswald and Paine would own the relatively uncommon Minox would be staggering). On top of that, they had the

incredible luck that the DPD inventory just happened to exclude Michael Paine's Minox light meter so that the person who did the tampering had this amazing cover story of a light meter mistaken for a camera.[17]

Bottom line? Here, as elsewhere, the hard evidence trumps. The Dallas Police were simply mistaken about this.

The Paraffin Test

Other cases of bureaucratic incompetence afflicted the Dallas cops. One that has echoed down through the decades in conspiracy books was the paraffin test administered to Oswald. It was supposed to show the presence of gunpowder residue on his hands and cheek, which might have proved he fired weapons that day, or exculpate him if no trace was found. Oswald tested positive on his hands and negative on his cheek, a result that (if taken at face value) would suggest he shot Officer Tippit (with a handgun) but not Kennedy (with a rifle). Conspiracists tend to accept the latter finding, but argue that the former was a false positive. Jim Marrs, in *Crossfire*, argues that "the results of this test presented evidence that Oswald may not have fired a rifle that day, yet these results were downplayed and even suppressed by the federal authorities."[18] And Mark Lane claims, "A positive response on both hands and a negative response on the face is consistent with innocence."[19]

In reality, the test did not provide any useful evidence. This is obvious if one reads modern forensics texts, but even in 1963 the test was known to be without value.[20] Indeed, as early as 1935 the *FBI Law Enforcement Bulletin* noted, "On the other hand, it is well to know the limitations of the diphenylamine [paraffin] test which are due to the fact that in a great many instances one may fire a revolver or pistol without leaving any trace of gunpowder on the hand which may be detected by this test."[21] FBI expert Cortlandt Cunningham explained the problems with the test to the Warren Commission, and then let slip: "There may be some law-enforcement agencies which use the test for psychological reasons." Allen Dulles replied, "Explain that." Cunningham started to explain: "Yes, sir; what they do is they ask, say, 'We are going to run a paraffin test on you, you might as well confess now,' and they will—it is—" And Dulles cut him off with "I get your point."[22]

Dallas Police forensics expert J. C. Day, when asked why he administered the test, replied lamely, "It was just something that was done to actually keep from someone saying later on, 'Why didn't you do it?'"[23] But of course, doing it resulted in conspiracy writers insisting that the test exculpated Oswald.

Dealing with Garrison: Fecklessness at Langley

For true-blue supporters of New Orleans district attorney Jim Garrison, it's a given that the federal government was heavily involved in sabotaging his investigation. For example, William Turner, an investigator who worked with Garrison, wrote, "Garrison's staff was penetrated by nine CIA agents."[24] Journalists who wrote articles critical of Garrison, or onetime staffers who became disgusted and defected, were uniformly accused of having been CIA plants.[25]

And it is true that the CIA was concerned about Garrison and what Garrison might find. A secret internal CIA memo alluded to "the impressive number of contacts we seem to have had who might now be implicated by Garrison."[26] Given Garrison's obsession with anti-Castro Cubans, and his ever-expanding list of suspects, this isn't surprising, since the CIA certainly had things it wanted to remain hidden. One thing they probably preferred to remain hidden (but only because Garrison might "misinterpret" it, according to the CIA) was that Garrison's target, Clay Shaw, had shared information on his foreign trips with the CIA Domestic Contact Service, just like thousands of other businessmen and ordinary tourists. But that had ended in 1956, and the CIA never paid Shaw for any services.[27]

So the Agency decided it needed a "Garrison Group" to deal with the troublesome DA. The first meeting of the group was on September 20, 1967.[28] That's right, September 20, seven months after the Garrison investigation began getting massive national and international attention when the New Orleans *States-Item* broke the story of his assassination probe on February 17. Indeed, if the CIA had the Garrison office infiltrated with spies as conspiracists claim, they should have known what Garrison was up to a couple of months earlier than this.[29] But it seems the CIA is more like the Department of Motor Vehicles than the well-oiled machine of conspiracy lore.

The records of the meetings of the Garrison Group show them pretty much spinning their wheels. The director of Central Intelligence, Richard Helms, was apparently not quaking in his boots in fear of being proven to have killed Kennedy. He didn't even attend the meetings, leaving the matter to subordinates. As a result, members of the group seemed especially interested in trying "to reassure the Director that we have the problem in focus."[30] Helms did complain of "the lack of explanation as to where and how he is liable to get into trouble" and "also wanted to know how he could fight back."[31] Of course, had he risked being revealed to be a JFK assassination conspirator, he wouldn't need any explanation about that.

Considerable befuddlement came to the surface when "the DD/S [Deputy Director/Support] said that he found it difficult to follow the cast of characters in Garrison's case and asked whether a chart could be provided."[32]

At two of the meetings, there was a discussion of the attempt of Clay Shaw's lawyers to contact the Justice Department in order to find out who "might be implicated at the trial."[33] But didn't these lawyers already work for the CIA? Hadn't they, as Garrison supporters claim, been part of the cabal from the start? In the actual event, they got stiffed. The verdict was that "Justice did not want the Agency to contact Shaw's lawyers, but rather to maintain the safety of our executive privilege."[34]

So what came of all this? A memo dated September 26 by Raymond Rocca outlined some possibilities for action. None of them involved any sort of dirty tricks or covert actions against Garrison. Some of the proposals involved legislative action ("an effort should be made to block or head off any attempts to put [Garrison's] *Playboy* article into the *Congressional Record*"), others involved appeals to public opinion ("file a specific bill of particulars on all aspects of the Garrison investigation that have become public"), and some involved going after people who had falsely claimed to be connected to the CIA ("initiate action with the Attorney General to bring charges of unlawful impersonation against Gordon NOVEL and Donald P. NORTON").[35] None would have done much good, and some (prosecution of Novel and Norton) would have doubtless backfired.

The helplessness of the CIA in mounting an effective response to Garrison is shown in a September 29, 1967, memo by CIA general counsel Lawrence Houston. The memo outlines all the persons Garrison claimed had a CIA connection, and explains what the connection, if any, was. But what could the CIA do if Garrison tried to convict Shaw using baseless charges of CIA connections to one or another of his suspects? Houston's conclusion was that the CIA could not refute any of Garrison's charges, since doing so would compromise the claim of "executive privilege," the right of one branch of government to resist having another branch intrude into its internal communications. The bottom line for Houston: "At the present time, therefore, there is no action we can recommend for the Director or the Agency to take."[36]

So instead of mounting a brilliant campaign of sabotage and disinformation, the CIA was fretting over legal niceties and was immobilized by the fact that it had no plausible options for action.

Other Examples of Incompetence

We won't deal here with the vastly more significant CIA fiascos like the Bay of Pigs, the plots against Fidel Castro and his regime, and the October 2002 National Intelligence Estimate (which concluded that Iraq had weapons of mass destruction, the justification for the Iraq War).[37] The key point is this: no conspiracy theory should posit a CIA vastly more competent than the CIA we see in the real world.

RISK-AVERSE BUREAUCRATS

While a lot of people associate bureaucrats with incompetence, one theme rather sophisticated people often stress is that bureaucrats are risk averse. They ask themselves: just what might get us in trouble, generate bad press, anger Congress, or just generally make life difficult?[38] When we find bureaucrats thinking like this, we don't need a conspiratorial explanation. It's a perfectly normal way for them to behave.

Oswald Allowed Back into the United States

Conspiracists almost uniformly find it very suspicious that Lee Oswald—who had defected to the Soviet Union in 1959, appeared before U.S. counsel Richard Snyder in Moscow to try to renounce his American citizenship, and promised to share military secrets with the Soviets—was allowed to return to the United States and was never prosecuted. Indeed, the State Department loaned him the money that allowed him and his wife and child to return. Author Sylvia Meagher found it highly sinister that in "decision after decision, the [State] Department removed every obstacle before Oswald—a defector and would-be expatriate, self-declared enemy of his native country, self-proclaimed discloser of classified military information . . . on his path from Minsk to Dallas."[39] Surely, this Cold War traitor should have been dealt with more harshly.

But how did the bureaucrats who decided to let him come back see the issue? One of them, an official in the Department of State (Virginia James), explained it this way:

> SOV [the Office of Soviet Affairs, Department of State] believes it is in the interest of the U.S. to get Lee Harvey Oswald and his family out of the Soviet Union and on their way to this country soon. An unstable character, whose actions are entirely unpredictable, Oswald may well refuse to leave

the USSR or subsequently attempt to return there if we should make it impossible for him to be accompanied from Moscow by his wife and child.[40]

Translation: this guy is trouble over there, and probably less trouble if we get him back in the States.

Apparently, similar logic caused Soviet officials to let him stay after he first defected to the USSR. Oswald had staged a suicide attempt, and as former KGB head Vladimir Semichastny explained to *Frontline* (speaking through an interpreter),

> If he is begging, to hell with him. Let him stay here in order to avoid an international scandal on account of such a nobody. We were not convinced this would be his last act of blackmail. We expected he would try again, which would be difficult to deal with in Moscow, so we decided to send him to Minsk.[41]

Of course, bureaucrats are not entirely without compassion. Conspiracy authors insist that Oswald should be seen entirely though Cold War lenses as a traitor. But there was a context to Oswald's defection. It's found in "The Defector Study" of the HSCA.[42] The study compared Oswald to eleven individuals who had defected to the Soviet Union between 1958 and 1964, who were at least roughly comparable to Oswald, and on whom fairly good information was available. The picture was not a pretty one. Virtually all had mental or family problems, and the vast majority eventually asked to return to the United States.

In this context, we can see how U.S. counsel Richard Snyder, when Oswald was applying to return to the United States, reported,

> Twenty months of the realities of life in the Soviet Union have clearly had a maturing effect on Oswald. He stated frankly that he learned a hard lesson the hard way and that he had been completely relieved about his illusions about the Soviet Union. . . . Much of the arrogance and bravado which characterized him on his first visit to the Embassy appears to have left him.[43]

Of course, compassion and risk aversion come together in cases like this. One may have compassion for a mixed-up kid, but it's also safer to have the mixed-up kid on U.S. soil, not likely to make trouble for the State Department.

GOING BY THE BOOK: GONORRHEA "IN THE LINE OF DUTY"

It's not terribly rare for soldiers to consort with prostitutes, so the fact that Lee Oswald, in the Marine Corps in September 1958, came down with gonorrhea should not seem strange. But the notation attached to the diagnosis on his medical record seems strange indeed. The disease was ruled "in the line of duty, not due to own misconduct."[44] Of course, you don't have to have much in the way of moral scruples about sex to view this as misconduct, since he at least should have used protection. But worse is the "in the line of duty" language. How does a Marine get clap "in the line of duty"?

This is where conspiracy logic kicks in. Intelligence services, for about as long as there have been intelligence services, have used prostitutes to get information. So perhaps Oswald was on an assignment to plant disinformation with the hookers he was consorting with. Conspiracy authors Ray and Mary La Fontaine observe, "The medical entry clearly suggests that if the Marine was involved in intelligence work, it was on the U.S. side."[45]

But suppose we try to go beyond speculation and find out what this notation actually meant. Author Anthony Summers phoned one of the doctors who treated Oswald and reported, "He did not recall the episode and explained that the notation was most probably a routine device to avoid jeopardizing Oswald's pay."[46] More specific information is available in the Warren Commission's Folsom Exhibit. Apparently, "not due to own misconduct" is a term of art. As explained by the judge advocate general, in a memo dated October 17, 1958,

> Misconduct is wrongful conduct. Simple or ordinary negligence, however, does not constitute misconduct. The fact that an act violates a law, regulation or order does not, of itself, constitute misconduct. In order to support a determination of misconduct, it must be found that the injury was intentionally incurred, or resulted from negligence that was so gross as to demonstrate a reckless disregard of the consequences.[47]

Translation: you can screw up to a degree, and we aren't going to call it "misconduct." Mark Zaid, a JFK researcher and a lawyer, notes that the Manual of the Judge Advocate General (section 0809 [b]) specifies, "Any disability resulting from venereal diseases shall not support a misconduct finding *if the member has complied with regulations* requiring him to report and receive treatment for such disease" (emphasis added).[48]

Oswald had done exactly this. Zaid further found that actions that do not rise to the level of "misconduct" will be ruled "in the line of duty" so as not to threaten a Marine's severance benefits.

There is one final piece of evidence: when Oswald shot himself with a Derringer pistol that he was not allowed to have in his possession, according to Marine rules, his injury was ruled "in the line of duty" and was "not the result of his own misconduct."[49] And this incident led to his being court-martialed. So screw-ups worse than contracting VD might still be ruled "in the line of duty" and "not the result of his own misconduct."

Of course, the Marine Corps could have mounted a crusade against VD, and harshly punished any soldier coming down with a case, but that would have invited large problems as Marines failed to get treated, and would have been a big hassle all around. So, the Corps had a rather forgiving and sensible policy. Oswald was dealt with in an entirely routine way. But you can't know that based on how the bureaucratic language *sounds*. You have to do a little research to find out what it *means*.

A GOVERNMENTAL BIAS TOWARD SECRECY

When we find the government keeping secrets, it's quite easy to jump to the conclusion that the bureaucrats must be concealing wrongdoing. After all, what *rational* reason would there be to keep something secret unless it reflects badly on you? Alas, bureaucrats often seem to have an irrational bias toward secrecy. Consider the following cases.

A Supposedly Obscene Song

In February 1964 an irate parent wrote to Attorney General Robert Kennedy to complain about the supposed obscenity of the song "Louie, Louie," asking, "How can we stamp out this menace?" The issue was kicked over to the FBI to investigate, with rather hilarious results. The FBI lab tried playing the 45 rpm record at 33 rpm in an effort to understand the lyrics, and simply could not. Members of the Kingsmen band were interviewed, and they insisted the lyrics were not obscene. The FBI, which had in its files several different versions of the "obscene" lyrics people thought they heard, obtained the real lyrics, which were quite clean.[50] But the documents relating to this episode have substantial portions redacted, including the name of the person who complained, the names of the special agents who investigated, the members of the band who were interviewed, and even the initials of one person who reviewed one of the memos.[51]

Writing in Secret Ink

In 1999 the James Madison Project, which specializes in trying to get secret documents released, asked the National Archives to specify the oldest classified document in their collection. They replied with information on six World War I documents dealing with "secret ink." The Archives would not release them without asking the CIA, and the CIA refused.[52] A CIA spokesman said, "We also don't want information that would be useful to terrorists and others who wish to harm Americans out in the public domain." James Madison Project lawyer Mark Zaid called secret ink writing "a fascinating but arcane science which today is more often the subject of comic book and cereal box advertising than spy craft."[53]

One would think that, with current technology, the CIA could read terrorist communications written in secret ink like a Microsoft Word document written in 24-point Times Roman. Further, terrorists now have computers and use the Internet to communicate, but in fact the CIA prevailed in court.[54] Finally, in 2001, the CIA approved the release of these documents. But why the delay? The answer is not much of value. This could be viewed as a deeply ingrained part of bureaucratic culture, or alternatively as the result of extreme risk aversion—not that these are really different phenomena.

THE HOSTY NOTE: A COVER-UP, BUT WHY?

Lee Oswald, after his return from the Soviet Union, was sometimes off and sometimes on the radar of the FBI. He was debriefed by agents Carter and Fain immediately on his return.[55] He was briefly "on" when he was arrested in New Orleans and asked to be interviewed by an FBI agent.[56] And he came to the attention of the Bureau again in the wake of his visit to the Soviet embassy in Mexico City. Dallas FBI special agent James Hosty was assigned to keep track of him. Hosty made two attempts to interview Oswald, going to Irving where Marina was staying with Mrs. Paine. Oswald was not there either time.

Several days before the assassination, Lee Oswald entered the Dallas FBI office and asked for Hosty. On being told that Hosty was not available, he produced a note for Hosty in an unsealed envelope and left it with the receptionist. The note eventually made its way to Hosty, who put it in his workbox. It remained there until the day of the assassination, when Hosty's supervisor Kenneth Howe found the note and took it to the special agent in charge of the Dallas office, Gordon Shanklin. Shanklin, rather disturbed, instructed Hosty to write a memo explaining the note, which the latter did.[57]

Two days later, on the afternoon Oswald was shot, Shanklin called Hosty into his office and showed him the note, saying (as Hosty recounted it), "Oswald's dead now, there can be no trial here, get rid of this." Hosty then went to the men's room, tore the note up, and flushed it down the toilet.[58]

This, of course, is an absolutely clear case of a cover-up. But covering up what? Conspiracists, of course, have their theories. Jim Marrs suggests, "Some researchers say a . . . plausible explanation is that Oswald, as an FBI informant, tried to warn the Bureau about the coming assassination."[59] Gerald McKnight argues that the note "was . . . a persuasive, if not absolutely convincing, countercheck to the official assertion that Oswald assassinated President John F. Kennedy."[60]

But what was in the note? There were three witnesses who saw the note and gave their accounts.[61] Receptionist Nanny Fenner said the note ended with the following message: "Let this be a warning. I will blow up the FBI and the Dallas Police Department if you don't stop bothering my wife." It was signed: Lee Harvey Oswald. Hosty's version, on the other hand, was, "If you have anything you want to learn about me, come talk to me directly. If you don't cease bothering my wife, I will take appropriate action and report this to the authorities."

Howe was quite vague about the note's contents, saying it contained "some kind of threat," but he knew nothing beyond that.[62] So there is no witness testimony supporting any notion that Oswald was reporting to Hosty as an FBI informer or asset. But of course, one could claim that all these people are FBI, and all are lying, although if so, it's interesting that they all tell somewhat different lies.

Ruth Paine, however, knew something about the note incident. When testifying to the Warren Commission, she described Lee's reaction when he found out that FBI agent James Hosty had been out to Irving to try to find him, but instead talked to Mrs. Paine and to Marina:

> **Ruth Paine:** I will go on as to the recollections that came later. He told me that he had stopped at the downtown office of the FBI and tried to see the agents and left a note. And my impression of it is that this notice irritated.
>
> **Albert Jenner:** Irritating?
>
> **Ruth Paine:** Irritated, that he left the note saying what he thought. This is reconstructing my impression of the fellows bothering him and his family, and this is my impression then. I couldn't say this was specifically said to him later.

Albert Jenner: You mean he was irritated?

Ruth Paine: He was irritated and he said, "They are trying to inhibit my activities. . . ."

Albert Jenner: Have you given all of what he said and what you said, however, on that occasion?

Ruth Paine: Yes. I will just go on to say that I learned only a few weeks ago that he never did go into the FBI office. Of course knowing, thinking that he had gone in, I thought that was sensible on his part. But it appears to have been another lie.[63]

Of course Lee, who lied all the time, was telling the truth about this.

Marina likewise testified about Lee's unhappiness upon finding out that Hosty was trying to reach him, and had been to Irving.

J. Lee Rankin: Now, what did you tell your husband about this visit by the FBI agent and the interview?

Marina Oswald: I told him that they had come, and that they were interested in where he was working and where he lived, and he was, again, upset. He said he would telephone them—I don't know whether he called or not—or that he would visit them.[64]

All of this, of course, is consistent with the fact that Oswald reacted strongly to Hosty when Hosty joined other law enforcement officers in the post-assassination interrogation of Oswald. According to Dallas Police detective Elmer Boyd, Oswald was "pretty upset with Mr. Hosty," because Oswald "said [Hosty] had been to the house two or three times talking to his wife, and he didn't appreciate him coming out there when he wasn't there."[65]

All the evidence adds up. The FBI witnesses disagree about just how overwrought the tone of the note was, but they all agree that Oswald was unhappy about Hosty talking to Marina; Ruth Paine's testimony, Marina's testimony, and the testimony from Oswald's post-assassination interrogation support that.

Think Scenario

If one is inclined to dismiss the witness testimony, one has to explain what the sinister purpose behind the note's destruction would be. If Oswald was some kind of agent or informant, one would think that he would have a more secure and reliable way of communicating with Hosty. Hosty's phone number was in Oswald's address book (Hosty had given it to Marina and Ruth Paine when he went out to Irving), and it makes no sense that an undercover asset or agent would leave a note with explosive information with a receptionist in an unsealed envelope.

Covering Up Something That Wasn't Misconduct

The guiding principle behind these actions is CYA: "cover your anatomy." It could be claimed that the FBI knew about Oswald being in Dallas, and therefore should have stopped the assassination. Indeed, when Dallas Police chief Jesse Curry told reporters that the FBI "knew about" Oswald and had not informed the Dallas Police, J. Edgar Hoover went entirely ballistic.[66] Further, it could be claimed that Hosty provoked an irate and unstable Oswald to shoot Kennedy. Neither charge would be fair, but fairness wouldn't have prevented it from being made. So ironically the FBI, afraid of unfair charges of misconduct, engaged in a genuine form of misconduct by destroying the note.

Of course, bureaucrats sometimes cover up genuine misconduct. Director of Central Intelligence Richard Helms, for example, ordered the destruction of files related to the agency's notorious MK/ULTRA program, which involved experiments in "mind control."[67] And the much more recent destruction by the CIA of hundreds of hours of interrogation of two al Qaeda lieutenants certainly raises the suspicion that what the tapes showed was rather unsavory.[68] But sometimes bureaucrats cover up stuff that's merely embarrassing. The CIA, for example, failed to inform the Warren Commission of CIA plots against Castro.[69] These were a source of embarrassment to the agency, but unless one believes that Castro had JFK killed in retaliation—something that a few people, but probably nobody in the CIA, believe—they have no relevance to the question of conspiracy.

IN SUMMARY

It's impossible to make a judgment on the validity of conspiracy theories without a sensible view of how government operates. Yes, bureaucrats sometimes do downright evil things. Quite frequently they are incompetent. Often they apply the rules and do things "by the book" even if it doesn't seem to make sense to outsiders. And they are quite generally sensitive to things that might generate "trouble," whether it's bad publicity, the ire of administrative superiors, or the attention of a legislature. That's the way real-world bureaucracies work, and none of it necessarily implies a conspiracy.

Chapter Fifteen

Putting Theory into Practice:
The Single Bullet Theory

Nothing about the Warren Commission's case has drawn more ridicule and scorn than the "single bullet" theory—universally dubbed the "magic bullet" theory by the conspiracists. As any conspiracy book will tell you, the theory requires that one bullet (Warren Commission Exhibit 399) inflict seven wounds on Kennedy and Connally: an entrance wound in Kennedy's back, an exit wound in Kennedy's throat, an entrance wound in Connally's back, an exit wound in Connally's chest, both an entry and an exit wound in Connally's right wrist, and an entrance wound in the governor's left thigh. The view of this theory in conspiracy books was best summarized by actor Kevin Costner, playing Jim Garrison in the movie *JFK*: "Never in the history of gunfire has there been a bullet like this."[1]

The conspiracists' critique of the single bullet theory is not an attack on one part of the theory. Rather, virtually every element of the theory has been labeled impossible. They have insisted that Kennedy's back wound was too low to be consistent with the theory. They have insisted that the wound in Kennedy's throat was in fact an entrance wound, not the exit wound that would fit the logic of the theory. They have insisted that Kennedy and Connally were not properly aligned for the trajectory to work, such that the bullet would have to zig and zag to hit both men. They have insisted that the Zapruder film shows Kennedy and Connally hit at different times, rather than at the same time. They have insisted that Connally could not have continued to hold his hat (as he is seen doing in the Zapruder film) if he had been hit in the wrist. They have insisted that the bullet is "pristine" and could not have inflicted all those wounds.

Conspiracists often depict Connally as holding his hat directly in front of his chest. If he did that at the moment the single bullet struck, the bullet leaving his chest directly below the right nipple would have to change direction and loop around to hit the dorsal side of Connally's right wrist (the top of the wrist when the hand is palm down), then exit the volar side (the bottom of the wrist when the hand is palm down) before going on to bury itself in Connally's right thigh.[2] So, if conspiracists have the geometry right, the single bullet theory is toast.

Another key issue is timing. Conspiracists usually assert that Kennedy has already been struck by a bullet when he appears from behind the Stemmons Freeway sign in the Zapruder film at frame 225. Yet, conspiracists typically insist, Connally shows no signs of being hit by a bullet until Zapruder frame 234 or so.[3] We have to do some very simple math to see the problem here. The FBI determined that Zapruder's camera ran at 18.3 frames per second. One good estimate of how quickly a very good shooter could cycle the mechanism of the Mannlicher-Carcano rifle was provided by FBI firearms expert Robert Frazier. He got off three accurate shots in 4.6 seconds. Since the clock starts the instant he fired the first shot, this means he could cycle and rifle and aim an accurate shot in 2.3 seconds.[4] Multiply 2.3 by 18.3 and you get 42 (rounding just a little), which is the minimum number of Zapruder frames between any two shots fired by a single gunman. Now bring in one more number: Kennedy appears to be unhurt when he disappears behind the Stemmons Freeway sign at Zapruder frame 210. Thus, if Kennedy was already hit when he reappeared from behind the Stemmons Freeway sign at Zapruder frame 225, and Connally was not hit at that point, they must have been hit by different shots. Given the 42 frames required to cycle and aim the rifle, no single shooter could have shot Kennedy at frame 210 and then hit Connally earlier than frame 251. But Connally is plainly hit by 235/236. So either a single bullet inflicted all these wounds on Kennedy and Connally, or there were two shooters.

All the issues surrounding the single bullet theory are interrelated. For example, if you are going to plot the trajectory of a hypothetical single bullet, you need to know where the wounds in Kennedy and Connally were. One does a trajectory analysis by connecting the wounds and seeing whether the line points back at the School Book Depository. If you don't know where the wounds were, you can't draw the line. If you have them in the wrong place, the line points somewhere it shouldn't.

Likewise, if one is going to plot a trajectory, one needs to know when Kennedy and Connally were hit. It might be that the trajectory works perfectly at

Zapruder frame 223, but not at all at Zapruder frame 237. In this latter case, hard evidence that one of the two men was hit at 237 blows the single bullet theory out of the water. But on the other hand, if it's unclear when the two men were hit, we might prefer a timing scenario that allows the single bullet theory to work—especially if the alternative is multiple shooters blasting away from various directions, all of them (aside from the shooter in the depository) leaving no evidence of being there.

KENNEDY AND CONNALLY'S BACK WOUNDS

Conspiracists, as noted, tend to insist that the wound must have been too low on Kennedy's back to allow a single bullet trajectory to work, and they point to four pieces of evidence. First, there is the autopsy face sheet that shows a dot on the back of the generic figure on the preprinted form.[5] If the face sheet is drawn accurately and to scale, the wound is too low to be consistent with the single bullet theory.

Second, there is Kennedy's death certificate, signed by his personal physician, Adm. George Burkley. It places the wound "at about the level of the third thoracic vertebra."[6] While "about" suggests a lack of precision, an actual entry at T3 would be too low for the single bullet theory to work. Third, conspiracists have combed through witness testimony to find witnesses who will put the wound in the lower location. For example, Secret Service agent Glenn Bennett, who was riding in the follow-up car, filed a written report saying that he "saw the shot hit the President about 4 inches down from the right shoulder."[7] Agent Clint Hill, who saw the body in the morgue at Bethesda told the Warren Commission, "I saw an opening in the back, about 6 inches below the neckline to the right-hand side of the spinal column."[8] Finally, conspiracists note that the hole in Kennedy's coat and the corresponding hole in his shirt appear too low to be consistent with the single bullet trajectory.

The Autopsy Face Sheet: The Wound Placement

In the mid-1960s, conspiracists quickly noticed and made an issue of the placement of the wound on the face sheet, and two of the three autopsists (James Humes and J. Thornton Boswell) were separately asked about it. The *Baltimore Sun*, in an article that ran on November 25, 1966, asked Boswell about this issue. Boswell said that the face sheet was not intended to be drawn to scale, and in the normal course of events would be superseded by photos of the body. Boswell put an "X" on the face sheet drawing perhaps three inches above the famous dot, explaining that that was where the entry wound was.

Humes was questioned by Dan Rather for a 1967 CBS News documentary *A CBS Inquiry: The Warren Report*, and he explained that the dot on the face sheet was merely an "aide–mémoire," and that the measurements written on the face sheet were accurate.[9]

Is this plausible, or just a mealy-mouthed excuse? Or worse, intentional disinformation?

Researcher Todd Wayne Vaughan analyzed materials from the autopsy of Lee Oswald, which was done by Dr. Earl Rose, the highly competent Dallas County medical examiner. Vaughan noted that

> I compared the locations of the wounds as marked on the body drawing with the measured location noted next to the wounds on the same sheet. It was obvious that they did not match, and that the marks on the body diagram were schematic and not to scale.[10]

One could argue, of course, that this just shows Earl Rose to have been incompetent—although this would be hard to square with Rose's stellar reputation.[11] More likely is what the HSCA Forensic Pathology Panel concluded—that "the drawing was merely a crude representation used as a worksheet primarily to assist in the preparation of the final report and was not necessarily an exact representation of the wound."

The panel further argued that "if the wound were located as low as represented on the worksheet, it probably would have penetrated and collapsed the right lung, an effect that would have been apparent on the initial chest X-ray."[12] Of course, the X-rays show the lung had not collapsed.

Since the Forensic Pathology Panel consisted of nine forensic pathologists, all among the most eminent in the nation who had been responsible for more than a hundred thousand autopsies, it would be hard to argue that they didn't know what was plausible with regard to autopsy face sheets.[13] Indeed, any reader who has had a minor auto accident and noticed the claims adjuster simply slapping an "X" on the dented fender (rather than trying to represent the damage precisely) should understand the principle.

Witness Testimony

We should know, by now, not to trust witness testimony. But it's worth noting that conspiracy authors are quite selective in how they quote "back wound" witnesses. Drawings done for the HSCA by Richard Lipsey and James Jenkins, both of whom were present at the autopsy, place the wound well above the T3 location that conspiracists prefer.[14] But like many witnesses, Jenkins has been inconsistent. In a 1998 interview with conspiracy author Charles Drago, he said the wound was "probably at T4."[15] This is hard to square with his drawing for the HSCA, but memory is fallible, and we can't assume that everybody (even all medical personnel) have a good knowledge of surface anatomy. An ignorance of surface anatomy may also explain why Admiral Burkley signed a death certificate placing the wound at T3.

The Face Sheet: Measurements

While conspiracy authors will tout the drawing on the autopsy face sheet, they are virtually unanimous in ignoring the measurements written on that same face sheet. The face sheet places the wound fourteen centimeters below the tip of the right mastoid process, the bony prominence of the skull directly behind the earlobe. This would be consistent with T1 (at the first thoracic vertebra, just below the seventh cervical vertebra) and not T3. This figure is repeated in the text of the autopsy report.[16] The autopsy also describes the path of the bullet through Kennedy's torso, saying it "traversed the soft tissue of the supra-scapular and supra-clavicular portions of the base of the right side of the neck." Further, the missile produced "contusions of the right apical parietal pleura and of the apical portion of the right upper lobe of the lung."[17] Decoding the medical jargon: the path of the bullet was above the shoulder blade, above the collarbone, and it bruised the tip of the right lung. To repeat, a bullet that hit Kennedy at T3 would have penetrated the lung and collapsed it, and neither the autopsy report nor any account from Parkland Hospital mentions a collapsed right lung. Conspiracists have been rather selective about citing evidence from the autopsy report. They have latched on to one very convenient dot, ignored the measurements in the report, and ignored specific anatomical statements about the path of the bullet.

Befuddlement at the Autopsy

Of course, one can challenge the autopsy report as a massive fake. Conspiracists, for example, like to quote nonsensical things that were said during the autopsy, or preliminary speculations of the autopsists, as though they are evidence of what the wounds *really* showed. The autopsists, for example, were unable to probe the wound through the torso, and speculated that the bullet had penetrated only shallowly and then been forced out by cardiac massage.[18] There was also speculation about a possible ice bullet that might have inflicted a shallow wound and then melted.[19] This, of course, is ballistics nonsense. But suppose you know there is a bullet entrance and cannot find any exit (the tracheotomy from Parkland obscured the exit). Suppose you can't find a bullet in the body. You might, in a moment of complete befuddlement, think about this.

But all this shows confusion, not conspiracy. For example, the autopsists said the bullet entered Kennedy's back at a 45–60 degree downward angle.[20] The angle from the sniper's nest would have been around 20 degrees, and above the sniper's nest was one more depository floor, and then sky.[21] Anybody want to look for evidence of a CIA stealth blimp over Dealey Plaza being used as a sniper's perch?

Supposedly, the conspiracy was covered up when Commander Humes wrote the autopsy report, by which time he knew what he had to say.

The Hard Evidence

But here, as is virtually always the case, hard physical evidence trumps witnesses, questioned official reports, and speculation: the autopsy photos and X-rays. As we have seen in chapter 11, these were authenticated by the HSCA using the best talent in a variety of disciplines. They were extensively analyzed by the HSCA Forensic Pathology Panel, which had the camera-original color transparencies and first-generation black-and-white prints. The Forensic Pathology Panel also had access to digitally enhanced versions of the photos, and could examine some of the wounds (including the back wound) through stereo visualization of pairs of photos. There happens to be a ruler in the photos of Kennedy's back. The HSCA concluded that "the midpoint [of the wound] is estimated to be 13.5 centimeters below the right mastoid process, with the head and neck, as positioned within the photograph, 6 centimeters below the most prominent neck crease and 5 centimeters below the upper shoulder margin."[22]

Remember, the autopsy said the wound was fourteen centimeters below the tip of the right mastoid process. The phrase "close enough for government work" comes to mind. This would be consistent with an entry at T1, which is high enough for the single bullet trajectory to work. The Forensic Pathology Panel, like the autopsists, noted an abrasion collar around the back wound, which clearly indicates an entrance wound.[23] So all the blather about witnesses, burned autopsy notes, face sheet drawings, and such really doesn't matter.[24] This is the "killer" evidence, and it places an entrance wound at C7/T1.[25]

Coat and Shirt Holes

One final argument, relevant to the back wound, is that the holes in Kennedy's jacket and shirt are too low to be consistent with a wound at T1. In reality, the hole in the jacket is 5.3 inches (13.5 cm) below the top margin of the collar.[26] The corresponding defect in the shirt was 14 cm below the upper collar border.

A generation of lone gunman theorists has accepted the assumption that this would be too low to be consistent with the single bullet theory, and have argued that Kennedy's coat and shirt were bunched up.[27] And indeed, photos of Kennedy in Dallas with Kennedy's coat obviously bunched up are plentiful.[28] But if the top of the coat collar was level with the tip of the right mastoid process, the hole in the coat and the back wound match up nicely, both 13.5 cm down. And indeed, multiple photos of Kennedy in the limo during the Dallas motorcade appear to show the top of his collar at his hairline, about level with the bottom of his earlobe, and therefore roughly level with the tip of his mastoid process.[29]

But if we believe the autopsy photos and X-rays—and we have seen that we should—this issue is largely moot. Since we know where the back wound was, the holes in the coat and shirt have to be consistent with that. The alternative is to believe the coat and shirt have somehow been forged to make the single bullet theory look impossible.

KENNEDY'S THROAT WOUND

If the location of Kennedy's back wound is controversial, both the location and the nature of the throat wound are subject to controversy. Conspiracists frequently insist that the throat wound was actually one of entrance. And they do indeed have some evidence for this. In the first place, the Parkland doctors seemed to *believe* that it was an entrance wound, since it was quite small and rather neat—unlike the large gory "stellate" wounds that are typical when a bullet exits. A press conference on the afternoon of the assassination included Dr. Malcolm Perry, who had headed the team trying to resuscitate the president. He was asked, "Where was the entrance wound?" and he responded, "There was an entrance wound in the neck."[30]

This, of course, is simply Perry's conclusion on an issue of wound ballistics, a matter about which he had no expertise. But it's easy to see why he reached it. The witnesses who saw the wound before it was obliterated by a tracheotomy incision gave essentially similar testimony to the Warren Commission. Perry said the wound was "situated in the lower anterior one-third of the neck, approximately 5 mm in diameter."[31] Dr. Carrico said there "was a small wound, 5 to 8 mm in size, located in the lower third of the neck, below the thyroid cartilage, the Adam's apple."[32] He was called to testify again, and said it "was probably a 4–7 mm. wound, almost in the midline, maybe a little to the right of the midline, and below the thyroid cartilage.[33] Dr. Roland Jones said that "the wound in the throat was probably no larger than a quarter of an inch in diameter. . . . It was a very small, smooth wound."[34] Finally, Nurse Margaret Henchliffe testified that "it was just a little hole in the middle of his neck. . . . About as big around as the end of my little finger."[35]

Shored Wounds

It is certainly true that exit wounds *tend* to be larger than entrance wounds. As wound ballistics expert Abdullah Fatteh notes,

> The increase in the area of the striking surface of a bullet at the point of exit due to deformation, yawing or tumbling explains why the *exit wounds are usually larger than the entrance wounds*.[36]

But there is an important exception: shored exit wounds. Again, from Fatteh:

> The presence of objects pressing against the skin in the area of exit of the bullet may affect the size of the exit hole. The pressure from such objects limits external stretching of the margins of the perforated skin. Consequently the subsidiary tears are not as extensive as they would otherwise be. The exit hole in such circumstances tends to be small and round with minimal tearing of the margins.[37]

And then, slightly later, Fatteh explains further,

> If a bullet exits from the skin without any resistance other than the tissue resistance, an exit hole with subsidiary tears results. . . . If, however, the bullet exits from the skin against pressure from a firm or hard object in

contact with the skin, the appearances of the exit wounds are different. . . . If the object in contact with the skin is hard and the bullet exits against considerable resistance from it, the exit wound may not only be round but it may show a rim of abrasion in its margins. Such exit wounds could easily be mistaken for entrance wounds. Exit wounds of this nature may be seen when the victim is lying on the ground or standing against a wall when shot and the exited bullet is stopped by the ground or the wall. They may also be caused when the exited bullet hits a belt, buckle, tough clothing or a similar object in tight contact with the skin.[38]

What shored Kennedy's exit wound? Simple: his shirt and tie. As his skin was stretched outward, the shirt and tie stopped the expansion before the skin ripped open. Thus, instead of leaving a stellate wound with nasty tears of the skin, the bullet punched through, leaving a relatively clean hole.

This is not mere speculation. John Lattimer simulated this shoring using pork legs that had the bone removed. He then fastened around the pork a shirt and tie like Kennedy's. Using his Mannlicher-Carcano rifle (every good assassination buff needs a Mannlicher-Carcano!) and ammunition identical to Oswald's (right down to the lot numbers), he shot through the simulated "neck," aiming so that the bullet exited at the same place, relative to the tie and collar, as the single bullet supposedly exited Kennedy's neck. The resulting wound was quite small, approximately ¼ inch in diameter. When he "undressed" the piece of pork by taking the tie off, he got a full-fledged stellate wound with large, nasty-looking tears.[39]

The HSCA Forensic Pathology Panel agreed with the Lattimer thesis, saying that a wound like Kennedy's neck wound could result "if the tissues through which the missile exited were shored, buttressed or otherwise reinforced by clothing or other external objects that would minimize the outward displacement of the skin and underlying superficial tissue and consequent tearing and distortion of these tissues." Further, the Forensic Pathology Panel agreed that the shirt and tie "might have served as sufficient reinforcement to diminish distortion of the skin."[40]

Unqualified Autopsy Doctors

The doctors who handled the autopsy of John Kennedy were not forensic pathologists. They were ordinary hospital pathologists with no expertise in making *forensic* determinations. If somebody died in a hospital, they doubtless were competent enough at determining the cause of death. But if somebody was shot, or poisoned, or shot himself, or died in an accident, they were not trained to do the sort of autopsy that the legal proceedings that followed would need.[41]

Bethesda was chosen as the site of the autopsy by Jackie Kennedy on the plane returning from Dallas to Washington. The president's aide, Admiral Burkley, told her that the autopsy needed to be at a military hospital for "security reasons," and added, "Of course, the President was in the Navy." Jackie responded with "Of course" and "Bethesda."[42]

One of the ironies of the case is that a skid-row bum found dead in a gutter in Dallas on November 22, 1963, would have been autopsied by Dr. Earl Rose. But the Kennedy family and its loyal retainers had the power—not to speak of the massive sympathy of the entire nation—to take the body out of Dallas and then choose the autopsy location, something no lesser mortals would ever have been allowed to do in a murder case.

But what about the Parkland doctors? Surely they had seen a lot of gunshot wounds, and their opinions should carry some weight. But actually no, they carry virtually no weight.

A study done at the Bowman Gray School of Medicine, Wake Forest University in Winston-Salem, North Carolina, looked at cases of people brought into the ER with multiple gunshot wounds. (If somebody has only a single wound, it's certainly an entrance wound, barring the unlikely possibility that they swallowed a gun that then discharged.) They looked at people who died and were autopsied by board-certified forensic pathologists. The researchers then compared the results of the forensic autopsy with the assessments of ER doctors as to whether each given wound was an entrance or an exit, and as to the number of shots that hit the deceased. Of the forty-six cases in their sample, ER doctors had been mistaken in twenty-four of them, including sixteen cases of errors in determining whether the wound was an entrance or exit wound, and fifteen errors in determining the number of bullets that had struck the deceased. While wounds caused by a single bullet had been misinterpreted 37 percent of the time, wounds caused by multiple bullets had been misinterpreted 75 percent of the time.[43]

Kennedy, of course, was a victim of two bullets—one in the head and one in the torso. And indeed, the early statements of the Parkland doctors clearly show the confusion that multiple wounds can cause. At the press conference on the afternoon of the assassination, Perry was asked of the head wound and the neck wound, "Could that be done by one shot?" He replied, "I cannot conjecture. I don't know." And then later, "There are two wounds, as Dr. [Kemp] Clark noted, one of the neck and one of the head. Whether they are directly related or related to two bullets, I cannot say." Further on, neurosurgeon Kemp Clark told reporters, "The head wound could have been either the exit wound from the neck or it could have been a tangential wound, as it was simply a large, gaping loss of tissue." Reporters really dogged the doctors on this issue, demanding, "Was there one or two wounds? Just give us something." Perry responded, "I don't know."

Given the Wake Forest study, none of this confusion and uncertainty should surprise anybody, but these statements at the news conference don't begin to show all the confusion among the Parkland doctors. Dr. Carrico told the Warren Commission,

> As I recall, Dr. Perry and I talked and tried after—later in the afternoon to determine what exactly had happened, and we were not aware of the missile wound to the back, and postulated that this [throat wound] was either a tangential wound from a fragment, possibly another entrance wound. It could have been an exit wound, but we knew of no other entrance wound.[44]

The notion that the throat wound was from a fragment is also found in the admission note of Dr. Robert McClelland, written at 4:45 on the afternoon of the assassination, saying that the president had "a massive gunshot wound of the head with a fragment wound of the trachea."[45]

But then Dr. Clark, who was in the ER, told the *New York Times* that one bullet hit Kennedy at about the necktie and "ranged downward in his chest and did not exit."[46] The ER doctors were, in sum, speculating wildly. And that was not because they were incompetent; the emergency room operation at Parkland was first-rate, and Kennedy could not have gotten better care, although he was beyond help. Forensic pathologists exist for a reason: they make the forensic determinations that other doctors don't do, and in fact shouldn't do, since that would interfere with keeping the patient alive.

Above or Below the Collar?

While conspiracists work to move the back wound down, they work to move the neck wound *up*. An example of this is found in Groden and Livingstone's *High*

Treason, which shows a drawing of a bullet hitting Kennedy low in the back, and another hitting him from the front in the Adam's apple. This is necessary since there were bullet defects in Kennedy's shirt, penetrating both the button and buttonhole portions of the shirt fabric, right below the collar button where they overlap.[47] According to the FBI, "the hole in the front of the shirt was a ragged, slit-like hole and the ends of the torn threads around the hole were bent outward. These characteristics are typical of an exit hole for a projectile."[48] The use of "projectile" rather than bullet is intentional. FBI firearms expert Robert Frazier told the Warren Commission, "I could not actually determine from the characteristics of the hole whether or not it was caused by a bullet."[49]

Perhaps the FBI was aware of the speculation about an exiting fragment, and was being extremely scrupulous in not ruling that out. A photo of the shirt, produced by the FBI, does indeed show ragged slits with the fibers pushed outward.[50]

Conspiracists have responded by claiming that the slits in the shirt were the result of scalpel-wielding nurses cutting off Kennedy's clothes. Indeed, nurses did cut off Kennedy's clothes, but why they would be fooling around with Kennedy's collar, piercing it from the *inside*, making a slit rather than the smooth long cut necessary to get the shirt off, is difficult to fathom, as is the claim that the very ragged holes were made by a scalpel. This claim, originated by conspiracy curmudgeon Harold Weisberg, reeks of desperation.[51]

If the defect in the front of Kennedy's shirt was not a bullet hole, and if one believes that the hole in Kennedy's throat was an entrance wound, it must follow that the wound was higher up, above the top margin of the collar. But the Dallas doctors clearly placed the wound well below the Adam's apple, consistent with the slits in the shirt collar. Kemp Clark, for example, said "lower third of the anterior neck."[52] Malcolm Perry said the wound was "in the midline of the neck, in the lower third anteriorly."[53] It's relevant here that these assessments come from admission notes of November 22, 1963. This is long before any of the doctors could have learned of any controversy over the issue and "regularized" their testimony.

But here, as elsewhere, arguing over witness testimony isn't terribly productive. Better evidence exists in the autopsy photos. Two of them in particular, the Stare of Death photo and a Left Profile photo, show the gash in Kennedy's throat where the tracheotomy obscured the neck wound. The gash is in the lower third of the neck, well below the Adam's apple, and where we could expect the wound to be if a bullet exited Kennedy's throat and tore through his shirt, nicking his tie.[54] As always, the hard evidence trumps. A bullet (or at least a "projectile") exited Kennedy's throat.

CONNALLY'S BACK AND CHEST WOUNDS

John Connally's back wound isn't particularly controversial. He was indeed hit in the back, and it was indeed a wound of entry. But there was one important thing about it: its oval shape. The HSCA Forensic Pathology Panel thought this important, since only two things could account for this. First, the bullet could have hit Connally's back at a sharp angle. But Dr. Shaw, who described the wound, made no mention of undermining of the contralateral margin of the wound, or of an abrasion collar on one margin, either or both of which might indicate a bullet hitting from an acute angle.[55]

So what is the other possibility? The Forensic Pathology Panel concluded "that the wound in Governor Connally was probably inflicted by a missile which was not aligned with its trajectory but had yawed or tumbled prior to entry into the Governor," and this was most likely "due to striking an intervening object."[56]

So if the bullet had hit something before it hit Connally, what is the most obvious thing it might have hit? Kennedy's torso, of course, although if Connally was hit by a bullet that did not hit Kennedy, some shooter's location (particularly in the Dal-Tex Building) would allow the bullet to hit a twig on the live oak tree in front of the depository.[57]

The chest wound is perhaps the least controversial of all the wounds. It was a large, nasty "sucking" wound right below Connally's right nipple.[58] Connally's back wound was clearly an entrance, and this wound is clearly an exit.

CONNALLY'S WRIST WOUNDS

Connally's wrist wounds are controversial for two reasons. First, conspiracists will insist that Warren Commission Exhibit 399 could not have left all the metal fragments that were in Connally's wrist and still weigh 158.6 grains, which is what it now weighs. Second, they claim that if Connally's wrist was shattered by the bullet that hit Kennedy (and Kennedy is clearly hit by frame 226), the governor could not have continued to hold his Stetson hat, which he is clearly holding in the Zapruder film for as long as the hit right hand is visible.

Both of these claims are weak. Frazier weighed three randomly chosen Mannlicher-Carcano bullets and got weights of 160.85, 161.5, and 161.1 grains.[59]

Doing some simple subtraction, this would imply that somewhere between 2.25 and 2.9 grains of metal should be left in Connally.[60] If there were more, Exhibit 399 could not have been responsible for all his wounds.

But there is indeed witness testimony that there was more. Nurse Audrey Bell, who said she took the fragments from the doctor who was removing them, put them in an envelope and turned it over to authorities. She has, several times, said that more lead was found in Connally's wrist than could have been missing from Exhibit 399. To conspiracy author Harrison Livingstone she said, "What we took off [Governor Connally] was greater than what is missing from this bullet [399]." "Much greater?" she was asked. She replied, "Yes."[61] She also said that "the smallest [of the fragments] was the size of the striking end of a match and the largest at least twice that big. I have seen the picture of the magic bullet, and I can't see how it could be the bullet from which the fragments I saw came."[62] In the 1970s, Bell was interviewed by the HSCA, and made a drawing of the fragments. Her drawing shows fragments much larger than the extant Connally fragments. She was shown Warren Commission Exhibit 842 (the purported Connally wrist fragments) by Assassination Records Review Board in 1997, and she said (in the words of Doug Horne, Review Board staffer) "that the fragment(s) photographed in the container were too small, and were too few in number, to represent what she handled on 11/22/63."[63]

Of course, one might wonder what the doctor who took the fragments out of Connally's wrist said. That doctor, one Charles Francis Gregory, told a rather different story. Before the Warren Commission he described the fragments as "varying from five-tenths of a millimeter in diameter to approximately 2 millimeters in diameter, and each fragment is no more than a half millimeter in thickness. They would represent in lay terms flakes, flakes of metal." And further, "They would be weighed in micrograms which is very small amount of weight. . . . It is the kind of weighing that requires a microadjustable scale, which means that it is something less than the weight of a postage stamp."[64]

So, we can accept the 1964 testimony of the doctor who removed some of the fragments from Connally's wrist (and left others, believing that trying to dig them out would do more damage than leaving them), testimony which is consistent with the fragments actually entered into evidence, or we can believe Nurse Bell, who went on record years later and whose version requires that the Commission

Exhibit has been tampered with, and indeed that the X-rays of Connally's wrist and thigh have been tampered with.[65]

Conspiracy author Josiah Thompson estimated the weight of all the fragments that would have been shed by CE 399 in the body of John Connally as "about 1.5 grains."[66] If anything, Thompson's estimate is on the high side, since he thought there were two fragments in the thigh (one lost, one visible on the X-ray) and one fragment visible in the chest X-ray. In reality, there was only one fragment in Connally's thigh and no fragment in Connally's chest.[67] Since the bullet could easily have shed between 2.25 grains and 2.9 grains, 1.5 grains shed in Connally's body isn't any sort of problem.

Connally Holding His Hat

If Connally was shot in the wrist, the question arises as to how he would hold onto his hat with his wrist shattered. And indeed, Connally is sitting in the limo holding his hat up in front of his upper cheek in Zapruder frame 230, which is after Kennedy is clearly wounded. Robert Groden, for example, notes that Connally is still holding his hat at Zapruder frame 274, and claims "this proves that Governor Connally was struck by two bullets."[68]

In reality, the bullet that smashed Connally's wrist damaged the radial nerve (which supplies sensation to part of the back of the hand) and not the ulnar and median nerves that enervate the muscles that maintain a grip.[69] But all this is rather moot when we consider the fact that John Connally most certainly *did* continue holding his hat. And he continued long past the point at which he has clearly been shot. Nellie Connally described the horror of the shooting to the *Texas Monthly*. She said of her husband,

> And he also, he has . . . he has . . . his hat in his hand. He always had that hat somewhere. He had the hat in his hand when I pulled him over and crouched him down and he was holding that hat up against him. He closed up that wound that would've killed him before we got to the hospital.[70]

The late Governor Connally was a loyal son of Texas. He's probably still holding that hat.

Michael Baden, chair of the HSCA Forensic Pathology Panel, told the committee that "Governor Connally did, in fact, hold his hat after he was shot, and after the bullet passed through his wrist." And further,

He did, in fact, not know that his wrist was injured after he was shot and it is not in our experience, investigation, unusual although it doesn't sound right but, in fact, people may be significantly injured and may have broken bones and may continue walking, continue holding a hat and not know it.[71]

Of course, people have suffered wounds much worse than Connally and still held objects. Consider, for example, Hawaii senator Daniel K. Inouye, who lost an arm in combat in World War II. He described the incident in his autobiography:

At last I was close enough to pull the pin on my last grenade. And as I drew my arm back, all in a flash of light and dark I saw him, that faceless German, like a strip of motion picture film running through a projector that's gone berserk. One instant he was standing waist-high in the bunker, and the next he was aiming a rifle grenade at my face from a range of ten yards. And even as I cocked my arm to throw, he fired and his rifle grenade smashed into my right elbow and exploded and all but tore my arm off. I looked at it, stunned and unbelieving. It dangled there by a few bloody shreds of tissue, my grenade still clenched in a fist that suddenly didn't belong to me anymore.[72]

So the fact that Connally continued to hold his hat appears to be, in fact, a non-issue.

CONNALLY'S THIGH WOUND

As with virtually every other wound in the body of either Connally or Kennedy, the thigh wound has created controversy. A key issue has been just how deep it was. An early report by Dr. George Thomas Shires stated that a missile fragment was deeply buried within the thigh in the femur.[73] Conspiracists quickly concluded that a bullet could not penetrate this deeply and then just fall out of the wound.

On this issue, as on every other, the best evidence is from the photos and X-rays. The Forensic Pathology Panel looked at the X-ray and concluded that "the 2 millimeter density is a missile fragment that was just under the skin and not deep within the thigh in the femur bone, as described in the Warren Commission Report."[74] Of course, a bullet that barely pierces the skin can easily leave a fragment and then fall out.

THE CONDITION OF THE BULLET

Warren Commission Exhibit 399 has been almost universally derided by conspiracists as "pristine." How could a bullet that inflicted seven wounds on two men be pristine?

Well, in the first place, it's not at all pristine. Viewed end-on, the tail of the bullet is badly mashed.[75] The muzzle velocity of a bullet fired from a Mannlicher-Carcano was between 2,100 and 2,200 feet per second.[76] Any bullet hitting hard bone at that velocity would certainly deform more than Exhibit 399; indeed, ballistics expert Larry Sturdivan told the HSCA that any velocity above 1,400 feet per second would cause deformation.[77]

In fact, the bullet never hit hard bone at full muzzle velocity. It lost about 400 feet per second in the air and in Kennedy's torso,[78] and then lost more velocity tumbling through Connally's chest, hitting only a "relatively thin and readily shattered rib" in the words of the HSCA Forensic Pathology Panel before finally hitting hard bone in Connally's wrist.[79] It's difficult to know how much velocity a tumbling bullet will lose, and conspiracists like John Hunt hold out for a higher velocity of about 1,300 feet per second.[80]

One key principle of physics is relevant here: kinetic energy varies as the *square* of velocity. Halve the velocity, and you have reduced the kinetic energy to only a quarter of what it was. Thus Martin Fackler fired a Mannlicher-Carcano round into the wrist of a human cadaver at 1,100 feet per second and the result was a bullet that appeared genuinely pristine (as opposed to the not-really-pristine Exhibit 399).[81] The HSCA Forensic Pathology Panel insisted that, in their considerable collective experience, a bullet that has been slowed by passage through soft tissue before hitting bone may be little more deformed than a bullet that has hit soft tissue only.[82]

That the bullet which hit Connally's wrist had been considerably slowed was shown by Warren Commission experiments that involved firing a Mannlicher-Carcano bullet into the wrist of a human cadaver. The cadaver wrist showed much more severe damage than Connally's. The clear implication is that the bullet which hit Connally's wrist had been slowed down by hitting something else first.[83]

TIMING OF THE SHOT

If it matters *where* Kennedy and Connally were hit, it matters equally *when* they were hit. For the single bullet theory to be valid, the first requirement, obviously, is that they were hit at the same time. Further, it must be at a time when both were aligned such that a single bullet trajectory works. Moreover, for the lone assassin theory to make sense, the shot must have been at a time such that one shooter could have fired not only the single bullet but also the other two shots fired in Dealey Plaza.

Since the release of the *Warren Commission Report* in 1964, lone gunman theorists have differed as to the timing sequence. For example, the report failed to specify an exact shooting sequence, but appeared to believe that the first shot came no earlier than Zapruder frame 210. At this point, Kennedy disappears behind the Stemmons Freeway sign, apparently unhurt. By the time he reappears at frame 225, he has obviously been hit. The Warren Commission tended to believe that the first shot would have been the most accurate (the shooter could take his time lining up the shot), so a first shot no earlier than frame 210 might seem likely.

The HSCA, trying to shoehorn their photographic analysis into the Procrustean mold formed by the acoustic evidence (which was discussed in chapter 11), put the single bullet at frame 190. This, of course, required that both Kennedy and Connally show a rather delayed reaction, especially since Connally does not show obvious pain until about 236–38.

More recently, however, a consensus has developed among lone gunman theorists that both Kennedy and Connally were hit at frame 223. The pieces of evidence supporting this consensus have been put into place slowly over the years, but they were assembled into a coherent whole by Johann W. Rush and Dr. Michael West in a video titled *Confirmation of the Single Bullet Theory*. First shown at the Midwest Symposium on Assassination Politics in Chicago in 1993, it brought together various pieces of evidence.

Although superficially Connally appears unhit until 234/235, a close scrutiny of the governor shows a lot going on in the frames following 223. In the first place, Connally's lapel, which is in place in 223, has flapped up in 224. This was first discovered by Robert P. Smith, a colleague of conspiracist Dr. Cyril Wecht in the 1970s, and Wecht noted it in a discussion with a Rockefeller Commission staffer, claiming that this established the passage of a single bullet.[84]

Considered in isolation, the lapel flap doesn't prove much. To begin, the bullet hole in Connally's jacket is not in the lapel, nor anywhere near it, but several inches below. Of course, the passage of a bullet could set up a wave in the fabric that would push the lapel outward. Dr. John Lattimer conducted an experimental recreation of the single bullet and did indeed create a lapel flap in the coat of his "Connally" mock-up.[85] The fact that it's possible for a bullet to create a lapel flap, however, doesn't prove that it happened in this case. There was a substantial breeze blowing in Dealey Plaza at the exact instant of the shot, although the photographic evidence (the blowing of the coats of Mary Moorman and Jean Hill in the Muchmore film, and the flapping of the flags on the presidential limo in the Zapruder, Nix, and Muchmore films) shows it was blowing head-on into the front of the limo. But who knows what eddies might have been created that could cause Connally's lapel to flap?

But between frames 224 and 225, we see something else happen. Connally shows a "hunching" reaction. When both these frames are registered on the knot of his tie, we see his shoulders hunch up and his head bob downward, suggesting a reaction to some external stimulus.[86] In the frames that follow, his hat, which has been out of sight (presumably resting on his left thigh), pops up. Photo analysts for the Itek Corporation, asked by CBS to examine the film in the 1970s, saw this. They reported the following:

> By frame 232–234 there is strong evidence that the Governor is reacting to a significant effect on his body; or from other data, to a bullet wound. [Connally] placed the time of his reaction at 234. We studied the film in this area to determine if there were any striking changes in his physical appearance which could be interpreted as the onset of a reaction. Five photo analysts studied the original film from frames 222–240. *They all concluded independently that somewhere between 223–226 there are signs of the beginning of a significant change in the governor's position and appearance.*[87]

So while a casual observer may see little evidence of Connally having been hit before frames 234–35, careful analysis shows that quite a lot was happening in the frames following 223.

Of course, for the single bullet theory to work, it isn't sufficient to establish that Connally was hit at Zapruder frame 223. It's also necessary to establish that Kennedy was (or at least could have been) hit at the same time.

Kennedy is not visible before frame 225, but one can see his right hand in frame 224. Between 224 and 225 his hand moves down, apparently being brought down from waving at spectators. Frame 225 is the low point, and frame 226 shows the beginning of the movement of his hands and arms up toward his neck. Forensics expert Robert Luis Piziali, testifying in a "mock trial" of Oswald sponsored by the American Bar Association in 1992, noted this, narrating a sequence of frames from the Zapruder film:

> As he emerges from the sign, you'll see that his hand is in a down position. As he was waving, he's now bringing it down. You can see that's his right hand right there. If we go to the next frame you will actually notice that the hand drops slightly. If we go back and forth, see the—the shiny part of the back seat of the car? You'll see his hand is still coming down from the wave. He has not yet reacted to the bullet that's gone through his body. If we now move on, what we'll see is in the next frame, there's his arm at the frame I was just talking about. Now watch it again. The elbow still hasn't jerked. Now the elbow jerks up. Okay, so it's a few frames later when you actually watch the elbow pop up. That is the President's first sign of reaction to being shot.[88]

If he, like Connally, was hit at frame 223, then he has to be reacting within approximately 100 to 150 milliseconds.[89] Is this possible?

If one assumes that Kennedy had to consciously perceive that he was hit, and then clutch his throat, it's not possible. But this isn't what happened. Kennedy's arm movements appear to be a neuromuscular reaction to a bullet that passed very close to his spine, shocking his spinal column. Thus, we aren't discussing a conscious reaction to a bullet, but rather a reflex. Nobody has investigated the exact kind of neuromuscular reaction that we see in Kennedy (experimental subjects willing to be shot in the back are scarce), but a variety of reflexes have been studied. One source, for example, notes that "one of the fastest loops is from arm sensors to spinal cord and back out to arm muscles: it takes 110 milliseconds for feedback corrections to be made to an arm movement." Other tests have been done on the speed of human reflexes, and the range is between roughly 60 to 200 milliseconds.[90] If Kennedy was hit at Zapruder frame 223, and first shows a reaction at frame 226, that's about 164 milliseconds. The timing seems to work.

THE SINGLE BULLET TRAJECTORY

For the single bullet trajectory to work, Connally must be well inboard of Kennedy, lower in the limo, and (probably) must have his torso turned somewhat to the right.

Just what is the evidence on this? Numerous photos show Connally well inboard of Kennedy during the motorcade. Duane Robinson, a freelancer whose work was later used by *Paris Match*, took several shots of the presidential limo earlier in the motorcade on Cedar Springs Road. Four of them show the limo from the right rear and make it clear that Connally is well inboard of Kennedy.[91] A compilation of amateur 8mm footage put together by a short-lived group called Dallas Cinema Associates shows at least two clips where the limo is photographed from the right rear. Both show Connally well to the left (inboard) of Kennedy. The same is true of amateur footage shot by presidential assistant Dave Powers, who was riding with Secret Service agents in the follow-up car. His film, shot from directly behind the limo, shows Connally well inboard of Kennedy.

Just exactly how *far* to the left of Kennedy was Connally? The answer is that we don't know exactly. Different sources show different things.

The Powers film, to which we have just alluded, shows Connally quite far inboard of Kennedy in some frames but not so far inboard in other frames. At the extreme, a frame from an 8mm film shot by Marie Muchmore shows the presidential limo turning from Main Street onto Houston Street, just a block short of the corner where it will turn left onto Elm. In this frame, Connally is far inboard of Kennedy, visible over the left shoulder of Secret Service agent Roy Kellerman in the front seat. Indeed, Connally is near the centerline of the limo, and is too far inboard for the single bullet trajectory to work.

Thus it appears that Connally moved around a lot. A large man, he was crammed into a jump seat with virtually no legroom.

But what of the instant the single bullet hit? Data are sparse. The Itek Corporation, in 1976, tried to estimate the position of Connally by using "stereo pairs" in the Zapruder film. We have already discussed the concept in connection with the authentication of the autopsy photos and the backyard photos. Typically, we can get a stereo pair by photographing a scene that is still, and moving the camera. But a wrinkle on this happens when the *camera* is still, and the *scene* moves in front of the camera. This is exactly what happened with the presidential limo moving in front of Zapruder's camera. Using three pairs of Zapruder frames from the 183–93 range, they concluded that Connally was 6.4 inches (plus or minus 2.2 inches) inboard of Kennedy.[92] This is hardly very precise. But note that it's radically at odds with the conspiracists' diagrams that show Connally directly in front of Kennedy.

Shortly after Itek completed its analysis, the HSCA commissioned a fellow named Thomas Canning to do a trajectory analysis of the single bullet. Canning was on loan from NASA to the HSCA: literally a rocket scientist. Canning approached the task of figuring out Connally's position using the Betzner photo—a photo shot by Hugh William Betzner Jr., who was standing behind and to the left of the limo.[93] Betzner tripped his shutter at Zapruder frame 186.[94] Interestingly, Connally is not shown in the Betzner photo, because a figure in the foreground obscures the Texas governor. But there is an open area between the foreground figure and Kennedy—to the right of the foreground figure and to the left of Kennedy in the limo. This establishes a line of sight to the left of which Connally must be. It turns out that this analysis shows that Connally was well inboard of Kennedy.[95]

What's the bottom line on this? Nobody can know exactly how Kennedy and Connally were positioned in the limo when the single bullet struck. But given the weight of the evidence, it's virtually impossible that Connally was directly in front of Kennedy. The range of estimates of the relative positions of the two men most certainly (as we shall see) encompasses any plausible number that's necessary for the single bullet theory to work.

For the single bullet trajectory to work, Connally also had to be lower in the limo than Kennedy, and have his torso turned to the right. There is no doubt about either point. Numerous photos show Connally—a tall man but seated in a jump seat barely above the floor of the limo—to be well below Kennedy in terms of head height. The HSCA determined the top of his head to have been 8 cm below Kennedy's.[96] Itek said, "We have estimated from the data that JFK sits about 1–2 inches higher than Governor Connally as measured at equivalent facial features." The HSCA then went on to note that the height difference in photos ranged from one to three inches, "depending on the relative posture of the two men."[97]

As for the rotation of Connally's torso, the HSCA noted, "The estimates of the angle of his twist vary from 30 degrees to slightly over 45 degrees."[98] Canning, in charge of this analysis, never states what number was used, but it appears to be nearer 30 degrees than 45 degrees. On the other hand Dale Myers, a computer animation expert and assassination researcher, notes,

> Computer analysis shows that JBC turned sharply to the right beginning at Z157. This right turn continues until Z193 where JBC's shoulders are rotated 48 degrees right, relative to the midline of the limousine. At this point,

JBC begins a slow rotation leftward. This smooth leftward turn continues until frame 223. At this point JBC's shoulders are rotated 37 degrees right, relative to the limousine.[99]

Myers's observations mesh well with Connally's own testimony. Connally said that, after hearing a shot, he turned to the right in an attempt to see Kennedy, and failing to do so, began to turn back to his left when he was hit by a bullet. In fact, a careful analysis of Connally's movements as seen in the Zapruder film supports his testimony.[100]

CONNALLY'S OPINION ABOUT THE SINGLE BULLET THEORY

If Connally's movements in the Zapruder film show his position and the timing of the shots to be consistent with the single bullet theory, why did Connally reject the theory? When pressed by CBS newsman Eddie Barker on whether the first bullet could have missed and the second hit both him and Kennedy, he admitted, "That's possible. That's possible. Now, the best witness I know doesn't believe that." The "best witness," Connally made clear, was his wife, Nellie.[101] And Nellie did insist that she had turned around in the limo and had seen that Kennedy had been hit, and then at a later point saw her husband hit by a bullet.

Yet a close examination of the Zapruder film shows that Nellie probably wasn't aware that her husband was shot as early as he actually was. In the key Zapruder frames 240–60 she is looking squarely at JFK. Her husband's face, contorted with pain, is turned away from her. After looking at her husband, she again turns to look at JFK, facing him squarely by frame 290. Nellie insisted, "I never looked back after John was shot."[102] But in fact she did look back after her husband was shot.

A key piece of data (although we already know not to lean too heavily on this kind of testimony) is the statement of John Connally that "I immediately, when I was hit, said 'Oh, no, no, no.' And then I said 'My God, they are going to kill us all.'"[103] But Nellie testified, "I recall John saying 'oh, no, no, no.' Then there was a second shot, and it hit John, and as he recoiled to the right, just crumpled like a wounded animal to the right, he said, 'My God, they are going to kill us all.'"[104]

Researcher Martin Shackelford had professional lip readers closely examine the Zapruder film, and they concluded that in frames 242–50 John Connally was saying "No, no, no, no."[105] So Nellie thought John had been hit after he said that, whereas John's recollection was that he was hit before he uttered those words. And the opinions of professional lip readers say he said that after he was wounded. It seems that Nellie was simply mistaken about the time at which her husband was hit.

Notwithstanding that Connally was telling the truth as he believed it, his opinions are not evidence. And Nellie's testimony, like that of many other sober and honest witnesses, was in error.

PUTTING IT ALL TOGETHER: TRAJECTORY ANALYSIS

If we can get good estimates of the relative positions and orientations of Kennedy and Connally in the limo, it's fairly straightforward to get a map of Dealey Plaza, and to figure out from various amateur films where the limo was at various times, in order to put it all together and see whether the single bullet trajectory works. In principle it does. In practice it's more complicated but quite possible.

The first serious attempt to do this came from the Itek Corporation in 1976. They sought to determine "whether the trajectory a bullet would follow from the sixth floor corner window of the TSBD is compatible with the relative positions of the two men and their wounds."[106] Their conclusion:

> If a bullet exited the President's body at about the center throat area, and it was following an approximate straight line trajectory from the sixth floor corner window, it would have struck Governor Connally at the approximate location which has been identified as a back wound he sustained. This conclusion is subject to the following conditions: (A) The President was struck in the interval from about Zapruder frame 212–223; and (B) there was little relative movement between the two men in the approximate 1.75 second interval between the film frame time of our measurements and the approximate time of impact of the bullet.[107]

Hard on the heels of the Itek analysis, the HSCA did a similar study. We have already discussed some of the data that went into their calculations. Their analysis had some advantages relative to that done by Itek—they had access to the autopsy photos and X-rays to determine the locations of Kennedy's wounds, for example. But it also had one big disadvantage: owing to the bogus acoustic evidence, the committee believed the single bullet hit Kennedy and Connally at Zapruder frame 190, and the analysis was done with that stipulation. The committee concluded, "Clearly, this analysis supports the single bullet theory."[108]

Aside from a rather perfunctory and simplistic analysis done for NOVA in 1988,[109] the next serious attempt to model the wounding of Kennedy and Connally was done by Failure Analysis Associates (FAA) in 1992 for a "mock trial" of Lee Harvey Oswald staged by the American Bar Association. FAA (which now calls itself Exponent) specializes in modeling accidents, disasters, and other things likely to lead to litigation. In effect, FAA was peddling its wares to the legal community. Using 3-D computer modeling, it showed that a single bullet shot from the Texas School Book Depository inflicting the torso wounds on Kennedy and all Connally's wounds was perfectly plausible.[110]

The most recent, and the best, of all attempts to model the single bullet trajectory was produced by Dale Myers and was featured in the 2003 ABC News documentary *The Kennedy Assassination: Beyond Conspiracy*. Myers's model is easily the most visually impressive of the lot—this after all is circa 2000 3-D computer animation and not circa 1992 3-D computer animation and certainly not circa 1988 3-D computer animation (as was the case with NOVA). It's also the most painstaking and probably the most accurate.

Myers works from the assumption that the single bullet hit Kennedy and Connally at Zapruder frame 223—which, as we have seen, is the consensus among lone gunman theorists.[111] By this time the reader will not be surprised to learn that Myers finds that a trajectory connecting Connally's chest and back wounds points right back through Kennedy's upper torso and right up toward the southeast window of the Texas School Book Depository.

Critiquing the Computer Models

Naturally, conspiracists have not been enamored of these trajectory models. One video, available on YouTube at this writing, accuses Myers of "Voodoo Geometry."[112] That's not true, but one can question the models. In the first place, they do start with somewhat different assumptions; Dale Myers and FAA, for example, modeled a shot at Zapruder frame 223, the HSCA at frame 190, and Itek a shot somewhere in the Zapruder 212–23 range. The HSCA and Dale Myers had Connally's torso rotated to the right in their models, but Itek and FAA seemed to have Connally facing straight ahead.[113] As for the difference in height of Kennedy and Connally, Itek went with 2 inches,[114] while the HSCA went with 8 cm (3.1 inches), and Myers apparently used 3 inches.[115] FAA has never released its data.[116]

Given these differences, it might seem odd that all these analyses support the single bullet theory. It might suggest a bit of reverse engineering. But before we reach that conclusion, we need to keep a few things in mind. None of these models claims to be perfectly accurate. The Itek, HSCA, and Myers models each come with an honest and admirable discussion of possible sources of error. And the HSCA, FAA, and Myers models all come with "error cones." When the trajectory line is run back in the direction of the School Book Depository, it usually doesn't point directly to the sniper's nest window. It usually points to somewhere close, and an "error cone" around the estimated trajectory line shows the area from which the shot might have come.[117] Dale Myers, for example, claims an error cone that, when projected on the face of the Texas School Book Depository, is about twenty-six feet in diameter.[118]

Different models, making slightly different assumptions and using slightly different measurements, may all produce error cones that include the sniper's nest. This is what is known in scientific research as "robustness." Getting the model to work does not depend on using one precise set of numbers. Rather, a range of reasonable numbers results in a model that works.

Of course, maybe the real error cones are larger than these models show. Let's suppose the real error cones are larger, maybe much larger. This would render the single bullet theory less *necessary*, but equally *possible*. Even if the real error cones are larger, they still encompass the sniper's nest window. And as we shall see, positing separate hits on Kennedy and Connally gets us into some nasty logical problems.

Think Scenario

One can't know the likelihood of any particular event without considering the probability of the alternatives. If you conclude that there is "only a 5 percent chance" that the single bullet theory is true, but then find only "a one in a thousand" chance that each of the four or five alternatives is true, you had better reconsider your "only a 5 percent chance" assessment. Put more formally, when you have an exhaustive and mutually exclusive set of contingencies, their probabilities must sum up to 1.0. After all, *something* happened.

This is most certainly true here. If we don't believe the single bullet theory, what *other* scenario do we believe?

Let's start with the bullet that hit Kennedy in the back. The wound is certainly an entrance wound, since it has an abrasion collar. Where did the bullet go? One theory, first suggested on the very night of the assassination by clueless autopsy doctors who were not aware of the exit wound in the throat (which had been obscured by the tracheotomy performed at Parkland Hospital), was that the bullet that hit Kennedy penetrated only an inch or two and then fell out—perhaps forced out by attempts at cardiac massage. The absurdity of this should be obvious. A bullet from a high-powered rifle hitting a human body is not going to penetrate only one or two inches. When pathology professor and assassination researcher John Nichols tested a Mannlicher-Carcano identical to Oswald's, he found that the bullet penetrated forty-seven inches of laminated, knot-free pine.[119] Of course, somebody could claim that this begs the question, since we might not want to assume that the shot came from a Mannlicher-Carcano. But would a conspiracy use a *less* capable weapon to shoot the president? They did want to kill Kennedy, didn't they?

If the bullet penetrated into Kennedy's body, what happened to it? It either remained in the body, or it exited. But autopsy X-rays show no bullets in Kennedy's torso; autopsists reported finding no bullets in his body. So if the bullet didn't remain in the body, it exited. And where might it have exited? The throat, which after all is where the other torso wound is.

If the bullet exited from Kennedy's neck, where did it go? If it didn't hit Connally, it should have hit the limo, but no bullet was found there.[120]

At this point, conspiracists will jump in with, "But the FBI examined the limo. They are the ones who say there was no bullet. You don't trust them, do you?"

However, a favorite conspiracist argument shows how lame this is. Critics of the single bullet theory have long pointed to the fact that the FBI and the Secret Service at first believed that one bullet hit Kennedy in the back, another separate bullet hit Connally, and a third bullet hit Kennedy in the head. Three shots, three hits. Indeed, the Warren Commission took a while to figure out the need for the single bullet theory. In an April 21, 1964, conference of Warren Commission staffers, doctors from Parkland Hospital, scientists called in by the Warren Commission, and even John and Nellie Connally looked carefully at the Zapruder film. According to a memo drawn up by Melvin A. Eisenberg discussing "conclusions" from this conference (there was much speculation and very few conclusions), the single bullet theory was never mentioned. Indeed, Arlen Specter, famous as the inventor of the single bullet theory, held out for the possibility that Connally was hit *after* frame

236—which would be well after Kennedy was clearly hit. Then an April 27, 1964, memo from staffer Norman Redlich to Chief Counsel J. Lee Rankin observed, "Our report presumably will state that the President was hit by the first bullet, Governor Connally by the second, and the President by the third and fatal bullet."[121]

So the problem that people who claim evidence tampering have is this: how could anybody tamper with evidence to make it fit a theory that didn't even exist yet? Why, for example, make a bullet "disappear" when you think that finding two bullets (one on Connally's stretcher and one in the limo) would be just fine?

The same goes for the autopsy. Why not report that you have found a bullet in Kennedy's body when you have no idea that in several months people will closely examine the Zapruder film and determine that the only bullet that's allowed is the one found on the stretcher? You can't successfully tamper with evidence until you know what theory your tampering is supposed to support.

If we reject the single bullet theory and are holding out for a conspiracy scenario, we need two shooters behind Kennedy and Connally. Connally was clearly hit in the back. The beloved grassy knoll shooter doesn't help us here. We need to posit a second shooter behind the limo—a shooter who left no evidence and was seen by no witnesses, not even witnesses of the caliber of the people who claimed to have seen a grassy knoll shooter. This is a jumbo-size ad hoc assumption, although we would cheerfully make it if other evidence really showed that the single bullet was vastly implausible.

But what about the "pristine" condition of Exhibit 399, the "magic bullet"? As we have seen, it wasn't really pristine, and shooting tests show that a bullet could do what it is claimed to have done and end up in the shape Exhibit 399 is in. But let's assume for a minute that it is absurdly implausible and ask whether it makes any sense that the bullet was planted, as conspiracists claim.

In the first place, why would a conspiracy plant the bullet? Presumably, to implicate Oswald by having a bullet that can be traced to his rifle—to the exclusion of all other weapons—turn up. If so, we have to assume, entirely ad hoc, that conspirators somehow got control of Oswald's rifle and fired some bullets, one of which could be planted.

But wouldn't it be dangerous to plant any bullet? The bullet was found by Darrell Tomlinson at Parkland Hospital at shortly after 1:00 p.m. (and certainly no later than 1:45 p.m.) on the very day of the assassination.[122] At this point, conspirators could hardly know what other bullets and fragments would turn up. Exhibit 399 could have been the "extra bullet" that could not be accounted for by any single shooter scenario. We can ask a similar question about two sizable fragments (presumably from the head shot) found in the limo after the shooting. They matched Oswald's Mannlicher-Carcano to the exclusion of all other weapons. Were they planted too? If so, why take the risk of planting redundant evidence when a single bullet or fragment would nail Oswald? If these fragments were not planted, they show that Kennedy was shot with Oswald's rifle.

This line of logic suggests that only a very boneheaded conspiracy would have multiple shooters in Dealey Plaza all blasting away at Kennedy. The more shots fired, the more likely it is that more bullets and/or fragments will turn up than can be explained by a single shooter. The more shooters you have, the more likely it is that *reliable* witnesses to more than one will come forward. Indeed, the more likely that somebody will actually produce photographs of some second shooter.[123]

Indeed, why allow any rifle other than the one that could be traced to Oswald to fire any bullets in Dealey Plaza? That would be absurdly risky, given the possibility that some bullet or fragment clearly fired from a rifle other than Oswald's would turn up. Conspiracists will insist that the conspirators "controlled the investigation" and thus could determine what *would* turn up. This, first, requires that the conspiracy have control of hundreds of people in the Dallas Police, FBI, Dallas County Sheriff's Office, and other agencies. It would also require that conspirators *know in advance* that all these people could be controlled. Or more precisely, that those persons who happened to stumble upon hard evidence of a conspiracy (and no conspiracy could know in advance who these would be) could somehow be controlled.

We need to follow a similar line of logic concerning the "pristine" nature of Exhibit 399. If the bullet really is so implausible, why would a conspiracy plant it? Given the necessary assumption that conspirators controlled Oswald's rifle, why not go out and shoot up some cattle until you produce a bullet that is suitably mangled, but with sufficient striations to match Oswald's rifle? And planting a virtually intact bullet is terribly dangerous. Suppose fragments weighing more than the metal missing from your planted bullet turn up? As we have seen, about 1.5 grains of fragments that must have come from Exhibit 399 have turned up—consistent with that bullet's loss of 2+ grains of metal. But suppose 5 grains or 8 grains or 20 grains of fragments turn up? The conspirators are screwed big time.

IN SUMMARY

As is often the case with these issues, evidence is important but logic produces the ultimate conclusion. The evidence can show that the single bullet theory is possible—the wounds are where they need to be, Connally and Kennedy are positioned where they need to be, the bullet is not implausibly "pristine"—but it can't show that it's necessary. Parsimony argues for the theory. Given that the theory fits the data adequately, why opt for extra shooters, extra bullets, faked autopsy photos showing the wounds in the wrong location, a planted bullet, and a whole Rube Goldberg scenario? And why posit a conspiracy that did a bunch of wildly reckless things that would most likely have blown up in their faces—having two shooters behind the limo, planting bullets, firing four or five or six shots in Dealey Plaza?

Once we clear away the factoids that a generation of conspiracists have slathered over the subject, we find that the single bullet theory is the prudent theory. The one most worthy of belief. The one that doesn't require you to have a lot of implausible notions buzzing around in your head like a swarm of bees.

Chapter Sixteen

Thinking about Conspiracy: Putting It All Together

It's doubtlessly clear to the reader by now that I believe Oswald killed Kennedy, and most likely did it by himself. Oswald owned the rifle that was recovered on the sixth floor of the Texas School Book Depository, a rifle that had disappeared from the Paine garage. The notions that the paper bag that Oswald took to work on the morning of the assassination contained "curtain rods" (which is what Oswald told Frazier) or a cheese sandwich (which is what Oswald told his interrogators after the assassination) are both implausible. Two fragments, presumably from the head shot, found in the front seat of the presidential limo matched Oswald's Carcano to the exclusion of all other weapons. And the famous "magic bullet" (Warren Commission Exhibit 399), in spite of all the controversy about it, is almost certainly the bullet that pierced the torsos of Kennedy and Connally, broke Connally's radius bone, and inflicted a minor wound in his thigh.

Oswald was one of the very few depository employees who cannot be accounted for at the moment of the shooting, and he is one of the very few who left immediately after the assassination—indeed the only male to have done so.[1] As discussed, the only person unfamiliar to depository employees who entered the building on the day of the assassination was an old man looking for a restroom.[2] It's exceedingly unlikely that an unknown assassin or team of assassins could have entered the building and set up shop in the sixth-floor sniper's nest with nobody in the depository noticing.

But suppose the reader does not agree that Oswald was the lone assassin. Are there any logical principles that ought to guide any serious thinking—lone assassin or conspiracy?

A LARGE CONSPIRACY ISN'T PLAUSIBLE

The first and most obvious principle is that a very large conspiracy simply isn't plausible. It's a simple matter of probabilities. Suppose, for example, a conspiracy of three people kill Kennedy, and then move on with their lives. Suppose, further, that there is a one-in-twenty probability that each of them will "defect" and "blow the whistle" on the plot. There are plenty of reasons why a plotter might defect. He might have an attack of conscience (although if he had much of that he would not have been part of the plot), he might want to make money with a book or a lecture tour, if caught in another crime he might want to use knowledge of a JFK conspiracy as leverage for more lenient treatment, or if he maintains any contact with his coconspirators, he might get crossways with them on a variety of issues.[3]

So the probability that any conspirator will defect is .05 (one in twenty), and the probability that the conspirator will *not* defect is .95. Then what is the probability that none of the conspirators will defect?

$$.95 \times .95 \times .95 = .857$$

Okay, this conspiracy probably will be a success. That's not quite three chances in twenty that one plotter will rat out the others.

But suppose there are twenty plotters. In that case the probability that nobody will defect and blow the whole project open is:

$$.95^{20} = 0.358$$

It seems that this plot has only about one chance in three of succeeding. Using the same logic for a conspiracy of thirty plotters, the probability that the plot won't be blown open is:

$$.95^{30} = 0.215$$

Is one in twenty (.05) the actual probability that a conspirator will defect? We have no idea, and the reader is invited to get out a calculator or pull up a spreadsheet on his or her personal computer and try different numbers. The general principle will always hold: the larger the conspiracy, the less likely it is to hold together.

Note that this kind of logic applies not only to conspirators defecting after the crime, but also to the need for each and every conspirator to do his or her job properly. The more elaborate and complicated the conspiracy, the more likely it is that somebody will mess up, and mess up in a way that leaves undeniable evidence of conspiracy.

Additionally, the logic applies to those witnesses who conspiracists think have been bullied, threatened, or intimidated to give "convenient" (nonconspiratorial) testimony. At some point, such a witness may decide to spill the beans—either due to scruples, an attack of bravery, hope of reward, or merely having figured out that the goons who intimidated him or her are all dead by now.

So let's posit twenty conspirators, each with a one-in-twenty probability of messing up a conspiratorial task, and a one-in-twenty probability of defecting at some future time, plus ten intimidated witnesses with a one-in-ten probability each of "spilling the beans." The probability that the whole thing will hold together is:

$$.95^{20} \times .95^{20} \times .90^{10} = .045$$

Not real good. Of course, these probabilities don't work unless each conspirator's decision to squeal is independent of each of the others, and the likelihood that a conspirator will mess up is independent of the others, and the probability that each intimidated witness will open up is independent of the others. This is probably a serviceable assumption.[4]

Obviously, the same logic applies to notions of a massive cover-up mounted in the wake of the assassination. Better that the conspirators leave a trail of evidence that honest (but not always perfectly competent) investigators would find to convict Lee Oswald, especially when it would be hard to know ahead of time just who would be willing to join the cover-up and who would be recalcitrant.

In spite of this logic, conspiracists seem to relish including as many people as possible in their theorized conspiracy. As *Time* magazine put it in a review of the movie *JFK*,

> So, you want to know, who killed the President and connived in the cover-up? Everybody! High officials in the CIA, the FBI, the Dallas constabulary, all three armed services, Big Business and the White House. Everybody done it—everybody but Lee Harvey Oswald.[5]

The reason so many conspiracists end up with theories involving a third of the population of the Free World is that they, as we have noted, tend to be collectors, collecting pieces of conspiracy evidence. And like, say, collectors of butterflies or antique firearms, they pride themselves on having the biggest and best collection.

Of course, the logical conclusion of the process is that you end up having all kinds of juicy evidence implicating almost everybody but the League of Women Voters and the ASPCA. And I hesitate to mention those two groups, lest some conspiracy theorist find a way to "link" them to the crime.

To actually solve a crime, you have to throw away most of your pieces of "evidence." You have to conclude that this sighting of the suspect where he could not have been is bogus, that the crackpot witness is not to be believed, and that a juicy-looking "connection" actually leads nowhere. When you do that, you are left with reasonably hard and reliable evidence, and with some luck, you can break the case. If you refuse to cull your evidence, you end up with suspicions out the ears, and no solution to the crime.[6]

HOW TO PRODUCE A CONSPIRACY THEORY THAT'S NOT INSANE

To begin with, any sane conspiracy theory has to include Oswald. And it's better if it includes Oswald pretty much the way the Warren Commission portrayed him. Keep in mind one simple fact: conspirators had to have enough control over Oswald and his movements to be certain he would not, when the shots rang out, be in front of the depository in plain sight of a dozen of his coworkers. Even worse, somebody like James Altgens might have taken a photo that showed Oswald, and not Billy Lovelady, standing in front of the building.[7]

This, of course, leaves open the possibility of Oswald being a manipulated patsy, perhaps told to "wait in the second floor lunchroom" for further instruction. But no conspiracy theory that excludes Oswald completely makes any sense.

Second, if the theory involves Oswald, it needs to involve a character very similar or identical to the Lee Oswald the Warren Commission described. Claiming that the backyard photos were faked, or that Oswald was impersonated in Mexico City, or that Oswald was a "fake defector," or that the Marine Corps should have expelled Oswald for his left-wing views but didn't because they knew about the conspiracy, or that Oswald didn't shoot at General Walker proliferates plotters too much. It requires a Herculean conspiracy that would make the Apollo program (which put American astronauts on the moon) look like a student's science fair project. Oswald wasn't Joe Average, but there are people like him in the world, and it makes a lot more sense for conspirators to pick a real disgruntled malcontent Marxist with delusions of importance and a checkered past than to manufacture one.

This view has huge logical advantages, but it has a big psychological disadvantage: it requires throwing away a large number of juicy pieces of "conspiracy evidence."

When Was Oswald Made a Patsy?

The "guiding hands" theory of how Oswald got a job at the Texas School Book Depository, as we have seen, is pretty unwieldy. Better to posit that some shadowy group of conspirators was tracking numerous possible patsies, and swung into action when a motorcade route was announced that ran right in front of the place of employment of one plausible patsy: Lee Harvey Oswald. This wouldn't rule out Oswald having had some connections with the CIA, or the FBI, or the Mafia, or any of the other favorite villains of conspiracy lore. If those "connections" made Oswald easier to manipulate, or perhaps blackmail, that would be a plus. But, given that there really are troubled malcontent loners in America, the fewer the "connections," the better for conspirators. Less possibility that a "connection" would prove embarrassing.

Of course, if Oswald was this sort of opportunistically chosen patsy, conspirators would need to, after they identified him, induce him to become part of the plot. A malcontent Marxist loner may be more likely to join a plot than an Eagle Scout, but it's not a given that he will.

A Theory of Two Conspiracies

One possibility is that Oswald was "set up" as a leftist precisely for the purpose of implicating Castro and provoking an invasion of Cuba. Then, this theory holds, a cover-up was launched by the U.S. government, motivated by the desire to defuse Cold War tensions. Conspiracy author John Newman tersely phrased the thesis as follows:

> In Phase I, immediately after the assassination, previously planted evidence of a Cuban/Kremlin plot surfaced in Oswald's files; this, in turn, precipitated Phase II, in which a lone-nut cover-up was erected to prevent a nuclear war.[8]

This theory does have certain advantages. You can posit that people in the "Phase II" cover-up are well motivated, just wanting to keep the country out of a dangerous situation that might lead to a nuclear war. But it has huge disadvantages too. It can't explain why, when the threat of nuclear war had subsided, nobody who was part of the "Phase II" cover-up came forward to explain what went on. Further, is assumes, ad hoc, that any evidence of a Cuban/Kremlin plot was "planted" by plotters, rather than simply appearing like tons of other spurious evidence—the result of lying or mistaken witnesses, bogus reports, and some people with an ideological agenda. In short, we just don't *need* a Phase I plot to explain Mexico City testimony tying Oswald to Communists since we have even more testimony, virtually all bogus, tying him to the CIA, or the FBI, or right-wing extremists.

In reality, lots of bogus stuff turned up. We don't need a conspiracy theory to explain it.

Then there is the fact that this "two conspiracies" theory lacks parsimony. Other things being anywhere equal, we should prefer a "one conspiracy" theory to a "two conspiracies theory" (if we adopt a conspiracy theory at all). And it resists falsification. Any evidence tying Oswald to left-wing forces is said to be the result of the Phase I conspiracy. Any evidence of Oswald being a loner is blamed on the Phase II conspiracy. Thus only evidence that Oswald was a right-winger or connected to U.S. intelligence or to anti-Castro Cubans or any force on the political right counts. Having accepted this, it becomes impossible to produce evidence that would falsify the favored theory of people who think Kennedy was the victim of right-wing forces.

That's terribly convenient. But it's bad science.

It also makes a lot of sense to posit that Oswald actually shot Kennedy. This could be consistent with other shooters in Dealey Plaza, or indeed conspirators who induced Oswald to shoot Kennedy. It has the advantage of not requiring an elaborate and arcane theory about how Oswald's rifle got into the depository, and how Oswald's prints got on the rifle and on the bag in which he apparently brought the rifle into the depository. Positing that Oswald brought the rifle to the depository to give to another conspirator isn't bad either, although if Oswald were involved this deeply, why not have him do the shooting?

Witting or Unwitting?

It's also best to posit that Oswald wanted Kennedy dead, and that he and his co-conspirators (if any such existed) were all witting participants in a plot whose goals and purposes they knew about. This relieves the theorist of the burden of positing a complex and convoluted theory of how the leftist Oswald was hoodwinked and manipulated, or worse a claim that Oswald was really a right-winger who pulled off an extensive, elaborate, and thoroughgoing charade (stretching back to his mid-teen years) pretending to be a leftist.

It would also explain why Oswald entirely stonewalled while he was in custody. If he had been set up and "patsyfied," he would have every incentive to rat out the coconspirators who had double-crossed him. But if he hadn't been double-crossed, he might have been inclined to protect his cohorts—or at least do so for a while.[9]

Why might Oswald have wanted Kennedy dead? Perhaps because he knew about Kennedy administration plots against Castro, and saw himself as the protector of the Cuban revolution. The most famous proponent of this theory, author Jean Davison, believes that Oswald did it alone, but a motive for a lone nut would also be a motive for a bunch of like-minded conspirators.[10]

Indeed, the simplest conspiracy theory I have heard has come from my history department colleague Stephen Hauser, who wonders why Oswald, in the wake of the assassination, was walking around the Oak Cliff neighborhood for no obvious reason. He suggests (but is not seriously convinced that it happened this way) that some scruffy guy in a Dallas auto-repair shop was listening to the radio about 12:45 p.m. and said, "The son of a bitch did it! I'll be damned if I'm going to go pick him up."

Set Up to Take the Fall, or Opportunistic Patsy?

Another possibility one might consider is that Oswald was not set up before the assassination at all. Perhaps the Dallas cops, suddenly the center of attention for the entire world and under huge pressure to find Kennedy's killer, simply seized upon a likely-looking suspect and then did what was necessary to frame him.[11]

Few if any conspiracy theorists believe this today, but there is one important historical figure who claimed it: Lee Harvey Oswald. In a statement to reporters as he was being hustled from one Dallas Police office to another, he said, "They're taking me in because of the fact that I lived in the Soviet Union. I'm just a patsy!" It's interesting that he did not say, "Mr. E. Howard Hunt told me to meet him in the domino room" or "I'm working for the U.S. government testing presidential security."

The problem with this theory, rather obviously, is that it would require the Dallas Police to manufacture, on very short order, a lot of hard forensic evidence pointing to Oswald, and do it for both the Kennedy and the Tippit murders. They would then have to either produce perjured testimony or have the absurd good luck of finding that Marina would testify that Oswald's rifle was missing from the Paine garage, and Frazier and Randle would testify to Oswald's long package, that no depository employee would mess things up by going to the media (who were all over the witnesses) and saying that Oswald was standing in plain sight during the shooting, and so on. The Dallas Police were not the hicks that some prejudiced authors have claimed (William Manchester is the worst example). But they weren't that good, or that lucky.

ANY ROOM FOR CONSPIRACY?

Is there any room for a sensible person to believe a conspiracy theory? Probably, given the fact that it's impossible in principle to prove a negative. But the sensible theories have psychological problems. They don't allow you to demonize your political enemies—or at least, not many of them. They don't allow you to savor a huge number of alluring pieces of "conspiracy evidence." They don't allow you to empathize with Lee Oswald as the hapless victim of massive sinister forces.

Sensible theories, in other words, are just no fun. And the most sensible theory—that Lee Oswald did it by himself—is the least pleasing of all.

Time Line

October 18, 1939	Lee Harvey Oswald is born in New Orleans. By then his father is already dead.
1939–1956	Oswald lives in twenty-one different residences, mostly with his mother. His two brothers are usually in an orphanage.
summer 1955	Oswald is a member of a Civil Air Patrol unit at Moisant Field Airport in New Orleans, with David Ferrie as his commander.
October 26, 1956	Oswald reports for basic training in the Marine Corps.
September 16, 1958	Oswald is diagnosed with gonorrhea and treated with penicillin. Infection ruled "in line of duty, not due to own misconduct."
September 11, 1959	Oswald is released from active duty by Marines on a hardship discharge, to look after injured mother.
September 20, 1959	Oswald sails for Europe on a freighter.
October 10, 1959	Oswald makes his way to London, and from there flies to Helsinki, Finland, and obtains visa to enter the Soviet Union as tourist.
October 16, 1959	Oswald arrives in Moscow.
October 21, 1959	After notification that his visa is about to expire, and that he must leave the country, Oswald makes an apparent suicide attempt.
October 31, 1959	Oswald visits the U.S. embassy and attempts to renounce his U.S. citizenship. Embassy official Richard Snyder informs him he must come back on a business day to complete the process, which Oswald never does.
January 7, 1960	Oswald arrives in Minsk.
March 17, 1961	Oswald meets Marina Nikolayevna Prusakova, whom he weds a few weeks later.
June 1, 1962	Lee and Marina leave from Moscow, headed for the United States.

June 14, 1962	Lee and Marina arrive in Texas, and move in with Lee's brother Robert in Fort Worth.
October 9, 1962	Lee rents a post office box in Dallas.
January 28, 1963	Lee orders .38 Special Smith & Wesson revolver.
February 22, 1963	Lee and Marina, having made a connection with the local Russian émigré community, meet Ruth Paine.
March 12, 1963	Lee orders war surplus 6.5mm Mannlicher-Carcano rifle from Klein's Sporting Goods in Chicago, under the name "A. Hidell." The rifle is shipped to the Dallas post office box.
March 31, 1963	Lee, in black "hunter of fascists" outfit, has Marina photograph him in the backyard of their Neely Street apartment, holding left-wing newspapers and Mannlicher-Carcano rifle. A revolver (apparently his .38 Special Smith & Wesson) is on his hip.
April 10, 1963	Lee attempts to assassinate right-wing general Edwin Walker at his Dallas home. Shot barely misses Walker, and Lee escapes.
April 24, 1963	Lee leaves Dallas for New Orleans. Marina and daughter June move in with Mrs. Paine in Irving.
May 10, 1963	Lee gets a job with the Reily Coffee Company.
May 11, 1963	Marina, June, and Ruth Paine arrive in New Orleans, where Marina and June rejoin Lee in apartment at 4905 Magazine Street.
May 26, 1963	Lee writes the Fair Play for Cuba Committee in New York, seeking a charter for a New Orleans chapter, which he will head.
May 29, 1963	Lee visits printer, orders a thousand handbills for "New Orleans chapter" of the Fair Play for Cuba Committee.
June 3, 1963	Lee rents post office box at the Lafayette Street station, lists "A. J. Hidell" as one of the people who may receive mail there.
June 16, 1963	Lee distributes Fair Play for Cuba handbills at the Dumaine Street wharf.
July 19, 1963	Lee is fired by the Reily Coffee Company.
August 5, 1963	Lee visits anti-Castro activist Carlos Bringuier, offers to help in the struggle against the Cuban dictator.

August 9, 1963	Oswald distributes Fair Play for Cuba handbills on Canal Street. Some of the leaflets list the address of the New Orleans chapter of the organization as "544 Camp Street." Lee is confronted by a very irate Bringuier and fellow anti-Castro activists. A scuffle ensues, and all are arrested.
August 21, 1963	Oswald debates Bringuier and anti-Communist activist Ed Butler on WDSU radio. Oswald is "outed" as someone who defected to the Soviet Union (information he has concealed), and feels he has been discredited and humiliated.
September 23, 1963	Marina and June leave New Orleans, headed for Dallas area to stay with Ruth Paine.
September 24, 1963	Someone from the office of G. Wray Gill (which David Ferrie frequented) calls a phone number in Chicago (a residential hotel where one Jean Aase lived). Aase later accompanies Lawrence Meyers (a friend of Jack Ruby's) to Dallas, where both of them socialize with Ruby on the night before the assassination.
September 25, 1963	Lee Oswald leaves New Orleans by bus, headed for Mexico City.
September 25, 1963 (evening)	Three men—two Cubans and an Anglo—visit the apartment of Sylvia Odio in Dallas. On the day of the Kennedy assassination, Odio recalls one of the men as being Lee Oswald.
September 25, 1963 (evening)	Lee Oswald calls Estelle Twiford in Houston, wanting to contact her husband, Horace Twiford, an official in the Socialist Labor Party of Texas.
September 26, 1963 (early morning)	Oswald leaves Houston on bus bound for Mexico.
September 27, 1963	Oswald arrives in Mexico City, rents room at Hotel del Comercio, visits Cuban and Soviet embassies wanting visa to enter Cuba.
October 2, 1963	Oswald leaves Mexico City, having failed to gain admittance to Cuba.
October 3, 1963	Lee arrives in Dallas, stays temporarily at YMCA. In later weeks he will live in rooming houses on Marsalis Street and North Beckley.

early October 1963	Oswald is looking for work with the assistance of the Texas Employment Commission.
October 14, 1963	Ruth Paine, Marina Oswald, Linnie Mae Randle, and Dorothy Roberts have coffee together, and Lee's job situation is discussed. Randle suggests a job may be available at the Texas School Book Depository, where her brother, Wesley Frazier, works.
October 15, 1963	Having learned of the opportunity, Lee applies at the depository, and is hired by supervisor Roy Truly.
November 1, 1963	FBI agent James Hosty visits Paine home in Irving, interviews Ruth and Marina.
November 5, 1963	Hosty returns to Paine home for another interview.
November 9, 1963	Joseph Milteer, right-wing racist activist, talks to a Miami police informant, and says it's "in the working" to shoot Kennedy. Supposedly, he will be shot "from an office building with a high-powered rifle."
November 12, 1963	Oswald, who was irate upon learning that the FBI had questioned his wife, leaves a note for Hosty at Dallas FBI headquarters demanding that Hosty leave his family alone.
November 19–21, 1963	Oswald presumably learns that the route of the Kennedy motorcade will pass directly in front of the depository. The route is published in both Dallas dailies on November 19, but Oswald may have seen the article on the 20th or 21st.
November 20, 1963	Rose Cherami, prostitute and drug addict, is found by law enforcement officer on a road in Louisiana, and then taken to jail, and soon afterward to a mental institution. There she says that Kennedy will be killed, supposedly before the event happens.
November 21, 1963 (morning)	Oswald tells Wesley Frazier that he wants to catch a ride to Irving that night, for the purpose of picking up "curtain rods."
November 21, 1963 (evening)	Oswald, at the Paine residence, implores Marina to come and live with him in Dallas. Marina refuses.
November 22, 1963 (morning)	Wes Frazier and Linnie Mae Randle see Oswald with a long paper bag, which Lee puts in the backseat of Frazier's car. Lee tells Frazier the bag contains "curtain rods," and both men drive into Dallas and report for work at the depository.

November 22, 1963 (12:30 p.m.)	John Kennedy is shot and killed in Dealey Plaza in Dallas.
November 22, 1963 (12:33 p.m.)	Oswald leaves the depository, takes a bus that gets stuck in traffic, and then a cab, and goes to his rooming house at 1026 North Beckley.
November 22, 1963 (1:15 p.m.)	Officer J. D. Tippit is shot and killed in the Oak Cliff section of Dallas by pedestrian whom he had stopped. Numerous witnesses observe either the shooting or the fleeing gunman.
November 22, 1963 (1:50 p.m.)	Oswald arrested in Texas Theatre after attempting to shoot Officer M. N. McDonald and scuffing with police.
November 22, 1963 (8:00 p.m.)	At Bethesda Naval Hospital, autopsy of the body of John Kennedy begins.
November 24, 1963 (11:21 a.m.)	Oswald is shot by Jack Ruby in the basement of Dallas city jail. Oswald dies shortly thereafter at Parkland Hospital.
November 24, 1963 (afternoon)	At Dallas FBI office, Agent James Hosty is summoned by Special Agent in Charge Gordon Shanklin and told to destroy the note that Oswald left for Hosty. Hosty tears it up and flushes it down the toilet.
November 25, 1963	Nicholas Katzenbach, assistant attorney general, writes a memo to White House staffer Bill Moyers arguing that "the public must be satisfied that Oswald was the assassin; that he did not have confederates who are still at large." Katzenbach further urges that "speculation about Oswald's motivation ought to be cut off."
November–December 1963	Numerous witnesses, most of them in Texas but some scattered throughout the nation, report having seen "Lee Oswald" in various locations, doing various things. Most of the "things" that this purported Oswald was engaged in have some connection to the facts about Oswald that were publicized in the wake of the assassination—getting a scope put on a gun, firing a rifle at a shooting range, trying to get an "undesirable discharge" changed.
April 30, 1964	John Bartlow Martin of the John F. Kennedy Library interviews Robert Kennedy. Bobby denies that his brother John had resigned himself to a Communist takeover in South Vietnam, and insists John felt it was vital to prevent that.

June 7, 1964	Jack Ruby testifies in Dallas before the Warren Commission. He begs to be taken to Washington so that he can prove to Lyndon Johnson that he was not part of a conspiracy to kill JFK.
February 17, 1967	*New Orleans States-Item* reveals that Orleans Parish district attorney Jim Garrison is investigating the Kennedy assassination.
February 24, 1967	Perry Raymond Russo tells the *Baton Rouge State-Times* that David Ferrie had discussed shooting John Kennedy about a month before the assassination. Russo is then interviewed by investigators from the Garrison office, and over time (with the help of Sodium Pentothal and hypnosis) his story morphs into an "assassination party" that includes David Ferrie, Lee Oswald, and Clay Shaw plotting to kill Kennedy.
June 28, 1967	Ed Hoffman, who was overlooking the area behind the stockade fence and the Texas School Book Depository at the time of the shooting, contacts the Dallas office of the FBI, and tells of two men whose actions he thinks suspicious.
September 20, 1967	The CIA convenes a "Garrison Group" to counter the charges against the agency made by Garrison.
1975	Rockefeller Commission investigates activities of the CIA, including some JFK assassination issues.
1977–1979	House Select Committee on Assassinations mounts a large-scale investigation of assassination.
February 6, 1985	Jury in Miami finds that E. Howard Hunt was not libeled by *The Spotlight*, which published an article claiming that he was an assassination conspirator, and one of the so-called three tramps in Dealey Plaza.

Notes

Much of the material related to the JFK assassination has its own peculiar conventions regarding citations, the result of how the evidence was collected and published.

The first-published and still critically important trove of primary-source materials encompasses the twenty-six volumes prepared by the Warren Commission, serving as the basis for the *Warren Commission Report*. These volumes (which can be accessed at the Mary Ferrell Foundation website, http://www.maryferrell.org/) contain testimony taken by the commission (with some witness affidavits mixed in), a series of commission exhibits, and then a collection of "named exhibits" (such as the Decker Exhibit and the Grant Exhibit). All of these can be cited by name (for example, Testimony of Ruth Paine) and also by volume and page number in the twenty-six volumes (so, 20 H 25 refers to page 25 of volume 20, which happens to be a letter that Lee Oswald, as a teenager, wrote to a socialist publication). Another large collection of documents is designated Commission Documents. Some of these were renumbered and included in the Warren Commission volumes as commission exhibits. Many were not. All are available from the National Archives and also on the Mary Ferrell Foundation website.

In the 1970s, the U.S. House of Representatives established the House Select Committee on Assassinations (HSCA), which investigated both the JFK and the Martin Luther King assassinations, and published a report (hereafter *HSCA Report*), as well as twelve volumes of evidence and exhibits. These volumes are cited in a way similar to the Warren Commission volumes. For example, 6 HSCA 138 refers to page 138 of volume 6 (which happens to be the first page of the HSCA authentication of the famous backyard photos of Oswald).

There is, of course, much relevant material not included in the Warren Commission volumes, the Warren Commission documents, or the HSCA volumes. Most (but not all) of this material is in the National Archives, and a Record Information Form (RIF) for any document can be located by a search of a web database (http://www.archives.gov/research/jfk/search.html). A key tool for finding any particular document is the Archives record number, usually in the form XXX-XXXXX-XXXXX. For example, record 180-10090-10316 happens to be a page of press clippings, from the files of the HSCA, about the Garrison investigation in New Orleans.

All of this doesn't exhaust the material relevant to the assassination, but if the reader understands the conventions surrounding this particular area of historical inquiry, the citations that follow will be much easier to understand, and the primary sources much easier to find.

A copy of these notes can be found online at jfkassassination.net/notes/. Many of the citations are in the form of hypertext links, which you can click through to see the primary source document.

Chapter 1. The Frailty of Witness Testimony

1. Transcript, "Who Was Lee Harvey Oswald?," *Frontline*, WGBH-PBS, November 16, 1993, http://www.pbs.org/wgbh/pages/frontline/programs/transcripts/1205.html.
2. Michael Leahy, "Oswald: A Brother's Burden," *Arkansas Democrat-Gazette*, November 16, 1997.
3. WordNet Search, s.v. "memory," http://wordnetweb.princeton.edu/perl/webwn?s=memory.
4. Decker Exhibit 5323 (19 H 492).
5. Ibid., 490.
6. Ibid., 480.
7. Testimony of Austin L. Miller (6 H 225).
8. Decker Exhibit 5323 (19 H 472).
9. Ibid., 486.
10. Tabulation by Joel Grant, "Earwitness Tabulation," Kennedy Assassination Home Page, http://mcadams.posc.mu.edu/earwitnesses.htm.
11. Dennis Ford and Mark Zaid, "Eyewitness Testimony, Memory, and Assassination Research," 1993, http://mcadams.posc.mu.edu/zaid.htm. The theory has been criticized on several grounds (for example, neither stress nor performance is one-dimensional), but the idea that very high stress levels can impede psychological performance is pretty robust.
12. Exhibit 1416 (22 H 833).
13. Exhibit 1418 (22 H 834).
14. *The Plot to Kill JFK: Rush to Judgment*, directed by Emile de Antonio (Oakland Park, IL: MPI Home Video, 1988), VHS. See also testimony of Sam Holland (6 H 247).
15. Exhibit 1419 (22 H 834).
16. *The Plot to Kill JFK*; testimony of Lee E. Bowers Jr. (6 H 288).
17. Richard B. Trask, *Pictures of the Pain: Photography and the Assassination of President Kennedy* (Danvers, MA: Yeoman Press, 1994), 175, 210, 218, 266, 335, 375, 427.
18. Officer Haygood said he "tried to jump the north curb . . . which was too high for me to get over" (6 H 298).
19. Daniel L. Schacter, *The Seven Sins of Memory: How the Mind Forgets and Remembers* (Boston: Houghton Mifflin, 2001), 112.
20. Sharon L. Hannigan and Mark Tippens, "A Demonstration and Comparison of Two Types of Inference-Based Memory Errors," *Journal of Experimental Psychology* 27, no. 4 (2001): 931–40.
21. Elizabeth F. Loftus, David G. Miller, and Helen J. Burns, "Semantic Integration of Verbal Information into a Visual Memory," *Journal of Experimental Psychology* 4, no. 1 (1978): 19–31.
22. Gary Mack, "The Man Who Named the Grassy Knoll," Kennedy Assassination Home Page, http://mcadams.posc.mu.edu/gk_name.htm.

23. John McAdams, "Earwitness Tabulation," Kennedy Assassination Home Page, http://mcadams.posc.mu.edu/earwitnesses.htm.

24. Exhibit 1425 (22 H 838).

25. There were actually three buildings on that corner.

26. Josiah Thompson, *Six Seconds in Dallas: A Micro-study of the Kennedy Assassination* (New York: Bernard Geis Associates, 1967), 25.

27. 2 HSCA 122.

28. Warren Commission, Document 87, 66, reprinted in Thompson, *Six Seconds in Dallas*, 311.

29. Testimony of Abraham Zapruder (7 H 571–72). Zapruder told newsman Eddie Barker that "I heard shots coming from—I wouldn't know which direction to say." CBS Television, "The Warren Report: Part 2," June 26, 1967.

30. Sam Malone, "Eyewitness Says: Connally Took First Shot, President 2nd" *Houston Post*, November 23, 1963. Readers might wonder whether there was a cop named "J. H. Hargis" riding in the motorcade. There was not. See Trask, *Pictures of the Pain*, 616–17.

31. Testimony of Bobby W. Hargis (6 H 294–95).

32. Trask, *Pictures of the Pain*, 156, 209, 373, 516. The Bothun photo doesn't establish that Hargis had dismounted, but the timing is consistent with his having done that, else we have to posit (contrary to his testimony and the Bond photo) that he just sat on his motorbike in the street for a minute or two.

33. Interview with the *Dallas Times Herald*, quoted in ibid., 209.

34. Testimony of Bobby W. Hargis (6 H 295–96).

35. Decker Exhibit 5323 (19 H 481).

36. November 26, 1963, FBI interview with Emmett Hudson, National Archives record 186-10006-10486.

37. On page 2 of the newspaper edition with the Moorman photo on the front page is indeed a photo of Dealey Plaza that shows the School Book Depository, so perhaps the FBI agents were confused about what Hudson had been looking at.

38. Testimony of Emmett J. Hudson (7 H 560).

39. *JFK: The Case for Conspiracy*, volume 2, produced by Robert J. Groden (Boothwyn, PA: New Frontier Productions and Grodenfilms, 1995), VHS.

40. Robert Blakey interview on February 3, 1979, National Archives record 180-10105-10394.

41. John McAdams, "Dealey Plaza Earwitnesses," Kennedy Assassination Home Page, http://mcadams.posc.mu.edu/shots.htm.

42. Stewart Galanor, "JFK: The Art and Science of Misrepresenting Evidence," History Matters, http://www.history-matters.com/analysis/witness/artScience.htm. Comparing Galanor's tabulation to those discussed earlier in the chapter, he has obviously inflated the number of Knoll witnesses.

43. James W. Douglass, *JFK and the Unspeakable: Why He Died and Why It Matters* (Maryknoll, NY: Orbis Books, 2008), 200.

44. *HSCA Report*, 231–32.

45. Ibid., 364.

46. National Institute of Standards and Technology, "What Are Outliers in the Data?," *Engineering Statistics Handbook*, http://www.itl.nist.gov/div898/handbook/prc/section1/prc16.htm.

47. Robert T. Carroll, *The Skeptic's Dictionary*, s.v. "Occam's razor," December 18, 2009, http://www.skepdic.com/occam.html.

48. Thompson, *Six Seconds in Dallas*, 25. Note that the subset of witnesses reporting the direction of the shots and the subset of witnesses reporting the number of shots were different in both the Thompson and HSCA studies.

49. 2 HSCA 122. Again, the subset of witnesses reporting the direction of the shots and the subset of witnesses reporting the number of shots were different.

50. "Dealey Plaza Earwitnesses." One of our five witnesses did not mention the Knoll as one of the two locations.

51. Stewart Galanor, "McAdams' Definitive Tabulation," alt.assassination.jfk newsgroup post, January 26, 2002.

52. National Archives document 124-10163-10435, FBI interview of Virgil Hoffman on March 28, 1977, 8–9; Ed Hoffman and Ron Friedrich, *Eyewitness* (Grand Prairie, TX: JFK Lancer Productions, 1995); and Bill Sloan, *JFK: Breaking the Silence* (Dallas: Taylor Publishing Company, 1993), 10–49.

53. Dallas office, FBI report dated June 28, 1967. Kennedy Assassination Home Page, http://mcadams.posc.mu.edu/hoffman1.htm.

54. Dallas office, FBI report dated July 6, 1967, http://mcadams.posc.mu.edu/hoffman2.htm.

55. Ron Friedrich, "Current Section: Ed Hoffman's Changing Story," *Kennedy Assassination Chronicles* 1, no. 2 (June 1995): 31–32, http://www.maryferrell.org/mffweb/archive/viewer/showDoc.do?docId=1319&relPageId=31.

56. Thompson, *Six Seconds in Dallas*, 121–22.

57. See *The Plot to Kill JFK*. Hoffman's claims of having seen the shooter in the location where Holland believed the shooter was could be seen as "corroboration" for both Hoffman's and Holland's accounts. But as we will see when we discuss "false corroboration," this possibility is only true if both accounts are independent. Hoffman's account of the shooter's position, however, came long after Holland's did.

58. CBS Television, "The Warren Report: Part 2," June 26, 1967.

59. Decker Exhibit 5323 (19 H 492).

60. Mark Lane, *Rush to Judgment: A Critique of the Warren Commission's Inquiry into the Murders of President John F. Kenney, Officer J. D. Tippit and Lee Harvey Oswald* (New York: Holt, Rinehart, and Winston, 1966), 33.

61. The Pentagon, however, was unable to identify who these agents were. See *HSCA Report*, 184.

62. Testimony of Jesse E. Curry (4 H 165).

63. Testimony of Bob Carroll (7 H 18).

64. Gerald Posner, *Case Closed: Lee Harvey Oswald and the Assassination of JFK* (New York: Anchor Doubleday, 1994 [paperback]), 268. Note that numerous other witnesses saw men in suits who they *thought* were Secret Service agents. Given the tendency, in the wake of the shooting, to assume that anybody in a suit must be with the Secret Service, this report proves little. The House Select Committee noted that these witnesses provided no corroborating details and that the majority "indicated that they were mistaken." *HSCA Report*, 183.

65. Testimony of Joe Marshall Smith (7 H 535).

66. Exhibit 2118 (24 H 548); Greg Jaynes, "Lee Bowers' View: A Photo Essay," *Kennedy Assassination Chronicles* 4, no. 2 (September 1998): 28–31, http://www.maryferrell.org/mffweb/archive/viewer/showDoc.do?docId=4263&relPageId=28.

67. Testimony of Lee E. Bowers Jr. (6 H 288).

68. Lane, *Rush to Judgment*, 32.

69. Decker Exhibit 5323 (19 H 510 and 517).

70. Testimony of Lee E. Bowers Jr. (6 H 285–86).

71. Ibid., 287.

72. Ibid., 287–88.

73. Josiah Thompson's interview with Marilyn Sitzman, November 29, 1966. Transcript in the Zapruder file at Assassination Archives and Research Center, Washington, DC, http://mcadams.posc.mu.edu/sitzman.txt.

74. Nigel Turner, "The Forces of Darkness," *The Men Who Killed Kennedy: The Definitive Account of American History's Most Controversial Mystery*, season 1, episode 2 (Alexandria, VA: TimeLife Video, 1993), VHS.

75. On badge man, see Dave Reitzes, "Nowhere Man: The Strange Story of Gordon Arnold," http://jfkassassination.net/arnold1.htm; and Dale K. Myers, "Badgeman: A Photogrammetric Analysis of Moorman Photograph No. 5 of the JFK Assassination," in *Secrets of*

a Homicide: JFK Assassination (Milford, MI: Oak Cliff Press, 2004), http://www.jfkfiles
.com/jfk/html/badgeman.htm.

Chapter 2. Problems of Memory

1. This report led the media to speculate that the cold-blooded assassin had eaten lunch
    while waiting for the president to appear.
2. Laura Hlavach and Darwin Payne, eds., *Reporting the Kennedy Assassination* (Dallas:
    Three Forks Press, 1996), 39.
3. Connie Kritzberg, *Secrets from the Sixth Floor Window* (Tulsa, OK: Under Cover Press,
    1994), 39–46.
4. Testimonies of Luke Mooney (3 H 288), E. D. Brewer (6 H 307), L. D. Montgomery (7
    H 97), Marvin Johnson (7 H 102), Elmer Boyd (7 H 121), Robert Studebaker (7 H 146,
    Studebaker Exhibit H), and Gerald Hill (7 H 46).
5. Testimony of William H. Shelley (6 H 330).
6. Testimony of Bonnie Ray Williams (3 H 169).
7. John F. Kennedy Assassination Records Collection, papers of C. Douglas Dillon, the
    President's Committee on the Warren Report to Columbia University Bureau of Ap-
    plied Social Research, box 3, National Archives, College Park, MD.
8. Richard B. Trask, *Pictures of the Pain: Photography and the Assassination of President
    Kennedy* (Danvers, MA: Yeoman Press, 1994), 423–31.
9. "JFK Shooting Recalled," *The Clifton (Texas) Record*, November 22, 2000, Kennedy As-
    sassination Home Page, http://mcadams.posc.mu.edu/couch.htm.
10. Testimony of Malcolm Couch (6 H 159–60).
11. Trask, *Pictures of the Pain*, 167–68.
12. *JFK: The Case for Conspiracy*, produced by Robert J. Groden (Boothwyn, PA: New Fron-
    tier Productions and Grodenfilms, 1993), VHS.
13. Testimony of Phillip Willis (7 H 496).
14. Testimony of Phil Willis in the Clay Shaw trial, February 14, 1969, http://www.jfk-online
    .com/pwillisshaw.html.
15. *JFK: The Case for Conspiracy*. Mrs. Willis's position was almost directly behind Ken-
    nedy, and she could not have actually seen whether his brains blew out backward or for-
    ward. The three films that show the head shot with sufficient clarity—those of Zapruder,
    Nix, and Muchmore—all show Kennedy's brains being blown upward and forward.
16. Nigel Turner, "The Forces of Darkness," *The Men Who Killed Kennedy: The Definitive
    Account of American History's Most Controversial Mystery*, season 1, episode 4 (Alexan-
    dria, VA: TimeLife Video, 1993), VHS.
17. Jim Marrs, *Crossfire: The Plot That Killed Kennedy* (New York: Carroll & Graf, 1989),
    341–42. Strictly speaking, Marrs doesn't quote Warren Burroughs as saying that Os-
    wald did these things, since Marrs believes that an Oswald impostor was the man who
    entered the theater.
18. Warren Commission Testimony of Julia Postal (7H10). Postal apparently inferred the
    man ducked into the theater, rather than actually seeing him do it.
19. Testimony of Warren Burroughs (7 H 15–16).
20. HSCA interview with David Osborne, June 20, 1978, National Archives record 80-
    10102-10415, 3.
21. 7 HSCA 15–16.
22. Jim Bishop, *The Day Kennedy Was Shot* (New York: Funk & Wagnalls, 1968), 452.
    Document 7: "Autopsy of Body of President John Fitzgerald Kennedy," 283, http://www
    .maryferrell.org/mffweb/archive/viewer/showDoc.do?docId=10408&relPageId=290.
23. HSCA hearings before the Medical Panel of the Select Committee on Assassinations,
    House of Representatives, March 11, 1978.
24. John Morris, "'Shooting' the Presidents," *Popular Photography* 81, no. 2 (August 1977).

25. Testimony given to the HSCA in Executive Session on August 11, 1978. National Archives record 180-10105-10333, http://mcadams.posc.mu.edu/knudsen6.txt.

26. Deposition of Saundra Kay Spencer, June 5, 1997, before the Assassination Records Review Board (ARRB), http://www.aarclibrary.org/publib/jfk/arrb/medical_testimony/Spencer_6-5-97/html/Spencer_0001a.htm.

27. Joseph Backes, "The State of the Medical Evidence in the JFK Assassination: Doug Horne's Presentation at JFK Lancer 1998 Conference," part 3, *JFK Lancer*, 1999, http://www.jfklancer.com/backes/horne/Backes3.html. The statement appears not to be a direct quote but rather Backes's characterization of what Horne said.

28. ARRB, "MD 13—Signed Military Inventory of Autopsy Photos and X-Rays (11/10/66)," http://www.aarclibrary.org/publib/jfk/arrb/master_med_set/md13/html/Image10.htm.

29. George Lardner Jr., "Archive Photos Not of JFK's Brain, Concludes Aide to Review Board," *Washington Post*, November 10, 1998, http://www.jfklancer.com/LNE/2brain.html.

30. ARRB, "Deposition of Francis X. O'Neill, Jr.," September 12, 1997, 164–66, http://www.maryferrell.org/mffweb/archive/viewer/showDoc.do?absPageId=68367.

31. Ibid., 158–62, http://www.maryferrell.org/mffweb/archive/viewer/showDoc.do?docId=792&relPageId=29.

32. ARRB, "Deposition of John T. Stringer," July 16, 1996, 85–90, http://www.maryferrell.org/mffweb/archive/viewer/showDoc.do?docId=798&relPageId=19.

33. Transcript of Jeremy Gunn's speech given at Stanford, May 18, 1998, http://spot.acorn.net/jfkplace/09/fp.back_issues/24th_Issue/gunn.html.

34. David S. Lifton, *Best Evidence: Disguise and Deception in the Assassination of John F. Kennedy* (New York: Macmillan, 1980).

35. Ibid., 592–94.

36. Ibid., 579.

37. Document 7: "Autopsy," 283.

38. Nobody would have known it was an Elgin Britannia, but the descriptions are consistent with a fancy coffin and not a simple metal shipping coffin. Regarding the bronze casket (as opposed to the gray metal shipping casket claimed by Lifton), see "MD 189: Document Provided to ARRB by Francis X. O'Neill, Jr. on September 12, 1997 Containing Recollections of Events Surrounding JFK Assassination," http://www.maryferrell.org/mffweb/archive/viewer/showDoc.do?docId=720&relPageId=5; ARRB, "Deposition of James W. Sibert, Jr.," September 11, 1997, 95–96, http://www.maryferrell.org/mffweb/archive/viewer/showDoc.do?mode=searchResult&absPageId=68500; Dennis L. Brio, "JFK's Death: The Plain Truth from the M.D.s Who Did the Autopsy," *Journal of the American Medical Association* 167, no. 20 (May 22, 1992): 2797 (Humes remembers the broken handle on the bronze casket); "ARRB Testimony of Dr. J. Thornton Boswell, 26 Feb. 1996," http://www.maryferrell.org/mffweb/archive/viewer/showDoc.do?docId=786&relPageId=16 (Boswell likewise remembers the broken handle on the bronze casket).

    On the body being wrapped in sheets (rather than arriving in a body bag) see ARRB, "Deposition of James W. Sibert, Jr."; "HSCA staff report of its interview of Dr. 'J' Thornton Boswell," http://www.maryferrell.org/mffweb/archive/viewer/showDoc.do?mode=searchResult&absPageId=1511292; "ARRB Testimony of Dr. James Joseph Humes, 13 Feb. 1996," http://www.maryferrell.org/mffweb/archive/viewer/showDoc.do?mode=searchResult&absPageId=67916; Brio, "JFK's Death" (Humes remembers body "wrapped in sheets in a swaddling manner"); "ARRB Testimony of Dr. J. Thornton Boswell" (Boswell remembers body arriving "wrapped in sheets and a pillowcase around his head"); "MD 189: Document Provided to ARRB by Francis X. O'Neill, Jr."

39. ARRB, "Deposition of James W. Sibert, Jr.," 95–96; and ARRB, "Deposition of Francis X. O'Neill, Jr.," 71.

40. Joel Grant, "Body Snatchers at Love Field?," Kennedy Assassination Home Page, http://mcadams.posc.mu.edu/b_snatch.htm.

41. "Burkley to HSCA, affidavit dated November 28, 1978, HSCA (RG 233), JFK Collection," *JFK Lancer*, http://www.jfklancer.com/burkleyhsca.html.

42. Brig. Gen. Godfrey McHugh, letter to the editor, *Time*, February 16, 1981, 5.

43. Kenneth P. O'Donnell, *"Johnny, We Hardly Knew Ye": Memories of John Fitzgerald Kennedy* (Boston: Little, Brown, 1972), 34.

44. William Manchester, *The Death of a President, November 20–November 25, 1963* (New York: Harper & Row, 1967), 314, 321.

45. *The Plot to Kill JFK: Rush to Judgment*, directed by Emile de Antonio (Oakland Park, IL: MPI Home Video, 1988), VHS.

46. Exhibit 1425 (22 H 838).

47. If Lane did ask, he chose not to use that footage. With Lee Bowers, Lane gets him to repeat the "flash of light" account and the details of the three cars, but he fails to ask Bowers where he heard the shots coming from. Lane apparently knew that Bowers would say that he could not tell whether the shots came from the depository or the underpass because "there is a similarity of sound, because there is a reverberation which takes place from either location" (6 H 287). This observation, of course, would throw doubt on all of the earwitness testimony.

48. Decker Exhibit 5323 (19 H 490).

49. Josiah Thompson, *Six Seconds in Dallas: A Micro-study of the Kennedy Assassination* (New York: Bernard Geis Associates, 1967), 103.

50. Gary L. Aguilar, "John F. Kennedy's Fatal Wounds: The Witnesses and the Interpretations from 1963 to the Present," August 1994, http://www.assassinationweb.com/ag6.htm.

51. For a more detailed critique, see "JFK Assassination: Kennedy's Head Wound—Parkland and Bethesda Eyewitnesses," Kennedy Assassination Home Page, http://mcadams.posc.mu.edu/head.htm#aguilar.

52. *National Geographic: Inside the U.S. Secret Service* (Burbank, CA: Warner Home Video, National Geographic Video, 2004), DVD, http://mcadams.posc.mu.edu/ClintHill.htm.

53. For a photo of Doris Nelson from November 1983, 57, see http://mcadams.posc.mu.edu/nelson.jpg.

54. JFK Lancer, "The Wounds at Bethesda," http://www.jfklancer.com/backes/horne/Backes2a.htm.

55. 7 HSCA 278.

56. JFK Library, Boston. See http://mcadams.posc.mu.edu/images/carrico_skull.GIF.

57. Ben Bradlee [Jr.], "Investigations: Dispute on JFK Evidence Persists," *Boston Globe*, June 21, 1981.

58. 7 HSCA 105, 109, 110.

59. "1968 Panel Review of Photographs, X-Ray Films, Documents and Other Evidence Pertaining to the Fatal Wounding of President John F Kennedy on November 22, 1963, in Dallas, Texas" *JFK Lancer*, http://www.jfklancer.com/ClarkPanel.html.

60. "Could the Parkland Doctors Have Seen the Back of Kennedy's Head?," http://mcadams.posc.mu.edu/faceup.htm. Some of the doctors report that the head was lifted and examined, but others—Robert McClelland, Gene Akin, and Paul Peters, for example—say they did not see that happen. Thus McClelland, Akin, and Peters could not be genuine "back of the head" witnesses.

61. ARRB, "Testimony of Charles Baxter, Ronald Coy Jones, Robert M. McClelland, Malcolm Perry, Paul C. Peters," August 27, 1998, 98, http://www.maryferrell.org/mffweb/archive/viewer/showDoc.do?mode=searchResult&absPageId=68410.

62. Russell Kent, "Wounds to the Left of JFK's Head?," *Dealey Plaza Echo*, July 1996, 40–42. Stewart described an entrance wound, and the others discussed what would appear to be the "great defect" that the vast majority of witnesses placed to the right of the centerline.

63. Report of the President's Commission on the Assassination of President John F. Kennedy, *Warren Commission Report* (Washington, DC: Government Printing Office, 1964), 315–16.

64. Ibid., 316–18;Warren Commission hearings (11 H 300).
65. Document 329, 190. However, Paine testified that by November he was making consid-
    erable progress (2 H 514).
66. Ian Griggs, "Oswald—a Driving Force?," *Fair Play* 14 (January–February 1997), http://
    spot.acorn.net/jfkplace/09/fp.back_issues/14th_Issue/lho_drive.html.
67. Exhibit 2976 (26 H 457).
68. Exhibit 2137 (24 H 732–33).
69. *Warren Commission Report*, 732.
70. Ibid., 320–21.
71. Testimony of Albert Bogard (10 H 353).
72. *Warren Commission Report*, 321.
73. Document 205, 739.
74. Testimony of Ruth Hyde Paine (2 H 515); Affidavit of Ruth Paine (11 H 153–55); tes-
    timony of Marina Oswald (1 H 58, 62); Priscilla Johnson McMillan, *Marina and Lee*
    (New York: Harper & Row, 1977), 500–2.
75. Document 6, 195.
76. *Warren Commission Report*, 318–19.
77. Testimony of Garland Slack (10 H 381).
78. Ibid., 380.
79. Testimony of Ruth Paine (3 H 125); Affidavit of Ruth Paine (11 H 153–55); testimony of
    Marina Oswald (1 H 62); and McMillan, *Marina and Lee*, 503–5.
80. Exhibit 2796 (26 H 185)
81. "FBI Clements Report of 03 April 1964 re: Ruby/Oswald," Document 736, 64, http://www
    .maryferrell.org/mffweb/archive/viewer/showDoc.do?docId=11134&relPageId=72.
82. "Odio: Proof of the Plot?," Kennedy Assassination Home Page, http://mcadams.posc
    .mu.edu/odio.htm.
83. *Warren Commission Report*, 323.
84. Exhibit 2335 (25 H 300).
85. Ibid.
86. Exhibit 2136 (24 H 726); "FBI Dalrymple Report of 18 Dec 1963 re: Oswald," Docu-
    ment 191, 6, http://www.maryferrell.org/mffweb/archive/viewer/showDoc.do?docId
    =10595&relPageId=7.
87. Exhibit 2136 (24 H 727); Affidavit of Mrs. Estelle Twiford (11 H 180).
88. *Warren Commission Report*, 731.
89. Testimony of Sylvia Odio (11 H 380).
90. Ibid., 384.
91. Exhibit 2335 (25 H 301).
92. Twiford Exhibit 1 (21 H 681). Unfortunately, no handwriting analysis was ever done to
    identify the writing on the envelope as Oswald's; so one can assume, ad hoc, that the
    envelope was forged if one wants.
93. Ibid., 682.
94. Exhibit 2335. One of the numbers was an old, disconnected one, and Oswald presum-
    ably got it from a phone book at (most likely) the bus station. Apparently he called the
    operator to get the other number, which was current.
95. Twiford Exhibit 1 (21 H 681).
96. Jean Davison, *Oswald's Game* (New York: W. W. Norton, 1983), 189.
97. Exhibit 2131 (24 H 716).
98. Ibid., 715.
99. Exhibit 2938 (26 H 386).
100. Exhibit 2940 (26 H 389).
101. Exhibit 2939 (26 H 388).
102. Ibid.
103. Davison, *Oswald's Game*, 190; and Exhibit 1781 (23 H 388).
104. *Warren Commission Report*, 308.

105. Exhibit 1161 (22 H 208).

106. Davison, *Oswald's Game*, 190.

107. Some conspiracists try to square this circle by pointing out that JURE was a rather leftist anti-Castro group that was often said to want "Castroism without Castro." But this position would seem to be a rather fine distinction in the media circus that would predictably follow Oswald being charged with killing Kennedy. Further, Oswald left a trail of having participated in *pro-Castro* (not just leftist) activities and statements.

108. *Warren Commission Report*, 728.

109. Exhibit 93 (16 H 341). Oswald's spelling errors corrected.

110. Davison, *Oswald's Game*, 195–98.

111. James Douglass, *JFK and the Unspeakable: Why He Died and Why It Matters* (Maryknoll, NY: Orbis Books, 2008), 298–302.

112. Ibid., 335.

113. Ibid.

114. As we shall see, many conspiracists insist that Oswald was impersonated in Mexico City in an obvious part of a setup. If he was not set up, perhaps "handlers" had told him to go to Mexico City. Either way, for conspiracy theorists, it was part of a plot.

115. Conspiracists usually insist that the backyard photos were faked. If so, they had to be faked before the assassination and be ready for discovery immediately after the president's assassination.

116. Leia Holland, "False Sightings of Escapees Keep Deputies Busy," *Pecos Enterprise*, January 12, 2001, http://www.pecos.net/news/arch2001/011201p.htm.

117. Emily Wheeler, "Sightings of Dubbo Murder Suspect Continue—Hunt Still on for Fugitive More than Two Years On," *Daily Liberal*, February 4, 2008, at http://www.daily liberal.com.au/.

118. Susan Caldor, "Remains in Gaffney May Be Suspected Serial Killer," *The Newberry (SC) Observer*, October 16, 2005, http://www.switchplates.netfirms.com.

119. Serial Killer Central, "Belle Gunness," http://www.skcentral.com/articles2.php?article_id=330.

120. James L. Swanson, *Manhunt: The 12-Day Chase for Lincoln's Killer* (New York: William Morrow, 2006).

121. Jeremy Pawloski, "After Four Months, Authorities Have Little Evidence in Lindsey Baum Case," *The Olympian* (WA), March 5, 2010, http://www.theolympian.com/670/story/1021596.html.

Chapter 3. Creating False Memories

1. "The Clay Shaw Trial Testimony of Perry Raymond Russo," *State of Louisiana v. Clay L. Shaw*, February 10, 1969, http://www.jfk-online.com/pr01.html.

2. Jim Garrison, *On the Trail of the Assassins: My Investigation and Prosecution of the Murder of President Kennedy* (New York: Sheridan Square Press, 1988), 151.

3. Both articles from the *Baton Rouge Morning Advocate* are online at http://mcadams .posc.mu.edu/russo1.txt.

4. "Russo Says on TV Didn't Know Oswald Before Assassination," *Baton Rouge Morning Advocate*, March 15, 1967, http://mcadams.posc.mu.edu/russo1.txt; Milton Brenner, *The Garrison Case* (New York: Clarkson N. Potter, 1969), 90; Gene Roberts, "Witness Says He Heard Oswald and 2 New Orleans Men Plot to Kill Kennedy," *New York Times*, March 14, 1967; and "The Clay Shaw Preliminary Hearing Testimony," transcript of interview of Perry Russo by Jim Kemp, http://www.jfk-online.com/pre31kemp.html.

5. Memorandum to Jim Garrison from Andrew J. Sciambra, February 27, 1967, http://mcadams.posc.mu.edu/russo2.txt.

6. Interview with Perry Raymond Russo at Mercy Hospital on February 27, 1967, from HSCA Administrative Folder-S7, David Ferrie, http://www.maryferrell.org/mffweb/archive/viewer/showDoc.do?docId=10083&relPageId=86.

7. Perry Raymond Russo, first hypnosis session, Exhibit F, http://mcadams.posc.mu.edu/session1.htm.
8. Perry Raymond Russo, "second" hypnotic session, Exhibit G, http://mcadams.posc.mu.edu/session2.htm. There is evidence of a hypnosis session held on March 9, which would actually have been the second session and thus would have made this "second" session the third one. See Patricia Lambert, *False Witness: The Real Story of Jim Garrison's Investigation and Oliver Stone's Film* JFK (New York: M. Evans, 1998), 76–79, 92–93.
9. Dr. Edward A. Weinstein, letter to the editor, *Washington Post*, March 27, 1967.
10. American Medical Association, *Encyclopedia of Medicine* (New York: Random House, 1989).
11. George H. Estabrooks, *Hypnotism* (New York: E. P. Dutton, 1957), 24.
12. Martin T. Orne, David A. Soskis, David F. Dinges, and Emily Carota Orne, "Hypnotically Induced Testimony," in *Eyewitness Testimony: Psychological Perspectives,* ed. Gary L. Wells and Elizabeth F. Loftus (New York: Cambridge University Press, 1984), 196.
13. James Phelan, *Scandals, Scamps, and Scoundrels: The Casebook of an Investigative Reporter* (New York: Random House, 1982), 165.
14. "Recovered Memory Therapy (RMT): Statements by Professional Organizations, 1993 to 1995," *Religious Tolerance,* http://www.religioustolerance.org/rmt_prof.htm.
15. Peter Brookesmith, *UFO: The Complete Sightings* (New York: Barnes & Noble Books, 1995).
16. Skeptics Dictionary, "Bridey Murphy," http://www.skepdic.com/bridey.html.
17. Phelan, *Scandals, Scamps, and Scoundrels,* 176.
18. James Kirkwood, *American Grotesque: An Account of the Clay Shaw–Jim Garrison Affair in the City of New Orleans* (New York: Simon & Schuster, 1970), 168.
19. Lambert, *False Witness,* 185–200; Dave Reitzes, "Impeaching Clinton," Kennedy Assassination Home Page, http://mcadams.posc.mu.edu/clinton1.htm.
20. Memorandum to Jim Garrison from Andrew J. Sciambra, January 31, 1968, http://mcadams.posc.mu.edu/collins1.txt; Kirkwood, *American Grotesque,* 216.

Chapter 4. Witnesses Who Are Just Too Good

1. It might seem strange that she was wearing a raincoat since it was not raining, but it had been raining in Dallas that day. Indeed, Mary Moorman is wearing a black raincoat, and the Babushka Lady, standing near Moorman and Hill, is wearing a white raincoat.
2. Jim Moore, *Conspiracy of One* (Chicago: The Summit Group, 1997), 30.
3. See Oliver Stone and Zachary Sklar, *JFK,* directed by Oliver Stone (Los Angeles: Warner Bros., 1991), VHS; Bill Sloan, *The Last Dissenting Witness,* with Jean Hill (Gretna, LA: Pelican Publishing Company, Inc., 1992); *Beyond JFK: The Question of Conspiracy,* directed by Barbara Kopple and Danny Schechter (Los Angeles: Embassy International Pictures, 1992), VHS. Primary sources on Hill also include Jim Marrs's book *Crossfire: The Plot That Killed Kennedy* (New York: Carroll & Graf, 1989) and Anthony Summers's book *Conspiracy* (New York: Paragon House, 1989). Both authors actually interviewed Hill.
4. Sloan with Hill, *The Last Dissenting Witness,* 21–22.
5. Testimony of Jean L. Hill (6 H 210).
6. Sloan with Hill, *The Last Dissenting Witness,* 24.
7. It is difficult to interpret the mangling of the name. Perhaps she did it to avoid making a charge of adultery against an identifiable person, although assassination buffs have no trouble identifying the officer in question.
8. Richard B. Trask, *Pictures of the Pain: Photography and the Assassination of President Kennedy* (Danvers, MA: Yeoman Press, 1994), 238.
9. Decker Exhibit 5323 (19 H 479).
10. *Warren Commission Report,* 334–35.
11. Sloan with Hill, *The Last Dissenting Witness,* 32.
12. The actual Warren Commission testimony shows Specter as not particularly hostile. Testimony of Jean L. Hill (6 H 205–23).

13. Sloan with Hill, *The Last Dissenting Witness*, 22.

14. Trask, *Pictures of the Pain*, 208–12.

15. Robert Richter, "Who Shot President Kennedy?," *NOVA*, season 15, episode 19, produced and directed by Robert Richter, aired November 15, 1988 (Princeton, NJ: Films for the Humanities and Sciences, 1992), VHS.

16. Sloan with Hill, *The Last Dissenting Witness*, 30.

17. Connie Kritzberg, *Secrets from the Sixth Floor Window* (Tulsa, OK: Under Cover Press, 1994), 31–33; Laura Hlavach and Darwin Payne, eds., *Reporting the Kennedy Assassination* (Dallas: Three Forks Press, 1996), 48–49.

18. Kritzberg, *Secrets*.

19. Testimony of Rufus Youngblood (2 H 148–49).

20. Exhibit 1024 (18 H 801).

21. Statement of Lyndon Johnson (5 H 562).

22. Joachim Joesten, *Oswald: Assassin or Fall Guy?* (New York: Marzani & Munsell, 1964).

23. *Warren Commission Report*, 28–40.

24. One final piece of evidence contradicting this notion of a changed parade route is the fact that the spectators, virtually all Dallasites who knew the traffic patterns, did not line up along Main Street in Dealey Plaza. Many clustered around the intersection of Houston and Elm (where the motorcade was scheduled to turn), along Houston Street, and (in smaller numbers) along Elm Street. They clearly didn't expect the procession to go down Main.

25. The film aired about 3:16 p.m., after being taken physically back to WBAP in Fort Worth and processed. See Trask, *Pictures of the Pain*, 238.

26. Exhibit 1967 (23 H 817).

27. *Two Men in Dallas: John F. Kennedy, Roger D. Craig*, produced by Lincoln Carle and Mark Lane (Vancouver: Alpa Productions, 1987), VHS; Roger Craig, "When They Kill a President" (unpublished manuscript, 1971), http://www.ratical.com/ratville/JFK/WTKaP.html.

28. *Two Men in Dallas*.

29. "When They Kill a President."

30. Testimony of J. W. Fritz (4 H 245); *Warren Commission Report*, 160–61.

31. Trask, *Pictures of the Pain*, 499.

32. Document 5, p. 70, FBI interview with Roy Cooper, November 23, 1963, National Archives record 124-10145-10036, quoted in John Kelin, "Yet Another Eyewitness," *Fair Play* 17 (July–August 1997), http://spot.acorn.net/JFKplace/09/fp.back_issues/17th_Issue/rambler_witness.html.

33. Testimony of Cecil McWatters (2 H 269).

34. *Warren Commission Report*, 159.

35. Testimony of Ruth Paine (2 H 506); Exhibit 2125 (24 H 696–97); Capt. W. P. Gannaway's memo to Jack Revill, Subject: Criminal Intelligence, December 23, 1963, in Dallas Municipal Archives, box 18, folder 05, document 031.

36. Testimony of Roger Craig (6 H 271).

37. Henry Hurt, *Reasonable Doubt: An Investigation into the Assassination of John F. Kennedy* (New York: Holt, Rinehart, and Winston, 1985), photo insert.

38. David B. Perry, "The Rambler Man," Dave Perry's John F. Kennedy Assassination Pages, 1993, http://davesjfk.com/rambler.html.

39. *Two Men in Dallas*.

40. Testimony of Roger Craig (6 H 267).

41. Exhibit 510 (4 H 250).

42. Trask, *Pictures of the Pain*, 524; and Marrs, *Crossfire*, 438.

43. Testimony of Luke Mooney (3 H 285); Exhibit 1974, 176 (23 H 919); Sims Exhibit A, 2 (21 H 511).

44. Sims Exhibit A, 3 (21 H 512).

45. Testimony of J. C. Day (4 H 253).
46. Exhibit 2003, 223 (24 H 314).
47. "Tom Alyea Film Clip: Finding the Shells," JFK Assassination Forum, May 24, 2010, http://www.youtube.com/user/assassinationforum#p/u/36/3tM7lY_z9t0.
48. Testimony of Roger Craig (6 H 267–68).
49. Ibid., 268; and Exhibit 2003 (24 H 228).
50. Decker Exhibit 5323 (19 H 507).
51. Exhibit 2169 (24 H 831).
52. Testimony of Seymour Weitzman (7 H 108).
53. Josiah Thompson, *Six Seconds in Dallas: A Micro-study of the Kennedy Assassination* (New York: Bernard Geis Associates, 1967), 221.
54. 7 HSCA 372.
55. Analysis of WFAA-TV video footage by Ethan Bercot, February 2009.
56. 6 HSCA 63–107.
57. "Texas Editor, Former Dallas Sheriff Tell FP Amazing New Information," *Los Angeles Free Press*, March 1, 1968, http://img254.imageshack.us/i/craigandjonespage1.jpg.
58. Richard Dudman, "Commentary of an Eyewitness," *New Republic*, December 21, 1963, 18.
59. Testimony of Eddy Walthers (7 H 550). When Garrison released the photos to the press that allegedly showed the recovery of a slug in December 1967, Walthers was interviewed and insisted that "nothing significant" was recovered.
60. Testimony of J. W. Foster (6 H 252).
61. Mark Oakes, *Eyewitness Video Tape*, Foster interview, July 9, 1991, available at http://www.lasthurrahbookshop.net/vidframe.html.
62. Trask, *Pictures of the Pain*, 497–98, 543.
63. Testimony of Roger Craig (6 H 265).
64. Testimony of Seymour Weitzman (7 H 109).
65. Testimony of Eugene Boone (3 H 294).
66. "Ruby Had 15,000 Bullets, Grenades, Rifles," *Los Angeles Free Press*, March 1, 1968, http://img36.imageshack.us/i/craigandjonespage10.jpg/.
67. Charles Crenshaw, *JFK: Conspiracy of Silence*, with Jens Hansen and J. Gary Shaw (New York: Signet, 1992). As a broad but fair generalization, we tend to "credit" Hansen and Shaw with the standard conspiracy factoids that litter the book and Crenshaw for his own first-person account, which is set off in a sans-serif typeface.
68. Ibid., 86.
69. Ibid., 153.
70. See Thompson, *Six Seconds in Dallas*; Harrison Edward Livingstone and Robert J. Groden, *High Treason: The Assassination of JFK and the Case for Conspiracy* (New York: Carroll & Graf, 1998); Harrison Edward Livingstone, *High Treason 2: The Great Cover-up; The Assassination of President John F. Kennedy* (New York: Carroll & Graf, 1992); David S. Lifton, *Best Evidence: Disguise and Deception in the Assassination of John F. Kennedy* (New York: Macmillan, 1980); Nigel Turner, "The Forces of Darkness," *The Men Who Killed Kennedy: The Definitive Account of American History's Most Controversial Mystery*, season 1, episode 1 (TimeLife Video, 1993), VHS; *JFK: The Case for Conspiracy*, produced by Robert J. Groden (Boothwyn, PA: New Frontier Productions and Grodenfilms, 1993), VHS; Richter, "Who Shot President Kennedy?"; Ben Bradlee [Jr.], "Investigations: Dispute on JFK Evidence Persists," *Boston Sunday Globe*, June 21, 1981.
71. Crenshaw, *JFK*, 79.
72. Ibid., 73–78; testimony of Dr. Robert McClelland (6 H 31).
73. Ibid., 32–33.
74. Testimony of Dr. Malcolm Perry (3 H 369, 370, and 377).
75. Crenshaw, *JFK*, 186–87. Of course, Oswald was too near death to give any sort of confession.
76. Alt.assassination.jfk newsgroup post, September 10, 1998.

77. William Manchester, *The Death of a President, November 20–November 25, 1963* (New York: Harper & Row, 1967), "Chronology" inside front cover.
78. Crenshaw, *JFK*, 188.
79. Harrison Edward Livingstone, *Killing the Truth: Deceit and Deception in the JFK Case* (New York: Carroll & Graf, 1993), 506. Livingstone cites as his source "various discussions with Dr. Charles Crenshaw" (607).
80. E-mail to the author, August 25, 2003. J. Gary Shaw adamantly denied this account in a response to Gary Mack's review of Livingstone's book. Mack responded that Jane Rusconi, Oliver Stone's research coordinator, confirmed the early version with LBJ wanting Oswald killed. Letters to the editor *The Fourth Decade* 2, no. 3 (March 1995): 19, http://www.maryferrell.org/mffweb/archive/viewer/showDoc.do?docId=48686&relPageId=19.
81. John McAdams, "Beverly Oliver: Babushka Babe? Or Bamboozling the Buffs?," Kennedy Assassination Home Page, http://mcadams.posc.mu.edu/Oliver.htm; David B. Perry, "Texas in the Morning Imagination," October 26, 2002, http://davesjfk.com/browns.html.
82. John McAdams, "Should We Believe Judyth Baker?," Kennedy Assassination Home Page, http://mcadams.posc.mu.edu/judyth.htm.
83. Judyth Vary Baker, "Before the Silence Came: Lee's Last Telephone Calls," draft of the final chapter of Judyth's book, http://mcadams.posc.mu.edu/endofline.pdf. Judyth's book has gone through many revisions, having been issued in 2006 as *Lee Harvey Oswald: The True Story of the Accused Assassin of President John F. Kennedy by His Lover* (Victoria, BC: Trafford) and in 2010 as *Me & Lee: How I Came to Know, Love and Lose Lee Harvey Oswald* (Walterville, OR: TrineDay). Each version of Judyth's book differs radically from the previous one, in large part because claims that have been exposed as bogus are sanitized from succeeding versions.
84. Paul Hoch, "Winnowing the Wheat and the Chaff," presented to the Second Annual Midwest Symposium on Assassination Politics, Chicago, 1993, http://mcadams.posc.mu.edu/hoch.htm.
85. A corollary of Hoch's ratio test holds that an account is suspect when it includes few or no names of people who are still alive and who might denounce the account or even sue for libel. Thus, the fact that one's roster of conspirators consists almost entirely of dead people doesn't suggest a sinister cleanup squad going around killing people off; rather, it suggests a story concocted to be "safe" in a way that a story accusing live individuals can't be.
86. The facts that the draft chapter in question had a note at the top obviously from Judyth and signed "j" and that Judyth herself sent the chapter via e-mail to several researchers didn't help, either. See "Should We Believe Judyth Baker?"
87. Motoko Rich, "Author Admits Acclaimed Memoir Is Fantasy," *New York Times*, March 4, 2008.
88. "A Million Little Lies: Exposing James Frey's Fiction Addiction," *The Smoking Gun*, January 8, 2006, http://www.thesmokinggun.com/archive/0104061jamesfrey1.html.
89. Constant Brand, "Author of Holocaust 'Memoir' Confesses She Made up Story," *San Francisco Chronicle*, March 1, 2008.
90. Hillel Italie, "'Angel at the Fence,' Holocaust Memoir, Publication Canceled," *Huffington Post*, December 27, 2008.

Chapter 5. Bogus Quoting: Stripping Context, Misleading Readers

1. David Scheim, *Contract on America: The Mafia Murder of President John F. Kennedy* (New York: Shapolsky Publishers, 1988), chapter 14. The real pioneer in misrepresenting Ruby's testimony, of course, was Mark Lane. See his *Rush to Judgment: A Critique of the Warren Commission's Inquiry into the Murders of President John F. Kenney, Officer J. D. Tippit and Lee Harvey Oswald* (New York: Holt, Rinehart, and Winston, 1966), chapter 19.
2. Ibid., 151.
3. Ibid., 155.

4. Testimony of Jack Ruby (5 H 181–213).
5. The script of the movie *JFK* quotes the "whole new form of government" passage, but it omits the "Jewish people are being exterminated at this moment" passage, apparently understanding that the latter statement would reveal Ruby as having been disturbed.
6. David Scheim's *Contract on America*, for example, quotes these two passages and nothing further (pp. 19–20, 209). Scheim calls this "a predetermined solution." Warren Hinckle and William Turner, in *Deadly Secrets: The CIA-Mafia War against Castro and the Assassination of J.F.K.* (New York: Thunder's Mouth Press, 1992), likewise quote these two precise passages. Some conspiracy books do quote a bit more of the context but virtually never enough to allow readers to question the "recipe for a cover-up" interpretation.
7. Katzenbach Memo, http://www.maryferrell.org/wiki/index.php/Katzenbach_Memo.
8. Gerald McKnight, *Breach of Trust: How the Warren Commission Failed the Nation and Why* (Lawrence: University of Kansas Press, 2005), 22, 27, 30, 45, 58, 102, 165, 166, 294, 355, 358.
9. Katzenbach memo, FBI 62-109060 JFK HQ File, Section 18, 29–30, http://www.mary ferrell.org/mffweb/archive/viewer/showDoc.do?docId=62268&relPageId=29.
10. Memorandum to Mr. Tolson from Mr. Belmont, November 24, 1963, FBI 105-82555 Oswald HQ file, section 3, http://www.maryferrell.org/mffweb/archive/viewer/show Doc.do?docId=57693&relPageId=13.
11. "A Note From Jack Ruby," *Newsweek*, March 27, 1967, 21.
12. Jim Marrs, *Crossfire: The Plot That Killed Kennedy* (New York: Carroll & Graf, 1989), 414; Noel Twyman, *Bloody Treason: On Solving History's Greatest Murder Mystery, the Assassination of John F. Kennedy* (Rancho Santa Fe, CA: Laurel Publications, 1997), 249. Twyman is quoting, with approval, the *HSCA Report*, 158.
13. Testimony of F. V. Sorrels (13 H 67–68); McMillon Exhibit 5017 (20 H 557–58); testimony of B. S. Clardy (12 H 413); Gerald Posner, *Case Closed: Lee Harvey Oswald and the Assassination of JFK* (New York: Random House, 1993), 398.
14. Dallas Police Department permit to visit prisoner in city jail issued to Tom Howard, dated 1:55 p.m., November 24, 1963, http://mcadams.posc.mu.edu/images/jail_pass.gif.
15. Ray Hall Exhibit 2 (20 H 42–43).
16. Bob Huffaker et al., *When the News Went Live: Dallas 1963* (Lanham, MD: Taylor Trade Publishing, 2004), 125.
17. *Dallas Times Herald*, November 24, 1963.
18. Alt.assassination.jfk newsgroup post, June 10, 2003.
19. Alt.assassination.jfk newsgroup post, June 11, 2003.
20. Mark Lane, *Plausible Denial: Was the CIA Involved in the Assassination of JFK?* (New York: Thunder's Mouth Press, 1991), 288, 322.
21. G. Robert Blakey and Richard N. Billings, *Fatal Hour: The Assassination of President Kennedy by Organized Crime* (New York: Berkley Books, 1992), 200.
22. *Warren Commission Report*, 333–34.
23. *Warren Commission Report*, 129–31, 740.
24. Photocopy of Marita Lorenz's deposition, 41, http://mcadams.posc.mu.edu/images/lorenz.jpg.
25. Lane, *Plausible Denial*, 288–303.
26. Lorenz deposition, 67.
27. Further, there could not have been any training for the Bay of Pigs invasion before Oswald left for the Soviet Union in 1959, because President Eisenhower did not sign off on a "Program of Covert Action against the Castro Regime," essentially the charter for what became the Bay of Pigs, in March 1960.
28. This error might also have been a minor misstatement by Walter Kuzmuk.
29. Lane, *Plausible Denial*, 287.
30. Trial notes of Kevin Dunne (Hunt's attorney), e-mail from Dunne, December 31, 2003.

31. Lane, prudently, declined to endorse the notion that Hunt and Sturgis were two of the tramps.
32. U.S. Commission on CIA Activities within the United States (Rockefeller Commission), *Report to the President by the Commission on CIA Activities within the United States* (New York: Manor Books, 1975), 253. The report added that one of Hunt's sons was too young to recall whether his parents were with him, and Hunt's wife was deceased while the commission was active.
33. Gaeton Fonzi, *The Last Investigation* (New York: Thunder's Mouth Press, 1993), 83–107.
34. Posner, *Case Closed*, 407.
35. Lane, *Plausible Denial*, 322.
36. This, remember, was a civil trial and not a criminal one, and therefore required only six jurors.
37. Stephen Doig, "Hunt-JFK Article 'Trash' but Not Libelous, Jury Finds," *Miami Herald*, February 7, 1985.
38. Ibid.
39. "Howard Hunt Loses Libel Suit Over Story He Helped Kill JFK," *New Orleans Times-Picayune*, February 7, 1985.
40. Jeff Hardy, "Jury Rules in Favor of Tabloid; Hunt Loses $1 Million Libel Case," *Tampa Tribune*, February 7, 1985.
41. Doig, "Hunt-JFK Article"; "Howard Hunt Loses Libel Suit"; Karen Payne, "Jury Here Rules Hunt Was Not Libeled," *Miami News*, February 6, 1985. When Hunt and his lawyers appealed the case, they argued that the judge's instruction to the jury directed it to take too narrow a view of "actual malice." See *Hunt v. Marchetti*, 824 F.2d 916, 1987 U.S. App. LEXIS 11080.
42. Hardy, "Jury Rules in Favor of Tabloid."
43. Lane, *Plausible Denial*, 234–35.
44. Lane says, "Judge Kehoe delivered his instructions to the jury carefully, reading a prepared statement that had been previously submitted for comment to counsel for each party," and provides no further information about the charge. Ibid., 318.
45. Henry Hurt, *Reasonable Doubt: An Investigation into the Assassination of John F. Kennedy* (New York: Holt, Rinehart, and Winston, 1985), 177.
46. Testimony of James B. Adams before the House of Representatives, Civil Rights and Constitutional Rights Subcommittee of the Committee on the Judiciary, October 21, 1975, FBI 62-109060 JFK HQ File, Section 183, 177, http://www.maryferrell.org/mffweb/archive/viewer/showDoc.do?mode=searchResult&absPageId=788061. The document says Ruby furnished "no information whatever."
47. Testimony of James B. Adams, assistant to the director, FBI, before the Select Committee on Intelligence (Pike Committee), November 18, 1975, part 3, 1036, http://www.maryferrell.org/mffweb/archive/viewer/showDoc.do?docId=145086&relPageId=102.

Chapter 6. Probability: Things that Defy the Odds

1. Exhibit 966 (26 H 447); Exhibit 1414 (22 H 828).
2. Ray La Fontaine and Mary La Fontaine, *Oswald Talked: The New Evidence in the JFK Assassination* (Gretna, LA: Pelican Publishing, 1996), 149.
3. Testimony of Sam Newman before the House Select Committee, Exhibit 1, National Archives record 180-10101-10379.
4. Transcript, "Who Was Lee Harvey Oswald?," *Frontline*, WGBH-PBS, November 16, 1993, http://www.pbs.org/wgbh/pages/frontline/programs/transcripts/1205.html.
5. Lee (Vincent T.) Exhibit 5 (20 H 524).
6. Edward T. Haslam, *Mary, Ferrie & the Monkey Virus: The Story of an Underground Medical Laboratory; a Non-Fiction Work* (Albuquerque, NM: Wordsworth Communications, 1995).
7. Milton Brener, *The Garrison Case: A Study in the Abuse of Power* (New York: Clarkson N. Potter, 1969), 49.

8. "How Many Spooks?" citing Memorandum: SUBJECT: Garrison Investigation: Queries from Justice Department, September 28, 1967, http://mcadams.posc.mu.edu/notcia.htm.

9. "Letter: I Am Attaching, In Answer to Your Request, CIA Comments," Reel 48, Folder GG, WC File (vol. 2) from Executive Registry, National Archives record 1994.03 .08.12:24:05:560005. See also Archives record 104-10406-10095 (same document), http://www.maryferrell.org/mffweb/archive/viewer/showDoc.do?docId=9532&relPageId=8.

10. Ibid.

11. Memorandum for Deputy Director of Support, from Howard Osborn, May 1, 1967, National Archives record 104-10105-10139, http://www.maryferrell.org/mffweb/archive/viewer/showDoc.do?docId=41374&relPageId=4.

12. 9 HSCA 104. Martin also said he thought he had seen a photo that included Oswald among Civil Air Patrol (CAP) members in Ferrie's home. This report, in fact, is possible.

13. 10 HSCA 128–29.

14. Ibid.

15. Ibid.

16. 9 HSCA 103–15.

17. Warren Commission Document 75, 314.

18. Jim Garrison, *On the Trail of the Assassins: My Investigation and Prosecution of the Murder of President Kennedy* (New York: Sheridan Square Press, 1988,) 110.

19. David Reitzes, "Phone Factoid: Tortured Connection," http://mcadams.posc.mu.edu/factoid.htm.

20. Ibid.

21. David Blackburst, e-mail to Dave Reitzes, August 22, 1999.

22. "Richard Billings' New Orleans Journal," December 1966–January 25, 1967, http://www.jfk-online.com/billings2.html.

23. Alt.assassination.jfk newsgroup posts, May 27 and 29, 1999.

24. "Richard Billings' New Orleans Journal."

25. Alt.assassination.jfk newsgroup post, June 4, 1999. In addition to the residential rooms, there would have been an unknown number of phone lines to hotel employees.

26. Peter Whitmey interview with Jean Aase, 1998, reported in May 26, 1999, post on alt.assassination.jfk newsgroup; alt.assassination.jfk newsgroup post, February 13, 1999.

27. Ibid.

28. 9 HSCA 905.

29. Exhibit 2267 (25 H 191); 9 HSCA 906.

30. 9 HSCA 805.

31. Bernard Fensterwald, *Assassination of JFK by Coincidence or Conspiracy?* (New York: Zebra, 1977), 288; Harrison Edward Livingstone and Robert J. Groden, *High Treason: The Assassination of JFK and the Case for Conspiracy* (Baltimore: Conservatory Press, 1989), 274; Anthony Summers, *Conspiracy* (New York: Paragon House, 1989), 454. Summers mitigates the silliness by writing, "All this one must add, wearily, may be coincidence," but then he presses ahead by saying that Ferrie "did move through Texas in a mysterious way in the days after the President's assassination."

32. Henry Hurt, *Reasonable Doubt: An Investigation into the Assassination of John F. Kennedy* (New York: Holt, Rinehart, and Winston, 1985), 284.

33. George Michael Evica, in *And We Are All Mortal: New Evidence and Analysis in the John F. Kennedy Assassination* (West Hartford, CT: Evica, 1977), 162–67; Noel Twyman *Bloody Treason: On Solving History's Greatest Murder Mystery, the Assassination of John F. Kennedy* (Rancho Santa Fe, CA: Laurel Publications, 1997), 273.

34. Jim Marrs, *Crossfire: The Plot That Killed Kennedy* (New York: Carroll & Graf, 1989), 338.

Chapter 7. More on Defying the Odds: The Mysterious Deaths

1. 4 HSCA 463. Note that the British use of "trillion" is different from the U.S. usage ("Table of Numbers," http://www.merriam-webster.com/table/dict/number.htm). This issue is actually moot, since the number is astronomical and, as we shall see, nonsense.

2. This is Teresa Norton, aka Karen Carlin (stage name: Little Lynn). See Jim Marrs, *Crossfire: The Plot That Killed Kennedy* (New York: Carroll & Graf, 1989). A Dallas Police report lists her name as "Karen Lynn Bennett" and notes that Bruce Carlin is her common-law husband. See Dallas Municipal Archives, John F. Kennedy Archive, Box 4, document 15.

3. Robert Groden, in *The Killing of a President: The Complete Photographic Record of the JFK Assassination, the Conspiracy, and the Cover-Up* (New York: Viking Studio Books, 1993), claims that "the complete list includes more than 300 individuals who have died under odd, and often violent circumstances" (p. xiv). Groden doesn't actually name the 300 people; however, all his mysterious deaths are people on Marrs's list.

4. David Flick, "On 45th Anniversary of JFK Assassination, Eyewitnesses Becoming Scarce," *Dallas Morning News*, November 22, 2008; and Eric Pace, "James Altgens, Photographer at Kennedy Assassination, Dies at 76," *New York Times*, December 17, 1995.

5. "A Matter of Reasonable Doubt," *Life* 61, no. 22 (November 25, 1966).

6. "Judge Joe Brown of Ruby Case Dies," *New York Times*, February 21, 1968.

7. Oswald left the depository perhaps three minutes after the 12:30 p.m. shooting. See *Warren Commission Report*, 155.

8. Chetta's brother-in-law, whose only connection with the case was his relationship with Chetta, is also on the list.

9. Of course, the House Select Committee on Assassinations (HSCA) had handwriting experts go over the same evidence that Cadigan did, and they came to the identical conclusions.

10. "Sylvia Meagher, 67, Former Health Official," *New York Times*, January 16, 1989.

11. 4 HSCA 464–65. The newspaper had an earlier version of the list, which only had fifteen mysterious deaths.

12. Marrs, *Crossfire*, 425.

13. Eric Paddon, "Dorothy Kilgallen and the JFK Assassination," http://mcadams.posc.mu.edu/kilgallen.txt, last accessed February 21, 2008.

14. Gary Wills and Ovid Demaris, *Jack Ruby* (New York: New American Library, 1968), 72.

15. "Dorothy Kilgallen Dead," *New York Journal-American*, November 8, 1965. Kilgallen stayed up very late to complete her column, sending it by courier to the *Journal-American* at 2:30 a.m.

16. Atra Baer, "Show Goes On . . . The Way Dorothy Would Want It," *New York Journal-American*, November 15, 1965.

17. National Archives record 180-100711-0433, agency file number 007250, HSCA, "Autopsy Report" and "Notice of Death" from the Office of Chief Medical Examiner of the City of New York.

18. Marrs, *Crossfire*, 560.

19. "Mrs. Earl E. T. Smith, Society Hostess, Dies," *New York Journal-American*, November 9, 1965.

20. Dr. Robert Artwohl, post on Compuserve, dated May 15, 1994.

21. Memorandum to Jim Alcock from Jim Garrison, Re: Autopsy of David Ferrie, not dated, http://mcadams.posc.mu.edu/proloid.gif.

22. John McAdams, "David Ferrie's 'Suicide Notes,'" Kennedy Assassination Home Page, http://mcadams.posc.mu.edu/death10.htm.

23. Patricia Lambert, *False Witness: The Real Story of Jim Garrison's Investigation and Oliver Stone's Film* JFK (New York: M. Evans, 1998), 57, 62–63.

24. Autopsy protocol, Orleans Parish Coroner's Office, dated February 22, 1967.

25. Marrs, *Crossfire*, 563.

26. "Dead in the Wake of the Kennedy Assassination: Clay Shaw: Mysterious Death?," New Orleans Department of Police, Hospitalization Case Report, August 16, 1974, http://mcadams.posc.mu.edu/death9.htm, last accessed February 21, 2008.

27. Marrs, *Crossfire*, 559.

28. James DiEugenio, *Destiny Betrayed: JFK, Cuba, and the Garrison Case* (New York: Sheridan Square Press, 1992), 27–28. Emphasis in original.

29. Ibid., 28.

30. Raymond G. Rocca, Memorandum, "Garrison Investigation: Queries from the Justice Department," September 28, 1967, 6. National Archives record 1993.08.20.15:17:33: 430028, http://www.maryferrell.org/mffweb/archive/viewer/showDoc.do?docId =104460&relPageId=8.

31. District of Columbia Department of Public Health, certificate of death, May 8, 1964.

32. James Ewell, "2-Car Smashup Kills Oswald Taxi Driver," *Dallas Morning News*, December 19, 1965.

33. *Coushatta Citizen*, February 17, 1966.

34. Phone interview with Harper on June 1, 2001. Interestingly, Harper had learned about Bogard's place on the mysterious deaths' list from a magazine he once read at the barbershop while waiting for a haircut. In a classic case of a witness becoming an assassination buff, he speculated that Bogard knew conspirators were out to get him and may have taken his own life for that reason. He didn't report any evidence, however, that the death was anything but a suicide.

35. Jodi Kantor, "Does Clinton Run Murder Inc.?," *Slate*, February 18, 1999.

36. Barbara Mikkelson, "The Clinton Body Count," *Snopes*, February 5, 2007, http://www .snopes.com/politics/clintons/bodycount.asp, last accessed January 25, 2008.

37. Bush Body Count, http://www.theforbiddenknowledge.com/hardtruth/bush_body _count.htm, last accessed January 25, 2008.

38. Ian Gurney, "The Very Mysterious Deaths of Five Microbiologists," December 20, 2001, http://www.rense.com/general18/five.htm, last accessed January 25, 2008.

39. "The Mysterious Deaths of Top Microbiologists," http://whatreallyhappened.com/ WRHARTICLES/deadbiologists.html, last accessed March 18, 2011.

40. "Did 22 SDI Researchers really ALL Commit Suicide?," http://www.fiu.edu/~mizrachs/ sdi-deaths.html, last accessed February 20, 2008.

41. Mike Gormez, "Deaths at Flag," http://www.whyaretheydead.info/, last accessed February 20, 2008.

42. "The Clinton Body Count," http://www.whatreallyhappened.com/RANCHO/POLITICS /BODIES.html, last accessed January 25, 2008, archived at http://mcadams.posc.mu .edu/ngarchive/Clinton_body_count.mht.

43. Owing to the Republican primaries, we were likely spared a "Mitt's Mormon Mortuary" tabulation or a "Huckabee's Homicides" count.

44. Webster G. Tarpley, "Is Gwatney Murder Part of Obama Body Count?" Rense.com, August 14, 2008, http://www.rense.com/general83/gwat.htm.

Chapter 8. Did People Know It Was Going to Happen?

1. Anthony Summers, *Conspiracy* (New York: Paragon House, updated 1991 edition), 404, ellipses in original.

2. Dan Christensen, "JFK, King: The Dade County Links," http://cuban-exile.com/ doc_101-125/doc0122.html.

3. Michael Benson's *Who's Who in the JFK Assassination: An A-to-Z Encyclopedia* (New York: Citadel Press, 1993) does not list him.

4. Henry Hurt, *Reasonable Doubt: An Investigation into the Assassination of John F. Kennedy* (New York: Holt, Rinehart, and Winston, 1985), 411. For similar assertions, see (for example) Harrison Edward Livingstone and Robert J. Groden, *High Treason: The Assassination of JFK and the Case for Conspiracy* (Baltimore: Conservatory Press, 1989), 408; Jim Marrs, *Crossfire: The Plot That Killed Kennedy* (New York: Carroll & Graf, 1989), 265.

5. Miami Police Informant, information on Milteer, November 26, 1963, National Archives record 180-10090-10307, 4, http://cuban-exile.com/doc_051-075/doc0062e.html.

6. Memorandum of conversation between [Bud] Fensterwald and Bill Somersett, June 5, 1968, from the files of the New Orleans District Attorney's office, National Archives record 180-10099-10133.

7. Secret Service, Atlanta Office, "Check on potentially dangerous persons November 22–25, 1963"; FBI memorandum to Alan Belmont from Alex Rosen, November 27, 1963, National Archives record 124-10012-10306; "Urgent" teletype from SAC [special agent in charge] Atlanta to "Director" [Hoover], November 26, 1963, National Archives record 124-10012-10384.

8. Secret Service memorandum, March 10, 1967, National Archives record 180-10091-10212.

9. FBI memorandum to Belmont.

10. See Dave Reitzes, "Impeaching Clinton, Part Two: Jackson," 2000, http://www.jfk-online .com/impeach2.html; 10 HSCA 199–204.

11. Memorandum to Jim Garrison from Frank Meloche, Re: Rose Cherami, March 13, 1967, http://www.jfk-online.com/cherdoc1.html.

12. Jim DiEugenio, "Rose Cheramie: How She Predicted the JFK Assassination," *Probe* 6, no. 5 (July–August 1999), http://www.ctka.net/pr799-rose.html.

13. 10 HSCA 202.

14. Reitzes, "Impeaching Clinton."

15. 10 HSCA 203.

16. Ibid., 201.

17. Ibid., 202.

18. Testimony of F. V. Sorrels (7 H 338).

19. Ibid., 456.

20. US Bureau of the Census, *Current Population Reports*, series P-25, nos. 311, 917, 1095, released June 4, 1999, http://www.npg.org/facts/us_historical_pops.htm.

21. Cherami's story is not reviewed here in detail, since it is quite convoluted and the primary sources are laced with hearsay.

22. *HSCA Report*, 230.

23. Dave Reitzes, "Truth or Dare: The Lives and Lies of Richard Case Nagell," http://mcad ams.posc.mu.edu/nagell1.htm.

24. Thomas Donnelly, *Rebuilding America's Defenses: Strategy, Forces and Resources for a New Century*, http://www.newamericancentury.org/RebuildingAmericasDefenses.pdf.

25. Ibid., 50–51.

26. "The New Pearl Harbor," Wikipedia, http://en.wikipedia.org/wiki/The_New_Pearl_Harbor, last accessed July 29, 2010.

Chapter 9. Signal and Noise: Seeing Things in Photos

1. Jane S. Halonen and John W. Santrock, *Psychology: Contexts of Behavior*, 2nd ed. (Dubuque, IA: Brown & Benchmark, 1996), 117.

2. Josiah Thompson, *Six Seconds in Dallas: A Micro-study of the Kennedy Assassination* (New York: Bernard Geis Associates, 1967), 126–28.

3. Warren Commission Document 5, 30, http://www.maryferrell.org/mffweb/archive/viewer/showDoc.do?mode=searchResult&absPageId=328791.

4. Thompson, *Six Seconds in Dallas*, 126.

5. Commission Document 962, 37, http://www.maryferrell.org/mffweb/archive/viewer/showDoc.do?mode=searchResult&absPageId=358094. Virtually nobody knows what a pergola is, but the pergola did include a pedestrian walkway, so "mall" was a perfectly fine description.

6. Thompson, *Six Seconds in Dallas*, 129.

7. Ibid., 224–25, 252–53.

8. "Orville Nix Film Overview and Time Line," Sixth Floor Museum at Dealey Plaza, http://www.jfk.org/go/collections/about/orville-nix-film-interview.

9. 6 HSCA 128.

10. Ibid., 130–31. Interestingly, Josiah Thompson had pretty decisively debunked this factoid in 1967. See Thompson, *Six Seconds in Dallas*, 224–25.

11. Livingstone and Groden, *High Treason*, 192–93.

12. Jim Marrs, *Crossfire: The Plot That Killed Kennedy* (New York: Carroll & Graf, 1989), 35.

13. 6 HSCA 44.

14. Robert Groden, *The Killing of a President: The Complete Photographic Record of the JFK Assassination, the Conspiracy, and the Cover-Up* (New York: Viking Studio Books, 1993), 192.

15. 6 HSCA 121–25.

16. Anthony Summers, *Conspiracy* (New York: Paragon House, updated 1991 edition), 215.

17. Groden, *The Killing of a President*, 124.

18. Testimony of Marina Oswald (11 H 304). Interestingly, Marina also said that the license plate had not been torn out when the FBI showed her the photo. But since the FBI got the photo from the Dallas Police, it's hard to view this discrepancy as anything but a failure of memory on Marina's part.

19. Mark Lane, *Rush to Judgment: A Critique of the Warren Commission's Inquiry into the Murders of President John F. Kenney, Officer J. D. Tippit and Lee Harvey Oswald* (New York: Holt, Rinehart, and Winston, 1966), 349.

20. "JFK Killing Witness Not Surprised Tests Indicated 2nd Gunman," *Fort Worth Star-Telegram*, December 22, 1978. Quoted in Marrs, *Crossfire*, 25.

21. Marrs, *Crossfire*, 25; Michael Benson, *Who's Who in the JFK Assassination*, 483; James P. Duffy and Vincent L. Ricci, *The Assassination of John Kennedy: The Complete Book of Facts* (New York: Thunder's Mouth Press, 1992), 511.

22. Richard Trask, letter to the editor, *Fourth Decade* 4, no. 3 (March 1997): 14–15, http://www.maryferrell.org/mffweb/archive/viewer/showDoc.do?docId=48698&relPageId=15.

23. 6 HSCA 258.

24. Benson, *Who's Who*, 173, 194, 385.

25. Alan J. Weberman and Michael Canfield, *Coup d'État in America: The CIA and the Assassination of John F. Kennedy* (New York: Third Press, 1975; rev. ed., San Francisco: Quick American Archives, 1992).

26. 6 HSCA 230.

27. U.S. President's Commission on CIA Activities within the United States (Rockefeller Commission), *Report to the President by the Commission on CIA Activities within the United States* (New York: Manor Books, June 1975), 257.

28. 6 HSCA 257–73.

29. *HSCA Report*, 92.

30. Ray La Fontaine and Mary La Fontaine, *Oswald Talked: The New Evidence in the JFK Assassination* (Gretna, LA: Pelican Publishing, 1996), 26–27.

31. "Time for the Truth," *A Current Affair*, June 25, 1992.

32. George Lardner Jr., "FBI Questions 'Tramp' at Slaying Site," *Washington Post*, March 4, 1992.

33. Kenneth Formet, "Gus Abrams: 'Yep, That's My Bill!,'" *Dateline Dallas* (Winter 1993): 24–25.

34. JFK Lancer's November in Dallas Research Conference, 2000, http://www.jfklancer.com/dallas00/Dallas00spea.html.

35. Weberman and Canfield, *Coup d'État in America*, 353.

36. Rockefeller Commission, *Report to the President*, 262–63. Emphasis in original.

37. 1 HSCA 417.

38. Ibid., 421.

39. *Who Killed JFK? Facts, Not Fiction*, CBS News (Beverly Hills, CA: CBS/FOX Video, 1992), VHS. See also Robert Richter, "Who Shot President Kennedy?," *NOVA*, season 15, episode 19, produced and directed by Robert Richter, aired November 15, 1988 (Princeton, NJ: Films for the Humanities and Sciences, 1992), VHS.

40. Magen Knuth, "Wecht and the Rockefeller Commission," http://mcadams.posc.mu.edu/wecht.htm.
41. Testimony online at "Back, and to the Left," http://mcadams.posc.mu.edu/wecht2.htm.
42. "*MythBusters* Revisited—Blown Away," season 3, October 12, 2005, http://www.youtube.com/watch?v=QCzD5uhSViY.
43. 6 HSCA 286–93; and Magen Knuth, "Was Oswald in the Doorway of the Depository at the Time of the JFK Assassination?," Kennedy Assassination Home Page, http://mcadams.posc.mu.edu/oswald_doorway.htm.
44. Groden, *The Killing of a President*, 141.
45. "Oswald Tied to Clay Shaw at New Orleans Trade Mart?," http://mcadams.posc.mu.edu/rush.htm.
46. Groden, *The Killing of a President*, 66.
47. See the excerpt of the letter from Anthony March to Robert Groden at Bogus Conspiracy "Photo Experts": Groden: Turning a Shotgun into a Rifle, Kennedy Assassination Home Page, http://mcadams.posc.mu.edu/experts.htm.
48. Peter Brookesmith, *UFO: The Complete Sightings* (New York: Barnes & Noble Books, 1995).
49. Bad Astronomy, "Fox TV and the Apollo Moon Hoax," February 13, 2001, http://www.badastronomy.com/bad/tv/foxapollo.html; and Anne M. Platoff, "Where No Flag Has Gone Before: Political and Technical Aspects of Placing a Flag on the Moon," National Aeronautics and Space Administration Contractor Report 188251, August 1993, http://www.jsc.nasa.gov/history/flag/flag.htm.
50. Arianne Cohen, "6 Debunked 9/11 Conspiracy Claims from NIST's New WTC 7 Report," *Popular Mechanics*, August 21, 2008, http://www.popularmechanics.com/technology/engineering/architecture/4278927.
51. 7 HSCA 128.

Chapter 10. Think Scenario

1. *Warren Commission Report*, 152.
2. Exhibit 1974, 176 (23 H 919). Richard B. Trask, *Pictures of the Pain: Photography and the Assassination of President Kennedy* (Danvers, MA: Yeoman Press, 1994), 523.
3. Jim Marrs, *Crossfire: The Plot That Killed Kennedy* (New York: Carroll & Graf, 1989), 53; Warren Commission Exhibit 2098 (24 H 531).
4. *Warren Commission Report*, 149–56.
5. The FBI questioned all depository employees, asking whether they had seen anybody they did not know in the building on the day of the assassination. The only stranger anyone reported seeing was an elderly man who had come in before the shooting and asked the location of the restroom. Exhibit 1381 (22 H 634).
6. Warren Commission Document 1420, 10–11.
7. Testimony of F. V. Sorrels (7 H 351–52).
8. Henry Hurt, *Reasonable Doubt: An Investigation into the Assassination of John F. Kennedy* (New York: Holt, Rinehart, and Winston, 1985), 114–16.
9. Decker Exhibit 5323 (19 H 483).
10. Warren Commission Document 205, 320.
11. For the route, see Decker Exhibit 5323 (19 H 483). Hurt also reports that Mercer had to wait "perhaps as long as three minutes" in traffic because of the blockage the truck caused.
12. Testimony of Lee Bowers Jr. (6 H 285–86).
13. For a map of the plaza's layout, including the railroad yard and the signal tower in which Bowers was perched, see *Warren Commission Report*, 73.
14. Ibid., 258.
15. Ibid.

16. Ibid., 690–97.
17. HSCA added some useful information on this issue, determining that the Soviet counsel in Helsinki, Gregory Golub, had permission from Moscow to give Americans visas without approval from Moscow if he was convinced they were "all right." In one documented case, two Americans got visas immediately upon showing they had Intourist reservations. *HSCA Report*, 212.
18. Jim Garrison, *On the Trail of the Assassins: My Investigation and Prosecution of the Murder of President Kennedy* (New York: Sheridan Square Press, 1988), 70.
19. Testimony of Robert Stovall (10 H 170–71).
20. Affidavit of Gary Taylor (11 H 480–81); testimony of Helen Cunningham (10 H 129–31); Cunningham Exhibit No. 1 (19 H 400). Oswald appears not to have shown up for the interview at Texas Power and Light.
21. Testimony of Roy Truly (3 H 213–14).
22. Conceivably, Roberts could have been an innocent party who merely witnessed a bit of playacting by Marina, Ruth Paine, and Linnie Mae Randle.
23. Joel Grant, "The 'Three Furies' that Brought Kennedy to Oswald," http://mcadams.posc.mu.edu/dallas.txt.
24. Anthony Summers, *Conspiracy* (New York: Paragon House, 1989), 188.
25. Summers does not say the contraband was documents. In fact, he doesn't even say it was contraband—he doesn't even guess at what it is. But if it wasn't, what was the point? Summers does not say, apparently because there is no conspiratorial interpretation that makes any sense.
26. Norman Mailer, *Oswald's Tale: An American Mystery* (New York: Random House, 1995).
27. "Another Oswald Sighting: Allegations of Lee Harvey Oswald in Alice, Texas," http://www.jfk-online.com/alicelho.html.
28. Chris W. Courtwright, "Oswald in Aliceland: A Tale of Two Days; a Tale of Two Oswalds," November 21, 1997, http://www.jfklancer.com/Courtwright1.html.
29. Ibid.
30. George Lardner Jr., "CIA Officer Rifled Files of Hill Panel," *Washington Post*, June 18, 1979. Several medical experts had, by this time, examined the materials at the National Archives. 6 HSCA 226, 316 (footnote 197); 7 HSCA 7, 75, 216.
31. Matthew Smith, *The Second Plot* (Edinburgh: Mainstream Publishing, 1992), 141.
32. Summers, *Conspiracy*, 13.
33. Robert Groden, *The Killing of a President: The Complete Photographic Record of the JFK Assassination, the Conspiracy, and the Cover-Up* (New York: Viking Studio Books, 1993), 161.
34. Jim DiEugenio, "The Sins of Robert Blakey, Part II," *Probe* 6, no. 1 (November–December 1999), http://www.ctka.net/pr1198-blakey.html, last accessed March 19, 2009.
35. U.S. Commission on CIA Activities within the United States (Rockefeller Commission), *Report to the President by the Commission on CIA Activities within the United States* (New York: Manor Books, 1975), 257–67; "1968 Panel Review of Photographs, X-Ray Films, Documents and Other Evidence Pertaining to the Fatal Wounding of President John F. Kennedy on November 22, 1963, in Dallas, Texas" (Ramsay Clark Panel), *JFK Lancer*, http://www.jfklancer.com/ClarkPanel.html.
36. See for example, Mark Lane, *Plausible Denial: Was the CIA Involved in the Assassination of JFK?* (New York: Thunder's Mouth Press, 1991), 39–87.
37. Michael Benson, *Who's Who in the JFK Assassination: An A-to-Z Encyclopedia* (New York: Citadel Press, 1993), 343.
38. One could argue, of course, that this was a brilliant ploy to *appear* incompetent, even though they knew that the fellow was not Oswald. If that were the case, then the tactic utterly failed. Four decades of conspiracy theorists have failed to make this obvious inference. Indeed, they appear not to have ever thought that the CIA might be incompetent.

39. Summers, *Conspiracy*, 351–53.
40. Exhibit 237 (16 H 638). Also see the photo insert in this book.
41. Anthony Summers, *Not in Your Lifetime* (New York: Marlowe & Company, 1998), 55–56; Warren Commission Document 205, 148. See also Gary Murr, "The Undeliverable Package," March 28, 2000, http://www.jfkresearch.freehomepage.com/murr.htm, last accessed April 20, 2009.
42. See the testimony of James Cadigan (4 H 97).
43. *Warren Commission Report*, 687.
44. Ibid., 388.
45. Transcript, "Who Was Lee Harvey Oswald?," *Frontline*, WGBH-PBS, November 16, 1993, http://www.pbs.org/wgbh/pages/frontline/programs/transcripts/1205.html.
46. *HSCA Report*, 219.
47. Testimony of K. W. Thornley (11 H 84). Thornley was wrong about Oswald losing his clearance, but it's significant that his roles and assignments created that impression.
48. Ian Griggs, "Firearms, Photographs, & Lee Harvey Oswald," *Kennedy Assassination Chronicles* 1, no. 1 (1995), http://www.jfklancer.com/bymain.html.
49. 6 HSCA 153; ibid., 141.
50. Gary Savage, *First Day Evidence: Stored Away for 30 Years in an Old Briefcase, New Evidence Is Now Revealed by Former Dallas Police Crime Lab Detective R. W. (Rusty) Livingston* (Monroe, LA: Shoppe Press, 1993).
51. "WTC 7: Silverstein's 'Pull It' Explanation Examined," http://whatreallyhappened .com/WRHARTICLES/silverstein_pullit.html. See video version clip of Larry Silverstein's "Pull it" statement at http://www.youtube.com/watch?v=7WYdAJQV100.
52. "WTC 7: Silverstein's 'Pull It' Explanation Examined"; and "Debunking the 9/11 Myths: Special Report," *Popular Mechanics*, February 3, 2005, http://www.popularmechanics .com/technology/military_law/1227842.html?page=5#wtc7.
53. Identical Internet searches (using the same dates and keywords) of "broadcast transcripts" turn up 496 mentions of the Twin Towers and only 50 mentions of WTC 7.
54. Ibid.
55. Jim Garrison, *Heritage of Stone* (New York: G. P. Putnam, 1970), 172.

Chapter 11. Not All Evidence Is Equal: Using Reliable Evidence

1. Dick Russell, *The Man Who Knew Too Much: Hired to Kill Oswald and Prevent the Assassination of JFK* (New York: Carroll & Graf, 1992). For a critique of the Nagell story, see Dave Reitzes, "Truth or Dare: The Lives and Lies of Richard Case Nagell," http:// jfkassassination.net/nagell1.htm.
2. John McAdams, "Did He Really Talk? Ray and Mary La Fontaine's Book," Kennedy Assassination Home Page, http://mcadams.posc.mu.edu/laf.htm.
3. Warren Commission Exhibit 773. Both documents were Exhibit 773, since Klein's put them together on microfilm and destroyed the originals.
4. Warren Commission Exhibit 788. This was the original document, canceled when it was cashed and obtained from the post office department.
5. *Warren Commission Report*, 567.
6. Ibid., 119.
7. 8 HSCA 226.
8. Ibid., 234.
9. Ibid., 246. Purtell did not examine the order coupon and return address, and complained that he had only a photocopy made from a microfilmed copy of the money order. See also p. 239.
10. Waldman Exhibit 7 (21 H 703).
11. *Warren Commission Report*, 119–21. The alias "A. Hidell," and P.O. Box 2915 and handwriting that can be identified as Oswald's, also applies to Oswald's purchase of the revolver that he used to shoot Officer Tippit.

12. 8 HSCA 234, 237, 244.
13. Anthony Summers, *Conspiracy* (New York: Paragon House, 1989), 59.
14. Testimony of H. D. Holmes (7 H 527).
15. Mark Lane, *Rush to Judgment: A Critique of the Warren Commission's Inquiry into the Murders of President John F. Kenney, Officer J. D. Tippit and Lee Harvey Oswald* (New York: Holt, Rinehart, and Winston, 1966), 414.
16. Ibid., 412.
17. Ibid., 414.
18. Exhibit 1158 (22 H 203).
19. Testimony of H. D. Holmes (7 H 527). The words are those of Commission Counsel Wesley Liebeler, who was questioning Holmes, and Holmes assented to that formulation.
20. Ibid., 528.
21. Lane, *Rush to Judgment*, 137–38.
22. *Warren Commission Report*, 557–56. HSCA had its own experts examine the fragments, and they verified the Warren Commission's finding (7 H 369) with the proviso that the Mannlicher-Carcano rifle had not been properly maintained, and the fragments were matched to bullets test-fired in 1963, rather than fired by the HSCA experts in 1978.
23. Ibid., 555–57; 7 HSCA 368.
24. Gary Savage, *First Day Evidence: Stored Away for 30 Years in an Old Briefcase, New Evidence Is Now Revealed by Former Dallas Police Crime Lab Detective R. W. (Rusty) Livingston* (Monroe, LA: Shoppe Press, 1993), 77–79.
25. Ibid.
26. Ibid., chapter 4.
27. Transcript, "Who Was Lee Harvey Oswald?," *Frontline*, WGBH-PBS, November 16, 1993, http://www.pbs.org/wgbh/pages/frontline/programs/transcripts/1205.html.
28. Exhibit 2003 (24 H 219).
29. Jim Marrs, *Crossfire: The Plot That Killed Kennedy* (New York: Carroll & Graf, 1989), 451.
30. Robert Groden, *The Killing of a President: The Complete Photographic Record of the JFK Assassination, the Conspiracy, and the Cover-Up* (New York: Viking Studio Books, 1993), 168.
31. 6 HSCA 141.
32. Priscilla Johnson McMillan, *Marina and Lee* (New York: Harper & Row, 1977), 340.
33. Gus Russo, *Live by the Sword: The Secret War against Castro and the Death of JFK* (Baltimore: Bancroft Press, 1998), 117.
34. Martin Shackelford, "Report from Dallas: The ASK Symposium, November 14–16, 1991," *The Third Decade* 8, nos. 2, 3 (January–March, 1992): 2, http://www.maryferrell.org/mffweb/archive/viewer/showDoc.do?docId=48764&relPageId=4.
35. We are passing over Michael Paine, who in the 1990s began saying that he had seen a copy of one of the backyard photos. See Russo, *Live by the Sword*, 117; Ray La Fontaine and Mary La Fontaine, *Oswald Talked: The New Evidence in the JFK Assassination* (Gretna, LA: Pelican Publishing, 1996), 225, 380. Testimony this belated simply has limited utility.
36. Groden, *The Killing of a President*, 168–71; and *Fake* (Fort Worth, TX: Third Coast Productions, 1990), VHS.
37. *Warren Commission Report*, 592–97.
38. 6 HSCA 146.
39. Ibid., 162–63.
40. Ibid., 167–72.
41. Ibid., 155–61. Conspiracists will claim that the Imperial Reflex is somehow "suspicious," since it only turned up several days after the assassination and in the possession of Lee's brother, Robert Oswald. The HSCA examined several family snapshots found among Oswald's possessions and found that they too had been shot with the same Imperial Reflex with which the backyard photos were taken. Ibid., 161.

42. Ibid., 212–15.
43. 8 HSCA 230.
44. Ibid., 234, 237, 244.
45. 6 HSCA 88. A "random patterning" is to be distinguished from, for example, the effects of normal wear, which might leave similar marks on all well-used rifles. See ibid., 106–7.
46. *Warren Commission Report*, 183–87.
47. Jean Davison, *Oswald's Game* (New York: W. W. Norton, 1983).
48. Michael Benson, *Who's Who in the JFK Assassination: An A-to-Z Encyclopedia* (New York: Citadel Press, 1993), 468.
49. Gerald McKnight, *Breach of Trust: How the Warren Commission Failed the Nation and Why* (Lawrence: University Press of Kansas, 2005), 46–59.
50. Warren Commission Document 1, 20–22.
51. *Warren Commission Report*, 184.
52. 2 HSCA 235.
53. "Marina Oswald Porter Talks to Oprah Winfrey," November 22, 1996, transcript by R. J. DellaRosa, http://www.jfkresearch.com/marina/marina.htm.
54. *Warren Commission Report*, 185.
55. Warren Commission Exhibit 1.
56. *Warren Commission Report*, 184–85.
57. 8 HSCA 235, 238, 243. McNally and Purtell unequivocally stated it was Oswald's handwriting, and Scott, for some unknown reason, didn't examine it.
58. McKnight, *Breach of Trust*, 57; Warren Commission Exhibit 2958.
59. Testimony of Linnie M. Randle (2 H 248).
60. Ibid., 226.
61. Sylvia Meagher, *Accessories After the Fact: The Warren Commission, the Authorities, and the Report* (New York: Vintage Books, 1992), 62.
62. Commission Exhibit 2974 (26 H 455); "Firearms Factoids: The 'Well-Oiled' Rifle," Kennedy Assassination Home Page, http://mcadams.posc.mu.edu/factoid8.htm.
63. U.S. Army, *Operator's Manual for the M16 and M4*, 0016 00-6.
64. Ibid., 0016 00-3.
65. Warren Commission Exhibit 2008; Warren Commission Exhibit 2009; testimony of Linnie M. Randle (2 H 250); testimony of Robert A. Frazier (3 H 395).
66. Testimony of P. M. Stombaugh (4 H 80–81).
67. Testimony of Arthur Mandella and Joseph Mooney (4 H 50–51).
68. Testimony of Sebastian F. Latona (4 H 44–45).
69. 8 HSCA 248.
70. Richard Trask, *Pictures of the Pain: Photography and the Assassination of President Kennedy* (Danvers, MA: Yeoman Press, 1994), 338.
71. Testimony of B. W. Frazier (2 H 222).
72. Testimony of Ruth Paine (3 H 72); testimony of Michael Paine (9 H 448).
73. Testimony of Gladys Johnson (10 H 297, 302).
74. Dale Myers, *With Malice: Lee Harvey Oswald and the Murder of Officer J. D. Tippit* (Milford, MI: Oak Cliff Press, 1998), 52–53.
75. Testimony of Marina Oswald (1 H 74).
76. Ibid.
77. Larry A. Sneed, *No More Silence: An Oral History of the Assassination of President Kennedy* (Dallas: Three Forks Press, 1998), 260.
78. Marina Oswald, Affidavit in Any Fact, November 22, 1963, http://mcadams.posc.mu.edu/aff-mari.gif.
79. Gerald Posner, *Case Closed: Lee Harvey Oswald and the Assassination of JFK* (New York: Random House, 1993), 345.
80. 2 HSCA 302.
81. Testimony of J. W. Fritz (4 H 217–18).

82. Testimony of B. W. Frazier (2 H 228).

83. Testimony of H. D. Holmes (7 H 305); testimony of J. W. Fritz (4 H 218).

84. Edward M. Hendrie, "Proving Guilty Knowledge," *FBI Law Enforcement Bulletin*, April 2000.

85. Testimony of Richard Stovall (7 H 192).

86. Warren Commission Document 5, 320, http://mcadams.posc.mu.edu/randle.txt.

87. Testimony of Buell W. Frazier (2 H 226–29). Emphasis added.

88. Exhibit 2444 (25 H 579).

89. Joseph P. McNally identified the signature on the hotel register as being Oswald's (8 HSCA 234). David Purtell declined to definitively link the signature to Oswald, noting that he had to work from "a photograph taken without a scale so that the magnification or reduction of the writing could not be determined" (p. 239). Charles C. Scott said the signature was Oswald's "tentatively and subject to modification should the original documents become available" (p. 245).

90. Exhibit 3127 (26 H 790).

91. *Warren Commission Report*, 304.

92. Again, McNally flatly authenticated the signature (8 HSCA 234), and Purtell demurred slightly, noting that the originals were poor-quality photos that lacked scales (p. 239). Charles C. Scott identified the photos of the signature as Oswald's, with the same "tentative" and "subject to modification" language.

93. McNally flatly declared the signature on the typewritten copy to be authentic (8 HSCA 234) while not mentioning the handwritten draft. Purtell for some reason failed to examine the draft letter, but he declared the signature on the typed copy to be Oswald's (p. 238). Scott identified both the signature on the typewritten letter and the handwritten draft with the now familiar caveats (p. 246).

94. Warren Commission Document 1084e, 4–5.

95. "The Warren Commission Was Right," *New York Times*, November 22, 1971. Reprinted in Peter Dale Scott, Paul L. Hoch, and Russell Stetler, eds., *The Assassinations: Dallas and Beyond; a Guide to Cover-ups and Investigations* (New York: Random House, 1976), 259–61. The Rosetta Stone was an artifact found in 1799 that was instrumental in the modern translation of previously obscure ancient Egyptian hieroglyphics.

96. Vincent Bugliosi, *Reclaiming History: The Assassination of President John F. Kennedy* (New York: W. W. Norton, 2007), 816. Emphasis in original. Bugliosi, of course, is going a bit overboard here. It's possible that Tippit was somehow tasked to kill Oswald, and the latter shot Tippit in self-defense. Or it's possible that a desperate Oswald, who had not shot Kennedy but had figured out that he was the designated patsy, killed Tippit to escape apprehension.

97. Exhibit 2003 (24 H 202); testimony of Mrs. Helen Markham (3 H 306).

98. Testimony of Mark Lane (2 H 51).

99. Markham Exhibit 1 (20 H 571).

100. *The Plot to Kill JFK: Rush to Judgment*, directed by Emile de Antonio (Oakland Park, IL: MPI Home Video, 1988), VHS; Lane, *Rush to Judgment*, 193–94.

101. Marrs, *Crossfire*, 341–42.

102. *Warren Commission Report*, 166–71.

103. Testimony of Cortlandt Cunningham (3 H 475–83).

104. *Warren Commission Report*, 172.

105. Testimony of Cortlandt Cunningham, 3 H 466. In the late 1970s, the HSCA reviewed the firearms evidence and confirmed the FBI's conclusions. All four spent cartridges had been fired from the Oswald revolver. The bullets were *consistent* with the Oswald revolver, but they could not be matched to it to the exclusion of all other weapons (7 HSCA 376–77).

106. The JFK Assassination Dallas Police Tapes, History in Real Time, Part 3, Channel 1, 1:34 p.m., http://mcadams.posc.mu.edu/dpdtapes/tapes3.htm.

107. Ibid., 12:44 p.m., http://mcadams.posc.mu.edu/dpdtapes.

108. Myers, *With Malice*, 260–61.

109. Gerald Hill: Transcript, "Who Was Lee Harvey Oswald?," *Frontline*, WGBH-PBS, November 16, 1993, http://www.pbs.org/wgbh/pages/frontline/programs/transcripts/1205.html.

110. Exhibit 2011, 8 (24 H 415); testimony of J. M. Poe (7 H 69).

111. Marrs, *Crossfire*, 343.

112. Lane, *Rush to Judgment*, 199.

113. Exhibit 2011, 8 (24 H 415).

114. Gilbert B. Stuckey, *Evidence for the Law Enforcement Officer* (New York: McGraw-Hill, 1968).

115. Exhibit 2011, 8 (24 H 414–15).

116. This was the only such revolver with this serial number. Testimony of Cortlandt Cunningham (3 H 458).

117. *Warren Commission Report*, 174.

118. Ibid.

119. 7 HSCA 39.

120. Ibid., 40–41. For the technical reports on the authentication, see ibid., 43–71; 6 HSCA 225–42.

121. 7 HSCA 103–35.

122. Rockefeller Commission, *Report to the President*, 257–67; "1968 Panel Review of Photographs."

123. Of course, the fact that Kennedy was not hit from the right front does not rule out a shooter from the right front, who simply missed. But as we have seen, the evidence of that is thin.

124. *HSCA Report*, 65–83.

125. National Academy of Sciences, *Report of the Committee on Ballistic Acoustics* (Washington, DC: National Academy Press, 1982), http://www.jfk-online.com/nas00.html.

126. *HSCA Report*, 80, 83.

127. *Warren Commission Report*, 101.

128. *HSCA Report*, 71–72.

129. Luis Alvarez, "A Physicist Examines the Kennedy Assassination Film," *American Journal of Physics* 44, no. 9 (September 1976): 819–22; John Lattimer, *Kennedy and Lincoln: Medical and Ballistic Comparisons of Their Assassinations* (New York: Harcourt Brace Jovanovich, 1980), chapter 12.

130. Lattimer, *Kennedy and Lincoln*, chapter 11; Bob Artwohl, post on Compuserve forum, April 6, 1994, http://mcadams.posc.mu.edu/thorburn.txt.

131. U.S. Const. art. II, §1.

132. Department of Health, State of Hawaii, Certification of Live Birth, http://msgboard.snopes.com/politics/graphics/birth.jpg.

133. Joe the Farmer, "Why the Barack Obama Birth Certificate Issue Is Legitimate," American Thinker, November 26, 2008, http://www.americanthinker.com/2008/11/why_the_barack_obama_birth_cer.html.

134. "Birth Certificate," *Snopes.com*, August 3, 2009, http://www.snopes.com/politics/obama/birthcertificate.asp.

135. "Obama's Birth Announcements," http://whatreallyhappened.com/WRHARTICLES/obamabirth.php.

136. If *one* parent is a U.S. citizen and the other parent is not, the child is a citizen if the U.S. citizen parent has been "physically present" in the United States before the child's birth for a total period of at least five years *and* at least two of those five years were after the U.S. citizen parent's fourteenth birthday. U.S. Department of State, "Documentation of U.S. Citizens Born Abroad," Travel.State.Gov, http://travel.state.gov/law/family_issues/birth/birth_593.html.

137. As early as March 26, 1790, Congress provided that people born outside the United States to parents who are U.S. citizens are considered "natural born." See "A Century of Lawmaking for a New Nation: U.S. Congressional Documents and Debates, 1774–1875, Statutes at Large, 1st Congress, 2nd session," ch. 3, 104, http://rs6.loc.gov/cgi-bin/ampage?collId=llsl&fileName=001/llsl001.db&recNum=227.

Chapter 12. Too Much Evidence of Conspiracy

1. David Perry, "Rashomon to the Extreme," David Perry's John F. Kennedy Assassination Pages, 2005, http://davesjfk.com/rashomon.html. This list, of course, does not include the hundreds of individuals fingered by this or that conspiracy book as part of the plot; rather, it includes only people claimed to have been conspirators who were present in Dealey Plaza.

2. In compiling this list, I have drawn on Michael T. Griffith's essay "Extra Bullets and Missed Shots in Dealey Plaza," April 28, 2001, http://www.mtgriffith.com/web_documents/extrabullets.htm, and the pioneering *J.F.K. Assassination: A Visual Investigation*, Medio Multimedia, 1993, CD-ROM. This list includes only shots clearly inconsistent with the consensus lone assassin scenario, which involves the single bullet and head shot and a bullet that missed the limo and hit the pavement.

3. Griffith, "Extra Bullets."

4. Ibid.

5. Ibid.

6. Medio, *J.F.K. Assassination*.

7. Ibid.

8. "J. Edgar Hoover: Clueless Bureaucrat?," memorandum for several FBI officials, November 29, 1963, http://mcadams.posc.mu.edu/clueless.htm.

9. John Connally, *In History's Shadow: An American Odyssey*, with Mickey Herskowitz (New York: Hyperion, 1993), 18.

10. 7 HSCA 15–16.

11. Ibid., 12.

12. "California Judge Delays Plot Probe Case Ruling," *New Orleans Times-Picayune*, November 1, 1968, http://www.maryferrell.org/mffweb/archive/viewer/showDoc.do?mode=searchResult&absPageId=779944; "DA Plot Probe Witness Beaten," *New Orleans States-Item*, January 11, 1968, http://www.maryferrell.org/mffweb/archive/viewer/showDoc.do?docId=62437&relPageId=9.

13. Jack Minnis and Staughton Lynd, "Seeds of Doubt: Some Questions about the Assassination," *New Republic*, December 21, 1963, 14–20, http://karws.gso.uri.edu/JFK/The_critics/Lynd/Seeds_of_doubt.html.

14. The JFK Assassination Dallas Police Tapes, History in Real Time, Inspector J. H. Sawyer, Channel 2, 12:45 p.m, http://mcadams.posc.mu.edu/dpdtapes.

15. NBC, *Seventy Hours and Thirty Minutes, as Broadcast on the NBC Television Network* (New York: Random House, 1966), 8. This volume is a transcript of the NBC-TV broadcast. The Enfield is a British rifle, although a .30 caliber isn't quite the same as a .303.

16. See "Confessions," Mary Ferrell Archive, http://www.maryferrell.org/wiki/index.php/Confessions.

17. 4 HSCA 428–53.

18. William Weston, "The Spider's Web: The Texas School Book Depository and the Dallas Conspiracy," *Dealey Plaza Echo*, March 2006, 3–26.

19. Barr McClellan, *Blood, Money and Power: How LBJ Killed JFK* (New York: Hanover House, 2003), 353.

20. Anthony Summers, *Conspiracy* (New York: Paragon House, updated 1991 edition), 187.

21. Peter Brookesmith, *UFO: The Government Files* (London: Brown Packaging, 1996), 27–29.

22. Barb Junkkarinen, Jerry Logan, and Josiah Thompson, "Eternal Return: A Hole Through the Windshield," JFK Lancer Forums, December 31, 1969, http://www.jfklancerforum

.com/dc/dcboard.php?az=printer_friendly&forum=3&topic_id=82475&mesg_
id=82475.

23. David B. Perry, "With Apologies to David Letterman: The Top Ten Reasons the Jim
Files' Story Needs Help," February 14, 1998, http://www.davesjfk.com/lettermn.html;
David B. Perry, "Texas in the Imagination," October 26, 2002, http://www.davesjfk.com/
browns.html.

24. Clint Bradford, "The Zapruder Film Is Authentic," http://www.jfk-info.com/moot1
.htm; Tony Marsh, "Critiques of Assassination Science," http://home.comcast.net/~the
-puzzle-palace.

Chapter 13. Beware False Corroboration

1. Jim Garrison, for example, in *On the Trail of the Assassins* (New York: Sheridan Square
Press, 1991), describes in great detail how he personally discovered the evidence of the
changed parade route (101–3). Inaccuracies in Garrison's account establish that he did
not independently make any such discovery and simply lied. See "Changed Motorcade
Route in Dallas?," Kennedy Assassination Home Page, http://mcadams.posc.mu.edu/
route.htm.

2. James E. Files, *The Murder of JFK: Confession of an Assassin* (Oakland Park, IL: MPI
Home Video, 1996), VHS. The "Secret Service identification" is a reference to the testimony of Joe Marshall Smith, which we have already discussed.

3. Edward Jay Epstein e-mail to Barb Junkkarinen, April 24, 2001. See also Richard Johnson, "Peacock Tempted to Buy News," *New York Post*, May 9, 1994.

4. Henry Hurt, *Reasonable Doubt: An Investigation into the Assassination of John F. Kennedy*
(New York: Holt, Rinehart, and Winston, 1985), 351.

5. Edward T. Haslam, *Mary, Ferrie & the Monkey Virus: The Story of an Underground
Medical Laboratory; a Non-Fiction Work* (Albuquerque, NM: Wordsworth Communications, 1995).

6. John Delane Williams and Kelly Thomas Cousins, "Judyth and Lee in New Orleans,"
Dealey Plaza Echo 11, no. 1 (March 2007), http://www.maryferrell.org/mffweb/archive/
viewer/showDoc.do?docId=109189&relPageId=27.

7. Edward T. Haslam, *Dr. Mary's Monkey: How the Unsolved Murder of a Doctor, a Se-
cret Laboratory in New Orleans and Cancer-Causing Monkey Viruses Are Linked to Lee
Harvey Oswald, the JFK Assassination and Emerging Global Epidemics* (Walterville, OR:
TrineDay, 2007).

8. Oswald 201 File, vol. 2, folder 6, p. 2, http://www.maryferrell.org/mffweb/archive/
viewer/showDoc.do?mode=searchResult&absPageId=992343.

9. Ibid., vol. 17, 4, http://www.maryferrell.org/mffweb/archive/viewer/showDoc.do?mode
=searchResult&absPageId=1006097.

10. *HSCA Report*, 250.

11. "Telephone Conversation between the President and J. Edgar Hoover," November 23,
1963, http://www.maryferrell.org/mffweb/archive/viewer/showDoc.do?docId=807
&relPageId=2; AARC Library, "LBJ Phone Calls—November 1963," http://www.aarc
library.org/publib/jfk/lbjlib/phone_calls/Nov_1963/html/LBJ-Nov-1963_0029a.htm.

12. Deb Riechmann, "Tape: Call on JFK Wasn't Oswald," Associated Press, November 21,
1999, http://www.jfklancer.com/LNE/LHO-Mexi.html.

13. Memorandum to Mr. Tolson from Mr. Belmont, Re: Assassination of President John
F. Kennedy, November 23, 1963, http://www.maryferrell.org/mffweb/archive/viewer/
showDoc.do?docId=1465&relPageId=14.

14. Memorandum to Senators Schweiker and Hart (Church Committee) from Staff, Re:
References to FBI Review of Tapes of Oswald's October 1, 1963 Mexico City Conversation, March 5, 1976, 5, National Archives record 157-10014-10168, http://www.mary
ferrell.org/mffweb/archive/viewer/showDoc.do?docId=1465&relPageId=5.

15. Ibid., 5–6.

16. SA Eldon D. Rudd to SAC, Dallas, November 23, 1963, National Archives record 124-10230-10430, http://history-matters.com/archive/jfk/fbi/105-3702/124-10230-10430/html/124-10230-10430_0002a.htm.

17. *HSCA Report*, 250.

18. Exhibit 2001 (24 H 30, 40); Warren Commission Document 1518, 2. Also see "Walker Shooting," http://whokilledjfk.net/Walker.htm.

19. The mangled state of the bullet precluded any determination that it was fired from the same rifle.

Chapter 14. How Bureaucrats Act

1. Memorandum for Mr. Tolson, Mr. Belmont, Mr. Mohr, Mr. Conrad, Mr. De Loach, Mr. Evans, Mr. Rosen, MR Sullivan, November 22, 1963, 4:01 p.m., FBI 62-109060 JFK HQ File, Section 1, 96, http://www.maryferrell.org/mffweb/archive/viewer/showDoc.do?docId=62251&relPageId=96.

2. Ibid., 95, http://www.maryferrell.org/mffweb/archive/viewer/showDoc.do?docId=62251&relPageId=95.

3. Oswald was shot deep inside the building basement, and daylight was not an issue.

4. Oswald went to his rooming house in Oak Cliff, miles from downtown, and then shot Tippit on an Oak Cliff street.

5. Memorandum, Washington, DC, to [several FBI officials] from J. Edgar Hoover, 1:39 p.m., November 29, 1963, http://mcadams.posc.mu.edu/clueless.htm.

6. 11 HSCA 485. The report is Warren Commission Document 1, http://www.maryferrell.org/mffweb/archive/viewer/showDoc.do?docId=10402.

7. The most notorious issue that had not been resolved was the single bullet theory.

8. "Cameras: Minox Camera," CIA Museum website, April 25, 2007, https://www.cia.gov/about-cia/cia-museum/cia-museum-tour/flash-movie-text.html.

9. Anthony Summers, *Not in Your Lifetime* (New York: Marlowe, 1998), 159.

10. Larry A. Sneed, *No More Silence: An Oral History of the Assassination of President Kennedy* (Dallas: Three Forks Press, 1998), 260.

11. Michael Russ, "Missing Minox or Major Mistakes?," http://jfkassassination.net/russ/minox.htm. Russ's essay is the definitive treatment of this issue.

12. Property Clerk's Invoice or Receipt, Police Department, City of Dallas, November 26, 1963, FBI 62-109060 JFK HQ File, Section 150, http://www.maryferrell.org/mffweb/archive/viewer/showDoc.do?docId=62437&relPageId=125.

13. Earl Golz, "Oswald Pictures Released by FBI," *Dallas Morning News*, August 7, 1978. Five of the photos were military scenes, which appeared to have been shot in the Far East or in Central America. If they were shot for espionage purposes, it's difficult to explain why the undeveloped film languished in the Paine house in Texas, rather than having been turned over to the CIA.

14. Bardwell D. Odum, interview of Michael Paine, Irving, Texas, January 31, 1964, Oswald 201 File, vol. 25, 98–99, http://www.maryferrell.org/mffweb/archive/viewer/showDoc.do?docId=111185&relPageId=98. Ruth Paine in fact produced the camera for the FBI.

15. Consistent with this hypothesis is the fact that Rose insisted that he examined the seabag on Saturday (November 23), but the photographic items were apparently taken on November 22, according to a sign in the Dallas Police evidence photo.

16. "Selective Pieces from My Personal Collection" (website with extensive photos of Minox cameras and light meters), 2010, http://www.minoxdoc.com/Collection.htm.

17. Russ, "Missing Minox or Major Mistakes?"

18. Jim Marrs, *Crossfire: The Plot That Killed Kennedy* (New York: Carroll & Graf, 1989), 442.

19. Mark Lane, *Rush to Judgment: A Critique of the Warren Commission's Inquiry into the Murders of President John F. Kenney, Officer J. D. Tippit and Lee Harvey Oswald* (New York: Holt, Rinehart, and Winston, 1966), 149.

20. Vincent J. M. Di Maio, *Gunshot Wounds: Practical Aspects of Firearms, Ballistics, and Forensic Techniques* (New York: Elsevier, 1999), 327; Charles O'Hara and Gregory L. O'Hara, *Fundamentals of Criminal Investigation,* 5th ed., rev. (Springfield, IL: C. C. Thomas, 1988), 771. Note that even in 2007, when vastly improved testing techniques had largely eliminated false positives, an authoritative text cautions that "a negative test for GSR [gunshot residue] is meaningless, as (a.) tests are only positive in about half of the cases when an individual is known to have fired a gun, (b.) tests are usually negative in relationship to rifles and shotguns." See Vincent J. M. Di Maio and Suzanna E. Dana, *Handbook of Forensic Pathology,* 2nd ed. (Boca Raton, FL: CRC Press, 2007), 151.

21. *FBI Law Enforcement Bulletin,* October 1935, 436–37. Of course, if false negatives are possible with a revolver, they are much more likely with a tightly sealed rifle mechanism. See testimony of Cortlandt Cunningham (3 H 492).

22. Ibid., 494.

23. Testimony of J. C. Day (4 H 276).

24. William Turner, *Rearview Mirror: Looking Back at the FBI, the CIA, and Other Tails* (Granite Bay, CA: Penmarin, 2001), 174. HSCA staffer Gaeton Fonzi made a similar claim, but with a similar lack of evidence. See *The Last Investigation* (New York: Thunder's Mouth Press, 1993), 239.

25. "Bedeviled by Spooks? CIA Plots to Undermine Garrison?," Kennedy Assassination Home Page, http://mcadams.posc.mu.edu/cia_garrison.htm.

26. Memorandum for the Record, Subject: Garrison Group Meeting no. 2—26 September 1967, National Archives record 104-10428-10022, http://www.maryferrell.org/mffweb/archive/viewer/showDoc.do?docId=6514&relPageId=2.

27. HSCA, Segregated CIA Collection, Staff Notes. National Archives record 180-10143-10221; HSCA, Segregated CIA Collection, box 42, National Archives record 104-10106-10772.

28. Memorandum for the Record, Subject: Garrison Group Meeting no. 1—20 September 1967, National Archives record 104-10428-10023, http://www.maryferrell.org/mffweb/archive/viewer/showDoc.do?mode=searchResult&absPageId=240344.

29. Fonzi, *The Last Investigation,* 239.

30. Garrison Group Meeting no. 2.

31. Garrison Group Meeting no. 1.

32. Memorandum for the Record, Subject: Garrison Investigation, September 29, 1967, National Archives record 104-10435-10052, http://www.maryferrell.org/mffweb/archive/viewer/showDoc.do?mode=searchResult&absPageId=255363.

33. Garrison Group Meeting no. 1 and no. 2.

34. Garrison Group Meeting no. 2.

35. Memo Surveying Possible Courses of Action Re: Garrison Investigation, September 26, 1967, National Archives record 1993.07.28.10:53:30:310620, http://www.maryferrell.org/mffweb/archive/viewer/showDoc.do?docId=101472&relPageId=1.

36. Memorandum for Director of Central Intelligence, Subject: Clay L. Shaw's Trial and the Central Intelligence Agency, September 29, 1967, National Archives record 1993.07.28.10:41:05:430620, http://www.maryferrell.org/mffweb/archive/viewer/showDoc.do?docId=101471&relPageId=5.

37. White House, "Iraq's Continuing Programs for Weapons of Mass Destruction," *National Intelligence Estimate,* October 2002, http://www.fas.org/irp/cia/product/iraq-wmd.html.

38. A classic in this genre is Charles Peters, *How Washington Really Works,* 4th ed. (Reading, MA: Addison-Wesley, 1993).

39. Sylvia Meagher, *Accessories After the Fact: The Warren Commission, the Authorities, and the Report* (New York: Vintage Books, 1992), 328–29.

40. James Exhibit 9 (20 H 248). The narrow issue here was whether Marina (who, unlike Lee, lacked U.S. citizenship) should be allowed in. But of course, this was all one "package."

41. Transcript, "Who Was Lee Harvey Oswald?," *Frontline*, WGBH-PBS, aired November 16, 1993, http://www.pbs.org/wgbh/pages/frontline/shows/oswald/etc/script.html.
42. 12 HSCA 435–73.
43. *Warren Commission Report*, 756.
44. Donabedian Exhibit no. 1 (19 H 605). Strictly speaking, the gonorrhea diagnosis was less than ironclad, since only a smear, and no culture, was done. Testimony of Capt. George Donabedian (8 H 313–14).
45. Ray La Fontaine and Mary La Fontaine, *Oswald Talked: The New Evidence in the JFK Assassination* (Gretna, LA: Pelican Publishing, 1996), 59.
46. Anthony Summers, *Conspiracy* (New York: Paragon House, 1989), 126.
47. Folsom Exhibit 1 (19 H 749).
48. Mark S. Zaid, "Oswald & VD: An Intelligence Connection?," *The Third Decade*, July 1992.
49. *Warren Commission Report*, 684.
50. The Kingsmen recording was in fact a cover version.
51. "The Lascivious 'Louie Louie,'" The Smoking Gun, August 8, 1998, http://www.thesmokinggun.com/louie/louie.html.
52. While there was no CIA when the documents were written, the CIA was the agency with the "most interest in the subject matter."
53. Bill Miller, "The Very Visible Battle over Invisible Ink," *Los Angeles Times*, June 13, 2001. See also "Central Intelligence Agency Refuses to Release Oldest U.S. Classified Documents Sought in Litigation," Washington, DC, March 30, 1999, press release of the James Madison Project, http://www.fas.org/sgp/news/jmpoldest.html.
54. Mark Zaid, in e-mail to author, September 2, 2009.
55. *Warren Commission Report*, 434.
56. Ibid., 436.
57. Final Report of the Church Committee, Book 5—The Investigation of the Assassination of President John F. Kennedy: Performance of the Intelligence Agencies, Appendix B: The FBI and the Destruction of the Oswald Note, 97, http://www.maryferrell.org/mffweb/archive/viewer/showDoc.do?docId=1161&relPageId=103.
58. Testimony before the House Committee on the Judiciary, Subcommittee on Civil and Constitutional Rights, December 12, 1975, 33. National Archives record 180-10086-10493.
59. Marrs, *Crossfire*, 234.
60. Gerald McKnight, *Breach of Trust: How the Warren Commission Failed the Nation and Why* (Lawrence: University of Kansas Press, 2005), 255.
61. Gordon Shanklin, when the incident later leaked, denied any memory of the whole affair. In 1975 testimony, he claimed, "I don't think I would have, under any circumstances, ordered the note destroyed." George Lardner Jr. and Walter Pincus, "FBI's Haste Sowed Seeds of Suspicion," *Washington Post*, November 15, 1993. There is probably nobody in the whole world who believes Shanklin about this.
62. Church Committee, Book 5, Appendix B, 96, http://www.maryferrell.org/mffweb/archive/viewer/showDoc.do?docId=1161&relPageId=102.
63. Testimony of Ruth Paine (3 H 18–19).
64. Testimony of Marina Oswald (1 H 57).
65. Testimony of Elmer Boyd (7 H 124).
66. Memorandum to Mr. Mohr from C. D. DeLoach, October 8, 1964, FBI 105-82555 Oswald HQ File, Section 217, 16–18, http://www.maryferrell.org/mffweb/archive/viewer/showDoc.do?docId=59647&relPageId=16.
67. Church Committee, Book 1: *Foreign and Military Intelligence* (Washington, DC: Government Printing Office, 1976), 403, http://www.aarclibrary.org/publib/church/reports/book1/html/ChurchB1_0206a.htm.
68. Mark Mazzetti and Scott Shane, "Destruction of C.I.A. Tapes Cleared by Lawyers," *New York Times*, December 11, 2007.
69. 11 HSCA 482–84.

Chapter 15. Putting Theory into Practice: The Single Bullet Theory

1. Oliver Stone and Zachary Sklar, *JFK: The Book of the Film; The Documented Screenplay* (New York: Applause Books, 1992), 153.
2. For a typical diagram, see Harrison Edward Livingstone and Robert J. Groden, *High Treason: The Assassination of JFK and the Case for Conspiracy* (New York: Carroll & Graf, 1998), photo insert.
3. Josiah Thompson, *Six Seconds in Dallas: A Micro-study of the Kennedy Assassination* (New York: Bernard Geis Associates, 1967), 75.
4. Testimony of Robert A. Frazier (3 H 407). In other tests, the best shooters equaled or nearly equaled Frazier, but nobody did better.
5. Autopsy descriptive (face) sheet, November 22, 1963, http://www.maryferrell.org/mff web/archive/viewer/showDoc.do?docId=582.
6. Requested Lists of Information Re: All of ARRB's Medical Witnesses, and All New ARRB Medical Evidence Not Previously in JFK Collection, 27, http://www.maryferrell .org/mffweb/archive/viewer/showDoc.do?mode=searchResult&absPageId=501149.
7. Exhibit 1024 (18 H 760).
8. Testimony of Clinton J. Hill (2 H 143).
9. George D. Lundberg, "Closing the Case in *JAMA* on the John F. Kennedy Autopsy," *Journal of the American Medical Association* 268, no. 13 (October 7, 1992): 1736.
10. Todd Wayne Vaughan, post to Compuserve "Politics" forum, October 25, 1995, http:// mcadams.posc.mu.edu/toscale.htm.
11. In 1977 Rose was chosen to be a member of the HSCA Forensic Pathology Panel, a body of the most respected forensic pathologists in the country.
12. 7 HSCA 88–89.
13. *HSCA Report*, 42.
14. See *Inside the ARRB: Appendices*, Appendix 51: HSCA staff report of its interview of Richard A. Lipsey, 266, http://www.maryferrell.org/mffweb/archive/viewer/showDoc. do?docId=145280&relPageId=266; ibid., Appendix 53: HSCA staff report of its interview of Navy autopsy technician James Curtis Jenkins, 295, http://www.maryferrell.org/ mffweb/archive/viewer/showDoc.do?docId=145280&relPageId=295.
15. Charles R. Drago, "New Interview with James Jenkins on JFK's Autopsy," *Kennedy Assassination Chronicles* 4, no. 3 (October 1998): 12.
16. *Warren Commission Report*, 540.
17. Ibid., 543.
18. Warren Commission Document 7: "Autopsy of Body of President John Fitzgerald Kennedy," 284–85, http://www.maryferrell.org/mffweb/archive/viewer/showDoc .do?docId=10408&relPageId=290.
19. ARRB, "Deposition of Francis X. O'Neill, Jr.," September 12, 1997, 30, http://www .maryferrell.org/mffweb/archive/viewer/showDoc.do?mode=searchResult&absPage Id=68344.
20. Warren Commission Document 7: "Autopsy," 284; ARRB MD 47, 4, http://www.mary ferrell.org/mffweb/archive/viewer/showDoc.do?docId=628&relPageId=5.
21. *Warren Commission Report*, 102–3.
22. 7 HSCA 84–85.
23. Ibid., 86.
24. John Lattimer, *Kennedy and Lincoln: Medical and Ballistic Comparisons of Their Assassinations* (New York: Harcourt Brace Jovanovich, 1980), 194–97.
25. The Forensic Pathology Panel was unhappy that the mastoid process is not a fixed body landmark. Move your head, and it moves relative to every other part of your body. But the photographic evidence is rock hard *for our purposes*, since it entirely rules out a wound at T3 and is absolutely consistent with a wound at T1. Indeed, had no ruler been in the photo, a good knowledge of surface anatomy would lead to that conclusion, which the Forensic Pathology Panel indeed endorsed (7 HSCA 87).

26. Ibid., 83.

27. Lattimer, *Kennedy and Lincoln*, 202–7.

28. Ibid., 205; John Hunt, "The Case for a Bunched Jacket," 1999, http://mcadams.posc .mu.edu/bunched.htm. Hunt has an extensive collection of photos showing Kennedy's jacket bunched.

29. Robert Groden, *The Killing of a President: The Complete Photographic Record of the JFK Assassination, the Conspiracy, and the Cover-Up* (New York: Viking Studio Books, 1993), 9, 14, 17, 18, 27, 32, 196.

30. Parkland Hospital Press Conference: Dallas Doctors' First Statements, Dallas, Texas, November 22, 1963, 2:16 P.M. CST, at the White House with Wayne Hawks, Kennedy Assassination Home Page, http://mcadams.posc.mu.edu/press.htm.

31. Testimony of Dr. Malcolm Perry (3 H 372).

32. Ibid., 361.

33. Testimony of Dr. Charles Carrico (6 H 3).

34. Ibid., 54.

35. Ibid., 141.

36. Abdullah Fatteh, *Medicolegal Investigation of Gunshot Wounds* (Philadelphia: Lippincott, 1976), 121. Emphasis in original.

37. Ibid.

38. Ibid., 124–25.

39. Lattimer, *Kennedy and Lincoln*, 234–36.

40. 7 HSCA 95.

41. Army doctor Pierre Finck, another autopsist, was a partial exception, being an actual forensic pathologist. But he arrived late and played a secondary role. Moreover, his normal army duties were administrative, and he lacked extensive experience in cutting up dead bodies.

42. William Manchester, *The Death of a President, November 20–November 25, 1963* (New York: Harper & Row, 1967), 349–50.

43. K. A. Collins and P. E. Lantz, "Interpretation of Fatal, Multiple, and Exiting Gunshot Wounds by Trauma Specialists," *Journal of Forensic Sciences*, January 1994, 94–99.

44. Testimony of Dr. Charles Carrico (6 H 5).

45. Exhibit 392 (*Warren Commission Report*, 526). Josiah Thompson (*Six Seconds in Dallas*, 53), who actually believed that the throat wound was the exit of a fragment, argues for this as follows:

    This same hypothesis was put forward by various government spokesmen in December, 1963. Citing governmental sources, *Newsweek* (Dec. 30, 1963), *Time* (Dec. 27, 1963), and the *Washington Post* (Dec. 18, 1963) all carried stories asserting that the autopsy had produced evidence that a fragment from the second bullet (the head shot) had been deflected downward and had passed out through the throat. *The Journal of the American Medical Association* (Jan. 4, 1964) reported that "a small fragment of this bullet [the head shot] angled down and passed out through Kennedy's throat."

    This, of course, is a massive case of the sort of "false corroboration" we have discussed. There is no way in the world that all of these secondary sources had independent information about any exiting fragment. However, Thompson's citations do show the sort of "legs" a bogus factoid can have, even in reputable journalistic outlets.

46. John Herbers, "Kennedy Struck by Two Bullets, Doctor Who Attended Him Says," *New York Times*, November 27, 1963.

47. 7 HSCA 89.

48. Letter to J. Lee Rankin from J. Edgar Hoover, March 23, 1964, FBI 105-82555 Oswald HQ File, section 111, p. 114. http://www.maryferrell.org/mffweb/archive/viewer/show Doc.do?mode=searchResult&absPageId=709880.

49. Testimony of Robert A. Frazier (5 H 61).

50. There is also a nick in Kennedy's tie, consistent with the location of the shirt defects, but it tells us nothing about entry or exit. Ibid., 62.

51. For a brief and readable recounting of the Weisberg thesis (Weisberg's own writings are hard to read), see Jerry McKnight, "Bugliosi Fails to Resuscitate the Single-Bullet Theory," http://www.maryferrell.org/wiki/index.php/Essay_-_Bugliosi_Fails_to_Resuscitate_the_Single-Bullet_Theory.

52. Exhibit 392 (*Warren Commission Report*, 517).

53. Ibid. (*Warren Commission Report*, 521).

54. For the Stare of Death photo, see Groden, *The Killing of a President*, 76. Interestingly, Groden reprints the Left Profile but crops it so that the gash in the neck is not visible (p. 72). For the entire set of available photos, including the Left Profile, check "JFK Assassination Evidence: Autopsy Photos and Xrays," *JFK Lancer*, http://www.jfklancer.com/photos/autopsy_slideshow/index.html.

55. 7 HSCA 144.

56. Ibid.

57. In an egregious violation of every rule of evidence and forensics, John Connally's clothes were dry cleaned before they were examined by any forensic or scientific experts. It's difficult to see how this could have been conspiratorial, however, since the nature of Connally's torso wounds has never really been in doubt.

58. The wound's name comes from the sound the air makes when it flows from the pleural cavity through the puncture hole.

59. Testimony of Robert A. Frazier (3 H 430).

60. Apparently, no metal fragments were left in Kennedy's torso.

61. Harrison Edward Livingstone, *High Treason 2: The Great Cover-up; The Assassination of President John F. Kennedy* (New York: Carroll & Graf, 1992), 312.

62. Livingstone and Groden, *High Treason*, 64.

63. Assassination Records Review Board Document MD 184, February 24, 1997, by Douglas Horne.

64. Testimony of Dr. Charles F. Gregory (4 H 120).

65. Exhibit 842 (17 H 841).

66. Thompson, *Six Seconds in Dallas*, 150.

67. The report of the Forensic Pathology Panel mentions no such fragment (7 HSCA 147), and Dr. Charles Petty, a member of the panel, testified to the HSCA that there was no fragment in Connally's chest (1 HSCA 378).

68. Groden, *The Killing of a President*, 27.

69. Dr. Charles Gregory, "Parkland Memorial Hospital Operative Record—Governor John Connally," November 22, 1963, in *Warren Commission Report*, 533–34; Bob Artwohl, "Prodigy Questions to Wecht," posted on the Prodigy Crime Bulletin Board, October 18, 1994.

70. Joe Nick Patoski, "The Witnesses," *Texas Monthly*, November 1998, 139.

71. 1 HSCA 321.

72. Daniel K. Inouye, *Journey to Washington*, with Lawrence Elliott (Englewood Cliffs, NJ: Prentice-Hall, 1967), 151–52.

73. 7 HSCA 157–58.

74. Ibid., 162.

75. Mary Ferrell Foundation, "NARA Evidence Photos: 'Magic Bullet,'" http://www.maryferrell.org/wiki/index.php/Photos_-_NARA_Evidence_-_Magic_Bullet.

76. Testimony of Robert A. Frazier (3 H 400).

77. 1 HSCA 396.

78. Testimony of Dr. Alfred Olivier (5 H 77–78); Testimony of Dr. Charles F. Gregory (4 H 122).

79. 7 HSCA 150.

80. John Hunt, "Breakability: CE-399 and the Diminishing Velocity Theory," History Matters, http://www.history-matters.com/essays/jfkmed/Breakability/Breakability.htm.

81. Gerald Posner, *Case Closed: Lee Harvey Oswald and the Assassination of JFK* (New York: Anchor Doubleday, 1993 [paperback]), 480.
82. 7 HSCA 172.
83. Testimony of Dr. Alfred Olivier (5 H 81–83); testimony of Dr. Charles Francis Gregory (4 H 122).
84. Todd Wayne Vaughan, in e-mail to the author, March 4, 2011. Wecht, of course, quickly backed off this conclusion.
85. John K. Lattimer, Angus Laidlaw, Paul Heneghan, and Eric J. Haubner, "Experimental Duplication of the Important Physical Evidence of the Lapel Bulge of the Jacket Worn by Governor Connally When Bullet 399 Went through Him," *Journal of the American College of Surgeons* 178, no. 5 (May 1994): 517–22.
86. "The Single Bullet Strikes John Connally," Kennedy Assassination Home Page, http://mcadams.posc.mu.edu/jbchit.htm.
87. Itek Corporation, *Kennedy Assassination Film Analysis* (Lexington, MA: Itek Corporation, 1976), 36–39. Emphasis in original.
88. Harrison Edward Livingstone, *Killing the Truth: Deceit and Deception in the JFK Case* (New York: Carroll & Graf, 1993), 214. Readers who find it a bit bizarre to read the narration of a film they can't see can go to Dave Reitzes's article "When Is JFK Seen Reacting to the Single Bullet? Too Late, Too Early, or Just Right?," Kennedy Assassination Home Page, http://jfkassassination.net/jfkhit.htm, to see the sequence.
89. Strictly speaking, the best estimate of the duration of a Zapruder frame is 54.64 milliseconds.
90. William H. Calvin, "The Unitary Hypothesis: A Common Neural Circuitry for Novel Manipulations, Language, Plan-ahead, and Throwing?," in Kathleen R. Gibson and Tim Ingold, *Tools, Language, and Cognition in Human Evolution* (Cambridge: Cambridge University Press, 1993); P. Brown et al., "New Observations on the Normal Auditory Startle Reflex in Man," *Brain* 114 (1991): 1891–902; C. Landis and W. Hunt, *The Startle Reaction* (New York: Holt, Rinehart, 1939).
91. "Kennedy marche vers la mort," *Paris Match*, November 26, 1968, 70–73.
92. Itek Corporation, *Kennedy Assassination Film Analysis*, 43–44. Itek would have preferred to use frames after 225, but it could not find usable pairs because (among other things) both men were moving around too much.
93. Richard Trask, *Pictures of the Pain: Photography and the Assassination of President Kennedy* (Danvers, MA: Yeoman Press, 1994), 159–66.
94. 6 HSCA 51.
95. Interestingly, nowhere in his testimony (2 HSCA 154–203) or in the written report of his findings (6 HSCA 32–62) does Thomas Canning say exactly *how far* inboard Connally must have been. But both an exhibit he supplied (Exhibit F-143, 2 HSCA 183) and the results of his trajectory analysis make it clear that Connally had to be well inboard.
96. 6 HSCA 54.
97. Itek Corporation, *Kennedy Assassination Film Analysis*, 47.
98. 6 HSCA 54.
99. Dale K. Myers, "Summary of Conclusions," *Secrets of a Homicide*, http://www.jfkfiles.com/jfk/html/concl1.htm.
100. 6 HSCA 17.
101. CBS Television, "The Warren Report: Part 2," June 26, 1967, transcript at http://www.maryferrell.org/mffweb/archive/viewer/showDoc.do?mode=searchResult&absPageId=1026337.
102. Robert R. Rees, "Nellie Connally: That Day in Dallas," CyberProfile, http://web.lconn.com/mysterease/connally.htm.
103. Testimony of Governor Connally (4 H 133).
104. Ibid., 147.
105. In frames 255 to 287, he may have been saying, "My God, they are going to kill us all." Martin Shackelford, "Listening to the Zapruder Film," Kennedy Assassination Home

Page, http://mcadams.posc.mu.edu/listen.htm.

106. Itek Corporation, *Kennedy Assassination Film Analysis*, 43.

107. Ibid., 50.

108. 6 HSCA 56.

109. The NOVA analysis was consistent with the single bullet theory if one made some modest assumptions as to Connally's posture.

110. *JFK Assassination Trial Exhibits* (Spectus Technologies: Menlo Park, CA, 1992), VHS. Some conspiracists will point out that FAA produced analyses for the "defense" in the trial, or analyses that claimed to support Oswald's innocence. This observation is true, but the firm produced nothing contesting the single bullet theory. Rather, they raised such issues as to why Oswald didn't shoot at the limo on Houston Street, rather than waiting for it to turn onto Elm, complete with fancy graphics of the limo on Houston.

111. Dale K. Myers, "JFK Assassination," *Secrets of a Homicide*, http://www.jfkfiles.com/index.html.

112. Bob Harris, *Dale Myers: Voodoo Geometry*, http://www.youtube.com/watch?v=kJrH62 TkCWE. A variety of somewhat less irrational criticisms of Myers work—as well as his responses—can be found at Dale K. Myers's "Frequently Asked Questions," *Secrets of a Homicide*, http://www.jfkfiles.com/jfk/html/faq_01.htm.

113. For the relevant frame from the FAA model, see illustration of the "magic bullet path" at http://mcadams.posc.mu.edu/sbt-faa.jpg. Itek does not mention any rotation of Connally's torso, so given the thorough descriptions of other parameters in its model, we have to assume it included no rotation.

114. Itek Corporation, *Kennedy Assassination Film Analysis*, 47.

115. I couldn't find a source in which Myers directly says "three inches," but the narrator in the ABC News documentary does say "three inches," a figure that apparently came from Myers.

116. ABC News, however, did commission animation experts from Z-Axis Corporation to conduct a peer review of Dale Myers's model. Their conclusion was that Myers had "taken a comprehensive and reasoned approach to animating this event and has successfully incorporated many diverse visual records into a unified and consistent recreation. We believe that the thoroughness and detail incorporated into his work is well beyond that required to present a fair and accurate depiction" (http://www.jfkfiles.com/jfk/html/zaxis.htm).

117. Myers's model is an exception, pointing directly into the sniper's nest window. Given his forthright discussion of possible error in the model, this isn't the result of some hyper-precision, but merely luck.

118. Dale K. Myers, "Summary of Conclusions: Potential Errors," *Secrets of a Homicide*, http://www.jfkfiles.com/jfk/html/concl2b.htm.

119. J. M. Nichols, "Assassination of President Kennedy," *The Practitioner* 211 (1973): 625–33.

120. There was one bullet strike to the chrome toping of the windshield, presumably caused by a relatively large fragment from the head shot. Also, a smaller fragment apparently cracked the windshield.

121. These memos are online at http://jfkassassination.net/wcsbt.htm.

122. Testimony of Darrell C. Tomlinson (6 H 129); Thompson estimates the time at 1:45 or 1:50, which is probably on the late side, *Six Seconds in Dallas* 156.

123. Photographer Robert Jackson narrowly missed getting an actual photograph of the sniper's nest shooter. His camera with the telephoto lens had no unexposed film in it, and he said everything "happened too fast" for him to get a shot with his other camera. Trask, *Pictures of the Pain*, 440.

Chapter 16. Thinking about Conspiracy: Putting It All Together

1. Exhibit 1381 (22 H 632–86).

2. Ibid., 634.

3. There is no statute of limitations for murder, but a bit player or somebody tangentially involved could probably easily trade inside knowledge for lenient treatment from prosecutors, particularly if that person could convincingly claim he or she was coerced or intimidated into staying quiet.

4. Of course, it's possible that a confession from one conspirator will provoke another conspirator to confess. This prospect, in fact, does not affect our probability calculations, since the relevant number is the probability of *any* confession, regardless of what the first confession provokes.

5. Richard Corliss and Patrick E. Cole, "Oliver Stone: Who Killed J.F.K.?," *Time*, December 23, 1991, http://www.time.com/time/magazine/article/0,9171,974523-1,00.html.

6. Fred Litwin, "A Conspiracy Too Big? Intellectual Dishonesty in the JFK Assassination," 1994–95, Kennedy Assassination Home Page, http://jfkassassination.net/toobig.htm.

7. 6 HSCA 286–93; Magen Knuth, "Was Oswald in the Doorway of the Depository at the time of the JFK Assassination?," Kennedy Assassination Home Page, http://mcadams .posc.mu.edu/oswald_doorway.htm.

8. John Newman, "Oswald, the CIA and Mexico City," *Probe* 6, no. 6 (September–October 1999), http://www.ctka.net/pr999-osciamex.html. Newman is summarizing the theories of Peter Dale Scott, the best-known proponent of this thesis.

9. Facing the electric chair in Texas would have given him a huge incentive to name his cohorts, although he might have believed that, in the murder of a president, such a revelation would not have been sufficient to save him. Further, he may have enjoyed playing the role of the innocent patsy, at least for a while.

10. Jean Davison, *Oswald's Game* (New York: W. W. Norton, 1983).

11. A variation of this theory might be that Oswald really did shoot Tippit and was then framed for shooting Kennedy.

Index

About the Author

John McAdams was a high school senior sitting in typing class when he heard that President John F. Kennedy had been shot. Along with his classmates, he rushed out to the cars parked in front of the school to hear occasional news bulletins that the local Top 40 radio station read from the wire. But the assassination did not become a big concern of McAdams's for decades. He earned a bachelor's degree from the University of Alabama (during the heyday of Bear Bryant), a master's degree from Columbia's Teachers College, and a doctorate from Harvard, then took a faculty position at Marquette University.

McAdams teaches courses in American politics, public policy, and political behavior. He has published in a wide array of scholarly journals, including the *American Journal of Political Science*, the *Journal of Politics*, *Sociological Quarterly*, and *Law and Contemporary Problems*.

His interest in the assassination was whetted in the early 1990s by the movie *JFK* and his participation in an Internet discussion group. This experience provoked him to start a website dedicated to the assassination and to teach a course on what was becoming an intense interest. The course was (and remains) extremely popular, and the website quickly became the top site on the Web dedicated to the assassination. Reviewers have called it "impressively comprehensive," "the best gateway to serious and reliable materials," and "the best collection of Kennedy assassination-related information."

McAdams describes himself as "a debunker by temperament." He is less willing to assert that he knows what is true than to be absolutely clear about what's *not* true. And, of course, the JFK assassination is a target-rich environment for a debunker. Yet McAdams has found the sorts of intellectual failures that afflict the JFK assassination literature also afflict the literature on other conspiracy theories: 9/11, the moon landing, Pearl Harbor, and so on.

McAdams insists that serious discussion of conspiracy issues can happen only when bogus factoids have been taken off the table. Failing to winnow the evidence leaves a huge psychological ambience of conspiracy without any possibility of solving the case.

McAdams and his wife, Lynda, live in the Milwaukee area. They have three grown children.

-